Enabling Access

Acknowledgements

We would like to acknowledge our debt to all of the contributors to this book. They approached their task with enthusiasm and commitment and we are grateful that they gave so freely of their time. Each one has been dedicated to ensuring that entitlement and access to education for pupils with special educational needs is not rhetoric but reality.

For editing and clerical support, we are indebted to Jo Egerton, whose skill and patience has enabled our work.

We are grateful to the support given by David Fulton and his team, who have kept special education as the key focus in their publications.

The book contains brief extracts from National Curriculum documentation. Material from the National Curriculum is Crown copyright and is reproduced by permission of the Controller of HMSO.

Enabling Access

Access

Effective Teaching and Learning
for Pupils with Learning Difficulties

Edited by
Barry Carpenter, Rob Ashdown
and Keith Bovair

David Fulton Publishers Ltd
2 Barbon Close, London WC1N 3JX

First published in Great Britain by
David Fulton Publishers 1996

British Library Cataloguing in Publication Data

A catalogue record for this book is available from the British Library

ISBN 1-85346-420-1

Typeset by Textype Typesetters, Cambridge
Printed in Great Britain by Cromwell Press Ltd, Melksham

Contents

Part III: The Context for the Whole Curriculum

Part IV: Conclusion

The Contributors

Rob Ashdown is Headteacher of St Luke's School for pupils with severe learning difficulties in Scunthorpe, North Lincolnshire. He has taught children with special educational needs in both the UK and Canada. He has contributed to various journals and books about aspects of the education of pupils with severe learning difficulties.

Sally Beveridge is Lecturer in Special Education at the University of Leeds. She coordinates and teaches courses which cover the full range of special educational needs, and her work embraces both initial teacher training and continuing professional development with experienced teachers. She has taught in primary and special schools and was formerly a director of an integrated preschool project at the University of Manchester.

Keith Bovair is Headteacher at Durants School for pupils with moderate learning difficulties, in Enfield, London. Keith was formerly Lecturer in Special Education and Educational Psychology at the University of Birmingham. He has edited several books: *Making Special Schools Ordinary Vols. 1 and 2* (Falmer, 1989/90), *The Curriculum Challenge* (Falmer, 1991), *Special Curricula Needs* (Fulton, 1992) and *Counselling in Schools* (Fulton, 1994). He is co-author of *Modern Foreign Languages for All* (Kogan Page, 1995).

Erica Brown is Senior Lecturer at the Centre for the Study of Special Education, Westminster College, Oxford. She has published widely on religious education in mainstream and special school settings and was the 1995 Fulton Fellow. Her books include *Opening Children's Eyes* (1991), *Mixed Blessings* (1993) and *Religious Education for All* (1996). She is editor and director of *Respect*, a journal of religious education for pupils with special educational needs. She lectures nationally and is a qualified Section 13 inspector for Denominational Worship and Religious Education. She is a bereavement counsellor working with children and parents.

Richard Byers is a member of the teaching staff at the Centre for the Study of Special Education, Westminster College, Oxford. He also tutors courses on a part-time basis for the University of Cambridge Institute of Education and for the Distance Education Unit of the University of Birmingham. Richard has contributed to a number of recent publications including *Planning the Curriculum for Pupils with Special Educational Needs* (Fulton, 1996) and *Implementing the Whole Curriculum for Pupils with Learning Difficulties.* (Fulton, 1994). Richard offers an independent school support and curriculum development service.

Barry Carpenter is Director of the Centre for the Study of Special Education, Westminster College, Oxford. He was formerly an inspector of schools and a headteacher. He publishes widely on a variety of special needs issues and has conducted lecture tours in Australia, New Zealand and Europe. His current research focuses on early intervention and family support. Barry is the father of a child with learning difficulties.

Tina Detheridge is Senior Lecturer at the Centre for the Study of Special Education, Westminster College, Oxford. Previously she was Manager for Special Needs at the National Council for Educational Technology (NCET). During that time she was responsible for many projects and publications on the application of information technology for pupils with special needs. Tina has also been involved in software development since 1983, as a partner in Widgit Software.

Bernard Gummett is Headteacher of George Hastwell School, Cumbria. Whilst studying for his MA (SEN) at Lancaster University he researched 'Sensory Stimulation in the Education of Pupils with Severe Learning Difficulties'. He was a major contributor to *Extending Horizons* (Ergent Publications, 1995) and also provided editorial support. George Hastwell School is involved in a project encouraging local schools to make educational use of e-mail and the Internet, promoting the opportunity inherent in these systems which provides all pupils with equal opportunities on a global scale.

Viv Hinchcliffe is the Headteacher at the Rectory Paddock School for pupils with severe learning difficulties in the London Borough of Bromley. He was formerly a lecturer in special educational needs in the School of Education at Brunel University. At Brunel he was the award leader for the in-service DPSE and M.Ed courses in the education of pupils with severe learning disabilities. He has published widely on aspects of special education, particularly on curriculum development.

Penny Lacey has worked for 20 years with pupils with special educational needs and as a specialist teacher of music, dance and drama. She has run workshops for non-specialists, believing that everyone can teach music. Penny was on the advisory body for writing the 1995 orders for music in the National Curriculum. She is a lecturer in special education at the University of Birmingham.

Ann Lewis is a Senior Lecturer in Education at the University of Warwick, and has taught in special and primary schools. She has been involved extensively in the development and evaluation of curricula for children with learning difficulties. Her current research concerns the impact of government policy on special needs provision. Publications include *Children's Understanding of Disability* (Routledge, 1995) and *Primary Special Needs and the National Curriculum* (Routledge, 1995). She is one of the editors of *Education 3 – 13,* a member of the editorial committee of *Special Children* and joint editor of the *British Educational Research Journal.*

Clare Martin is Deputy Headteacher of George Hastwell School, Cumbria. Whilst studying for her MA (SEN) at Lancaster University she researched 'The Impact of the National Curriculum on Schools for Pupils with Severe Learning Difficulties'. She has recognized the importance of information technology for providing access to the curriculum for all pupils and her pupils have won National Multimedia in Education Awards. She was a major contributor to *Extending Horizons* (Ergent Publications, 1995) and also provided editorial support. She has been involved in a Schools Curriculum and Assessment Council project to produce guidance on access to the whole curriculum for pupils with profound and multiple learning difficulties.

Peter Mittler is Emeritus Professor of Special Education at the University of Manchester where he was formerly Dean and Director of the Faculty of Education. He is a consultant for UNESCO, the World Health Organization, and the UN. Throughout his distinguished career he has contributed to significant national and international developments in the field of special education. His publications are well-known world-wide.

Helen Mount is Head of Language and Communication at Mont Varouf School for pupils with severe learning difficulties, Guernsey. She was formerly coordinator of the MENCAP Profound Intellectual and Multiple Disabilities section. Prior to that Helen was Head of

Lower School in a Manchester special school for over seven years, including a period of secondment as a Manchester Teacher Fellow, co-writing *Literacy for All* (Fulton) and *Technology for All* (Fulton).

Carol Ouvry has worked in the field of special education for 20 years; much of this time was spent in schools, working with pupils with profound and multiple learning difficulties. She has also worked in the field of in-service training as course coordinator, as trainer, and as editor and writer of distance learning materials. She has maintained her particular interest in all aspects of work with children and adults with profound and multiple learning difficulties and in collaborative working with parents and professionals from other disciplines. She is Associate Tutor at the Centre for the Study of Special Education, Westminster College, Oxford and is editor of *PMLD Link*.

Melanie Peter is Lecturer in the Centre for the Study of Special Education, Westminster College, Oxford. A trained and widely experienced teacher of pupils with special educational needs, she has a national profile for her work in this field. She is author of *Drama for All* (Fulton, 1994), *Making Drama Special* (Fulton, 1995), *Music for All* (Fulton, 1995), *Art for All: Vols. 1 and 2* (Fulton, 1996) and *Making Dance Special* (Fulton, in press).

Jill Porter is an experienced teacher of children with severe learning difficulties. She has been involved in training teachers for a number of years at a variety of levels (B Ed, PGCE, Advanced Diploma, Masters) about severe learning difficulties and special educational needs in general. She has recently served on the working party of the Special Educational Needs Training Consortium compiling core competences for teacher education in special educational needs.

Ron Ritchie is Head of the Department for Professional Development at Bath College of Higher Education. He has written widely in the area of science and technology including *Primary Science: Making it Work* (Fulton, 1993) and *Primary Design and Technology: A process for learning* (Fulton, 1995). He was an advisory teacher for science and has taught in primary and secondary schools.

Brian Robbins is Headteacher of Hallmoor School, Birmingham. He has worked in schools for pupils with learning difficulties for over 20 years. He is the author of *Mathsteps* (LDA, 1993) and has published articles and chapters on mathematics for several books and journals. He provides INSET for teachers in mainstream and special schools in the UK and in other European countries.

Philippa Russell is Director of the Council for Disabled Children. She was consultant to the Department of Health on the guidance for the Children Act 1989 and for the DfEE on the *Code of Practice for the Identification and Assessment of Special Educational Needs*. She is a consultant for the Disability Unit on the forthcoming inter-departmental guidance on transition to adult services. Philippa is the parent of a young man with learning disabilities. She is widely known for her distinguished contribution to the area of special needs.

Suzanne Saunders has taught in special schools for 16 years, both in the UK and the USA. The last ten of these were as Head of Education in a residential special school for children with profound and multiple learning difficulties. She is currently working as Research Fellow and tutor in the Centre for the Study of Special Education, Westminster College, Oxford. She is undertaking research in the areas of Fragile-X syndrome and family support.

Chris Stevens is the Manager for Special Needs at the National Council for Educational Technology (NCET). He was formerly Professional Officer for Special Educational Needs at the Schools Curriculum and Assessment Authority with a responsibility for all areas of special educational needs and able children. His previous background is in schools and his most recent post was as headteacher of a school for pupils with severe and profound and multiple learning difficulties.

David Sugden holds the Chair of the School of Education (1995–1999) and is Professor of Special Needs in Education at the University of Leeds. He is the author of four books and over 70 articles on special educational needs and child development. David has taught in the UK and USA in primary, special and secondary schools. He is a regular presenter at national and international conferences.

Christina Tilstone has taught children with special educational needs for more than 30 years in a range of special schools. She was a major supporter of the transfer, in 1971, from health to education for pupils with severe learning difficulties. In her work in educating children to take their place in society, she believes that all schools have a curriculum responsibility to decrease society's negative impressions. She is now a Lecturer in Special Education at the University of Birmingham, and is responsible for the learning difficulties distance education course. She has written widely on teaching children with special educational needs, and on the professional development of teachers. She is the present editor of the *British Journal of Special Education.*

Helen Wright is presently a research student in the School of Education, University of Leeds, studying children with Developmental Coordination Disorder. She is seconded for three years (1993–1996) from her lecturing position in the School of Physical Education, Nanyang Technological University, Singapore.

Foreword

Chris Stevens

In 1988, when the Education Reform Act (ERA) became law, I was head of a school for pupils with severe learning difficulties. Together, the school staff considered the implications of ERA for our pupils and decided that this law did not actually apply to us. In fact, we felt that if we kept our heads down, the whole thing would go away. The wisdom of this strategy, we felt, was confirmed when the government decided that special schools would be allowed to delay implementation of the provisions of the Act for one year.

While we did not claim that our school curriculum was perfect, we were committed to the principles on which that curriculum stood. In particular we knew that the development of communication and life skills for our pupils was the top priority. The idea of a curriculum based on ten subjects, where progression was defined through statements of attainment on ten levels, seemed alien to us and, in many ways, irrelevant. Setting clear teaching and learning objectives based on developmental models and related to the needs of individuals had served us well in the past and we believed that this new-fangled curriculum threatened this approach. I believe that the priorities we identified for our pupils then still remain the basis of the whole curriculum for many pupils with special educational needs today. They are the way in which schools implement and translate the overriding aims of ERA to promote the spiritual, moral cultural, mental and physical development of pupils at school and of society, and prepare such pupils for the opportunities, responsibilities and experiences of adult life.

With implementation of the new National Curriculum came the realization that all pupils would be expected to participate. The principle of entitlement was embraced by teachers. Circular 5 (NCC, 1989a) and Curriculum Guidance 2 (NCC, 1989b) from the National Curriculum Council reinforced the principle that this should be a curriculum for all.

The notion of a curriculum for all was an appealing one and, as a staff, we looked afresh at the National Curriculum and began to think about incorporating it into our whole curriculum provision. Why am I telling you all this? I suppose it is because these experiences were not unique and I am sure most of you recognize the feelings, both positive and negative, that we as a staff were sharing. Some schools rejected the National Curriculum, arguing that they could not and should not change their way of working. Others risked stretching credulity by identifying all their curricular activities as National Curriculum programmes of study. We were determined to do neither of these things.

We believed that for all pupils, and in particular for pupils with severe learning difficulties, the curriculum should incorporate teaching and learning objectives which would require work beyond National Curriculum subjects. We were equally sure that many teaching and learning objectives we identified for our pupils could be pursued through National Curriculum programmes of study. By planning to meet the full range of curricular needs within a broad and balanced approach, we would embrace the principle of entitlement and ensure our pupils were included in the mainstream of educational developments.

This whole curriculum beyond the National Curriculum is not something special or different, which only applies to pupils with learning difficulties. It is, I believe, the approach every teacher adopts. However, the balance of emphasis within that curriculum ensures provision is tailored to individual needs.

In 1993, Sir Ron Dearing reviewed the curriculum (SCAA, 1994) and addressed some of the inflexibilities which had been built into the statutory orders and their assessment. I am pleased to say that today few teachers of pupils with special needs feel that the National Curriculum programmes of study have nothing positive to offer their pupils. Changes in end of key stage assessment, giving greater emphasis to teacher assessment, mean that it is possible to report all pupils' achievements in positive ways.

We are now a decade on from the conception of the National Curriculum. In special education we are, at last, in a good position to offer pupils a broad and balanced curriculum which is relevant to their needs and which is based on the same range of provision enjoyed by all pupils. Such a curriculum can only be planned as a cohesive whole; compartmentalizing aspects of the whole curriculum risks seeing one part as having more merit or worth than another. The whole curriculum in all schools will vary, depending on local needs and opportunities. In special education it is important that we embrace that whole curriculum, using its diversity and opportunity to plan for breadth, balance and relevance. Too often in the past we have been too ready to identify the things about pupils with special needs which make them different. Individual needs will always be there and will need to be addressed, but opportunities to address them can and should reflect the opportunities given to all pupils.

This book makes a significant contribution to the developments in planning for access to the whole curriculum and I commend the work to you.

References

National Curriculum Council (1989a) *Circular No. 5*, York: National Curriculum Council.
National Curriculum Council (1989b) *Curriculum Guidance 2: A Curriculum for All*, York: National Curriculum Council.
School Curriculum and Assessment Authority (1994) *The National Curriculum and its Assessment*, London: SCAA.

Chapter 1

Enabling Access

Barry Carpenter and Rob Ashdown

Enabling Access, the title of this book, challenges us all to go beyond the original debates that emerged in 1989 from the introduction of the National Curriculum in relation to pupils with special educational needs (SEN). The dialogue then was about *entitlement,* and the challenge then was how, through creative and innovative teaching, pupils with a whole range of SEN could receive their entitlement to the statutory curriculum. These debates were not without their merits. They enabled the teaching profession to recognize that there were common curriculum principles for all and that the aims of education could relate broadly to pupils of all ages and abilities. In the conversations that took place between all members of the teaching profession, much clarification of a variety of issues was given and, in many ways, a deeper understanding of the learning needs of children with SEN was reached.

Entitlement is now broadly accepted, but that does not bring with it automatic solutions. It is one thing to be entitled to a curriculum; it is another to be engaged actively in that curriculum. Entitlement alone does not meet needs, nor does entitlement mean that that curriculum is appropriately designed or delivered to meet the diversity of needs that exist within our pupil population. We now need to look at *access*. How do we enable all pupils to have access to a curriculum that is dynamic, coherent, meaningful and will allow them to prepare themselves, with the support and guidance of their teachers, for the challenges of adulthood? Various authors have illuminated the entitlement debate (e.g., Ashdown *et al.*, 1991; Jordan and Powell, 1994), and many have stressed the need for a whole curriculum that addresses every facet of each individual pupil's development (Bovair *et al.*, 1992; Sebba *et al.*, 1995). Throughout this book, the contributors strive to articulate quality classroom practices which will genuinely engage each child as a learner in that dynamic process of teaching and learning.

Who are the children?

The pupil group debated in this book are largely those students with moderate learning difficulties (MLD) or severe learning difficulties (SLD). Many of the latter group are said to have profound and multiple learning difficulties (PMLD). It is unnecessary to debate here the aetiology and nature of their learning difficulties; readers wishing to read more

...ld refer to introductory readers (e.g., Gulliford and Upton, 1992) or more advanced ...xts (e.g., Clements, 1987; Ware, 1994) as appropriate. The target audience for this book is the teachers of these pupils, who may work in nursery, primary, secondary or special schools. Inevitably, in articulating curriculum opportunities for these pupils, much is said that has relevance for the far wider group of pupils with SEN too; indeed, it could be argued that what is good practice for pupils with SEN is good practice for all pupils.

In the context of this book, the pupils in focus are those who require particular learning pathways to be charted for them if they are to be given access to the statutory curriculum. They are pupils for whom imaginative and creative programmes of study (PoS) are necessary to enable them to receive their curriculum entitlement; pupils who, without PoS personalized to their particular needs, would be alienated from the flow of learning experience in the classroom; pupils who need specific engagement strategies to be employed to ensure their participation in the curriculum; and pupils who, without learning routes which mirror their learning styles, would remain on the periphery of curriculum activity when their right is to be active participants at the heart of the learning process. They are pupils for whom teachers are, through their innate creativity, *enabling access*. Our goal as teachers of pupils with learning difficulties, and an aim of this book, is to afford each pupil learning experiences which are both empowering and dignifying. Ultimately our desire is to build an inclusive curriculum (Carpenter, 1995).

Curriculum development since 1988

We are concerned here with access to a whole curriculum rather than just the National Curriculum. Nevertheless, we must begin by considering the major impact that the National Curriculum has had on curriculum development in schools before we turn to the other developments which we would like to see happening in schools.

From 1989 onwards, school curricula have changed dramatically as teachers have tried to apply fully the National Curriculum. It is plain that the introduction of the National Curriculum has forced a wholesale rethink in schools about long-established curriculum models and approaches to curriculum planning. On the whole, this can be viewed as a positive change, but it has been a painful process for all schools, due in part to inconsistent messages and a lack of clear guidance from the central authorities. However, in their determination to interpret the National Curriculum and implement it in ways which were meaningful for the pupils, and which met their highly individual needs, schools and various consortia have actually achieved much impressive progress in curriculum development.

This commendable work owes much to the ability of the teachers and their belief in the value of a National Curriculum for all. However, in part, especially for teachers of pupils with SLD or PMLD, this effort was fuelled by a concern to establish an entitlement to the National Curriculum because there were real fears that exclusion from the National Curriculum was a possibility and that this might lead to eventual exclusion from the education service. After all, only two decades beforehand many pupils with SLD were regarded as unsuitable for education at school and did not enjoy the same rights to education by qualified teachers as other children.

From the outset there was a degree of resistance from teachers of pupils with SEN to the National Curriculum. Many teachers were convinced that its advent would divert attention away from the paramount needs of the pupils, especially as regards their personal and social development. Also, they did not like the its subject emphasis and found it hard to see the relationship of many of the National Curriculum PoS to the school curricula that had been painstakingly developed prior to 1988. Finally, there was much anxiety that lack of teaching time would mean that the National Curriculum would squeeze out major elements of the traditional curricula in schools (e.g., elements of personal and social education (PSE), use of community leisure facilities, etc.).

In answer to such concerns, non-statutory guidance was developed by the National Curriculum Council (NCC) which stressed the importance of entitlement to a whole-school curriculum made up of the National Curriculum, religious education and other curriculum areas (NCC, 1990). As Carpenter (1992) points out, the cross-curricular elements described by the NCC actually constituted powerful justifications for continuing to provide all of the valued elements of the traditional curricula. Unfortunately, however, this non-statutory guidance never had the prominence of the statutory orders. NCC did produce non-statutory guidance which demonstrated, with examples, how relevant activities for pupils with SLD could be delivered through the National Curriculum (NCC, 1992). Whilst this guidance was very helpful, it was somewhat marred by its focus on the core subjects; many teachers would have welcomed examples of activities, especially for pupils with PMLD, which demonstrated meaningful involvement with the National Curriculum foundation subjects.

Another step towards meeting teachers' concerns was taken in 1993 when the NCC published a booklet called *Opportunity and Challenge* (NCC, 1993) which was the result of a consultation exercise with teachers of pupils with a range of disabilities and learning difficulties. In this document, the NCC acknowledged that:

- the National Curriculum is only one part of the whole-school curriculum;
- there should be access to other developmental work across the curriculum, particularly as regards PSE, and various therapies;
- priorities for meeting the needs of individual pupils must be addressed;
- many pupils need to work partly or entirely at National Curriculum levels below those originally designated for Key Stages 2, 3 and 4;
- the procedures for changing the statements of pupils to reflect modifications and/or exceptions to the National Curriculum were generally viewed by teachers as negative or complicated;
- teacher assessment offered better opportunities than the existing national tests for celebrating achievements and diagnosing difficulties;
- there was a need for guidance on the moderation of teacher assessment, formal recognition of proven assessment instruments, and the development of accreditation for assessment schemes;
- there is a need to achieve consensus on curriculum content and that this might be met by the establishment of a national network for sharing good practice and schools' experiences;
- teachers were looking for substantive non-statutory guidance which could give more examples of how the needs of pupils with MLD, SLD and PMLD could be met through all of the National Curriculum subjects.

In April 1993 the Secretary of State for Education invited Sir Ron Dearing, Chairman of the NCC and the Schools Examination and Assessment Council (SEAC), and Chairman designate of the new School Curriculum and Assessment Authority (SCAA), to review the National Curriculum in England. The so-called Dearing Report acknowledged that aspects of the National Curriculum had not served well some pupils with SEN and it expressed the view that the proposed slimmer National Curriculum would give teachers enough time to meet their needs in relevant ways (SCAA, 1994).

Following consultation on draft proposals in Summer 1994, the final recommendations on the revised National Curriculum were accepted in full by the Secretary of State in November 1994. The revised National Curriculum was first taught in September 1995. There is a special significance to the *common requirements,* which are a series of requirements applying to the statutory orders for each subject. These refer to *access to the curriculum* for all pupils, but particularly for pupils with SEN and able pupils. They stress the PoS for each Key Stage (KS) should be taught to the great majority of pupils in the key stage, in ways appropriate to their abilities. For the small number of children who may need the provision, it is stated that material may be selected from earlier key stages where this is necessary for individual pupils to progress and demonstrate achievement. This is significant because it legitimizes the fact that, say, pupils with PMLD may need to continue to follow elements of the KS1 PoS well after 7 years of age. The common requirements also stressed the need to use augmentative means of communication, non-sighted methods, technological and other aids or adapted equipment as appropriate.

As regards assessment, national Level 1 and Level 2 assessment tasks were introduced as an alternative to written tests at KS2, KS3 and KS4. In addition, SCAA commissioned research from the National Foundation for Education Research into good practice in assessment for pupils with significant learning difficulties (NFER, 1995).

Despite these important changes, some teachers still complain that, in terms of the content of the PoS for each subject and each key stage, the National Curriculum remains a curriculum designed primarily for the average learner in mainstream schools. It seems that SCAA, the Office for Standards in Education (OFSTED) and their advisers still have a long way to go before they can convince all teachers that the National Curriculum can be truly regarded as inclusive. Yet, SCAA has made plain that the PoS for each subject and key stage should be regarded as a minimum entitlement that serve as a basis for planning the curriculum. The message is that it is for schools to decide how and in what depth to teach the material contained in the PoS. No methodology is implied; this is a matter for the professional judgement of teachers. Moreover, SCAA does not insist that all individual priorities for pupils can be met entirely *through* the statutory PoS and recognizes that they may have to be met through additional activities that occur *alongside* the PoS (SCAA, 1996).

Schools do have considerable freedom as regards the content of the whole-school curriculum and teaching approaches. The significance for teachers of all statemented pupils of the SCAA's own guidance on planning the curriculum for pupils with PMLD should not be underestimated (SCAA,1996). It reiterates that:

- there is an entitlement to a whole curriculum, not just the National Curriculum;
- not all individual priorities can be met through the National Curriculum;
- tokenism should not be tolerated and there must be meaningful involvement in subject-focused activities;
- teaching priorities may relate to cross-curricular skills such as communication, personal and social development, information technology capability, and the cross-curricular processes of investigation and problem-solving;
- unavoidable routines and care procedures should not be viewed as interruptions to teaching but as valuable teaching opportunities that should not be rushed and should be planned carefully;
- teachers should not be anxious to count the hours and minutes allocated to each subject of the National Curriculum, although there is still a need for rigorous planning of the curriculum;

- breadth and balance in the curriculum is something to be achieved over a year or a key stage rather than a week or half-term.

Schools were promised in the Dearing Report a period of relative stability and autonomy as regards the curriculum (SCAA, 1994). Now they have an opportunity to systematically review, evaluate, modify and consolidate all aspects of the whole curriculum. Schools are not the victim of a system or events beyond their control; it is possible and desirable for schools to re-establish control over their curriculum (Byers and Rose, 1994).

What remains to be achieved?

We must remember that the National Curriculum is not in its final form and that there will be other reviews in due course which will offer opportunities to incorporate changes that will make it more flexible. Therefore, there is a need for positive suggestions about ways it may be changed. In addition, it is timely and essential to recall the agenda for action which existed prior to the introduction of the Education Reform Act in 1988, including:

- the introduction of more rigour into the process of curriculum planning and a greater degree of breadth and balance in the curriculum;
- a move away from prescriptive, teacher-led activities, which did little to empower pupils and encourage personal autonomy, to a more interactive style of teaching;
- building on the new ideas which were suggested by research into children's cognitive development and styles of learning at different ages, taking into account the implications of new findings about the learning and development of children with different disabilities and learning difficulties (e.g., Clements, 1987);
- the development of positive approaches to teaching self-control to pupils who present seriously challenging behaviours;
- the development of effective partnerships between teachers, parents, pupils and others concerned with the development of effective individual education plans (IEPs) for pupils with learning difficulties;
- the introduction of new technologies which have the potential for transforming the curriculum for pupils with a range of disabilities and learning difficulties.

Articulating purposes and values

In recent years, the needs of pupils have been defined and a curriculum has been handed down to schools by central agencies working to realize a government programme of radical curriculum reform. As a result, there has been a considerable erosion of the school-based initiatives for pupil-centred curriculum development which were once the hallmark of special education. Instead, teachers have had to work very hard to interpret the statutory content of the basic curriculum and to bring it to life. This process was probably all the harder because teachers were not directly involved in the centralized process of curriculum development (which was carried out by remote working groups of experts) and they may not have understood fully the rationale behind the design or content of the various subject orders.

The National Curriculum was originally handed down to schools in a series of jigsaw puzzle-type pieces that failed to fit together. In fact, the National Curriculum as a whole still suffers from the fact that it has no underpinning philosophy other than the basic requirements stated in the Education Reform Act 1988: that it should be broadly based and balanced; that it should promote spiritual, moral, cultural , mental and physical development; and that it should prepare pupils for the opportunities, responsibilities and experiences of adult life.

The thrust of all National Curriculum documentation, both statutory orders and non-statutory guidance, is to give a rather sterile presentation of what schools should teach. Various politicians have their particular views about what all pupils should be taught, and they tend to focus upon the need to teach a rather narrow range of competences and the desirability of using only a small number of the whole range of teaching techniques which are actually available and of proven worth. Inevitably, the guidance from OFSTED and SCAA reflects the views of the politicians as expressed through the media and the Department for Education and Employment (DfEE). The result is that there is no real vision of what school curricula should make available for pupils; there are no statements of purposes or values that can be called inspirational or enthusing. In practice, this rich vision has always been provided by teachers and others working in close contact with the pupils.

Of course, the curriculum does not exist in isolation; in many ways it is a reflection of society and the demands that society is placing upon its future adults. A good example of this would be to compare the cross-curricular skills identified by the NCC in 1990 with those identified by the Confederation of British Industry (CBI) in June 1994 (c.f. Carpenter, in press). The lists below illustrate the high degree of correlation between the education arena and the employment marketplace:

NCC	CBI
Communication	Communication
Numeracy	Numeracy
Problem-solving	Problem-solving
Study	Modern Foreign Languages
Information Technology	Information Technology

These are valuable skills for life that students with learning difficulties as lifelong learners can use and apply in a variety of contexts. Hence, in this book several chapters are devoted to debating key issues, such as working with families and changing public attitudes, all of which influence either the curriculum, pupil advocacy or the potential of the student with SEN to engage in his or her own citizenship.

What are the needs of these pupils?

It is important that we listen to the views of influential members of society. However, at the end of the day, when all of the politicians and experts have had their say about the content of the curriculum and when the latest curriculum reforms and transformation in schools are complete, the all-important question is this: what has been the personal gain for the individual learner during his or her formative school years?

Regardless of the structure or content of the curriculum, each learner has the right to ask his or her teachers, 'What do I get out of this?' Ideally, each learner would articulate (by whatever means) the outcomes of his or her learning experiences. Indeed, the learner's views would be a far richer measure of the validity of a curriculum than any existing criteria identified by OFSTED or SCAA. If the pupils cannot do this themselves, for whatever reason, we should be their advocates. At a series of workshops organized by one of us, teachers considered these theoretical questions and they decided that through their educational experiences learners should expect to:

- gain self-esteem
- increase independence
- develop knowledge
- make choices
- express preferences
- be active participants
- gain communication skills
- broaden their horizons
- gain access to a wide variety of resources including IT and multimedia
- have expectations of themselves and of others
- develop awareness of themselves and of others
- have opportunities for socializing and socialization
- develop their citizenship
- develop their self-esteem.

This list could go on. Readers will wish to add their own thoughts, but, as an exercise, it is well worth staff teams or individual teachers looking at the curriculum and, without any reference to its subject content or headings, project for and with their students what the eventual gains may be.

If the curriculum is to achieve any of the above, then it should be relevant and appropriate – *enabling access*, promoting empowerment, facilitating achievement, meeting individual needs and allowing the attainment of personal goals. There must be consideration of both objectives and methodologies. The curriculum is underpinned by four key curriculum tenets: breadth, balance, relevance and differentiation. These concepts have been discussed and debated many times, but they require consideration at a personal level. How does each teacher know that these principles are embodied in his or her classroom practice? What evidence can he or she produce?

A group of teachers working with one of us produced some examples of evidence that they would be able to offer to indicate that these four principles were very much alive as dynamic features of the teaching and learning process in their classrooms. These examples are shown in Table 1.1.

Of course, the process of producing a quality curriculum is not simply a question of modifying or simplifying an established core curriculum; the result might only be a watered-down curriculum of no real benefit to the learner. The individual circumstances of pupils and their daily living environments must also be taken into account if we are going to achieve any sort of coherence within the curriculum for each pupil. For example, Sue Fagg and her colleagues give some excellent examples of how we should take an holistic overview of the learning needs of our pupils (Fagg *et al.*, 1990).

To ensure that the various curriculum areas and learning experiences impact upon the pupil in a coordinated manner, teachers may wish to look at the real-life experiences of their pupils and the naturalistic settings with which they engage over a weekly or monthly cycle. It is then possible to undertake an environmental analysis of the curriculum and to use this as the context for plotting the critical learning experiences which may be derived from the curriculum. The key features of this approach are:

- an holistic overview of the pupil's life
- an identification of the key environments experienced, over time, by the pupil
- negotiation of priorities for learning with the pupil based on their potential application
- an attempt to meet individual needs within naturalistic settings
- an increased sensitivity of the educational processes within the pupil's life through seeking ecological validity
- a blending of negotiated goals with the pupil's lifestyle.

The family have a large part to play in this process and their views should also be taken into consideration.

Breadth	schemes of work displays timetable IEPs range of resources teaching and learning styles students' own work
Balance	balance of time curriculum audit continuing and blocked work lesson plans/balance of knowledge, skills attitudes students' own work IEPs
Relevance	matched needs through IEP talking to students (voice of the child) displays transition plans environments records of achievement resources and equipment
Differentiation	lesson plans use of human and other resources use of different environments IEPs curriculum documents teaching and learning styles integration students work (including portfolios, video, photos, etc.)

Table 1.1 Classroom evidence of breadth, balance, relevance and differentiation

What forms should their education take?

As noted above, there is no specification of the methodology that teachers must use. In terms of actual objectives, schools do have to respond to the challenges posed by an altered National Curriculum and the new discretionary powers that they now have of deciding what to teach in detail and what to teach more superficially. However, SCAA has provided non-mandatory models for planning the whole curriculum (SCAA, 1995; 1996) which offer teachers the opportunity to take back the ownership of the curriculum.

SCAA has suggested that in planning for the curriculum, a school should consider their aims, objectives, policies and priorities as an initial step. Schools will need to consider:

- *statutory* curricular provision
- areas in which they are *required* to have policies which may lead to additional curricular provision being made
- areas in which they have *chosen* to develop policies which may lead to additional curricular provision being made
- particular *school priorities* within the curriculum.

These four strands in combination should offer both access and flexibility for pupils with learning difficulties in that the curriculum then incorporates not only the National Curriculum subjects, religious education and sex education (statutory), but also such areas as careers education (required), health education, personal and social development, information technology (chosen), or physiotherapy or speech therapy (school priorities).

It is also encouraging to find within the SCAA documentation a recognition of the value of experimentation. This is crucial when educating many pupils with learning difficulties. Their patterns of learning are so complex that it is impossible for the teacher always to meet individual needs accurately at the first attempt.

SCAA (1996) offers a six-phase systematic approach to planning the curriculum which is discussed in more detail later in this book (see Chapter 14). These six phases are:

Phase 1:   policy-making
Phase 2:   developing schemes of work/long-term planning
Phase 3:   developing schemes of work/medium-term planning
Phase 4:   developing schemes of work/short-term planning
Phase 5:   assessment and recording
Phase 6:   review and evaluation.
(SCAA, 1996, pp. 24–5)

It is possible to apply this model of planning to developing any aspect of the curriculum, even those areas which may fall outside the defined National Curriculum. The three levels of long-term, medium-term and short-term planning are also helpful in designing learning experiences which truly address the experiences of individual children with learning difficulties. The statutory PoS alone will not meet those needs; teachers will need to add supplementary learning experiences, thus extending the PoS. In applying these specifically to individual pupils within their classrooms, teachers will personalize the PoS, by means of the resources and the communication and interaction strategies used. These three variants of PoS correlate very well with the three planning phases suggested by SCAA:

- long-term planning – statutory PoS
- medium-term planning – extended PoS
- short-term planning – personalized PoS.

Recognition of these three levels of planning in relation to both the whole-school curriculum and the individual pupil is essential. The *Code of Practice for the Identification and Assessment of Special Educational Needs* (DfE, 1994) calls for statements of SEN which specify long-term objectives, regular reviews which set medium-term targets, and short-term planning by teachers on a termly or more frequent basis. Each child with SEN should have an individual education plan (IEP) which will set out the nature of his or her learning difficulties, the action required to meet these, the staff involved, and any resources which are required. Typically, a series of targets will be generated to be reviewed at least termly and always at the annual review.

Targets in IEPs often range widely over the child's development and do not always express themselves in terms of curricular objectives that can be met in the classroom. Hence, without careful planning, teachers could find themselves keeping records against the IEP targets as well as the whole range of normal school curricular records, with no direct correlation between the two. In addition, the school curriculum policies and schemes of work may not reflect the needs of the individual as expressed in the IEP targets. Finally, the IEP does not necessarily specify the teaching methodology by which targets are to be delivered. It is in this respect that a personalized PoS is a useful concept; the teacher can look to the strategies for teaching each target within the context of the curriculum as it is personalized for each child. Therefore, this model for curriculum planning, shown in Figure 1.1, and the guidance in the Code of Practice have the potential to give teachers the means of constructing a range of learning experiences that accurately match the learning needs of the individual pupil.

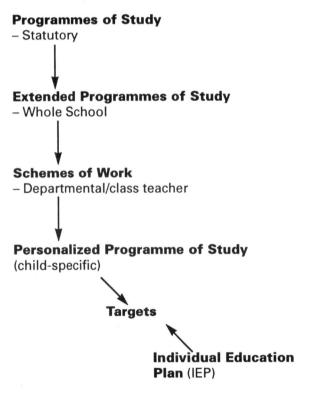

Programmes of Study
– Statutory

Extended Programmes of Study
– Whole School

Schemes of Work
– Departmental/class teacher

Personalized Programme of Study
(child-specific)

Targets

Individual Education Plan (IEP)

Figure 1.1 Reconciling the curriculum and individual needs

The content of this book

Section 1: Perspectives on the National Curriculum

The first section of the book consists of chapters about every National Curriculum subject, each of which has been written by one or more people who have a special enthusiasm and expertise in the subject as well as awareness of the needs of pupils with MLD, SLD or PMLD. They do not necessarily treat every aspect of the statutory PoS for every key stage for their assigned subject. Also, they do not describe the whole range of activities and experiences which are possible. There simply is not the space to do so within the confines of a chapter of only several thousand words. Therefore, readers will find some obvious omissions; for instance, there is nothing specific about teaching literacy or dance. However, we believe that readers will recognize that each author's particular interests and enthusiasm result in a fresh perspective on their subject. Each chapter offers new ideas or models for developing further the schemes of work which already exist in most schools. Where appropriate, authors list resources and make recommendations for further reading which readers may wish to pursue. As regards the omissions, we believe that they have all had treatment elsewhere recently and in considerable detail.

Section 2: Access and entitlement to the whole curriculum

The next section mainly addresses the concerns of teachers about the relevance of the National Curriculum to pupils with SEN and strategies by which all pupils may be guaranteed access to a whole curriculum which includes the National Curriculum. However, the section begins with an insightful chapter by Erica Brown which demonstrates the importance of religious education for all pupils and offers suggestions about the range of activities which are possible.

The chapter by Carol Ouvry and Suzanne Saunders specifically tackles questions concerning access and entitlement to the whole curriculum for pupils with PMLD. They demonstrate that the subject-led National Curriculum and the needs-led developmental and other additional curricula (e.g., therapies) have parallel and interrelated strands which come together in each pupil's IEP. Ouvry and Saunders stress that each pupil must have an individually designed curriculum in which the relationship between the National Curriculum, the traditional developmental curriculum, and additional curricula will vary from pupil to pupil and for the same pupil over time. The model that they describe has implications for teachers of all pupils with SENs precisely because it has been developed in relation to pupils with the most profound learning difficulties.

Of course, a school curriculum is more than the actual content of skills, knowledge and understanding which teachers traditionally aim to impart; it is also very much to do with the processes of teaching and learning, which are effectively explored in the chapter by Richard Byers. Equally important is the need for teachers to have a clear understanding of what each pupil can do with knowledge and understanding; hence the inclusion of a chapter by Ann Lewis on what makes for effective assessment and which identifies important issues and principles.

One of the major requirements for sound curriculum development is the need for it to be pursued by teachers who are prepared to reflect on their own practice and modify it in the light of their experiences and new models of learning and teaching. This need to develop a committed force of reflective teachers was the major motivation behind our decision to ask Sally Beveridge to contribute a chapter on action research in the context of the classroom.

Finally, the development of the whole curriculum requires careful planning; the SCAA model for curriculum planning and other influences on curriculum development and review are described in the chapter by Rob Ashdown.

In combination, the chapters in this section show that, as long as there is rigour in curriculum planning and schools have arguments to justify their policies, teachers should feel able to pick and choose the elements of the National Curriculum and other curriculum areas which are appropriate to the individual pupil and still ensure that there is sufficient breadth and balance in the curriculum.

Section 3: The context for the whole curriculum

Schools do not conduct their business of education in a vacuum. Schools depend for their success on having the active support and cooperation of parents who, by and large, see the pupils for more of their waking hours than the school staff do. In the past, all too often, schools have paid much lip-service to the concept of partnership with parents without doing enough to create the conditions for this to develop. In his chapter, Barry Carpenter explores the problems experienced by families which have a child with learning difficulties. He shows how much can be done, and is being done, to realize the ideal of a home-school partnership. The theme is continued by Philippa Russell in a chapter which explores the rights and the responsibilities of parents and does not neglect to consider the need for the involvement of the children themselves.

Schools also need well-qualified staff who are equipped to meet the demands of a complex curriculum and a complex role. In recent years, there have been reasons to doubt whether the country is keeping pace with demand for a supply of well-trained teachers of children with SEN, as discussed in a report by the Special Educational Needs Training Consortium (SENTC, 1996). Jill Porter has been close to this issue for a long time as a provider of teacher training for student teachers and experienced, qualified teachers. In her chapter she discusses the nation's requirements for competent, reflective teachers, how training was provided in the past and how it might be provided in the future.

In the final chapter of this section, Christina Tilstone reminds us that schools and all those people associated with them (i.e., parents, pupils and professionals of all kinds) have a wider obligation in their curriculum development than satisfying outside agencies like SCAA and OFSTED. There is a life beyond school and the home and all of these people have to do what they can to ensure that any obstacles that prevent children with SEN from exercising their rights and freedoms are removed so that they can participate fully in the activities of their societies at the levels and in the ways which are appropriate for each individual.

This goal has profound implications for curriculum development in schools, because at every step of curriculum planning there needs to be careful consideration as to whether it limits or extends opportunities. The extent to which the curriculum of a school permits its pupils to participate in normal community activities (e.g., education, leisure, work, living in one's own home) can have a pervasive effect on the lives of the pupils, as children and as adults, as well as on the attitudes of the general public towards all children and adults with learning difficulties and disabilities. In a climate of financial constraints, schools may be less inclined to put resources into, say, links with colleges and schools, the development of effective PSE programmes or the use of community facilities, but these opportunities serve to break down barriers to socialization in communities as well as provide opportunities for pupils to learn new skills and practise learned ones. Surely, this is the ultimate test of the ability of schools to provide an effective curriculum that guarantees access to all things which we value.

Section 4: Conclusion

Peter Mittler, who is well known for his work in the field of special education, is the final contributor to this book. His chapter brings together many of the different strands which run throughout the book and it is to him that we leave the final words. However, we would like to take this opportunity to make a few concluding remarks of our own.

Despite the promises of a period of stability for schools, we expect that there will continue to be rapid educational change. Teachers should be prepared for this. To a certain extent, future changes will affect the pertinence of all of the material that is presented in this book, but readers should find that the content remains relevant for many years to come. Each chapter contains material of interest to all teachers and gives clear pointers for the way forward in enabling all pupils to gain access to effective school curricula which, as demanded by the Education Reform Act, will equip them to benefit from the opportunities and experiences that they encounter in adult life as well as meet their responsibilities as adults. We hope that the book will be a useful resource for them in their work.

Teachers badly need opportunities for an effective debate about the nature and content of the whole curriculum. They need to widen the debate beyond the present narrow concentration on a circumscribed set of pupil competences and a small number of techniques which are in favour. Although it raises many questions as well as providing answers, we believe that this book is an effective contribution to that debate.

No longer should the National Curriculum be viewed as a straitjacket, but rather as the basis for making a response to the individual pupil. The pupil stands before us with a range of learning needs; we are teachers, and the tool of our trade is the whole curriculum. Through that curriculum we make a response to the learning needs of the pupil. In educating pupils with learning difficulties the diversity of their needs means that no one form of education will ever totally predominate. There is an ever-changing landscape of learning difficulties and this means that each year a child may appear in our classrooms the likes of whom we have never seen before, and will demand of their teachers new and innovative ways of teaching.

References

Ashdown, R., Carpenter, B., Bovair, K. (1991) *The Curriculum Challenge: Access to the National Curriculum for pupils with learning difficulties,* London: Falmer Press.

Bovair, K., Carpenter, B., Upton, G. (1992) *Special Curricula Needs*. London: David Fulton.

Byers, R. and Rose, R. (1994)' Schools should decide...', in Rose, R., Fergusson, A., Coles, C., Byers, R. and Banes, D. (eds) *Implementing the Whole Curriculum for Pupils with Learning Difficulties,* London: David Fulton.

Carpenter, B. (1992) 'The whole curriculum: meeting the needs of the whole child', in Bovair, K., Carpenter, B. and Upton, G. (eds) *Special Curricula Needs,* London: David Fulton.

Carpenter, B. (1995) 'Building an inclusive curriculum', in Ashcroft, K. and Palacio, D. (eds) *The Primary Teachers Guide to the* New *National Curriculum,* London: Falmer Press.

Carpenter, B. (in press) 'Curriculum and achievement: planning for transition', *International Journal of Adolescence and Youth.*

Clements, J. (1987) *Severe Learning Disability and Psychological Handicap,* Chichester: John Wiley.

Fagg, S., Aherne, P., Skelton, S. and Thornber, A. (1990) *Entitlement for All in Practice,* London: David Fulton.

Gulliford, R. and Upton, G. (eds) (1992) *Special Educational Needs,* London: Routledge.

Jordan, R.R. and Powell, S.D. (1994) 'Whose curriculum?: critical notes on integration and entitlement', *European Journal of Special Needs Education,* 9, 1, 27–39.

NCC (1990) *Curriculum Guidance 3: The whole curriculum,* York: NCC.

NCC (1992) *Curriculum Guidance 9: The National Curriculum and pupils with severe learning difficulties,* York: NCC.

NCC (1993) *Special Needs and the National Curriculum: Opportunity and challenge,* York: NCC.

NFER (1995) *Small Steps of Progress in the National Curriculum: An executive summary,* Slough: NFER.

SCAA (1994) *The National Curriculum and its Assessment; Final report,* London: SCAA.

SCAA (1995) *Planning the Curriculum at Key Stages 1 and 2,* London: SCAA.

SCAA (1996) *Planning the Curriculum for Pupils with Profound and Multiple Learning Difficulties,* London: SCAA.

SENTC (1996) *Professional Development to Meet Special Educational Needs: Report to the Department for Education and Employment,* Stafford: Staffordshire County Council and SENTC.

Sebba, J., Byers, R. and Rose, R. (1995) *Redefining the Whole Curriculum for Pupils with Learning Difficulties,* London: David Fulton.

Ware, J. (1994) *Educating Children with Profound and Multiple Learning Difficulties,* London: David Fulton.

Part I:
Perspectives on the National Cu

Chapter 2

English

Vivian Hinchcliffe

Introduction

Speaking and listening, reading and writing, represent the channels through which the whole-school curriculum is taught and by which children's knowledge, skills and understanding are demonstrated. The general requirement for English across the Key Stages (KSs) is that English should develop pupils' abilities to 'communicate in speech and writing and to listen with understanding' (DfE, 1995). Teachers of children with special needs may have difficulties understanding what is meant by 'effective' here (and elsewhere in the general requirements: 'effective speaking and listening pupils', 'effective readers' and 'effective writers'). However, most teachers will interpret this as a challenge to provide a curriculum which enables pupils to communicate *as effectively as possible.* Teachers working with children with special educational needs will interpret communication (within the three attainment targets (ATs) for speaking and listening, reading and writing) in its widest sense, to include augmentative communication for some pupils, e.g., objects of reference, manual signs, and symbols as identified in the access statement in the Common Requirements of the orders. The Common Requirements state that appropriate provision should be made for pupils who need augmentative communication, thereby giving pupils opportunities to use whatever means of communication is available to them (e.g., communication aids, manual signs, symbols, gesture, facial expression, vocalizations, etc.) This has raised the status of augmentative communication and has helped focus our attention on what pupils with special needs can already do with their existing communication skills in modes other than, or supplementary to, speech.

In this chapter, I intend to show how drama can be used to demonstrate children's achievement in the English ATs, especially in AT1: speaking and listening. I also hope to demonstrate how drama can offer children with special educational needs access to the programmes of study (PoS) in ways appropriate to their age, interests and abilities. Drama holds some unique merits for children with special needs. Through drama children can learn much about what Bruner calls the 'narrative mode of thought', i.e., 'human acts of imagination', such as 'good stories, gripping drama, believable (though not necessarily 'true') historical accounts' (Bruner, 1986). References to children's perience of narrative, both real and imagined, permeate the English PoS. It is my intention to show that drama can represent a powerful medium in which children can actively experience the 'narrative mode of thought'. Drama can also provide meaningful contexts in which children can learn about the social and psychological world, i.e., about people's intentions, desires, beliefs and feelings. I shall describe some drama in which these themes are explored alongside the statutory requirements for English in the National Curriculum. I will attempt to show how some of the English PoS can be taught through drama in interactive and meaningful ways.

The demise of drama

Prior to the Dearing Report (SCAA, 1994), the early demands of the National Curriculum stifled some of the work hitherto done in drama in special education. This was also true of some of the other expressive arts, even though subjects like music and art became National Curriculum subjects. The teaching time allocated to the core curriculum subjects: English, maths and science put a squeeze on the expressive arts. Drama was not a National Curriculum subject in its own right and it soon became marginalized. Other parts of the curriculum also suffered, for example, personal, social and health education (PSHE), which was once considered as the mainstay of special education. The preoccupation with the three core subjects and the heavy administrative demands on teachers meant that some of the more creative and pastoral aspects of the curriculum took a back seat. I have written elsewhere (Hinchcliffe, 1994) that the implementation of the National Curriculum in special schools militated against curriculum development in some important areas, e.g., PSHE, and effectively redirected teachers' attention away from a number of innovative approaches to teaching and learning. Since the introduction of the streamlined 1995 National Curriculum, the gradual 'freeing-up' of subject study and administrative demands has given teachers more opportunities to re-focus their attention on some of these areas of the curriculum, for example the creative arts.

The quality of drama in special schools, especially in schools for children with severe learning difficulties (SLD), can be rather patchy. To some extent this may be due to teachers' poor expectations. Some teachers are overly pessimistic of what the less-able child can understand and achieve in drama. Consequently, some of the drama that I have seen in special education is, in my opinion, unnecessarily simple and at times superficial. Drama can be constrained by too much external control (see Table 2.1); this can occur when drama becomes preoccupied with performance, for example, when children play 'walk on, walk off' parts in the Christmas nativity. The type of drama which is described towards the end of this chapter is much more spontaneous: pupils are encouraged to take control, problem-solve and improvise. This type of drama work bears a strong resemblance to children's improvisation in symbolic play (column 3, Table 2.1). Some teachers are also inexperienced in teaching drama. This is not helped by the paucity of good quality in-service training in drama (a legacy of the National Curriculum squeeze on drama in the late 1980s).

Reality ———————————————————————— Pretence				
functional play	functional / pretend play	symbolic play	drama	
e.g., parking cars in garages; dusting in imitation	habitual schemas	less contextual support	scripted	improvised
	'external control' scripts, e.g., home corner play with miniature pots and pans (props represent same objects and are used functionally)	'internal control' flexible scripts improvisation 1) object substitution e.g., blocks as cars, banana as telephone; 2) refers to absent objects as if they were present; 3) attributes properties to an object which it does not have (Lewis *et al.*, 1992)	'external control'	'internal control'
	dolls as passive recipients (to be fed/clothed)	dolls as active agents seen as having internal states – perceptions, intentions, desires, beliefs		
	compliant participants in pretend play routines, e.g., 'baby' in mummy-baby play with older siblings	dominant participants in pretend play routines, e.g., 'mummy' in mummy-baby play with younger siblings		

Table 2.1 Pretence and drama

The value of drama

I confess to being a passionate advocate of drama. I shall show later that there are sufficient references to drama in the revised English National Curriculum for schools to attach to it greater emphasis than many currently do. Below, I list the benefits of involving children at all ages and levels of ability in drama. In the next section, which describes children's work, some of these aspects are explored in greater depth.

- Drama is part of people's cultural tradition. It is a medium through which we can explore both our own, and other people's, cultural identity.

  The Education Reform Act (1988) states that all state schools must provide pupils with a curriculum that promotes their spiritual, moral, cultural, mental and physical development. Defining the first three dimensions – spiritual, moral and cultural development – is not without its problems, yet they are recognized in the 1988 Act as being 'fundamental to the process of education'. However, as has been alluded to earlier, in the years immediately following the Act, the concentration in schools on the subjects of the National Curriculum led to the issue of Circular 1/94, in which concern was expressed that 'insufficient attention has been paid explicitly to spiritual, moral and cultural aspects of pupils' development' (DfE, 1994). It is significant that the 1992 Education (Schools) Act, which instituted the current systems of school inspections, included spiritual, moral, social and cultural development prominently as one of the four statutory elements for inspection. Spiritual, moral, social and cultural development permeate the life and work of the school: the task of identifying where these dimensions are found in the curriculum is often difficult because they can be implicit and subtle. Drama is one area of the curriculum in which these elements are made explicit, indeed, as we shall see later, drama can become a medium in which to highlight, express and reflect upon spiritual, moral, social and cultural awareness, particularly the complexities of human relationships.

- Through drama, children can explore what Bruner (1986) calls the 'narrative mode of thought', i.e., human acts of imagination, e.g., 'good stories, gripping drama, believable (though not necessarily 'true') historical accounts'.

  The PoS for English in ATs 1–3 across the Key Stages make continuous reference to the narrative mode, for example at KS1:

  AT1: Speaking and Listening
  Pupils should be given opportunities to talk for a range of purposes, including:
  - telling stories, both real and imagined; imaginative play and drama... (PoS, 1.1.a).
  AT2: Reading
  The literature read should cover the following categories:
  - poems and stories with familiar settings and those based on imaginary or fantasy worlds
  - retellings of traditional folk and fairy stories; etc. (PoS, 2.1.d).
  AT3: Writing
  They should be taught to write in a range of forms, incorporating some of the different characteristics of those forms. The range should include a variety of narratives, e.g., stories, diaries, poems, etc. (PoS, 3.1.c).

  Bruner (1986) describes two types of thinking about the world: the 'paradigmatic mode of thought', which deals with the logical, systematic or scientific aspects of mental life, i.e., the kind of thought processes associated with solving puzzles, testing hypotheses and offering explanations; and the 'narrative mode of thought' which is essentially imaginative and social. According to Bruner, this is the side of the mind which allows us to make experience meaningful, and which leads to 'human acts of imagination'. For children with special educational needs, who often find their creativity suppressed by inherent difficulties with literacy skills, drama can offer a channel of expression which is dynamic and immediate.

- Drama can offer pupils valuable opportunities to learn about symbolism and representation, and can offer older pupils with learning difficulties age-appropriate opportunities to engage in pretend play.

  Representation is at the heart of the English curriculum: words, signs, gestures, rebuses are all forms of representation, symbols of meaning. Most contexts in drama make demands upon a person's representational abilities. Appreciation of drama, either watching or doing it, is dependent upon our awareness that those involved are playing parts. Drama is a representation of reality, but not reality itself (even a reenactment of a real-life event by original characters is a simulation of reality, because it is outside the current time-frame). A powerful catalyst to representational thinking, needed for most aspects of the school curriculum, e.g., number, literacy, etc., is pretend play. Pretend play and drama are closely linked and may be viewed at different points along a continuum (see Table 2.1). Most non-learning disabled children are able to play symbolically, achieving all of Lewis *et al.*'s (1992) criteria, by the time they reach 4 years of age (column 3 in Table 2.1). Teachers typically provide younger pupils with special education needs contexts in which they can engage in pretend play, e.g., the home-corner. However, teachers of older pupils, such as those with severe developmental delay, experience difficulties finding age-appropriate contexts in which to provide them with the same kind of symbolic experience. Drama can offer these older pupils similar opportunities to learn about representational thought. Young people with autism have impoverished experience of pretend play. A strong indicator of autism is a person's inability to engage in pretend play; the absence of imaginative pursuits, including this form of play, is one of the three features of impairment known as the 'triad of impairment' (Wing and Gould, 1979). Autistic children's difficulties with symbolic play have been fully documented in the literature (see Baron-Cohen, 1995). Drama may provide these children with valuable experience of representation.

- When children involve themselves in playing parts in drama, it may help them to see the world from someone else's perspective, what Piaget called the ability to 'decentre' (Piaget and Inhelder, 1956).

The ability to see the world from another person's point of view is critical to our successful integration into social life. The drama narratives used in the work cited below focus on why the central characters act in the way that they do, what they think and how they feel. Involvement in drama can highlight these implicit features of daily life, inferences which we may take for granted but which may be more confusing to some of our pupils with special needs. Role-play and debriefings afterwards may encourage children to think about the consequences of one's actions, and provide opportunities to see the world from a different perspective. Similar potential benefits can be achieved by the next point, which requires no amplification.

- Drama can offer a safe avenue in which to learn about the social world: 'the arts, by their nature of being like life but not life itself, free us temporarily from the burden of the future. They hold this feature in common with play, ...they (the arts) can take liberties with time, places and perspective...' (Heathcote, 1980, p.4).

- Drama provides pupils with opportunities to learn about their own and other people's psychological states, i.e., their intentions, desires, beliefs and feeling states.

Returning to his thesis on narrative, Bruner writes about two story landscapes on which narratives are based. One is the 'landscape of action' (which contains the constituents of the action), the sequence of events which make up the story (which Bruner likens to a 'story grammar'), and the 'landscape of consciousness' (what those involved in the action 'know, think, or feel, or do not know, think, or feel', which may also be regarded as people's psychological states) (Bruner, 1986). The ability to appreciate our own and other people's mental states is critical to our understanding of human behaviour. All of us, most of the time, take account of the way people's inner psychological states affect their behaviour. Indeed, whether we mean to or not, we are constantly striving to make sense of people's behaviour by inferring something about their 'internal states', i.e., their intentions, beliefs and feeling states (Bretherton *et al.*, 1981). For example, if a teacher asks a child a question and the child does not answer, the teacher may think that the child does not *know* the answer, does not understand, was not *attending*, has not *heard*, does not *want* to respond, etc. All the words underlined refer to the child's possible internal states. We shall see in the next section that one of the specific aims of involving the children in drama is to focus their attention upon people's internal states.

Dennett (1978) calls the human ability to understand and predict people's behaviour by reference to beliefs and desires, 'folk psychology'. Staff of Rectory Paddock School (1983) refer to this ability as 'personal-social cognition', highlighting the importance of people's knowledge and awareness of their own psychological states as well as other people's. Most of us have a strong urge to understand what 'makes people tick' and, in many ways, the better we are at 'folk psychology', the better we may fare in the social world. The consequences of not being able to represent other people's mental states, or at least not being very good at it, has been demonstrated by researchers and teachers working with certain groups of children with special educational needs. Baron-Cohen's (1995) thesis on 'mindblindness' provides a convincing account of autistic children's difficulties in contemplating other people's psychological states. Hinchcliffe and Roberts' (1987) survey of the frequency and type of internal state language (language related to intentions, beliefs and feeling states) among children with severe learning difficulties indicated a poverty of spontaneous internal state reference. A larger follow-up study by one of the authors added weight to these findings (Hinchcliffe, 1995). Hinchcliffe and Roberts found drama to be a valuable teaching context in which to develop children's conscious awareness of mental events and feelings, as well as the ability to talk about them.

- Drama can provide meaningful contexts in which children can use 'interactional speech' (Moffett, 1968).

Heathcote (1980) writes about the spontaneity of drama and how it requires participants to engage in 'interactional speech' or conversational dialogue (after Moffett, 1968). Heathcote states that the 'give and take of dialogue' in drama can represent a powerful context in which children can learn about higher level thinking and language use. She adds that drama capitalizes on interactional dialogues, stimulated by the need for individuals to collaborate in meaningful tasks and experiences.

- Participants in drama can make good use of the non-linguistic context of spoken language: body expression, gesture, facial expression, intonation of voice, etc. In addition, people can use space, time and movement to communicate meaning.

In my work with pupils with SLD over the years, some of the most memorable and expressive moments in drama have been performed by children with limited spoken language. One teenager with Down's Syndrome with whom I worked had very limited speech, but any shortcomings in verbal expression were compensated for by her ability to use sign, gesture, body language and facial expression.

A way in to drama

I wrote earlier that the PoS for English make several references to drama. In the key stages for speaking and listening, they are graded in ascending order of sophistication.

Key Stage 1, AT1: Speaking and Listening
Pupils should be encouraged to participate in drama activities, improvisation and performances of varying kinds, using language appropriate to a role or situation. They should be given

opportunities to respond to drama they have watched, as well as that in which they have participated (PoS, 1.1.d).

Key Stage 2, AT1: Speaking and Listening

Pupils should be given opportunities to participate in a wide range of drama activities, including improvisation, role-play, and the writing and performance of scripted drama. In responding to drama, they should be encouraged to evaluate their own and others' contributions (PoS, 1.1.d).

Key Stages 3 and 4, AT1: Speaking and Listening

Pupils should be given opportunities to participate in a wide range of drama activities, including role-play, and in the performance of scripted and unscripted plays. Pupils should be encouraged to develop both their communication skills and their ability to evaluate language use. In responding to drama, they should be given opportunities to consider significant features of their own and others' performances (PoS, 1.1.d).

In addition to actively participating in drama, the PoS above state that pupils should be given opportunities to respond to drama they have watched as well as that in which they have participated. In teaching drama to pupils with special needs, I prefer to encourage them to watch drama before I invite them to actively participate in drama.

Watching is easier than doing

In terms of child development, young children learn a great deal about the social world by watching (and listening to) people interact. Young children learn about pretend play by observing their siblings and parents at play, long before they become participants in pretend play. Parents and care-givers predispose young children to see the world symbolically by drawing them into pretend play routines, for example, pretending to drink from miniature cups, pretending to clear up an imaginary spillage of tea, etc. Demonstrating the representational nature of drama by doing it in front of the children capitalizes on the learning potential offered by observation. The attention of pupils at all levels of ability can be transfixed when their teachers pretend to be someone or something else, handle and use imaginary objects, etc. Demonstrating drama allows teachers to make the symbolic nature of drama explicit to their children and provides them with useful preliminary representational experience.

Children like to watch their teachers doing drama

Teachers represent powerful role models to children. Demonstrating drama allows teachers to use their total repertoire of communication skills, e.g., gesture, intonation of voice and body language: powerful clues to help children engage in drama. Children's experience of drama is likely to be richer when their teachers enter whole-heartedly into it.

Encouraging pupils to watch drama is an ideal way to ease them into doing drama

Teachers might begin by presenting scenarios which contain familiar 'scripts': representations of personally experienced events which enable children to interpret and predict people's behaviour (Nelson, 1981). Pupils can be gradually drawn into drama in the same way that mothers draw their children into play, within 'routinized settings' where teacher and pupils act within a familiar domain.

Debriefings following drama offer pupils valuable opportunities to listen and learn from one another

The PoS in speaking and listening emphasize this:

> They [pupils] should be encouraged to relate their contributions in a discussion to what has gone before, taking different views into account (KS1, PoS, 1.2.b).
> In responding to drama, they should be encouraged to evaluate their own and others' contributions (KS1, PoS, 1.1.d).
> In responding to drama, they should be given opportunities to consider significant features of their own and others' performances (KS3 and 4, PoS, 1.1.d).
> In discussions, they should be encouraged to take different views into account (KS3 and 4, PoS, 2.2.a).

Involving pupils in drama

The following work was undertaken with a group of senior pupils aged 14–18 years attending a school for pupils with SLD. The drama centred around 11 short narratives, written specifically for this group of students. The first eight narratives were performed by the teachers in front of the students; in the following three narratives, students were gradually drawn in to participate in the drama. A great emphasis was placed on discussion during debriefings following drama.

Design criteria for writing narratives for drama

All of the narratives used contained some element of conflict. Central characters were seen to deceive each other, play tricks on people, or attempt to avoid trouble by putting the blame on other characters. Some characters were shown to be jealous, envious or disappointed. Conflict was an essential design criterion. This feature drew on some of Judy Dunn's research. Her longitudinal observation of young children in the home identified certain types of domestic situation which seemed to accelerate children's learning about the social world, particularly their awareness of psychological states (Dunn,1991). Two of these conflict situations were:

- situations when children attempt to alter other people's psychological states, for example, teasing behaviour, comforting, helping and joking
- contexts in which they try to avoid some kind of disapproval (from parents or siblings), including: a) behaviour which deliberately thwarts others' intentions; b) children's excuses to evade trouble or punishment; and c) their fibs and lies.

Elements of conflict permeated all the narratives. In addition, there were other design criteria. The narratives:

- were free-standing – i.e., they were 'context-rigid' and coherent. They were short and they had clear beginnings and ends. They were all prefaced by a brief introduction, describing the characters and the scene
- were strongly emotive – they included characters deceiving each other, evading trouble, feigning illness, etc.
- were visually very powerful – the actors explicitly showed their emotions and gave strong visual and auditory clues as to their states of mind, using clear mime, gesture, facial expression and exaggerated intonation of voice

- used few real props – there was a preference for strong mime and imagery
- involved characters who sometimes thought out loud, wore their hearts on their sleeves and made occasional asides to the audience
- contained natural language – the type of language which is heard and used in real life, i.e., deliberately not differentiated to the linguistic abilities of the children, but accompanied by strong visual clues to meaning.

Clarity of intent

The intentions of this work and some examples of the relevant PoS for AT1: 'speaking and listening' are provided below. During the drama and afterwards in debriefings, students were encouraged to:

- retell (through speech and/or sign) the sequence of the main events of the story, i.e., relate what the main characters did and what they said, (KS1: to describe events, observations and experiences; KS2: to identify and comment on key features of what they see and hear in a variety of media; KS2: to recall and re-present important features of a presentation)
- discuss characters' behaviour in reference to their internal states, i.e., their beliefs, desires, intentions and feelings, for example to offer possible reasons why characters acted in the ways they did, why they said the things that they did, what were their intentions, what they may have wanted, what they may have thought and how they may have felt (KS1: to give reasons for opinions and actions; KS1, Key Skills: to use talk to develop their thinking and extend their ideas in the light of discussion; KS2: to use vocabulary and syntax that facilitate the communication of more complex meanings)
- discuss, in relation to specific narratives, what may have gone before and predict what may happen next (KS1: to explore, develop and clarify ideas; to predict outcomes and discuss possibilities; KS2: to share ideas, insights and opinions)
- generalize and relate some of the events in the narratives to real-life occurrences, for example, identifying episodes in their own lives when they have acted in the same way as story characters, felt the same emotions, etc. (KS1 and 2: as above)
- actively participate in a re-run of the story narrative, to play the parts of the main characters (KS1–4: to participate in drama activities, improvisation and performances of varying kinds, using language appropriate to a role or situation…)
- actively participate in a continuation of the story narrative, to improvise within the general story framework, along lines chosen by the students (KS1–4: as above).

Results

One of the narratives, 'The Dirty Coffee Cups', is contained in the appendix to this chapter. It shows a transcription of the adults' and students' discussion during the debriefing and demonstrates how video-recording can be used for a variety of purposes: to assess the students' abilities in the points above; to use again with the students at a later date to allow them to stand back and reflect upon the whole process; and to celebrate students' success as video Records of Achievement. Note the way some of the students were gradually drawn into the drama and were encouraged to improvise within a similar theme. Their improvisation was seen to be coherent and showed great potential for future work in this area. Although the improvisation was short, video-recording of their action revealed their ability to use facial expression and intonation of voice: for instance, Simon's statement that he was not going to school was said in a very lethargic manner; Janet's instructions were very matriarchal; David's improvised solution to the problem was very spontaneous; and David's mime (filling a receptacle with water and throwing it over Simon) was well executed, humorous, and provided further evidence of the students' ability to improvise and use mime. This work revealed how readily some of these students engaged in role play. As a small group, they were able to portray 'laziness' in an appropriate way.

Conclusion

Space does not permit me to do justice to the achievements of this group of students in their response to this work. The potential for extension of this type of work into AT2 Reading and AT3 Writing and other areas of the curriculum is great. All of the students were shown to respond to the 'narrative mode of thought' (Bruner, 1986). The less-able students were able to respond to the actions of characters using very few props, to engage in the make-believe world of drama and demonstrate an awareness of representation. Other students were shown to enter into what Bruner calls the 'landscape of consciousness', demonstrating an awareness of characters' internal states, i.e., their intentions, beliefs, desires and feelings.

In conclusion, it has been proposed that drama offers a powerful medium in which children can learn about people's internal states. This is an important focus for work in drama. Learning about people's psychological states is a necessary prerequisite to self-advocacy. Self-advocacy is one of the ways that we actively direct our own destiny; it is a means by which we make our desires, beliefs and intentions known, usually to people who have some control over us (Hinchcliffe, 1994). In order to do this, children with special needs have to learn more about emotion and the mental world; about what 'makes people tick'. I do not think that we give our pupils enough opportunities to express their thoughts, desires and feelings. Drama can open up these channels of expression.

Heathcote once wrote, 'Educational use of drama has a long way to travel' (Heathcote *et al.*, 1988). I hope that I have demonstrated some of the merits of drama for children with special needs. I hope that the revised English Orders will encourage teachers to assign to drama greater emphasis than has generally been seen in recent years.

References

Baron-Cohen, S. (1995) *Mindblindness: An Essay on Autism and Theory of Mind*, Cambridge, Mass.: Bradford Books.
Bretherton, I., McNew, S. and Beeghly-Smith, M. (1981) 'Early person knowledge as expressed in gestural and verbal communication: When do infants acquire a "theory of mind"?', in Lamb, M.E. and Sherrod, L.R. (eds), *Infant Social Cognition*, Hillsdale, NJ: Erlbaum.
Bruner, J.S. (1986) *Actual Minds, Possible Worlds*. Cambridge, Mass.: Harvard University Press.
Dennett, D.C. (1978) *Brainstorms*, Cambridge Mass.: Bradford Books.
DfE (1994) *Religious Education and Collective Worship*, Circular 1/94, London: DfE.
DfE (1995) *English in the National Curriculum* London: HMSO.
Dunn, J. (1991) 'Understanding others: evidence from naturalistic studies of children', in Whiten, A. (ed.) *Natural Theories of Mind*, Oxford : Blackwell.
Heathcote, D. (1980) *Drama as Context*, Huddersfield : NATE.

Heathcote, D., Bell, E., Bowmaker, M., Chilley, M., Gibbon, J., Oakes, S., Pivars, M. and Vause, M. (1988) 'Drama', in Roberts, T. (ed.) *Special Needs in Ordinary Schools: Encouraging expression: the arts in the primary school,* London: Cassell.

Hinchcliffe, V. and Roberts, M. (1987) 'Developing social cognition and metacognition', in Smith, B. (ed.) *Interactive Approaches to the Education of Children with Severe Learning Difficulties,* Birmingham: Westhill College.

Hinchcliffe, V. (1994) 'A special special need: self-advocacy, curriculum and the needs of children with severe learning difficulties', in Sandow, S. (ed.) *Whose Special Need?,* London: Paul Chapman.

Hinchcliffe, V. (1995) 'The social cognitive development of children with severe learning difficulties', unpublished PhD thesis, Brunel University.

Lewis, V., Boucher, J. and Astell, A. (1992) 'The assessment of symbolic play in young children: a prototype test', *European Journal of Disorders of Communication,* 27, 231–45.

Moffett, J. (1968) *Teaching the Universe of Discourse,* Boston, Mass.: Houghton Mifflin.

Nelson, K. (1981) 'Social cognition in a script framework', in Flavell, J.H. and Ross, L. (eds) *Social Cognitive Development,* Cambridge: Cambridge University Press.

Piaget, J. and Inhelder, B. (1956) *The Child's Conception of Space,* London: Routledge & Kegan Paul.

SCAA (1994) *The National Curriculum and its Assessment; Final report,* London: SCAA.

Staff of Rectory Paddock School (1983) *In Search of a Curriculum,* Sidcup: Robin Wren Publications.

Wing, L. and Gould, J. (1979) 'Severe impairments of social interaction and associated abnormalities in children: epidemiology and classification', *Journal of Autism and Developmental Disorders,* 9, 11–30.

Appendix

(Viv and Keith are teachers; the rest are students.)

Narrative: The Dirty Coffee Cups

(Keith in the living room watching television, lots of dirty cups are lined up on the floor.)

Keith: Right it must be time for Neighbours (turns on the television and lounges right back in the chair, legs outstretched, hands behind his head).

(enter Viv)

Viv: Don't you think it's about time that you cleared this mess up? (points to the line of dirty cups)

Keith: What mess?

Viv: How many cups have you got there?

Keith: (pensively, counting) Six!

Viv: You're not going to leave them there until mum gets home?

Keith: (gesturing with his arm) Oh, just leave it, leave it. ...let's watch Neighbours.

Viv: Ok, (sits down) you're the one who will get into trouble. (watches television). Don't you think that you should do something about these cups?

Students: Yes.

Keith: (again lethargically) Oh, leave them.

Debriefing

Viv: What happened in that story?

Simon:	He couldn't be bothered to clear them up.
Viv:	Yes, he had all his cups on the floor....and he just left them there.
Viv:	What did Keith say?
Peter:	Leave it.
(simultaneously)	
Janet:	Leave it.
Anna:	Leave it.
David:	Leave it.
Viv:	And how was he sitting on that chair?
Simon:	(stretching back on his chair) Like this.
Viv:	Yes, stretched back. How did he look?
(no response)	
Viv:	(to Janet) You're right in saying that he couldn't be bothered...
Janet:	Lazy.
David:	Lazy, lazy.
Viv:	Lazy...he was being a lazy bones wasn't he?
David:	(laughing) Lazybones.
Viv:	What does it mean to be lazy?
Simon:	You just sit there and do nothing.
Peter:	Not bothered to do anything.
Viv:	You just sit there, waiting for things to be done for you....I'm a bit lazy sometimes...expecting people to clear up after me...
Simon:	Yep (with amusement).
Janet:	Lazybones! (pointing to Simon) He's a lazybones.
(laughter)	
Molly:	He's quite sad.
Janet:	Everyone do it for him.
Viv:	Is there another way that we can play a part and show that someone is lazy? Who would like to show a lazy person...show someone being lazy?
Peter:	Stay in bed.
David:	Stay in bed.
Viv:	Staying in bed, right. Can we get anyone else involved?
(no response)	
Viv:	You could stay in bed...you don't want to get up...you could play that part. Can we get anyone else to play a part?
Simon:	Get up.
Viv:	Yes, we could have another person saying, 'Come on, get up'.
Janet:	This is mum.
Viv:	What would she say, then?
Janet:	Lazy bones, get up.
Viv:	Yeah, say a bit more, anything else?
Janet:	Get up for school....Or get up to go to work.
Viv:	Which would be better?
Janet:	School.
Viv:	You want to do the school. Let's try it out, we've got something here. Anyone want to play a part?
Janet:	Me, mum.
Viv:	You want to play mum, all right, come over here. Now, who wants to play someone being lazy?

(Anna points to Simon, gets up and comes to front)

Viv: Good, you're going to do some acting.

(Viv puts two easy chairs together to make a bed)

Viv: Let's say that this is a bed (Simon lays down on the bed)

Molly: Dad.

Viv: What are you going to say to Simon?

Janet: (to Simon) Lazybones get up.

Viv: Good. Can you say something else?

Molly: Dad.

Viv: You want a dad to be in this?

Molly: Yeah.

Viv: Who's going to play dad?

Anna: Peter.

Peter: What about David?

(David comes out to front)

Viv: (to Janet) Now, you and dad can think about what you are going to say.

Janet: Got to get him up for school, because he's late for school.

Viv: Good, (to David) now, you could say something about Simon, you could say
            that he has been getting a bit lazy, lately....

David: Lazy.

(students, laugh)

Janet: He never has breakfast...

Viv: We're going to leave you (gesturing to Janet, David and Simon) to do some
            acting together. Have a go.

(Janet and David approach Simon, Janet tugs on Simon's wrist)

Janet: Come on, get up!

Simon: No, I'm not going to get up for school.

(Janet begins to tug him rather vigorously)

Viv: Don' t pull him too hard. Say something else to him.

Janet: (to David) Say something to him.

David: Water.

Janet: Get some water (students pretend to get some water and throw it over
            Simon).

Chapter 3

Mathematics

Brian Robbins

Is National Curriculum mathematics relevant?

> I still can't see the point of forcing our kids through National Curriculum maths. What use will it
> be to them when they leave school?

Sandra, an experienced special school teacher, had sat through the mathematics
coordinator's presentation on the Dearing Review and was experiencing an
overwhelming sense of *déjà-vu*. When the National Curriculum was first introduced she
had expressed doubts about its relevance to her pupils. She couldn't understand why her
headteacher had been so determined that the school should follow it and she was
convinced that the new orders made it no more likely that her pupils would achieve an
acceptable standard in the subject.

Sandra could contain herself no longer: 'At the beginning of term the special needs
adviser said we should remember what Dearing said, that the curriculum has to be
"wholly relevant and meaningful" to the children we teach. Surely if the National
Curriculum isn't relevant we should disapply them and save them and ourselves a lot of
anxiety.'

Support for this view could be gained from much that was written about mathematics
in special education prior to and following the introduction of the National Curriculum.
The report of Schools Council Low Attainers in Mathematics Project (Denvir *et al.*, 1982)
pointed out that mathematics curricula for low attainers had been derived from those
which are seen to benefit the more able pupils. It referred to the practice of
concentrating on number work with lower achieving children and quoted a primary
school where the work being done by the 'remedial' group was both harder and less
motivating than the parallel topic work being done by the rest of the class and required
those very skills, such as formal recording, at which the children were weakest.

The National Curriculum with its set standards of expectation had the potential to take
us down the same road. Many pupils in special education spend the whole of their
school careers not achieving Level 1, supporting the predictions of O'Toole and O'Toole
(1989). The phrase, 'Working towards Level 1' was introduced. It may have been
intended to suggest that progress was taking place but like so many well-meaning
phrases, it quickly became a euphemism for failure.

Dearing – a gain or a loss?

The relief felt when the Dearing Review made the primary curriculum more manageable has been tempered by a tinge of regret amongst many teachers in special education at losing the greater detail of the original Statements of Attainment. Teachers who need to pace learning more carefully have taken the opposite view to those who perceive the National Curriculum as a syllabus to be worked through by the end of each Key Stage. This indicates different perspectives on teaching, which is a significant factor in the much wider debate around inclusive education. In terms of teaching and learning mathematics, teachers in special education were probably more comfortable with the precision of the original orders than mainstream colleagues.

Mathematics as a subject

Standards or quality?

The debate on standards in mathematics continues with Jagger (1996) being critical of the concern to teach secondary mathematics in the context of real-life problems and seeing the need to focus on mathematics as a subject. From a special education viewpoint this is counter to much of the work done under such headings as 'social arithmetic' and currently being promoted at the vocational education level by City and Guilds Numberpower.

The crux of this argument is whether we view mathematics as a subject, as a means of accessing other areas of the curriculum, or as an essential skill for adult life. It is, of course, all three and we need to take the argument a step further to consider the balance that needs to be struck in mathematics teaching between each of these requirements.

The debate usually centres around 'standards', and comparisons are drawn between the relative ease with which children of a particular age in different countries can handle complex numerical problems. A good example of this line of criticism was contained in the headline 'British maths fails to add up' (Pyke, 1996) and the report below it continues in this narrow-minded vein. It is only by reading beyond this and looking more closely at the research (Burghes, 1996) that we can appreciate that the introduction of the National Curriculum has created uncertainty amongst teachers. Laying the blame at the door of, on the one hand 'traditional', or on the other 'progressive', methodologies is unfair and a waste of time and energy. Many teachers can quote examples of children who could 'number-crunch' but would have no idea how to apply that knowledge. Using computation as a measure of mathematical standards is as reliable as selecting grand prix drivers on the assumption that their technical knowledge alone is an accurate indicator of their ability to handle a car at high speed.

We need to draw the distinction between 'quality' and 'standards' of learning. Whatever standards or national norms are strived for, it is the usefulness of that knowledge to the learner that is the test of the quality of what he or she has achieved. It is not sufficient to set hurdles for the pupil to jump and, if he or she doesn't succeed, to make them higher. Skemp (1971) distinguished between 'understanding' and 'learning without understanding'. He illustrates it as the difference between a person with a plan who, if he or she takes one wrong step will be lost and the person with a mental map of the town who will be able to construct a route wherever he or she starts from and adapt that route as they proceed.

Teachers' skills in teaching mathematics

The talented special needs teacher, and there are many in our schools, will guide the pupil along the pathway of learning, using imagination and knowledge of the pupil to find ways of achieving success so that interest and motivation are maintained and self-esteem restored. In doing so they will have helped the pupil to develop their own 'mental maps' so that they can use the skills they possess to deal with new challenges.

This is basic good practice in many of our special schools and learning support teams, and there is clearly a need to 'go back to basics', but perhaps not in the way that tabloid headline writers mean. We need to appreciate that if learning is, as it has to be if it is to be truly effective, an interactive partnership between learner and teacher, then we must address what each brings to the learning and teaching process.

Teachers bring to their daily task a history of their own mathematics learning which may not have been a satisfying experience. Now they face the pressures of getting their pupils through the National Curriculum and scoring well in the Standard Assessment Tests, the demands of the reluctant learner, the slow learner and those who seem to them bent on preventing anyone else learning, and the knowledge that beyond the schools walls is an army of experts, each with a view to express on what is wrong with mathematics teaching.

They will be drawn towards finding the 'best maths scheme'. Publishers have successfully promoted the idea that maths can be taught through schemes, and then failed, inevitably, to publish schemes that meet everyone's needs.

Schemes won't meet teachers' needs in full because every teacher has a different level and type of background knowledge, differing amounts of confidence in teaching maths, different levels of personal mathematical competence, different understanding of the process of learning mathematics and a different appreciation of how that process can break down in the minds of individual children. They won't meet pupils' needs because every pupil comes to learning with a unique body of mathematical knowledge.

Pupils' skills

Some will come with a clear understanding and well-developed skills built on sound early mathematical experiences provided by parents, siblings, playgroup, nursery school and capable infant teachers. Others will have a jumbled set of specific, semi-formed and probably unrelated bits of learning seasoned with quite fundamental misconceptions. Some will be given the encouraging label 'good at maths', others will be identified by less complimentary epithets.

Mathematics in particular is built on previous learning, and certain key elements of knowledge and skill are prerequisites to successful new learning. Donaldson (1978) recognizes that the work of Piaget (1952) made a fundamental contribution to our understanding of how children learn basic mathematical concepts, but questions whether he was right to assert that the learning of these concepts cannot be hastened. When faced with pupils who do not possess these concepts in any way that enables them to apply them, we need as teachers to find strategies to enable them to understand and be able to apply these essential tools.

This is one example of the tensions that have been created for teachers who know that it is unrealistic to push their pupils towards unachievable targets and yearn for a more realistic and meaningful approach to mathematics teaching.

The Cockroft influence

Sandra had done her special education training in the days when the Cockroft Report (DES, 1982) was the most-quoted guide to mathematics teaching. The report recognized that mathematics is used in a number of contexts and she was convinced that it should be taught not in an abstract manner but in situations that could be understood by the pupils. She found strong echoes of those sentiments in the Dearing Report (SCAA, 1994).

Have we been through one of those cycles of history where we appear to have returned to the point we started from? Has the National Curriculum been an unfortunate blip which has distracted us from the real business of teaching children with special needs appropriately and forced us down the wrong alley?

Many people, the writer included, have tried to match pre-National Curriculum materials to the structure it imposed. Some, the present writer not included, have rewritten all their work to that structure, which must make the frequent changes to that structure, from the original 14 attainments targets (DES, 1989) to five in the first revision (DES 1991) galling for writers and expensive for publishers, not to mention the confusion it has caused and the many valuable teacher-hours taken up in revising schemes of work and record-keeping systems.

So has the whole thing been a waste of time and energy and would we have been better avoiding being caught up in the National Curriculum exercise?

Inclusion

Those of us who pushed for inclusion (Robbins, 1989) did so in the belief that to argue otherwise would sideline our pupils at a time when the pressure for inclusion was mounting and would marginalize teachers. Certainly there were difficulties for special schools (Robbins, 1992) but where teachers from special education worked alongside mainstream colleagues there was mutual benefit. In that sense the process that has taken place since 1988 could be said to have promoted an acceptance of the right of pupils identified as having special needs to have the same entitlement as others. It is hard to measure the degree to which the National Curriculum has been responsible and the extent to which other forces, such as a wider acceptance of the desirability of including special schools in mainstream projects at both local and national levels, have played their part.

The OFSTED factor

At a classroom level the beleaguered teacher in a moderate learning difficulties (MLD) school, anxious whether an OFSTED inspector is going to criticize her for not teaching multiplication to her 8-year-old pupils, is unlikely to appreciate these fine nuances of changes in educational practice. She might not thank those who pushed for involvement in the National Curriculum and look back with nostalgia to a time when she could teach her pupils what she and her colleagues thought was best for them. For her the whole exercise has been stressful, time- and energy- consuming and of limited value educationally.

The concern at its introduction was that children with learning difficulties should have an entitlement to participate in the National Curriculum. Perhaps in retrospect what we desired was equality of opportunity and the National Curriculum seemed the obvious vehicle for achieving that. The challenge then was to achieve access and vast amounts of midnight oil were burned in matching schools' mathematics schemes to the National Curriculum. 'Making the National Curriculum accessible' was a major drive that is still a sought-after topic for in-service education.

Published schemes

Publishers have sought to respond to the demand for materials for pupils who are not considered capable of following mainstream mathematics schemes to work through at their own pace. The search for this particular Holy Grail has led in the past to a continuous diet of simplified worksheets and pages of rote number-crunching exercises.

The National Curriculum subject order has influenced what is available for teaching mathematics to the extent that most schemes are now structured to match it. If schemes aren't so structured then publishers will have included guidance on how the contents can be related to the National Curriculum. Personal experience of doing it for Mathsteps (Robbins 1987,1993a) showed that it wasn't always straightforward.

Worryingly, this focus on the National Curriculum might lead authors and publishers to exclude items which they had previously thought necessary.

Meaningful mathematics

The 1995 National Curriculum loosened the straitjacket and gave us the scope to address the legitimate concerns of people like Sandra without forgoing the potential benefits for our pupils of being associated with the main flow of mathematics education. This is particularly important at the interface between mainstream and special education.

Having recognized that the National Curriculum gave us a common language for setting expectations and providing appropriate teaching, the battle for acceptance has been won. The battle now is to make the pupil's mathematical experiences meaningful and relevant.

Some reasons for learning mathematics

- To acquire the basic skills for everyday life
- To develop the ability to think logically
- To encourage an independent approach to learning by equipping children with the skills of observation, recording and appraisal of information
- To provide a wide range of interesting experiences
- To use mathematics as a means of understanding their environment
- To gain skills that will be needed in adult life
- To develop each pupil's full potential.

(This list draws on the findings of the Low Attainers in Mathematics Project – Denvir *et al.*, 1982.)

Differentiation

This appears a great freedom, but it brings with it an awesome responsibility that is encapsulated in that over-used word, 'differentiation'. We may find it hard to define but we know it when we see it being done well or when it is not being done.

The topic is dealt with in much more detail elsewhere (e.g., Peter, 1992); it is sufficient in this context to recognize that differentiation in mathematical education can be achieved by setting different tasks for individual pupils or by working towards a range of outcomes in a group or class activity. Both have their place and it would be unwise to ignore the strengths and drawbacks of each approach. Children gain a lot from working together but the teacher needs to be aware of what each one brings to the task and what each can be expected to gain from it.

Differentiation of input need not mean 'death by a thousand worksheets'! There are many ways in which activities can be individualized without resorting to this strategy. It is worth reiterating the dictum of the Cockroft Report that mathematics should involve practical, oral and written work. 'Written' products may not be achievable by some pupils and this latter item should perhaps be redefined as 'representational,' to include drawn outcomes.

Staff at a special school were reminded of a drawback of differentiation by input when some but not all of the pupils were given tasks in the National Curriculum Key Stage 3 SATs. Those left out, because the tasks were considered too difficult for them, were upset at not being given the opportunity to do them. They had certainly made a clear statement on 'inclusion'!

Programmes of study

In the original National Curriculum order (DES, 1989) some aspects of mathematics, which in previous studies had been highlighted as of particular importance to pupils with learning difficulties, were not clearly identified, or were included in unexpected, and to many of us inappropriate, places.

Time and money were all given a significant status in previous work which Robbins (1981) surveyed, and from his analysis he set out the main strands of a consensual mathematics curriculum. The foundations of mathematical concepts were not given due attention. The work on early mathematics is almost dismissed in that dreadful phrase 'Working towards Level 1'.

Aspects of mathematics considered most significant for pupils with learning difficulties

Number
Fractions
Money
Measure
Time
Pictorial representation
Shape
Sets
Pattern
Geometry

(Robbins, 1981)

Using and applying mathematics

When the original National Curriculum orders were published (DES 1989) many teachers in special education realized that AT1, Using and Applying Mathematics, was a challenge, and yet it was the area where we should have been making most effort. We have been aware for many years that many pupils with learning difficulties do not generalize knowledge readily and that for them to transfer to an unfamiliar situation what has been learned in one particular context has not come easily. It is often as, if not more, difficult to apply what might has been presented to them in rote fashion with no contextual reference. 'I hear and I forget, I see and I remember, I do and I understand' – the Chinese proverb that influenced 'modern mathematics' – may not sit easily alongside the strenuous efforts to cover enough in the mathematics curriculum at KS1 and KS2 for some pupils to reach the highest expected levels for number or algebra. And yet it may well be that the pupils of those teachers who, working to the kind of policy that contains the points made in the 'School's Mathematics Policy Checklist', below, have been able to provide a range of mathematical experiences, and taught the mathematical knowledge and skills in a way that has enabled the children to form accurate and meaningful concepts, are those that are equipped for secondary mathematics.

The demand to 'get through the levels' led to the temptation to feed pupils a diet of repetitive exercises as a means of meeting the requirement to 'do some maths', often reinforced by parental pressure for their children to be able to count and calculate and demands to see evidence that they were 'doing proper maths'.

Appropriate, relevant and meaningful

The phrase in the 1995 National Curriculum orders that the curriculum for each pupil should be 'wholly relevant and meaningful' gives us the scope and the confidence to apply an 'appropriate, relevant, meaningful' test to the new Programmes of Study (PoS) from the point of view of pupils with varying degrees of learning difficulty. Guidance on adapting them for pupils with profound and multiple learning difficulties (PMLD) is contained in a booklet produced by the Schools' Curriculum and Assessment Authority (SCAA, 1996). Teachers of pupils with other types of learning difficulty would find that many of the points made in this document have relevance for their curriculum planning.

School's Mathematics Policy – Checklist

Entitlement
– does your mathematics policy recognize:
entitlement for all pupils to the National Curriculum PoS?
mathematics as an essential means of communication?
the place of mathematics in the development of logical thinking?

Expectations
– does your school's mathematics teaching:
give all pupils the chance to succeed?
challenge them to achieve more?

Equal opportunities
– is your mathematics curriculum:
free from gender and racial stereotyping?
accessible to all pupils?

Experiences
– do pupils have a broad range of mathematical experiences?
– do pupils experience working individually, in groups
and as part of a whole class?
– is there a balance between practical, oral and written activities?

Goals of a Mathematics Curriculum

Pupils should learn relevant factual information
  – mathematical terms and notations (such as 'sets', +, - , x)
  – mathematical conventions (such as standard units)
  – results (such as number bonds)

Pupils should develop basic mathematical skills
  – performing basic operations
  – communicating in mathematical terms
  – using information technology

Pupils should develop mathematical concepts
  – recognize relationship between one concept and other (e.g. addition and subtraction)
  – select appropriate data to find the solution to a problem

Pupils should develop basic strategies for problem solving
  – make an estimation
  – use trial and error methods
  – look for patterns
  – reason logically

Pupils should develop personal skills
  – good work habits
  – positive attitude to mathematics

Early mathematical experiences

Learning theorists from Piaget onwards have given us insights into how children learn mathematics. By its structure the National Curriculum has compartmentalized that learning under artificial headings. The National Curriculum structure has one fatal flaw: it fails to give the proper value to the learning that underpins achievement in KS1.

The weasel phrase 'Working towards Level 1' has crept into educational jargon. This is a meaningless and totally unjustified down-grading of the vast richness of experiences that children bring to school. It is as if the pioneering work of Matthews (1990) never happened. It is that learning, or the lack of it, that makes or breaks achievement in mathematics.

There are many ways in which teachers can encourage pupils to have a positive attitude towards mathematics; examples are given of some approaches that have been successful.

A positive attitude to mathematics – 1

Mathematics in history

Have you thought how mathematics began?
The farmer in times before recorded history needed to know how many sheep he had to make sure they hadn't been eaten by wolves or stolen by his neighbour. His solution was to have a pile of stones and, in the same way a cricket umpire keeps count of the number of balls to go in each over, moves one from one pile (or in the umpire's case 'pocket') to the other, each time a sheep goes past him into the next field.

Extension
What were the difficulties with this system?
Can you think of a better way?
Why didn't the Stone Age farmer use a calculator?

A positive attitude to mathematics – 2

Mathematics in history

The Roman Empire
The Romans were great engineers and without mathematics they could not have made the impressive buildings and roads that have survived 2,000 years. Their mathematics is based on a system of numerals, Roman numerals.

Have you thought about the relationship between fingers and Roman numerals?
I – one finger.
V– a full hand. Hold your hand in front of you with the fingers spread and you will see the outline is roughly a 'V'.
X – two 'V's.

Extension
A history/mathematics topic could be built around school children in Roman times learning mathematics. For example, think of number words like 'centurion'.

A positive attitude to mathematics – 3

Mathematics and English

Many children's stories can be used for developing mathematical concepts. Next time you are browsing in the children's section of a bookshop look at the vocabulary and see how it matches many of the mathematical concepts your pupils have been struggling with. For example:

Classifying words: same, match, different, big, small ..., circle, square, triangle, oblong...
Number words: one, two..., first, second..., each, every, enough, too many, less, more...
Sequencing words: bigger, smaller, shorter, heavy, light
Spatial words: in, inside, out, on, under, above, between, over, across
Time words: morning, breakfast, night, days, winter, birthday....
(A fuller vocabulary list is in *Mathsteps*, Robbins 1993a. Examples of the story approach are given in *Don't you Enjoy Maths?*, Robbins, 1990.)

A positive attitude to mathematics – 4

Mathematics, French, geography, history and food technology

A special school (MLD) visits Brittany with its Year 8 pupils as part of their annual programme. The visit is part of a cross-curricular topic entitled 'Food and markets'.

In preparation for the visit they learn French; they have 'hands-on' experience of French currency; they learn about the country and the route they will travel and they visit their local markets.

During their time in Brittany they go to markets and many other places of interest.

Each evening they discuss what they have seen and learned and then hear a story about one of the heroes of Breton history whose memorial they will have seen or heard about that day.

They will draw a time-line with the dates of all the events and the lifetimes of the historic figures.

(Robbins, 1993b; 1995).

A positive attitude to mathematics – 5

Mathematics in the workplace

A recent event run by an education and business partnership involved special school pupils alongside mainstream primary pupils in a mathematics day.

All the activities were based on the KS2 PoS, 'Using and applying mathematics'. The pupils were in mixed special school/mainstream school groups and each group spent 20 minutes on four of a series of six activities. Each activity was run by a teacher and an employee of one of the companies involved, which were a distribution company, a bank, a travel agent, a large building company and a manufacturing company.

The distribution company's task involved the pupils in studying the schedule for a lorry and, working as a team, answering questions based on it. The mathematical skills involved were time, distance, the 24-hour clock and interpreting tables and clocks.

Other activities included one on eating abroad, designing a drive and creating a 'net' of a cereal box and comparing the weights of different goods (this activity is described later).

(Arranged by Liz Nasta of Birmingham Education and Business Partnership and Jane Davis of the Birmingham Curriculum Support Service.)

Success in mathematics can support progress in other areas, particularly by promoting the pupil's self-esteem.

A positive attitude to mathematics – 6

Mathematics and PSE

D had been placed in a special school following considerable difficulties in a primary school. He was always recognized as being amongst the more able pupils in his MLD school and return to mainstream was a realistic option. There were two concerns: primarily his tendency to disrupt the work of his peers by sudden outbursts, and secondly whether his core skills were sufficiently developed to meet the demands of a secondary curriculum.

After a considerable amount of liaison between the special school and a neighbouring secondary school, several false starts because of cold feet on D's part and his mother, he transferred successfully during Year 9. One positive factor was his ability at mathematics and he was able to cope successfully in a higher mathematics set than most of his peers in the supported learning group.

After one or two initial *contretemps* with his peers he has recognized that his annoying habits are unacceptable and has settled down to work. After six months there is every indication that his return to mainstream will be permanent.

The following are examples at each Key Stage of how items in the PoS can be adapted for pupils with particular types of learning difficulty.

Key Stage 1 PoS

Understanding relationships between numbers and developing methods of computation

Activity with a class of pupils in an SLD school.
Learning objective: Clapping a rhythm of three claps.
Materials: None
Activity: Clap twice. Ask the pupils to do the same in time with you. If successful, clap three times and ask the pupils to clap three in time with you.
Success criteria: Clapping three in time with the teacher.
(This activity is one of a progressive series in *Mathsteps*, Robbins, 1993a.)

Key Stage 2 PoS

Shape, space and measures

Activity with a class of 8- and 9-year-old pupils in an MLD school
Learning objective: To make a box capable of holding a variety of dried goods which will also protect the goods.
Materials: Nets, drawn to the shape required to make a box.
A variety of dried goods (cereals, oats, rice, dried peas).
Scissors, sellotape, scales, weights.
Activity: A discussion about packaging and the definition of dried goods. Pupils each cut out a net and sellotape it together. Fill it with one type of dried good and weigh. Record the findings and repeat with other dried goods. Compare the weights to find the lightest and heaviest. Discussion about value for money, how the same size box can hold different quantities.
Success criteria: All pupils actively involved and enjoying the activity. Pupils able to give reasons why one box held different quantities. Able to state that when shopping it is important to look at the weight displayed on the box. Mess on table and floor indicating the active participation of pupils!

Using mathematics

The KS2 activity contributes to the mathematics curriculum by utilizing knowledge and skills, and concepts in varying stages of development, that can be described within the headings 'understanding and using properties of shape' and 'understanding and using measures'. It also contributes to the design and technology curriculum.

A teacher who is confident with both the mathematics and design and technology curricula can provide learning opportunities within the PoS of the National Curriculum, and by using imagination and resourcefulness, reach beyond the constraints of each one and achieve meaningful experiences. Teachers skilled at differentiation will lead every pupil to achieve something in this activity.

All will construct the box from the net, all will participate in the filling and weighing. Some will grasp the underlying concepts of conservation and comparison, others may have to return to it in another activity.

A criticism of mathematics schemes is that they jump from one topic to another and do not allow for sufficient consolidation of learning. In the example quoted above the teacher would develop this theme over a series of lessons, giving opportunities for those who have understood to take the topic further, while those who have not yet reached that point are able to experience similar activities.

There is little point in presenting the next topic if the pupil has not achieved some of the learning inherent in the present one. This seems obvious but there are still examples to be found of pupils being presented with work because it comes next on the syllabus and not because it is the next logical stage in their progression to mathematical understanding.

Key Stage 3 PoS

Understanding and using measures

Activity with a class of pupils in an MLD school
Learning objective: Estimating and measuring time.
Materials: Clock or stop watch, recording sheets with columns headed: 'Guess' and 'Actual time'.
Activity: Working with a partner discuss how long you think it would take to undertake familiar tasks, such as: counting to 100, writing your name, making a wall with 20 cubes, boiling a kettle, getting to school.
Success criteria: Making an accurate measurement of the actual time taken and comparing it with the estimate.

(Similar activities are in the SMILE materials.)

Key Stage 4 PoS

Processing and interpreting data

Activity with a class of pupils in an MLD school
Learning objective: Undertaking purposeful enquiries. This activity encourages pupils to find out information and develop their personal skills.
Materials: Recording sheet. Airport information brochure and timetables.

Activity: Pupils find out:
- the airport telephone number
- which flight would get you to each destination by midday
- which flight would get you back to Birmingham by 1800
- the time taken from departure to arrival for each flight.

Success criteria: Each pair successfully completes the recording sheet through their own investigations.

Maths across the curriculum

We have seen examples of how mathematics need not be a stand-alone subject but a body of knowledge applied in other aspects of the curriculum.

Many teachers felt that the National Curriculum led to the popular means of cross-curricular activity, topic work, being frowned upon. There was certainly a strenuous effort to justify it in terms of the National Curriculum, the most common manifestation being the ubiquitous topic web which seemed to cascade triffid-like from every in-service course! But if we regard the school curriculum as, amongst other things, a means of learning those skills that will stand young people in good stead in adult life, then we don't need to contrive a set of subject-suckered tentacles!

The view of the School Curriculum and Assessment Authority is that curriculum planning should take account of issues which permeate the whole curriculum but be based upon a subject-focused process (SCAA, 1996). For instance, a significant amount of relevant work is carried out in food technology. It requires the application of a wide range of mathematical skills and it has been used as a vehicle in special education for teaching not only maths but other subjects such modern foreign languages (Robbins, 1993b; 1995).

Conclusion

Whatever changes are made to the National Curriculum, now or in the future, we must not lose sight of the requirement that the curriculum be 'wholly meaningful and relevant'.

This chapter began by reminding ourselves how mathematics became an accepted part of the curriculum for pupils with learning difficulties. It was there because it was relevant, and we must always guard against introducing the irrelevant or the inappropriate in response to external pressures. It has to be meaningful, not in a contrived way but in a manner that links with previous learning, current experience and an appreciation of what mathematical knowledge will be useful in adult life. The targets set in Individual Education Plans should project forward from previous learning, project back from future needs and reach across the range of educational activities, subjects and cross-curricular dimensions.

Rather than be either excited or disappointed about National Curriculum mathematics, we should take hold of the flexibility we now have and construct our school curriculum in a way that gives us scope to pitch mathematics-based activities at many levels.

Above all we must be wary of lowering expectations by dismissing something as 'totally inappropriate'. The more positive approach is to say, 'In my professional judgement, knowing the current achievements, level of understanding and learning characteristics of this individual pupil, this is not yet an appropriate target. However, I can see how it might in the future be something well worth him learning and this is how I intend to introduce activities to develop the knowledge, skills and understanding underlying this target.'

We must endeavour to approach the teaching of mathematics with dynamism and imagination, recognizing that it is a living subject that should not be contained within sterile subject boundaries. Teachers who approach it in this way will find their own fascination with mathematics grows as they appreciate the creative possibilities in what they might previously have seen as a dull and demotivating part of their own experience as a pupil. We must be alert to ways of developing mathematical knowledge in contexts that are relevant, meaningful and motivating to each learner, whatever their learning characteristics. Above all, we must aim to increase every young person's facility with the powerful range of skills that come under the umbrella of mathematics.

Acknowledgements

The author is grateful to the Mathematics Curriculum Team at Hallmoor School for the policy document and several of the activities included in this chapter.

References

Burghes, D. (1996) 'Why we lag behind in maths', *Times Educational Supplement,* 15 March.
Denvir, B., Stolz, C. and Brown, M. (1982) *Low Attainers in Mathematics,*
Schools Council Working Paper 72,London:Methuen.
DES (1982) *Mathematics Counts* (The Cockroft Report),London: HMSO.
DES (1989) *Mathematics in the National Curriculum,* London: HMSO.
DES (1991) *Mathematics in the National Curriculum (1991),* London: HMSO.
DfE (1995) *Mathematics in the National Curriculum,* London: HMSO.
Donaldson, M. (1978) *Children's Minds,* Glasgow: Fontana/Collins.
Jagger, J. (1996) 'First of all, what's the question?', *Times Educational Supplement,* 15 March.
Matthews, G. (1990). *Early Mathematical Experiences* (3rd edn), Harlow: Longman.
O'Toole, B. and O'Toole, P. (1989),. 'How accessible is Level 1 Maths?', *British Journal of Special Education,* 16, 3,115–18.
Peter, M. (ed.) (1992) *Differentiation: Ways forward,* Tamworth: NASEN Enterprises.
Piaget, J. (1952),. *The Child's Conception of Number,* London: Routledge and Kegan Paul.
Pyke, N. (1996) 'British maths fails to add up', *Times Educational Supplement,*
15 March.
Robbins, B. (1981) 'Mathematics for slow-learners: curriculum development through materials evaluation', unpublished M.Ed. dissertation. University of Birmingham.
Robbins, B. (1988) *Mathsteps* (1st edn), Wisbech: LDA.
Robbins, B. (1989) 'There's a place for us', *Junior Education,* October, 35.
Robbins, B. (1990) 'Don't you enjoy Maths?', in Smith. B. (ed.) *Interactive Approaches to Teaching the Core Subjects,* Bristol: Lame Duck Publishing.
Robbins, B. (1992) 'No easy option', *Junior Education,* April, 50–51.
Robbins, B. (1993a) *Mathsteps* (2nd edn), Wisbech: LDA.
Robbins, B. (1993b) 'Sans Frontieres', *Special Children,* April, 18–20.
Robbins, B. (1995) 'Links across Europe', *Special,* Spring, 4, 15–17.
SCAA (1994) *The National Curriculum and its Assessment; Final report,* London: SCAA.
SCAA (1996) *Planning the Curriculum for Pupils with Profound and Multiple Learning Difficulties,* London: SCAA.

Skemp, R. (1971) *Psychology of Learning Mathematics,* Harmondsworth: Penguin.
SMILE individualized mathematical activities and resources, details from: SMILE Centre, 108a
    Lancaster Road, London W11 1QS.

Chapter 4

Science

Ron Ritchie

Introduction

When the National Curriculum was first announced in 1986, the inclusion of science as a core subject came as a surprise to many teachers. At that time, science was effectively an 'optional extra' in the curricula of the majority of primary and special schools. However, a decade later science can be regarded as one of the success stories of the National Curriculum. It has become generally accepted by teachers that all pupils have an entitlement to a science education, although there is still some way to go to make such an entitlement a practical reality. The government had originally indicated its intention of introducing 'Science for all' in a policy document (DES, 1985). This set an agenda covering breadth, balance, relevance, differentiation, equal opportunities, continuity, progression, links across the curriculum, teaching methods and assessment that led to the science National Curriculum. This chapter explores the implications of a science curriculum for all pupils from 5 to 16 and addresses the particular opportunities and challenges this provides for teachers working in special schools.

Science was by no means universally welcomed into the curriculum. It was introduced as a core subject at a time when Her Majesty's Inspectorate was reporting inadequate provision for science in special schools (HMI, 1986; 1990). In some, the introduction of science meant a move away from a relatively narrow curriculum that focused on language and mathematics skills. Some teachers remained to be convinced that science was appropriate for their pupils. Others saw science as a means of enriching the curriculum as well as adding breadth, recognizing the enthusiasm pupils with SEN often had for science (Carter, 1994). Indeed, science was argued to have particular benefits for such pupils. Guidance material from the National Curriculum Council (NCC) states that 'activities in science have characteristics which will help pupils with SEN achieve success' (NCC, 1992). The following reasons are cited: science activities are based on direct first-hand experiences; skills and knowledge and understanding can be developed in small steps through practical activity, so helping concentration; science activities can capture the imagination and may reduce behavioural problems; working in groups can encourage participation and interpersonal communication.

Teaching science poses considerable challenges for many teachers, including those working in special schools. Perhaps of most significance is some teachers' lack of confidence to teach science. This results from a number of factors, but especially lack of subject knowledge (Wragg *et al.*, 1991). The perceived problems of organizing science in a practical way also inhibits its development. Teachers may recognize the importance of their pupils learning through doing but often find such activities difficult to manage. Add to this a lack of resources in many schools, lack of suitable accommodation and technician support for older pupils, concerns about health and safety and lack of in-service education and training (INSET) opportunities for teachers and the reasons for the somewhat uncertain development of science become apparent. The introduction of science as a core subject did not guarantee all pupils had opportunities to learn science.

The nature of science and science education

The key purpose of science is to enable us to understand the physical and biological world. In this sense it could be argued that science is clearly of relevance to everyone. Science provides a particular means, or method, of gaining knowledge and understanding through a process of investigation. This usually involves the collection of empirical evidence to test out ideas, or hypotheses, in order to falsify or support them, drawing on a range of skills such as predicting, estimating and measuring, fair testing, recording and pattern-seeking. Such skills are used by scientists working on new explanations for materials' behaviour in a laboratory, or pupils learning about the properties of materials in the classroom. Scientists spend much of their time on routine laboratory work, perhaps of an observational nature. This can also be reflected in the way we teach science. Regardless of the nature of pupils' particular difficulties, it is important for them to use their senses effectively. Indeed, the 'sensory curriculum' is common in special schools as a means of facilitating this aim. For example, much work associated with the early sensory cognitive areas of the curriculum for pupils with profound and multiple learning Difficulties (PMLD) have direct links with science (Gibson, 1991). Science provides a context for pupils' observations to be carried out with purpose.

Scientists are curious: their observations often lead to questions that can be answered by investigating. Fostering pupils' curiosity is an aim of science education. It is, of course, more challenging with some pupils than others. However, most pupils have a natural interest in the world around them, which can be built on through science. Attitudes (such as curiosity, perseverance, independence and respect for evidence) are fundamental to learning, but do not feature explicitly in the National Curriculum, although they are included in OFSTED's criteria for inspecting the quality of learning in science (OFSTED, 1995). Fostering such attitudes can be a positive outcome of science work, contributing to pupils' self-esteem and learning in other areas of the curriculum.

Science as a process leading to provisional understanding, rather than a fixed body of knowledge, is another potential benefit of science education. The way pupils work scientifically is as important in terms of learning as the ideas about science that they develop. Supporting pupils to approach activities systematically, perhaps using a framework such as 'plan/do/review', can make an important metacognitive contribution to their learning, helping them understand *how* they learn as well as *what* they learn. Science provides opportunities for pupils to work at their own level, testing their ideas systematically alongside those of others. The way in which they work can, in many ways, mirror the work of real scientists.

Pupils' learning in science

Pupils learn best in science when they engage in a practical way with the world around them. However, experience alone is rarely enough; we need to recognize the part that communication and the social context play. The way in which learners interact with each other and with their teacher, or other adults, is an essential element of the learning equation. Over the last decade a great deal of research has been conducted into pupils' learning in science (e.g., CLIS, 1988–92; SPACE, 1990–93). From this research, it is evident that learners (of all ages and levels of capability) approach new experiences in science with existing ideas about the world and that these ideas, however naive and undeveloped, will significantly affect their future learning. Learning is an active process of structuring existing understanding prior to restructuring ideas as a result of new experiences or teacher intervention. Consequently, research would suggest that it is important for teachers to elicit children's existing ideas and use these to inform decisions about appropriate interventions. 'Starting from where the learner is' is hardly a new idea. However, the insights offered by research concern the nature of pupils' existing ideas and the prevalence of 'common alternative ideas' which can help teachers plan their science work. For example, it is common for pupils to think that: their eyes actively send out light when they see; that plants get their food from the soil; that evaporation is caused by water soaking into a surface; that electricity comes from both sides of a battery and 'clashes' in a bulb; that 'cold' is something that travels into the body when a cold object is touched. Each of these has implications for the way we teach. To focus on the evaporation example, research (SPACE, 1991) indicates that another common explanation amongst young learners for evaporation, when asked to explain why the level of water goes down in a tank, was the idea that small creatures came out at night and drank the water. Their teachers asked them how this could be tested. One suggestion was to leave a lump of cheese by the tank, because, according to the pupils, a small creature would be sure to eat it and so if it did not get eaten an alternative explanation would be needed. An activity like this is unlikely to be found in a traditional science book but could be argued as the 'right' one for these pupils.

Research like this has led to the development of 'constructivist approaches' to teaching science (Ollerenshaw and Ritchie, 1993). Such approaches usually include the following phases:

- orientation – the teacher sets the scene and seeks to arouse learners' interest and curiosity
- elicitation – the teacher helps learners find out, clarify and share what they already think (structuring their existing ideas)
- intervention – the teacher encourages learners to test their ideas, to extend, develop and replace them (restructuring their understanding)
- review – the teacher helps learners recognize the significance of what they have found out/learnt and how (metacognitive dimension)
- application – the teacher helps learners to relate what they have learned to their everyday lives.

Each learner actively constructs a unique understanding of the world, therefore learning must be differentiated. Each learner will have a unique starting point and will follow a unique route to understanding. Progression in science is not something that can be easily documented as a linear path. Take the following example related to dissolving a spoonful of sugar in a mug of tea – does the level go up or stay the same? Very young children will usually say the level remains the same because the sugar 'disappears'. Slightly older children often claim that the level goes up, based on an understanding of conservation of matter – the sugar 'must go somewhere'. Pupils who have met and understood ideas concerning the particulate nature of materials through school science will, like the first group, recognize that the level stays the same, but have a different more sophisticated explanation. In other words as children learn they may go 'backwards' before they progress. Ensuring progression in science requires a teacher to make an appropriate intervention based on evidence of a pupil's existing skills, knowledge and understanding. Eliciting children's existing understanding and skill level in order to plan appropriate next steps is ongoing formative assessment that is integral to teaching. An effective teacher has to be a good assessor; the two go hand-in-hand (Ritchie, 1996a).

The approach discussed above has important implications when working with some pupils with SEN. They may need particular support in tackling investigations, especially if they have experienced failure in mainstream classes or been banned from practical work in laboratories and established negative attitudes. Initially, such pupils may react more positively to learning basic scientific ideas – taking pride in aspects of recall. Another problem arises from asking some pupils to express their own, perhaps naive, ideas in front of their peers. A fear of failure is common, and strategies for more private elicitation of existing ideas may be needed. For the same reason, too much emphasis on pupils devising investigations to test their own ideas, before their confidence in science is established, could be detrimental. A sounder starting point will often be an investigation to test the teacher's idea or a teacher-directed illustrative activity. Some pupils may well hold unexpected and unusual ideas that are difficult to discover and even harder to modify. Pupils determinedly hold on to their own ideas unless they have good reasons for changing them. Those with SEN often exhibit a more irregular profile of achievement than others. Their learning can be more of a patchwork of concepts that may never link up. The challenge for a 'constructivist' teacher is to support the learner as she or he builds up a cognitive map of 'scientific' ideas that progressively gets closer to accepted scientific ideas.

Science in the National Curriculum

The history of the National Curriculum for science is a complicated one (Ritchie, 1996b) with ten versions prior to the current orders (DfE, 1995). All versions have sought to provide a balanced science curriculum including two main aspects, one concerned with 'behaving scientifically' (the process dimension) and the other related to the knowledge and understanding that pupils should learn (the content dimension). In the latest version the content has been reduced and made more manageable, the nature of the process aspect of the curriculum has been revised, and level descriptions have been provided for assessment purposes. The new orders place emphasis on the programmes of study (PoS), rather than the assessment requirements.

At each Key Stage the PoS is divided into five areas (with reference below to KSs 1 to 3 Attainment Targets (ATs) only):

General requirements which apply across the other areas. These cover systematic enquiry; science in everyday life, the nature of scientific ideas, communication and health and safety.

Experimental and Investigative Science (AT1) – what pupils should be taught about planning experimental work, obtaining evidence and considering evidence (at KS1 and 2) and planning experimental procedures, obtaining evidence, analysing evidence and drawing conclusions, considering the strength of evidence (at KS3).

Life Processes and Living Things (AT2) – what pupils should be taught about life processes (and cell activity, at KS3), humans as organisms, green plants as organisms, variation and classification (and inheritance, at KS3), living things in their environment.

Materials and their Properties (AT3) – what pupils should be taught about grouping and classifying materials, changing materials, separating mixtures of materials (KS2 only), patterns of behaviour (KS3 only).

Physical Processes (AT4) – what pupils should be taught about electricity (and magnetism at KS3), forces and motion, light and sound, the Earth and beyond (KS2 and 3), energy resources and energy transfer (KS3 only).

These areas (except the first) are designated as ATs in terms of the assessment requirements and, for each, level descriptions are provided which are to be used by teachers to make summative end of Key Stage assessments on a 'best fit' basis, although they can also serve a formative function. For reporting purposes, at the end of each key stage, the weighting between AT1 and ATs 2–4 varies: it is 50 per cent at KS1 but in later key stages AT1 is given less weighting.

It is likely that many pupils with severe learning difficulties (SLD) or moderate learning difficulties (MLD) will spend much of their time in science working within Level 1 and 2 and, therefore, this is the focus of the next sections. Finally, it is important to remember that the National Curriculum is not the whole curriculum, nor should it restrict pupils' learning opportunities. There are aspects of science which teachers may wish to cover even though they are not statutory requirements. The National Curriculum offers a framework for science which seeks to ensure continuity between classes and schools and to support teachers in planning for progression. It is not 'a right answer' nor does it prescribe the only opportunities pupils should be offered.

Experimental and Investigative Science (AT1)

One of the battles that the profession won during the evolution of the National Curriculum was the retention of a process strand, despite political pressure to restrict the science curriculum to its content. The importance of pupils behaving scientifically has already been stressed. However, the inextricable links between the two aspects of science must not be lost. The key purpose of behaving scientifically is to gain knowledge and understanding. The development of process skills is best (although not always) in the context of activities which are also intended to improve pupils' knowledge and understanding.

Pupils' learning in AT1 will result from a variety of different types of practical work:

- observation activities;
- exploratory activities (structured or unstructured);
- pupil-devised investigations;
- teacher-devised and directed investigations;
- illustrative activities, planned by a teacher and carried out by pupils;
- focused practical tasks to develop and practise particular skills;
- teacher demonstrations;
- research using first-hand and/or secondary sources.

All these have their place and can support and lead into each other (see Ritchie 1995). For pupils with SEN, some of these approaches will be more appropriate than others. Often, exploratory activities will be of most value to pupils with SEN. Pupil-devised investigations offer potential, but only if the pupils are ready to deal with the demands involved. If these investigations become too complex any development of new knowledge and understanding may get lost in pupils' attempts to deal with the sophistication of the skills and processes involved. Therefore, at times, teacher-directed activities may be more successful in developing specific knowledge and understanding (linked to ATs 2–4).

The sensory curriculum (Longhorn, 1991) provides a good starting point for science work in special schools. It encourages the development of all the senses and can be implemented through science activities. Such work can have the added advantage of drawing attention to enhanced skills of certain pupils; for example, the hearing of a pupil who is partially sighted. To provide a variety of opportunities for pupils to use their senses many schools build up resource banks of suitable collections, such as shiny things, strong smelling items, scratchy objects, squashy objects, smooth objects, things that make sounds, containers, wooden objects, metal objects, toys, elastic items, bottles, fasteners, markers, strings and threads, gloves, footwear, sugars, powders, breakfast cereals. Each of these can be used to practise and develop observation using particular senses, or mixed for more open-ended activities. Pupils should be encouraged to share their experiences in whatever way they can, and be supported in using appropriate vocabulary (when possible). Activities linked to these collections should be systematically built into pupils' programmes, ensuring there is adequate time, space and adult support available. (For more detailed guidance on developing auditory, visual, kinaesthetic and olfactory awareness within AT1 see Jones *et al.*, 1993.) The school environment (inside and out) offers opportunities for extending observational activities like these, or as a starting point for such work.

After basic experiences, with a focus on observation skills, some pupils will be ready to use the collections in other ways. They can be supported in a range of exploratory activities, using skills such as sorting, classifying, trying things out and, ideally, raising questions and talking about their ideas. Such work has considerable potential for pupils working within Level 1 and 2. As an example, consider the following sequence of work with a collection of fruits (developed from a case study in Ollerenshaw and Ritchie, 1993, p.20) for a small group of pupils, working with their teacher, or another adult. It can be adapted for the particular needs of the pupils involved and spread over more than one session. Provide the pupils with a collection of about six to eight different fruits, including some uncommon ones. Invite the pupils to handle the collection and talk about each item: *What are they called? What do they notice about each? How does it feel? What smell (or taste) does it have?* Use a 'feely bag' to focus on the feel of each. Give them plenty of time, and allow them to follow their own lines of discussion or activity. Encourage them to share what they already think or know about fruit. When they need more guidance, ask them to choose two examples that are different and say why. Ask them to choose two which have something in common. Devise other 'games' linked to similarities and differences. Introduce activities to encourage the pupils to order the collection: biggest to smallest, lightest to heaviest, thickest to thinnest, etc. Their work could be recorded in a variety of ways – drawing around, sticking on pictures etc. Devise memory games (e.g., 'Kim's game'), perhaps played blindfold. *Which examples can be identified by their touch or smell?* Sort the collection yourself using an obvious criterion (shape) and ask them to decide why you have put them in the groups that you have.

Now ask the pupils to think of ways to sort the collection into two or more groups. Suggestions might be colour, those eaten peeled or unpeeled, smoothness of surface or whether the pupils predict there are seeds or stones inside (later tested by cutting each in half). The pupils could be asked to record their method of sorting in some way (for example drawing them in two shopping basket outlines). The next stage might be to play '20 questions': tell the pupils you have chosen one fruit, in your head, and they have to find out which, but you will only answer their questions with 'yes' or 'no'. If this is successful one of the pupils can choose an item for others to guess. More capable pupils could develop this work into simple identification trees, perhaps using a computer programme (see Ollerenshaw and Ritchie, 1993, p.126). Raising questions of a more open-ended type than those involved above would be the next stage of development. Brainstorm questions that the pupils have about the collection. Encourage *How?, Why?, What will happen if ...?* questions. The children's questions could be written down and discussed. How can they be answered? For example, by looking (*Can you see where it was attached to a tree?*), some by watching it over a period of time (*Does the apple stay shiny?*), some by looking in books or asking someone (*Which countries do oranges come from?*), some may not have an answer (*Where did the first apple come from?*). The 'best' questions from a scientific point of view are those that can be answered by carrying out some kind of investigation or test (*Does it contain seeds? Does it float? Does it bruise if dropped? Why do some fruits go rotten before others?*) It may require considerable help before pupils can raise such questions and can devise ways of answering them, but it is an important goal.

Another approach to planning AT1 activities for pupils with SEN is to break down the statements in the PoS into component parts and think of a range of activities which will support learning in each part. For example, at KS1 pupils should be taught 'to turn ideas suggested to them, and their own ideas, into a form that can be investigated'. This leads to questions such as:

Whose ideas? (teacher, other adult helpers, peers, from books, from TV)

What kind of ideas might the pupil have? (scientifically acceptable, partially acceptable, scientifically unacceptable).

How might the ideas be communicated? (talk, draw, make, write, act, sing, sign).

How might ideas be turned into ones that can be investigated? (turn into 'action' questions, simplify, limit the options or items, think of analogies, select more appropriate equipment).

What support does the pupil need for this? (peer group discussion, adult prompts, adult guidance, adult demonstration).

What kinds of investigations might be involved? (simple tests, repeated, one-off, observations over a period, collaborative or individual).

In the context of the work with fruit, a pupil may have said, 'I like bananas best'. The teacher could facilitate learning in this aspect of the PoS by asking the pupil whether she or he thought others did as well? The question, *How could we find out?* could lead to a simple investigation into other pupils' preferences, recorded on a tick chart.

Jones *et al.* (1993) provide a thorough treatment of the previous National Curriculum orders using this method (described as 'milestones' to each statement at Level 1 and 2) and their analysis and useful examples remain highly relevant to the new orders. A similar approach to amplifying statements in this way can be taken to the Level Descriptions (Russell, 1995).

The emphasis of this section has been on pupils working within Levels 1 and 2 of Sc 1. For further guidance on pupils devising more complex investigations see ASE (1994).

Knowledge and understanding (ATs 2–4)

The links between the process and content of science have already been stressed. It is evident that pupils will, potentially, be developing new knowledge and understanding in the context of any of the practical activities discussed above. This section addresses other content areas of science.

Life skills is a common and important aspect of special schools' curricula. Much of the work related to this theme has direct links with science. For example, the following areas are included in the PoS for AT2:

> that humans need food and water to stay alive;
> that taking exercise and eating the right types and amount of food help humans to keep healthy;
> about the role of drugs and medicine;
> that humans can produce babies and that these babies grow into children and then to adults (KS1).
> the functions of teeth and the importance of dental care;
> that tobacco, alcohol and other drugs can have harmful effects (KS2).

The general requirements state that pupils should be given opportunities to 'recognize hazards and risks when working with living things and materials and follow simple instructions to control the risks to themselves' (KS1); 'they should take such action themselves to control these risks' (KS2).

Such an agenda is clearly appropriate to all pupils, regardless of their specific difficulties. Each of the above statements can be amplified as a set of intermediate goals, or targets, for pupils. As an example (drawing on the work of Jones *et al.*, 1993) consider the following intermediate targets for the statement 'humans need food and water to stay alive':

- communicate about sources of food or drink (eye contact, vocalization, gesture, speech or pulling adult);
- know that a person needs to eat or drink (communicates when thirsty/hungry or takes direct action to get a drink or eat);
- know that not eating causes hunger, and lack of fluids causes thirst (asks for a drink on a hot day and gives reasons);
- know that humans die if they get no food or drink (understands starvation in the context of a story, through pictures or video).

Analyses of statements in this way enable a teacher to plan work for individual children to progressively build on their existing understanding, ensuring repetition of experiences when necessary. Clearly, with some pupils who lack sophisticated language skills there will be problems of assessing and developing their knowledge and understanding. There is considerable scope for oral work in science and, of course, there are other means of communicating. Pupils with SEN may be capable scientific thinkers who lack the means to communicate their ideas – they need support in doing this.

Other areas of experience that are common in special schools, and relate directly to the science curriculum include:

AT 2 keeping animals and plants in the classroom
       maintaining a school garden or pond
       visits to a local farm, park or woods
       visits of doctor or nurse
AT 3 sand and water play
       clay and plasticine modelling
       collecting and sorting rubbish
       cooking
       choosing clothes
AT 4 using toys, construction kits and large play equipment
       using mains electrical appliances
       using kitchen tools and equipment
       working with construction kits
       dancing, swimming and sports
       listening to sounds/singing/playing instruments.

For more information concerning activities such as these see Jones *et al.* (1993), Ginn Science (1994) and Nuffield Science (1993).

The role of the teacher

The non-statutory guidance for science (NCC, 1989) outlines the varied roles an effective teacher of science should adopt. These include:

enabler (facilitates learning opportunities);
manager (coordinates activities and organizes the pupils);
presenter (sets the scene, clarifies ways of working and gives information);
adviser (actively listens and offers ideas and alternatives);
observer/assessor (gathers evidence of progress against learning objectives);
challenger (comments critically on procedures and outcomes);
respondent (answers questions).

The earlier discussion about a constructivist approach indicates all of these roles are likely to be used by a teacher working in that way. Teachers also need to be questioners: nothing facilitates learning more effectively than asking the right question at the right time. This is not always easy and will not necessarily be an 'open' question; 'closed' questions can be just as valuable, especially with pupils who may initially find open-ended questions too threatening. Harlen (1985, pp. 47–57) provides useful guidance on the types of questions a teacher should be asking, as well as exploring the way in which teachers can turn children's questions from being non-scientific or non-productive into action or productive ones.

Teachers have to ensure that all pupils have access to a science curriculum. Access can be facilitated through differentiation. In science, differentiation by task requires a teacher to consider aspects which will affect its difficulty: how familiar the pupils are with the materials and equipment used; how familiar the pupils are with the concepts and vocabulary involved; the required accuracy of measurements; the number and type of factors involved; the extent to which the teacher leads or prompts (NCC, 1991, p.2). The alternative is to plan a task suitable for learners with a range of competences and recognize that outcomes will be differential, and interact with the pupils to support their individual learning. This chapter has already stressed the need for precisely defined learning objectives to encourage small and manageable steps forward. This can also encourage pupil autonomy if pupils are made aware of the targets and take responsibility for aspects of their own learning.

Access is also helped by ensuring science is made meaningful for all learners: that activities are introduced in relevant contexts, possibly through an integrated topic approach (see Coulby and Ward, 1996). This reinforces cross-curricular links and can increase pupils' motivation and interest in science. The National Curriculum, with its subject labels, should not deflect us from implementing science in a manner which allows all pupils to appreciate its relevance to their everyday lives. The manner in which work is presented to pupils can raise issues of access. This is clearly the case if written material is used and guidance on presenting work, found elsewhere in this volume, should be applied to science as much as to any other subject. For older pupils, working at lower levels, it is essential to set activities in contexts suitable for their ages and ensure that materials provided do not contain inappropriate language and images.

The final consideration when thinking about access is deciding how to cope with pupils' particular difficulties: physical disabilities may require the use of technical aids, say when observing or measuring; hearing impaired pupils will need to be offered more pictorial clues and simple language; visual impairment will need enhanced aural and tactile information, and adapted equipment; those with emotional and behavioural difficulties will need activities planned to build on a particular interest. For further guidance on improving access to the curriculum, see Curriculum Council for Wales (1993), Gibson (1991) and Sherrington (1993, pp.73–6). Information technology, as discussed elsewhere in this book, can provide important tools to facilitate access. It can also enhance and enrich science work (Frost, 1995).

The implementation of science activities in a special school is never going to be easy. However, there are ways of easing the problems, for example, making use of other adults in the classroom (support teachers, parents or helpers). Key to making this strategy work is ensuring that the individual is well briefed and has a clear understanding of your objectives for the activity. A good way of using another adult is to get them to ask questions you have formulated and scribe the pupil's responses in a large format book (see Ollerenshaw and Ritchie, 1993, p.55) during the elicitation phase of work. There are many advantages to organizing practical science as a small-group or paired activity. Some pupils will however need a great deal of support in working with others during practical tasks and another adult enabler can be essential. If school policy allows for parental help in the classroom, an additional benefit can result from encouraging parents to support their children's learning in science at home, building on experiences in school (ASE, 1995).

Conclusion

To conclude, let me revisit what pupils will learn through science and why it should be regarded as a fundamental and enjoyable facet of children's education:

- an appreciation and understanding of the natural and made world through first-hand experiences wherever possible or second-hand experience where appropriate;
- skills, processes and ways of working which will help them cope with everyday living and which may be useful for future work and leisure activities;
- positive attitudes towards science and the development of attitudes such as curiosity,

perseverance, independence and respect for evidence which can be applied in other situations.

'Science for all' should mean exactly that, and not be allowed to become a meaningless slogan: it is for us, as teachers, to make it a reality

References

ASE (Association of Science Education) (1994) *Making Sense of Primary Science Investigations*, Hatfield: ASE.
ASE (Association of Science Education) (1995) *Primary Science: a Shared Experience* (revised edn), Hatfield: ASE.
Carter, P. (1994) 'Getting special needs in science', *Primary Science Review*, 33, June, 21–4.
CLIS (Children's Learning in Science) (1988–92) *Various Project Reports*, Leeds: University of Leeds.
Coulby, D. and Ward, S. (eds) (1996) *The Primary Core National Curriculum*, (2nd edn), London: Cassell.
Curriculum Council for Wales (1993) *Design and Technology – One in five*, Cardiff: CCW.
DES (1985) *Science 5 – 16: A Statement of Policy*. London: HMSO.
DfE (1995) *Science in the National Curriculum*, London: HMSO.
Frost, R. (1995) *IT in Primary Science*. Hatfield: ASE.
Gibson, P. (1991) 'Science for all', *Primary Science Review*, 17, 20–21.
Ginn Science (1994) *Primary Science*, London: Ginn.
Harlen, W. (1985) *Primary Science: Taking the plunge*, London: Heinemann.
HMI (1986) *A Survey of Science in Special Education*, London: HMSO.
HMI (1990) *Education Observed: Special needs issues*, London: HMSO.
Jones, L, Skelton, S., Fagg, S. and Thornber, A. (1993) *Science for All* (2nd edn) London: David Fulton.
Longhorn, F. (1991) 'A sensory science curriculum', in Ashdown, R., Carpenter, B and Bovair, K. (eds) *The Curriculum Challenge: Access to the National Curriculum for pupils with learning difficulties*, London: Falmer Press.
NCC (1989) *Science: Non-statutory guidance*, York: NCC.
NCC (1991) *Science for Pupils with Special Educational Needs. A workshop pack for Key Stages 1 and 2*, York: NCC.
NCC (1992) *Teaching Science to Pupils with Special Educational Needs: Curriculum guidance 10*, York: NCC.
Nuffield Science (1993) *Nuffield Primary Science*, London: Collins Educational.
OFSTED (Office for Standards in Education) (1995) *Inspection Handbook*, London: DfE.
Ollerenshaw, C. and Ritchie, R. (1993) *Primary Science: Making it Work*, London: David Fulton.
Ritchie, R. (ed.) (1995) *Primary Science in Avon: A handbook for teachers by teachers*, Bath: Bath College of Higher Education Press.
Ritchie, R. (1996a) 'Assessment and recording as a constructive process', in Cross, A. and Peet, G. (eds) *Developing Science in Primary Education – The reader*, Plymouth: Northcote House.
Ritchie, R. (1996b) 'Science in the National Curriculum', in Coulby, D. and Ward, S. (eds) *The Primary Core National Curriculum* (2nd edn), London: Cassell.
Russell, T. (1995) 'Progression in the post-Dearing curriculum: getting a feel for levels', *Primary Science Review*, 37, 8–11.
Sherrington, R. (ed.) (1993) *Primary Science Teachers'* Handbook, Hemel Hempstead: Simon and Schuster Education.
SPACE (Science Processes and Concept Exploration) (1990–93) *Primary SPACE Project Reports*, Liverpool: University of Liverpool Press.
Wragg, E.C., Bennett, S. and Carre, C.G. (1991) 'Primary teachers and the National Curriculum revealed', *Junior Education*, 15, 11.

Chapter 5

Physical Education

David Sugden and Helen Wright

Requirements of the National Curriculum

Physical education (PE) is one of the seven foundation subjects in the basic National Curriculum with three components: attainment targets (ATs), programme of study (PoS) and assessment arrangements. For PE there is one single AT which is the summation of all the end of Key Stage descriptions, and to meet this AT pupils should be able to demonstrate the knowledge, skills and understanding in the areas of athletic activities, dance, games, gymnastic activities, outdoor and adventurous activities and swimming. Teachers are given the discretion to design schemes of work, assessment tasks and criteria, all based on the PoS and the pupil's ability.

At KS1 pupils pursue three activities: dance, games and gymnastic activities. At KS2 the above activities are continued and developed with the inclusion at points during the Key Stage of athletics, swimming and outdoor and adventurous activities. At KS3, pupils should be taught games plus one other full unit of activity and at least two additional half units of an activity area drawn from athletics, dance, gymnastics, outdoor and adventurous activities and swimming. Games should be taught in each year of KS3. In KS4, pupils should be taught a minimum of two different activities, one of which should be a game.

The National Curriculum in PE states that all pupils are entitled to and should have access to the PE programme at school from KS1 to KS4. The requirements of the PE programme are that the pupils should be physically active, demonstrate knowledge and understanding mainly through physical actions rather than verbal explanations, be aware of relevant terminology and engage in activities that involve the whole body, maintain flexibility and develop strength and endurance. The pupils should be helped to become independent learners through the processes of problem-solving, evaluation of self and others, and consolidate skills through practice and repetition. Positive attitudes should be developed by way of fair play, an understanding of personal successes and failures, plus an appreciation of strengths and weaknesses in others and oneself. To ensure safe practice pupils should be taught rules, their relevance and other codes of conduct, and the appropriateness of various forms of clothing.

All pupils, including those with special educational needs (SEN), are entitled to a comprehensive PE programme which takes into account their individual needs and interests. They are also entitled to appropriate allocations of time to enable them to make progress and reach appropriate levels of attainment. Almond (1995) notes that every pupil is entitled to activity, fun, achievement/progression, recognition and self-worth from a PE programme.

The PE curriculum has a number of fundamental principles underlying it and these hold for all pupils. At each Key Stage the curriculum should be broad and appropriate to the age of the pupils; it should be balanced, with each area being given sufficient attention; as a whole the curriculum should have coherence, embracing a rich variety of interconnected activities; the curriculum should have relevance in accounting for the needs and previous learning of the pupils; and of particular importance for pupils with SEN is the requirement of the curriculum to be differentiated to meet the needs of pupils.

Access for pupils with learning difficulties to the PE programme will affect the teaching and planning of the PE lesson and this access should be framed in terms of inclusion and integrity. *Inclusion*, in that planning for pupils with SEN should be from first principles that all pupils are a valued part of the school community and the school is enriched by their presence. Difference and diversity are principles to applaud as they are the stuff of life; thus their inclusion is built into the system from the beginning and not tacked on at some later stage. *Integrity*, in that activities and the learning context are challenging and realistic. It is not enough to simply engage pupils in physical activity, it needs to be purposeful physical activity. The statutory framework for PE is such that schools and teachers have wider discretion in teaching the subject than in many other areas on the National Curriculum. This allows for the four end of Key Stage statements to be broad enough to cover the substantial majority of the ability range without resorting to a statement for disapplication or modification of the requirements of the National Curriculum. The Dearing Report (SCAA, 1994) also recommended that pupils with learning difficulties who need to work at levels below those defined in National Curriculum orders for each Key Stage should be able to do so without recourse to a statement. To do this, Key Stage advisory groups were asked to write Key Stage PoS in such a way that there are elements of the programme that can be taught to all pupils in ways appropriate to their abilities. It is hoped that with greater flexibility at this stage of planning, the need for disapplication and modification can be eliminated or reduced and that all can be readily included in the PE programme.

Acquisition of motor skills with pupils with learning difficulties

The PE curriculum involves pupils acquiring motor skills, and in order to establish what we know about how pupils with learning difficulties acquire, retain and generalize motor skills, it is appropriate to examine the learning process to determine what is involved in the acquisition of motor skills. A simple model of motor skill acquisition involves three phases: understanding, acquiring and refining, and automating. This old but classic model has stood the test of time, and has been refined and elaborated to involve instructional variables (Henderson and Sugden,1992). Certainly the early part of any motor skill is cognitive in nature; the pupils need to understand what is required of them and how this requirement is linked to their previous knowledge and experience and their ability. This in turn has enormous implications for how the skill is presented, introduced and demonstrated. The situation has to be meaningful to the pupil, or the pupil has to abstract meaning him or herself, and in many pupils with learning difficulties this ability is at a lower level than their peers. The more complex the situation, demanding choices, memory and selection, the more cues the teacher will need to provide. This early part of the learning process is crucial to pupils with learning difficulties as research has shown us that very often they fail to acquire a skill because of a lack of understanding, not because of their motor ability. The associative stage of learning is when the pupil is acquiring and refining the skill and traditionally involves the presentation of appropriate tasks, structured in such a way as to lead the pupil through progressively more complex practices. Careful observation and matching the task to the resources of the pupil is a fundamental principle during this stage. Finally, a pupil may reach the automatic stage of acquisition, where the task is performed almost without thought and with few errors. Even when a pupil reaches this stage, it is still possible to facilitate more complex and advanced skills. For example a pupil with severe learning difficulties may have a balance difficulty and she or he may have been working towards walking on a wide bench. Once this has been accomplished, the pupil can be asked to modify the walk by placing targets to walk into (or avoid), by walking backwards or sideways, by counting steps as they walk, by carrying or throwing a bean bag to themselves as they walk, etc. Most skills can be modified, made simpler or more complex by changing the demand, adding or taking away a sub-component, facilitating creativity by asking the pupil to provide alternatives.

We have begun this section by describing the learning process, rather than by describing motor skills of pupils with learning difficulties. The reason for this is that we are demonstrating what areas need to be examined to provide access effectively and concentrating on the learning situation and context which can be modified by the teacher to facilitate learning in all pupils.

For purposes of delivery of the curriculum to individuals it is not particularly worthwhile to compare pupils with learning difficulties to their peers. We do know that as a group they have a slower rate of learning, may not reach the same levels as their peers and have some difficulty with spontaneous generalization (Sugden and Keogh, 1991). But this tells us little about developing programmes for individuals. What is required is a careful analysis of the learning context for groups of individuals such that it can be optimally tailored to their needs. For example, level of performance is an individual issue and should be utilized to match the learning situation/context to the resources of the pupil. The knowledge on variability can be used positively for motivational purposes: e.g., 'Remember when you did this yesterday'. The information on generalization and the difficulties some pupils face enables us to structure the learning context in a manner that facilitates this process, pointing out similarities, verbal elaboration of actions, providing and fading out of verbal and physical assistance and the structuring of the tasks.

Outcomes in PE

The AT and end of Key Stage statements naturally determine the aims and objectives of the PE curriculum. However, there is a case for taking a wider view on outcomes and asking two very simple yet quite profound questions. In any PE lesson, or part of a lesson, where does the emphasis lie? Does it lie in the pupils learning how to move or is the emphasis more on pupils moving in order to learn? Naturally any answer would have to include both of these as desirable outcomes, and this is confirmed by looking at the attainment targets, but a closer examination may reveal that the emphasis of one or the other may change according to the needs of the pupils. For example, a class teacher may be using an activity circuit with pupils showing severe learning difficulties to start a lesson trying to involve all the pupils. A number of outcomes are desirable from this activity. If there is a range of tasks such as jumping, crawling, balancing and climbing, the teacher may be reinforcing these by simple repetition in this activity circuit. It may be that part of the circuit is quite difficult or involves the pupils performing an activity that they have not perfected. In this case it may desirable to provide support and help at this part. In both of these the pupil is learning how to move, perfecting a behaviour they have done many times before or acquiring a previously partially learned skill. The pupils are learning how to move. However, using the same activity the teacher can change the emphasis according to the needs of the group. She or he may have pupils who show inappropriate behaviours such as pushing and poking other pupils, not being able to take turns and/or being inattentive and distractible. The objectives of the circuit could then change with simple rules being introduced about not touching other pupils, and only one person being on the apparatus at any one time with a range of rewards (choice of activity) being available for the appropriate behaviour, and the withdrawal of privileges for inappropriate behaviour. A second example concerns decision-making and choice. The pupils may evidence appropriate behaviour and they can perform on the circuit quite competently, but you wish to stretch their learning capacity. At various parts of the circuit decisions can be inserted such as jumping into the 'red hoop', 'small square', crawl 'under' the mat. This can be made more demanding by asking the pupils to set the tasks for each other. A final example involves pupils cooperating with each other on the circuit to achieve a joint objective. Two pupils could start at the beginning and end of the circuit and move towards each other but can only pass by giving each other physical support. These examples are illustrating how the pupils are moving in order to learn. In every physical education lesson these twin outcomes are being set and achieved, but with pupils showing learning difficulties, it is more important that these outcomes are clear and planned for.

Planning a programme

To ensure that the curriculum is coherent, a breakdown of the total time allocation for each area is a useful exercise. It enables the teacher to see how activities are distributed across the year and to determine how continuity and progression is achieved. It is not simply a matter of allocating a half-term block to an activity; it involves determining how much time is required for a particular programme of study and allocating accordingly. For example, double lessons raise a number of issues. First there is considerable variability in the length of such lessons; perhaps 60 to 100 minutes. Effective working time is also dependent upon changing times, which again vary considerably. In these lessons it may be more appropriate to present two activities rather than spread out one activity over the whole session. Maximizing the available time is the key issue, because time spent learning a skill is an important variable affecting the outcome.

Assessment and recording

The revised National Curriculum does not require statutory teacher assessment at the end of a Key Stage, but the end of Key Stage descriptions set the standards against which pupils achievement can be measured, and provide the basis for reporting on pupil progress. Pupil achievement and progress should be monitored throughout a unit of work, helping to plan lessons and inform individual programmes. The school-based stages of the *Code of Practice for the Identification and Assessment of Special Educational Needs* (DfE, 1994), particularly the Individual Educational Programmes, require that the teacher has an assessment and recording system in place such that information about a pupil's progress can be communicated to other appropriate professionals. Almond (1995) suggests that teachers assess pupils by allocating a measure of degree of performance such as 'needs help with', 'working towards', 'achieving', and 'achieving well'.

Grouping and support issues in the PE lesson

When planning and organizing a lesson or programme of work, the starting points are the needs of the pupil and the situation that already exists. More often than not it is minor changes in this area which can lead to a substantial change in the accessibility of the curriculum for the pupil with learning difficulties.

The grouping of pupils is an important issue within any PE lesson. A PE lesson can be divided into a number of sections which require the pupils to work on their own, in pairs, in large or small groups, with or without support. Accessibility to the PE curriculum for a pupil with learning difficulties can be helped or hindered by the teacher's ability to group the pupils. Both the demands of the situation and the resources of the pupil must be considered, and our experience in this area leads us to recommend flexible grouping. For example, a class of 30 primary school pupils may contain two pupils with learning difficulties, who are having difficulty in understanding, acquiring and performing the motor skills that will allow them to successfully participate in some activities in the PE lesson. When the pupils are working individually, grouping is not a problem as the pupil will be choosing their own level of performance. However, when these pupils are required to work in pairs for skill learning, or sequence building, then the teacher must decide how best to group the pupils. For activities such as sending and receiving objects, it may be advisable to pair the pupil with learning difficulties with a pupil who is competent in these activities. In this way the partner will be a good enough 'sender' to provide the pupil with learning difficulties with accurate feeds, thus facilitating practice and receiving. In addition, the capable pupil is competent enough to deal with any awkward throws or kicks that may come from the pupil with learning difficulties. Schmidt (1991) has suggested that more varied experiences during skill acquisition can have beneficial learning effects through the transfer of skills to novel situations. If this is the case, not only is the pupil with learning difficulties benefiting from a stable, predictable environment set up by the capable pupil, but the pupil with difficulties provides the variable practice for the able pupil to develop their skills. In this case both pupils are served from the pairing. On other occasions it may be more beneficial to place the pupil with learning difficulties in pairs or in groups of pupils with similar ability. For example, the pupils may be asked to perform a joint sequence involving a roll, a jump and a balance in a gymnastic lesson. Two pupils of similar ability will complement each other, and will not feel that one is exemplifying the other's difficulties or holding back the other. The pupils can perform to the best of their ability level and this should be remarked upon by the teacher.

When pupils are expected to work in larger groups, the nature of the activity and desired outcome will influence the make-up of the group. For competitive activities, random selection of the groups will usually bring parity. If, however, the pupils are involved in skill acquisition practices, it is important to have pupils in the group who are physically and emotionally supportive of pupils with learning difficulties. The physical support is seen by their skilled feeding in ball situations, for example. Their emotional support is shown by their constant encouragement, and praise of the pupil with learning difficulties. This provides an atmosphere which motivates the pupil with learning difficulties to strive to gain the skills, and makes the pupil feel welcome.

The needs of the pupil, linked to the desired outcome for the activities, give the lead to the teacher with respect to grouping. The needs of pupils with learning difficulties are both emotional and physical, and as such demand that the teacher examines the grouping issue thoughtfully. Flexibility in this dimension of lesson planning, rather than a teacher who responds to each situation with a rigid doctrine, can bring great rewards for the pupil with learning difficulties.

Adapting and analysing the learning context

Teaching is an interactive process, involving the resources of the pupil, the activities to be learned and the context in which these are learned. Of these three variables, the teacher is able to control the last two. The context can be arranged in terms of grouping, as seen above, and activities can also be manipulated. In order to do this we are concentrating on two related concepts, which are explained separately for practical purposes but in reality merge into each other. These concepts are task adaptation and task analysis. The terms 'learning context adaptation and analysis' are preferred as they help focus the attention on all the players in the situation, not just the task (Sugden and Wright, 1996). However, adapting and analysing tasks has come to be a recognized role for teachers when working with pupils with learning difficulties. Entitlement to participation is a fundamental right for all pupils, and this often requires modifying the activity to meet the resources of the pupils. Task adaptation involves changing the task, rules of the game, requirements of the activity, and modifying equipment and apparatus such that all pupils can take part in the activity. These changes need not be massive. A ball that moves more slowly through the air such as a sponge ball makes catching or trapping easier; hitting a ball off a cone rather than from a thrown ball gives the pupil more control over contact with the ball, as well as placement; altering rules so that all pupils in a game situation have to pass the ball before a score can be registered; adjusting the height of equipment for pupils; offering a choice of difficulty in an activity circuit – all these facilitate the participation of pupils. Increased participation in this way leads to increased learning (see Brown, 1987).

A direct way of facilitating skill learning is to analyse the task to be learned and break it down into its component parts such that it is easier to approach. The parts can be considered wholes in themselves, but they can also be reassembled to make the original whole again. This offers the opportunity for the pupil to be successful throughout the learning experience. The guiding principle behind task analysis is that the teacher orders the components of a tasks from simple to more complex. This not only includes the task itself but should include the environment in which the task occurs. Gentile *et al.* (1975), Spaeth-Arnold (1981) and Henderson and Sugden (1992) all consider the mover-environment interplay to be crucial to task analysis. A stationary pupil in a stable environment is dealing with a less complex situation than when the pupil is moving and the environment is changing. The demands of the environment should not be overlooked when trying to simplify a task. Physical activities are made up of perceptual, cognitive and motor components, and therefore any simplification of activities or tasks involves reducing the demands in one or more of these three areas. For example, in receiving a moving ball the perceptual demands can be reduced by having a brightly coloured ball or one with a bell in it for pupils with visual impairment; cognitive components can be reduced by taking out the parabola, by rolling a ball along the ground to intercept; motor demands can be reduced by slowing the ball down, by using a bigger ball, one that is easier to catch. All of these practices are progressive in that the initial step is to find the level where the pupil can be successful. Incorporated in this approach is encouragement and praise for this successful completion followed by a progressive increase of the task demands. This moves the pupil through in small successful stages (see Brown,1987; Henderson and Sugden, 1992; Sugden and Wright, 1996).

From principles and guidelines to practice

In the first example we highlight a gymnastic-cum-movement lesson for 7–8-year-olds that includes two pupils who have learning difficulties and shows how the lesson can be planned and organized to ensure that these two pupils are involved and profit from the lesson. Pupils with learning difficulties can and do have difficulties understanding the requirements of set tasks. Before the teacher is in a position to deal with the practical situation it must be established that the pupil with learning difficulties has understood what is being asked of them. The teacher needs to simplify instructions, offering a visual representation via demonstrations. It may be necessary to reduce the requirements of the task for the pupil with learning difficulties such that the number of components within a task are less for the learning difficulties pupil than for the other pupils in the class.

Pupils with learning difficulties are often lacking in confidence through a perceived reduced ability when they compare themselves to their peers. This can be because their shyness for instance has limited their experiences or that their poor motor skills have led to failure and a subsequent lack of belief in themselves. Either way, it is the case that the learning difficulties pupil's self-concept has to be improved and nurtured in a positive way through their PE experiences, before the more specific motor skills that cause them difficulties can be tackled. Improving the pupil's confidence through adapted movements can be achieved. Curriculum gymnastics offers an ideal opportunity for individualized learning to take place where the pupil can visibly take part and progress despite not performing exactly the same skills as their peers. The opportunities for task adaptation and task simplification to meet the learning difficulties pupil's needs abound.

The two pupils with learning difficulties in this example are different from each other despite both finding certain movements difficult to execute and control. For pupil A there is an overall impaired ability across the movement spectrum which has in turn led to a desire to withdraw from PE activities where possible. For pupil B the problems arise more specifically when the environment around them is changing and not directly under their control, e.g. when asked to move in sequence with others or change direction suddenly in a crowded gym with all the class on the move. When left to his or her own devices from a stationary position and in his or her own timing, pupil B has a lot more success. Pupil A needs to be encouraged to participate and become more involved, while pupil B needs to have the opportunity to develop control in his or her own time before tackling the complexities of a changing environment not under his or her control.

Working on a thematic approach to curriculum gymnastics allows the material within the lesson to be challenging and different for each and every pupil if necessary. In this example the main theme is 'travelling' with the sub-theme for the lesson being stretching and curling. Each lesson taught, based on this overall theme, is expected to include a warm up session containing large body movements, flexibility work specific to the sub-theme of the lesson, skill development, strength work and a cool down.

The aim of this example gymnastics lesson is to develop a sequence of different movements on the floor which transport the pupil from point A to point B using alternate stretched to curled movements.

The warm up will begin with a game that the pupils work on alone, called 'body parts', where they start slowly jogging around the gym avoiding each other; when the teacher calls out a certain body part they must put that body part on the floor and then get up and jog around again. The game is simple enough for pupil A to take part in successfully so long as the teacher starts with easy-to-place body parts such as the hands, bottoms or backs, and keeps the game at an orderly pace. Even though the teacher would want the game to speed up from its initial slow pace, in order to allow pupil B to remain in control and participate, he or she should ensure that pupil B has enough time to start jogging again before the next body part is called. Manipulating the warm up in this manner will mean that while all the pupils participate, both pupil A and B have not encountered a threatening environment at the start of the lesson. For the flexibility work, again the pupils are working individually so that as long as pupil A can follow the teacher's lead, and pupil B has enough room to operate within, neither of them should experience difficulties here. It is important for both pupils that they are encouraged by being successful right from the start of the lesson and that they enter the major part of the lesson, the development of the theme, with a positive experience from the warm up.

Moving onto the next part of the lesson, the teacher must ensure that the pupils have a practical as well as theoretical concept of the task requirements and the notion that these tasks, whilst challenging, are within their capabilities. In this case the pupils must be sure what constitutes stretched and curled movements. The teacher can introduce simple stretched and curled shapes for the pupils to try, followed by the opportunity to use some of those shapes to move from one place to another plus add their own ideas too. Pupil A should be physically close to the teacher so that the teacher is in a position to encourage, reinforce and help correct or develop the pupil's attempts. Pupil B should be given plenty of space within which to work so that he or she can have the chance to learn to control the movements in the first place without being encumbered by the close presence of others. All the pupils should be encouraged to identify the movements that they enjoy best and practice them so as to improve upon their quality – tighter curl, longer stretch or more fluid transition from one movement to the other. All the pupils can be congratulated on their level of control and persistence to 'smooth' their attempts.

From individual work the pupils can further be grouped in pairs to learn from each other their favourite sequence. The teacher should organize the grouping; for pupil A the partner should be someone who is working at a similar level and it not seen as a threat. For pupil B the partner should be one who has a good level of control and can act as a role model. As the pupils work in pairs the teacher can privately set differing tasks for the respective pairs according to their abilities. For instance, the pair which includes pupil A can continue to simply teach each other their sequences while the pair that includes pupil B can be asked to do their respective sequences in unison, mirroring each other and by so doing giving pupil B the opportunity to work to someone else's timing. Providing the teacher feels that either or both pupil A or pupil B has mastered the sequence sufficiently well, and can cope with the publicity, the pupil's efforts can be reinforced and rewarded by showing the other pupils their efforts.

For the closing part of the lesson the strength work can be done in pairs with the pupils partnered in the same manner, with pupils that complement them in a non-threatening way but are different from their earlier partners, and the cool down done individually using the stretches and curls from the sequence. In this manner the teacher has managed to cover the aim of the lesson in such a way that the two learning difficulties pupils are included with integrity while the others in the class have been sufficiently challenged at the same time.

The second example lesson offers guidelines and suggestions for the inclusion of two pupils with learning difficulties in a mainstream basketball class for 12-year-olds. As previously stated good practice must prevail and this lesson is organized to include a warm up, revision of previous work, new work and a cool down.

The aim of this particular basketball lesson is to use dribbling and passing skills, previously taught, in a small-sided game of three versus three to achieve a position on court where a high percentage shot (i.e., a shot with a good chance of success) at the basket may occur. The basketball lesson begins with a dribbling tag warm up using the lines of the basketball court. At least five of the class will dribble the basketball and attempt to tag their classmates whilst remaining on the lines of the court. Once tagged the basketball is passed to the next pupil. The game begins with walking and develops into running. The idea of tag with a basketball is an easily understood concept for the pupil with learning difficulties to grasp quickly. Revision work in this lesson focuses on passing the ball forward and ahead of your team mates in order to attack the basket area. The pupils work in threes across the court, passing the ball to a team mate who is slightly ahead of them, trying to use a chest pass and timing the pass to reach the player's hands without them having to reach back for the ball. If the receiving player is not in a forward position, the passer of the ball will dribble forward until their team mate has got slightly in front. A clear demonstration of the task will ensure that the learning difficulties pupil understands.

The lesson will then develop into a conditioned game which through its design will highlight certain high percentage areas of the court (i.e., areas from which one can shoot with a good chance of success) to score a basket from. The basketball court or teaching area will be divided into three separate sections for three games to be played simultaneously. Nine pupils will be assigned to each small court and three teams established; two teams will play while the third team watches. Alternatively the third team of three could be split into one referee and one coach for each of the two playing teams. The pupils will be asked to use their forward movement skills to attack the target, in this case two skittles inside a circle placed near but not at the base lines of the courts. If the pupils knock down one skittle with one shot, 10 points will be awarded; however, if the pupils manage to knock down both skittles from one attempt 30 points will be given, so encouraging the pupils to get into a position for a high percentage shot. At the same time this will encourage the defence to take up positions to defend high percentage shots, which can be discussed with the class as a whole or in their small groups.

As the 'full' game of basketball includes time-outs for the discussion of tactics and this conditioned game encourages the pupils to think of tactics to achieve the best chance of a 30-point score, the teacher can schedule time-outs for the pupils too. To include the pupil with learning difficulties in the discussion the teacher can ask the pupil to show the others the best place to stand for the best chance of a 30-point shot. A rotation of teams will allow the pupils to play against all the other teams.

After a discussion of the tactics required to be successful in the small-sided game, followed by the transferable use of the tactics to the 'full' game, the pupils will cool down by working in pairs doing ball handling skills with the basketball. These skills should include those that demand control and stretching from a stationary position, easy to follow by demonstration for the inclusion of the learning difficulties pupil; as the skills are done using the hands from a stationary position, a stable and simple environment, the demands placed on the pupil are reduced.

A problem often encountered for the pupil with learning difficulties is that of acceptance from the other pupils. He or she must believe in him or herself, and to help the pupil, the teacher's feedback and inclusion of the pupil in discussions are vital. If the pupil with learning difficulties can be with pupils who ask 'What do you think?' with regards to tactical discussions and solutions to problems, then the pupil's difficulties are halved. Thoughtful presentation of material in such a way that communication is not impeded for the pupil with learning difficulties will allow the same inclusion and access to the curriculum that the other pupils experience.

Concluding comments

Whatever resources the pupil brings to the PE situation, the processes of providing access are the same. Careful planning of outcomes linked to the particular activities; suitable grouping of pupils including the provision of support; the adaptation of games and activities such that all children can participate and the analysis of individual tasks facilitating learning; sensitive presentation of tasks with explanations, demonstrations, instructions and feedback all geared to the individual needs of the pupils; and finally a commitment to inclusion, with an attitude which welcomes and celebrates differences.

References

Almond, L. (1995) 'Introduction to the National Curriculum', in Sports Council/BAALPE/NDTA. *Teaching physical education*, London: PEA.

Brown, A. (1987) *Active Games for Children with Movement Problems*, London: Harper and Row.

DfE (1994) *Code of Practice on the Identification and Assessment of Special Educational Needs*, London: Department for Education.

Gentile, A.M., Higgins, J.R., Miller, E.A. and Rosen, B.M. (1975) 'The structure of motor tasks', *Movement*, 7, 11–28.

Henderson, S.E. and Sugden, D.A. (1992) *Movement Assessment Battery for Children*, London: The Psychological Corporation.

National Curriculum Council (1992) *Physical Education: Non-statutory guidance*, York: National Curriculum Council.

SCAA (1994) *The National Curriculum and its Assessment; Final report*, London: SCAA.

Schmidt, R.A. (1991) *Motor Learning and Performance: From principles to practice*, Champaign, Ill: Human Kinetics Publishers.

Spaeth-Arnold, R.K. (1981) 'Developing sports skills', *Motor Skills: Theory into practice, Monograph 2*.

Sugden, D.A. and Keogh, J.F. (1991) *Problems in Movement Skill Development*, Columbia: University of South Carolina Press.

Sugden, D.A. and Wright, H.C. (1996) 'Curricular entitlement and implementation for all children', in Armstrong. N. (ed.) *New Directions in Physical Education Vol. 3: Change and innovation*, London: Cassell.

Further reading

Allen, A. and Coley, J. (1995) *Dance for all (2 and 3),* London: David Fulton.

Bidabe, L., Lollar, J.M. and others (1990) *Mobility Opportunities Via Education (MOVE),* Bakersfield, CA.: Kern County Superintendent of Schools Office.

Golding, R. and Goldsmith, L. (1986) *The Caring Person's Guide to Handling the Severely Multiply Handicapped* London: Macmillan.

Gray, J. (1995) 'Physical education', in Ashcroft, K. and Palacio, D. (eds) *The Primary Teacher's Guide to the New National Curriculum,* London: Falmer Press.

Law, I.H. and Suckling, M.H. (1983) *Handling When Children are Profoundly Handicapped* Jordanhill College.

Sherborne, V. (1990) *Developmental Movement for Children,* Cambridge: Cambridge University Press.

Stewart, D. (1990) *A Right to Movement,* London: Falmer Press.

For further information about Sherborne movement activities and regular in-service sessions contact Sherborne Foundation UK, The Sherborne Centre, Office No. 5, Old School House, Britannia Road, Kingswood, Bristol Road, Bristol BS15 2DB.

For further information about MOVE and in-service sessions, contact MOVE International, Centre for Educational Development, University of Wolverhampton, Gorway Road, Walsall WS1 3BD. The MOVE Curriculum and associated equipment are available from Rifton, Robertsbridge, East Sussex TN32 5DR.

Chapter 6

History

Clare Martin and Bernard Gummett

We are not the first who have fried our sousages in Grønavika! (e-mail message from Øystein Olsen, grade 9, Røvær skole, Norway)

Introduction

The Education Reform Act of 1988 gave all pupils of compulsory school age, including those with a wide range of special educational needs (SEN), a legal entitlement to the National Curriculum Programmes of Study (PoS) for history. This chapter will look at the requirements of the statutory orders, revised in 1995, explore some of the issues concerned with relevance and access for pupils with learning difficulties and give examples of activities in history with reference to the relevant PoS.

History within the National Curriculum

The introduction of the original statutory orders for National Curriculum history were marked with controversy, including what focus should be placed on British history and whether the subject should be more concerned with the processes involved with learning history or the acquisition of historical facts. There have also been tensions about the relevance of history for pupils with SEN and about the ways in which it might be taught (Sebba and Clarke, 1993; Ware and Peacey, 1993).

If history is defined as the study of the past in order to better understand the present, then clearly history is more than just learning lists of dates or studying the lives of former kings and queens. The study of history can 'give pupils a sense of identity' (DES, 1990) and that in itself is central to the process of education. As Sebba and Clarke (1991) assert:

> In all the strategies which teachers adopt to heighten their pupils' perceptions of their individual identities, they can remind themselves that not only are they attempting something which has always been a pre-eminent aim of the personal and social curriculum, but also that they are working within the framework of National Curriculum history.

If the study of history can help pupils with learning difficulties develop a greater awareness of their own existence, this provides a powerful justification for history having a place within their curriculum.

The Dearing Report (SCAA, 1994) was followed by the publication of the new statutory orders for all the subjects in the National Curriculum including history. In an attempt to address the problems caused by there being too much material to cover, the subject matter has been reduced. The number of attainment targets (ATs) has been reduced from three to one. In KS1 and 2 the number of core units has been reduced and there is a greater flexibility with regard to the extension studies which have replaced the supplementary study units.

The KS1 PoS states that 'pupils should be given the opportunity to develop an awareness of the past and of the ways in which it is different from the present' (DfE, 1995). The areas of study and the key elements are then outlined, with the requirement that they should be taught together. The areas of study do not refer to any specific periods of history but indicate that pupils should be taught about everyday life, and progress to changes in their own lives and in the lives of those around them. There is also the requirement that pupils should be taught about the lives of a range of famous men and women and about different types of past events. For KS2 and 3 the areas of study are replaced by study units which refer to specific periods such as Romans, Anglo Saxons and Vikings in Britain (KS2) and mediaeval realms: Britain 1066–1500 (KS3), with schools able to choose between some of the options. These study units are also to be taught in conjunction with the key elements which for the first three Key Stages are:

1. Chronology
2. Range and depth of historical knowledge
3. Interpretations of history
4. Historical enquiry
5. Organization and communication.

As the Key Stages advance, the content of what should be taught in relation to these key elements becomes more demanding. For example at KS1, within chronology, pupils are to be taught:

> to sequence events and objects, in order to develop a sense of chronology (PoS, Key Element 1a)
> to use common words and phrases relating to the passing of time, e.g., *old, new, before, after, long ago, days of the week, months, years* (PoS, Key Element 1b).

At KS3 the requirement for chronology is for pupils:

> to place the events, people and changes in the periods studied within a chronological framework (PoS, Key Element 1a)
> to use dates, terms and conventions that describe historical periods and the passing of time, e.g., *era, mediaeval, Reformation, Industrial Revolution, Hanoverian, Georgian* (PoS, Key Element 1a).

The new orders have introduced a major change in that the ATs are replaced by level descriptions for assessing pupils' progress. Teachers are required to judge which level best fits the pupil's performance at the end of each Key Stage. But as Byers (1994) indicates questions remain about assessment. For example, will teachers use the level descriptions to assess pupils in mid-Key Stage or will they use the PoS? There will also be a strong temptation for teachers to break down the level descriptors into individual elements, yet such an approach is against the spirit of the new orders which seek to encourage a move away from checklists.

Whether the level descriptors or the PoS are used will also influence the recording and reporting of progress in history. Schools are legally required to report the progress of pupils in all subjects covered by the National Curriculum. Care will need to be taken to ensure that what is reported actually represents what pupils with learning difficulties have achieved and not merely what they have experienced. For pupils with learning difficulties who may make progress in small steps, achieving this aim will present staff with a major challenge.

The executive summary following research by the National Federation for Educational Research (NFER) into assessment, recording and accreditation commissioned by the School Curriculum and Assessment Authority (SCAA), makes several recommendations which teachers should take into consideration (NFER, 1995). These include the suggestion that 'Record keeping systems in school should be manageable yet provide sufficient information to enable teachers, parents and other professionals to maintain an overview of pupils' progress'. The summary also recognizes the value of pupils being involved in their own learning and assessment.

It is important that each pupil's Record of Achievement should cover all areas of their individual curriculum, including history, and that these records should continue to be meaningful to the pupil even years after they have been compiled. The use of photographs and video can help to achieve this, as can the use of information technology in conjunction with symbol writing software (e.g., the Rebus Symbol Collection from Widgit Software). Indeed, as Sebba (1994) points out, Records of Achievement capture part of the pupil's own personal history. Of pupils with severe learning difficulties (SLD), Carpenter (1995) asks, 'can symbols enable our pupils to participate in the assessment process, to gain some degree of control over this formative process and begin to make judgements about their own learning?' He demonstrates that they clearly can and concludes that

> Symbols enhance the participation of students with learning difficulties in a range of social and educational activities. They help to bring a sense of achievement, a precious tool in building self esteem, and as such can make a valuable contribution to the lives and education of those with learning difficulties.

Planning to teach history

The teaching of history requires careful planning in order to ensure coverage, continuity and progression. Schools will have, or will be developing, policies for National Curriculum subjects including history and will have recognized the value of identifying a history coordinator. Sebba (1994) suggests that the responsibilities of the coordinator might include:

- drafting of the policy statement, long-term plans (across Key Stages) and schemes of work;
- planning for progression and differentiation;
- auditing current curricular coverage;
- developing a good understanding of the curricular requirements;
- creating resource 'boxes';
- developing a range of appropriate activities for others to use;
- monitoring progress across the school;
- listing and acquiring resources for teachers;

- ensuring history is prioritized on the school development plan when appropriate;
- providing staff development through team teaching, staff meetings.

One of the major issues to be addressed when planning the teaching of history is whether pupils will follow PoS for the age-appropriate Key Stage, possibly covering the material identified for that Key Stage but at the earlier levels, or continue to work on material from earlier Key Stages. The advice from SCAA is that the age-appropriate Key Stage PoS should be the starting point for teachers when they are planning pupils' work and that material should only need to be selected from the earlier Key Stages for a small number of pupils (SCAA, 1996; Stevens, 1995). To illustrate the opportunities this presents, a theme can be taken from KS3 and explored to discover how coverage is possible at level one. The PoS for KS3, Study Unit 6, specifies that pupils should study a past non-European society. It offers a list from which a suitable society can be selected, and for this example a study of the indigenous peoples of North America has been chosen. This area of study provides an appropriate framework within which pupils can be taught 'to use common words and phrases relating to the passing of time', a phrase taken from the key elements listed for KS1. The study of Native Americans provides an ideal opportunity for pupils to talk about *'old, new, before, after, long ago'* within a new and interesting framework.

Many pupils with learning difficulties are placed within a mainstream school or within a teaching group which has a wide range of learning difficulties. This will increase the likelihood of material from the age-appropriate Key Stage being used, but will present teachers with the challenge of differentiating the teaching material so that it is accessible to all the pupils in the group and of ensuring that all the pupils are able to demonstrate achievement and progression.

It is also necessary to decide whether to teach history as a separate subject or as part of an integrated theme, or indeed as a combination of the two approaches. Much has been written about the use of themes, sometimes referred to as topics or projects (Byers 1990; Sebba *et al.*, 1995). One of their strengths is that themes allow the cross-curricular links between subjects to be fully exploited, but the demands of the National Curriculum do not allow teachers and pupils to pursue themes guided solely by the way the theme evolves.

Themes can be used to ensure curriculum coverage for history. In order to do this, one school drew up a four-year cycle of themes. During a curriculum planning meeting the staff identified elements and study units to be covered within history and copied them onto small cards. The cards were shuffled and distributed among staff who were then responsible for placing their cards onto a large grid containing the four year cycle of termly themes. It was quite easy to decide the place of some cards, but others were not so easy and for some the connection to the theme was more tenuous. One of the chosen themes is Buildings and under this, at KS1, the card was placed which contained 'everyday life in the past including houses, shops and other buildings'. The card containing Study Unit 3b 'Britain since 1930; the Blitz and evacuation' was placed at KS2 and at KS3 one of the cards was for Study Unit 1, '1066 to 1500; Arts and architecture, including castles, cathedrals, monastic buildings and parish churches'.

The session stimulated a very useful discussion about what might be covered within each area and how it might be possible to differentiate activities so that they were accessible to pupils of all abilities within each of the teaching groups. It was agreed that at the end of each theme the staff would meet to review whether or not it had been possible to cover the identified material and to share what had and what had not worked well. This theme grid will allow the teachers to ensure that pupils are covering the PoS for history because it contains all the areas required within the programmes of study.

Including pupils with profound and multiple learning difficulties

It has to be recognized that it may not be possible to cover all the areas required by the National Curriculum for pupils with profound and multiple learning difficulties (PMLD) because of the competing demands made on their time in school. For example, some pupils may need daily physiotherapy sessions and it may take them longer than usual to eat their midday meal. Guidance from SCAA (1996) indicates that for this group of pupils it may be necessary to cover material from later Key Stages in outline rather than in depth, or that teachers might plan work for pupils in KS2 and 3 using material from an earlier Key Stage but presented in an age-appropriate way.

The biggest question about relevance and access has been about whether or not history should have any place within the curriculum of pupils with PMLD. Ware (1994), talking about the National Curriculum in general, suggests that 'the imaginative use of the programmes of study can both provide a wider range of teaching contexts for essential skills and offer pupils the opportunity to develop these skills in meaningful contexts'. Ware outlines some of the arguments for and against the inclusion of pupils with PMLD in the National Curriculum and concludes that it serves 'as a useful reminder that knowing about science, history, geography, etc. can contribute to a full life'.

Some pupils with PMLD have a minimal ability to demonstrate their understanding of what is happening around them. However, these pupils should not be excluded from activities which might provide them with enrichment and enjoyment.

Many pupils with PMLD are placed within groups alongside pupils whose learning difficulties are less severe. The use of carefully planned group work can increase the access of all pupils, including those with PMLD, to activities within history. Sebba *et al.* (1995) explore the value of group work and, while recognizing the need for all pupils with learning difficulties to have access to individual teaching, they argue that 'all pupils, regardless of need, have a right to participate in education alongside their peers'. They describe different methods of grouping pupils such as jigsawing and pairing: 'Often the teaming of a skilled pupil with one whose needs are greater and in some cases profound can have mutual benefits' (Sebba *et al.*, 1995).

Historical resources

When planning to teach history the provision of, or access to, the necessary resources has to be considered. Once a school has decided what study units to cover, the resources for that period can be acquired. This will involve finding books which cover the chosen periods at the correct level of difficulty, a task which is becoming easier as publishers respond to the demand which the National Curriculum has created. It is also extremely beneficial to give pupils access to objects and artefacts which stimulate thought and discussion about a particular period and encourage them to become more aware of change. Giving pupils the opportunity to look at and handle a flat iron, for example, can lead to them deducing that in the times when the iron was used there was no electricity and to then contemplate what life was like without electricity. Being able to handle the large iron shoe from a cart horse can stimulate a discussion about how horses used to do the work which is now done by tractors and other vehicles.

It is also important that schools make good use of the physical resources within their local environment. Not only are local museums rich sources of historical artefacts but there are now many opportunities to experience living history, for example, at Jorvik, Stott Park Bobbin Mill, Beamish and the Iron Bridge Gorge museums.

People are also resources for teaching history. During the 1995 commemorations surrounding the fiftieth anniversary of the end of the Second World War, the period was brought alive, for some pupils, by the school caretaker who was able to talk about a wartime childhood and tell tales of ration books and gas masks.

Other resources which can help to bring periods of history to life are computer programs, CD-ROMs and virtual reality. Mention has been made of the use of symbol writing software to increase pupil access to written material and to increase their ability to write about history. Other computer programs follow an adventure game format or allow the production of time-lines. An increasing number of CD-ROMs permit pupils to explore a wide range of historical data. For example, the Dorling Kindersley CD-ROM, 'Stowaway!' (see the resources list at the end of this chapter) enables pupils to examine an eighteenth century warship. As the ship is explored, animation and sound augment the knowledge of what it must have been like to be aboard such a vessel, including having a limb amputated! The interactivity of these computer programs is both engaging and informative.

The Internet has been described as the world's biggest library of information. Pupils studying a particular subject may be able to go 'on-line' in order to find out more about it. As the 'net' moves from containing mostly text-based data towards information illustrated with pictures and sound, it will become more relevant to pupils with learning difficulties.

The technology of virtual reality, which is currently being developed, presents the exciting possibility of allowing pupils to visit historical sites and to actually experience involvement in historical events. Jonathan Grove, at Sheffield Hallam University, is conducting research into whether or not virtual reality can work in the classroom. As part of this project he has developed a virtual Greek villa. Pupils can move through the building, and pick up and examine artefacts. Another example is the 'virtual' reconstruction of Fountains Abbey. These developments are new but it is easy to imagine how they will provide pupils with experiences which will increase their awareness of what it might have been like to have lived during a particular period.

Teaching history

The following examples of activities concerned with the teaching of history to pupils with a range of learning difficulties are offered, not as perfect examples but, to illustrate ways in which the teaching of history has been approached and to highlight some issues about relevance and access. A common thread running through the examples is that they are all, in some way, linked to the pupils' own experiences.

During a term when the theme was 'Work', a group of KS3 pupils studied the history of Barrow-in-Furness (KS3: Study Unit 3: industrial change and its impact on the way of life of people at different levels of society). The pupils were encouraged to think about the time before Barrow existed. They talked about how there were very few houses on the map and lots of fields. A series of maps of Barrow, showing its historical development, helped illustrate the changes. The pupils talked about how people needed iron to make things, how iron was found in the land around Barrow and why the iron works were built. They talked about the iron being used to build ships – hence the development of Vickers Shipbuilding and Engineering Limited (VSEL). The iron works and VSEL needed people to work in them so houses were required. The people needed shops and leisure facilities and so the town continues to grow, even though the shipbuilding is in decline.

This was a little too theoretical, so to make the subject come alive the pupils reconstructed the growth of Barrow-in-Furness and they did it in one afternoon. They started with a very large sheet of white card. On this was drawn the outline of Barrow. The group were equipped with smaller sheets of card, coloured pens, glue and scissors. The first thing to be added to the map was the iron works, then some houses for the workers to live in. The pupils drew the buildings which were cut out and stuck onto the map. VSEL, the main employer in the town and closely associated with many of the pupils' families, was added to the map along with some cardboard ships and submarines.

The most important feature of the activity was that it made the pupils really think about how the town evolved. For example, as soon as the pupils had put some houses on the map they were encouraged to think about where the people would buy their food, hence the need for shops. The group talked about what the people would do in the time when they were not working, so the park and the cinema were constructed and added to the map.

In response to questions about how people might travel out of Barrow, for example to go on holiday, the railway station was added to the map. Roads, schools, churches, the bus depot and the hospital were all added as the group considered how people lived and what they needed. The pupils were enthusiastic about the activity and were able to make good deductions. For example, one pupil spotted that a bridge was needed between Walney Island and mainland Barrow, a requirement quite overlooked by the staff. At the end of the afternoon all the pupils had increased their awareness of the history of Barrow-in-Furness. The theme had relevance for this group of pupils because it was concerned with their town and involved places that were within their experience.

One of the key elements to be taught in history is 'interpretation', by which pupils need to develop the ability to identify different ways in which the past is represented. This includes being able to differentiate between fact and fiction. During a term when 'Media' was the integrated theme, a group of pupils tackled this issue. Many of the pupils were keen television viewers and it was apparent that many of them thought that the events on programmes like Coronation Street and Neighbours were true. For this reason the theme 'Soap operas are not real!' was introduced. In order to elucidate that these programmes are written and then acted, the group wrote a script, selected the cast and rehearsed their own soap opera. Script writers' meetings were convened and the pupils sat around a large table. Each pupil had a pen and paper arranged in front of them with glasses, a jug of water and a dish of refreshments.

The pupils went on to complete a range of work sheets associated with the same theme. The activity illustrated a number of cross-curricular links. There were many strong links with English and also with religious education, as the pupils discussed which characters in the soap operas were good or bad. The pupils also considered what behaviours or characteristics were significant in making these deductions.

A study of Vikings, by a group of KS3 pupils with learning difficulties, was enhanced by an e-mail link which the pupils had with Rovaer School, an all-age mainstream school situated on a small island off the coast of Norway. The pupils had already taken part in a simulated archaeological dig and had unearthed the foundations of a model Viking farmhouse, which they reconstructed using timber and small pieces of green cord carpet for turf. The group then considered what questions they would like to ask the pupils in Norway about the Vikings.

The questions included, what sort of animals did the Vikings have? What were their houses like? What sort of food did they eat? What were their clothes like? What did the Vikings do in their leisure time? Did the Vikings have shops and money? The response from Rovaer School exceeded the request and a pupil called Oystein provided some magnificent material:

> Our forefathers called their country Norvegr, which we have shortened to Norge. It means simply 'the way to the North' – or Norway. The archaeologist Per Haavaldsen and his assistant Helge Viken from Archaeological Museum in Stavanger visited Røvær from 2/8–4/8–1988. The reason was that a new economic map was to be made. Relics of antiquity were to be included. The discoveries at Røvær were very interesting, indeed!
>
> In Grønavika (The Green Bay) which is the people of Røvær's bathing place, 12 sites were found, and maybe there are more. The experts don't think that people have been living there the whole year. It may have been a site people were living at in seasons, during the fisheries. People living on Røvær today think it's funny that there have been people here for a long time ago. We are not the first who have fried our sausages in Grønavika!

The reply from Norway seemed particularly vibrant because it was such a direct source of information. The whole group gathered around the computer while the data was down-loaded and printed out. The study was extended by the availability of a set of Viking symbols (Widgit Software). Pupils were able to use a computer, some with the support of an overlay keyboard, to produce their own written material to include in their booklets on the Vikings. The pupils enjoyed being able to read from their booklets in a group, and in order to include a pupil who had no speech, some phrases about the Vikings were programmed into an ORAC communication device. The pupil was then able to use a string switch to activate a phrase when it was his turn to speak. His response indicated that he was pleased to be able to join in with the other pupils in this historical activity.

A theme on 'Materials' provided the impetus for some pupils to study the Bayeux Tapestry and subsequently the Battle of Hastings (KS3; Study Unit 1, mediaeval realms: Britain 1066–1500). It was noted that if the pupils could memorize the date of the Battle of Hastings they would know as many historical dates as a large proportion of the population. Scenes from the tapestry were enlarged and then coloured. The pupils were encouraged to think about the content of the picture they were working on and to comment on how the people were dressed, what weapons they used in the battle and why the Normans needed to take horses in the boats with them. The pupils made quite sophisticated observations during these sessions and then made their own tapestry about life at their school. They included all the pupils in the school, the mini buses, the classrooms and the sensory room. In this way they were able to make links between the past and the present.

A group of Year 10 pupils, with a wide range abilities, followed programmes of studies from KS3 at different levels. Some pupils considered and understood why the Domesday Book was written, while for others the study presented a further opportunity to practise recalling their names and addresses within a different framework. Names and addresses also featured on each pupil's page in their updated version of the Domesday Book which they produced using computer-based multimedia. They looked at how the book was originally written by hand and then were questioned about how a task of this magnitude would be tackled now. As the use of technology is an important element in their daily life it was not long before computers were suggested.

During a theme on 'Dwellings' (KS1: Pupils should be taught about...aspects of the way of life of people in Britain in the past beyond living memory), a group of pupils with learning difficulties constructed a time-line arranging pictures of dwellings into chronological order. The first picture in the time-line was a cave. The pupils were encouraged to think about what it was like to live in a cave, and what modern-day comfort they would most miss. The list included television, videos, washing machines and tea bags! This activity not only encouraged the pupils to think about life in the Stone Age but also increased their awareness of their own environment and way of life.

Conclusion

History is a subject which is accessible and has relevance for all pupils, including those who have learning difficulties. It has the potential to enrich the curriculum and provide many interesting contexts in which learning can take place. It also provides a framework for other skills to be practised and developed. The teaching of history will be most effective where teachers have a positive attitude to the benefits of the subject for their pupils. The 1995 statutory orders for history have increased the amount of flexibility with which teachers can plan interesting and imaginative work in order to enable pupils to gain access to the programmes of study for history. Studying history will encourage all pupils to develop a sense of time and to be more aware of and interested in the world around them.

References

Byers, R. (1990) 'Topics: from myths to objectives', *British Journal of Special Education*, 17, 3, 109–12.

Byers, R. (1994) 'The Dearing Review of the National Curriculum', *British Journal of Special Education*, 21, 3, 92–96.

Carpenter, B. (1995) 'Self assessment using symbols', in *Extending Horizons*, Coventry: National Council for Educational Technology.

DES (1990) *History for Ages 5 to 16*, London: HMSO.

NFER (1995) *Small Steps of Progress in the National Curriculum: Executive summary*, Slough: NFER.

Sebba, J. (1994) *History for All*, London: David Fulton.

Sebba, J. and Clarke, J. (1993) 'A response to "We're doing history"', *British Journal of Special Education*, 20, 4, 141–2.

Sebba, J., Byers, R. and Rose, R. (1995) *Redefining the Whole Curriculum for Pupils with Learning Difficulties* (2nd edn), London: David Fulton.

SCAA (1994) *The National Curriculum and its Assessment; Final report*, London: SCAA.

SCAA (1996) *Planning the Curriculum for Pupils with Profound and Multiple Learning Difficulties*, London: SCAA.

Stevens, C. (1995) 'News from SCAA', *British Journal of Special Education*, 22, 1, 30–31.

Ware, J. and Peacey, N. (1993) '"We're doing history" – What does it mean?', *British Journal of Special Education*, 20, 2, 65–9.

Resources

Widgit Software, 102 Radford Road, Leamington Spa, Warwickshire CV31 1LF (Tel.: 01926 885303).

Dorling Kindersley, 9 Henrietta Street, London WC2E 8PS (Tel.: 0171-836 5411).

Chapter 7

Geography

Bernard Gummett and Clare Martin

At 12.40pm Sulphur Mountain Doppler Radar showed the showers moving into the mountains. Four to seven inches of snow has fallen in the Big Bear area. New showers were blossoming over northern Ventura County and north-western Los Angeles County and these showers were likely producing snow above 2500 feet. Travel to the mountains and north-western desert areas is discouraged. If you absolutely must travel to these areas today ... Remember to take emergency supplies and tire chains in preparation for hazardous winter weather conditions (National Weather Service, Oxnard, California, USA).

Why study geography?

Geography can be defined as the 'science of the earth's surface, form, physical features, natural and political divisions, climate, productions, population, etc.' (*Concise Oxford Dictionary*) but in the introduction to *Geography for All*, Sebba (1995) defines geography more simply as being 'about the relationships between people and places'. Sebba goes on to state that geography 'aims to help pupils make sense of their surroundings and develop an understanding about the interaction of people with the environment'. The dictionary definition provides a more traditional view of geography but it does not conflict with Sebba's definition.

The HMI Curriculum Matters document *Geography from 5 to 16* (DES, 1986) suggests (pp.5–6) the study of geography will enable pupils to:

- extend their awareness of, and develop their interest in, their surroundings;
- observe accurately and develop simple skills of enquiry;
- identify and explore features of the local environment;
- distinguish between the variety of ways in which land is used and the variety of purposes for which buildings are constructed;
- recognise and investigate changes taking place in the local area;
- relate different types of human activity to specific places within the area;
- develop concepts which enable them to recognise the relative position and spatial attributes of features within the environment;
- understand some of the ways in which the local environment affects people's lives;
- develop an awareness of seasonal changes of weather and of the effects which

weather conditions have on the growth of plants, on the lives of animals and on their own and other people's activities;
- gain some understanding of the different contributions which a variety of individuals and services make to the life of the local community;
- begin to develop an interest in people and places beyond their immediate experience;
- develop an awareness of cultural and ethnic diversity within our society, while recognising the similarity of activities, interests and aspirations of different people;
- extend and refine their vocabulary and develop language skills;
- develop mathematical concepts and number skills;
- develop their competence to communicate in a variety of forms, including pictures, drawings. simple diagrams and maps.

This list has been reproduced elsewhere (Sebba, 1995; Sebba and Clarke, 1991) but bears repetition because it removes geography from being the study of glaciers, volcanoes and peninsulas to being a subject which is accessible to and which has relevance for all pupils, including those with learning difficulties.

Geography in the National Curriculum

In September 1995, following a complex consultation process, the new statutory orders for geography came into effect. The Dearing Report on the National Curriculum (SCAA, 1994) was followed by a reduction of content for all subjects, and in the statutory orders for geography the detail of what was to be studied was markedly diminished. Byers (1994) suggests that 'Geography and history have borne the brunt of the slimming down process'. He goes on to say,

> Geography has undergone a great reduction in terms of detail. At each Key Stage, there is reduction in the requirements to study different places against the geographical 'themes'. The 'themes' are themselves focused, in order that continuity and progression are clarified and reduced in number at each Key Stage.

The review of geography also took the opportunity to clarify the knowledge, understanding and skills to be taught, to remove areas of overlap between Key Stages and across subjects and to replace the five former attainment targets (ATs) with a single AT called geography.

One of the objectives which the review of the National Curriculum sought to achieve was to,

> create a National Curriculum framework which was sufficiently flexible to enable teachers of pupils with special educational needs (SEN) to plan relevant and suitably challenging work (Stevens, 1995).

The subject and Key Stage groups which produced the new Programmes of Study (PoS) were charged with the need to produce material that could be taught at an appropriate level to all pupils, including those who have special educational needs. Another element which achieved the flexibility that Stevens described was the access statement that,

> For the small number of pupils who may need the provision, material may be selected from earlier or later Key Stages where this is necessary to enable individual pupils to progress and demonstrate achievement. Such material should be presented in contexts suitable to the pupil's age (Stevens, 1995).

It is important that teachers, especially those working with pupils whose learning difficulties are severe, do not just use the PoS for KS1 when planning work for pupils who may be working within level 1 for most, if not all, of their school careers. Indeed the advice from the School Curriculum and Assessment Authority about pupils with profound and multiple learning difficulties (PMLD) is that 'teachers should familiarise themselves with the full range of programmes of study in all National Curriculum subjects before making decisions on which is the most appropriate content' (SCAA, 1996). Within the same document there is also advice that teachers of pupils with PMLD might wish to select material from the later PoS, 'for coverage in outline rather than depth'.

For each of the three Key Stages covered by the current statutory orders, the PoS for geography are divided into four sections. The first section lays out some general guidelines and details what pupils should be given the opportunity to do within that Key Stage. As pupils progress through the Key Stages these guidelines become extended and more complex, but they are still covering the same aspects of geography. For example, pupils at KS1 should be given the opportunity to:

> undertake studies that focus on geographical questions, e.g., *'What/Where is it?'*, *'What is it like?'*, *'How did it get like this?'* and that are based on direct experience, practical activities and fieldwork in the locality of the school; studies should involve the development of skills, and the development of knowledge and understanding about places and themes (PoS, 1b).

KS3 requires that pupils should be given the opportunity to:

> undertake studies that focus on geographical questions, e.g., *'What/Where is it?'*, *'What is it like?'*, *'How did it get like this?'*, *'How and why is it changing?'*, *'What are the implications?'* and that involve fieldwork and classroom activities; studies should involve the development of skills, and the development of knowledge and understanding about places and themes (PoS, 1b).

The second section of the PoS for each Key Stage outlines the geographical skills which are to be developed and the context within which this development should take place. At KS1 these skills are at an elementary level and the appropriateness of their place within the curriculum of pupils with learning difficulties is unlikely to be disputed. For example, within this section pupils are required to be taught to 'follow directions, including the terms up, down, on, under, behind, in front of, near, far, left, right, north, south, east, west' (PoS, 3c). At KS2 and 3 the geographical skills which are outlined become increasingly complex, though it is still possible to see how some of these geographical skills might have relevance to pupils with learning difficulties. For example the PoS for KS3 include the geographical skills of using and making maps and plans at a variety of scales (PoS, 3c). Working toward the acquisition of these skills can provide stimulating work for pupils with learning difficulties and may provide an additional dimension to educational visits out of school.

The third section of the PoS states what is required to be covered under the heading of 'places'. At KS1 pupils are required to study the locality of the school plus one other, either in the United Kingdom or overseas (PoS, 4). At KS2 three localities are to be studied: the wider locality of the school, another locality in the United Kingdom and one locality in a country in Africa, Asia, South America or Central America (PoS, 4). In studying the locality of the school it is important to remember that for many pupils with learning difficulties the school they attend is not necessarily in the same locality as their homes. At KS3 the study of places changes from localities to the study of countries (PoS, 4). The requirement is that two countries other than the United Kingdom should be studied and that these two countries, one each to be selected from two lists, should be at significantly different stages of development. As with the geographical skills it is possible to see that the study of places at each of the Key Stages might provide interesting contexts for pupils to learn about places, but the depth of the pupils' studies will be dependent on the degree of their learning difficulties.

The fourth section at each Key Stage is concerned with thematic study or studies. The thematic study at KS1 requires pupils to investigate the quality of the environment in a locality (PoS, 6a, b, c). At KS2 four themes for investigation are listed (PoS, 6–10) and at KS3 there are nine themes to be studied (PoS, 6–14). The suggestion is made that these themes might be taught separately, in combination with other themes, or as part of the study of places. At KS3 the terms 'tectonic' and 'geomorphological processes' are used to describe two of the themes. These terms might make some teachers recoil in horror, yet a closer examination of the PoS reveals that tectonic processes actually involve studying earthquakes and volcanoes. Consequently these areas will provide stimulating contexts for learning.

Another major change which took place following the Dearing Report (SCAA, 1994) was the move away from the use of statements of attainment for assessing achievement, towards the use of level descriptions. It has been suggested that the use of level descriptors is advantageous for pupils with learning difficulties because they allow for the pupils' achievements to be matched against a best fit and will encourage teachers to move away from detailed checklists. In contrast, other educationists predict that it will be necessary to fragment the level descriptors into their constituent elements in order to be able to assess and record pupil progress, particularly when the pupil is making progress in small steps.

SCAA commissioned the National Foundation for Educational Research to carry out research into effective practice in assessment, recording and accreditation (NFER, 1995). Their recommendations include the following:

- assessment procedures and materials, incorporating a small steps approach within the revised PoS, should be developed to take account of the needs of pupils with learning difficulties. Publishers could play an important role in this.
- approaches to assessment should be developed through collaboration between specialists in learning difficulties and disabilities and specialists in subject areas, not only within schools but within clusters of schools. Such cooperative working could also be linked to the development of Individual Education Plans (IEPs).

The recommendation that teachers should collaborate in order to assist with the teaching of subjects like geography is an important and potentially convincing one. However, the realization of this may be constrained by the demands being made on teachers' time and by the inexorable contraction of the local advisory services as personnel increasingly become absorbed within the inspection process.

The teaching of geography has been influenced by the advent of school inspections by the Office for Standards in Education (OFSTED). If the arrival of the National Curriculum did not stimulate the development of policies in curriculum areas, including geography, then the expectation of an OFSTED inspection is almost guaranteed to do so. Prior to an inspection schools are required to provide 'curriculum plans, policies and guidelines or schemes of work, already in existence' (OFSTED, 1995). Bines (1993) points out that 'the National Curriculum requires collaborative planning of the curriculum, to map and ensure coverage of National Curriculum requirements and promote progression and continuity'.

Planning to teach geography

The formulation of policies and the identification of subject coordinators for geography has resulted in a good deal of positive curriculum development. The role of the subject coordinator is an important one and should include playing a key role in drafting the policy statement, monitoring the delivery of geography and progress throughout the school and maintaining the resources required for the successful teaching of the subject. Ideally the coordinator will be a teacher who has a specialism in geography, but in many schools this is not possible and the school will rely on a teacher who has an interest in the subject and who is committed to developing their expertise, possibly by pursuing in-service training opportunities.

Sebba (1995) lists seven principles which will assist in developing a coherent structure for planning, recording and assessing in geography:

1 Ensure the planning system in the school provides a broad and balanced curriculum which is planned sufficiently far ahead to ensure continuity and progression.
2 Include opportunities for assessment at the planning stage rather than bolting them on as an afterthought.
3 Ensure that the primary reason for assessing pupils is to identify what they have learnt so that the teacher knows what to do next.
4 Adopt a recording system that enables pupils' progress in geography to be noted in sufficient detail to inform assessment but does not generate volumes of unused information.
5 Assess pupils through a variety of methods to ensure they can demonstrate what they have learned.
6 Involve pupils where possible in planning, recording and assessing.
7 Define a clear, realistic role for the coordinator and ensure adequate support is provided.

The school's policy for geography should contain the aims and objectives in geography and the curriculum plan for how the subject will be taught. It is important that the policy should reflect the actual practice in the school; this can only be achieved if all the staff are actively involved in preparing the policy. Another issue which has become increasingly significant, particularly in the light of OFSTED inspection reports, is the time allocation of each subject, including geography. The advice from SCAA (1996) with regard to pupils with PMLD is that planning needs to take account of the learning time available for each individual and that:

> It is important to avoid anxiety over allocation of specific hours and minutes to each subject: schools will wish to aim for balance and breadth in the time available over the year or Key Stage, utilising the time most profitably and ensuring a productive atmosphere is established (p.17).

Although there is a general consensus that geography has a place in the curriculum for pupils with learning difficulties, there remains some contention about its relevance for pupils with PMLD. The consultation exercise which took place after the publication of the draft proposals for the new orders for each subject indicated that many teachers were concerned about providing access for this group of pupils. Ware (1994) reviews the debate and concludes that the introduction of the National Curriculum has had a positive effect on the curriculum for pupils with PMLD. It should also be recognized that the PoS for geography can provide an interesting framework for the development of other skills. Ware also points out that the National Curriculum, has reminded us that that there is more to being a member of the human community than the acquisition of minimal independence skills. The National Curriculum has served as a useful reminder that knowing about science, history, geography, etc. can contribute to a full life (p.81).

An important planning decision to be made by schools is what teaching style to use for geography. In some schools geography is taught as part of an integrated theme while in others it is a separate subject. A solution which has been reached by some schools, including some special schools, is that geography is taught as part of a integrated theme for pupils within KS1 and KS2, while for pupils at KS3 and KS4 it is taught as a discrete subject. This model has the added advantage that it also replicates the way geography is often taught in mainstream schools (Halocha and Roberts, 1995). The way in which pupils are grouped will also influence how geography is to be taught and the way in which the differentiation of learning will be managed.

One of the strengths of using themes is that they allow the cross-curricular links between subjects to be fully exploited, but it has to be recognized that the demands of the National Curriculum do not allow teachers and pupils to pursue themes guided solely by the way a theme evolves.

The 1995 statutory orders for each subject in the National Curriculum are prefaced by a page entitled 'Common requirements', which specify that:

> Appropriate provision should be made for pupils who need to use means of communication other than speech, including computers, technological aids, signing, symbols or lip reading (DfE, 1995).

For many pupils with learning difficulties, the use of technology, symbols and signing has a tremendous relevance because these systems have the potential to dramatically increase the access of pupils to all curriculum areas, including geography.

It is possible to use symbols in conjunction with technology to accompany words so that written material becomes accessible to pupils who have little or no 'reading' skills. Some pupils with learning difficulties may not be able to recall all the symbols but, nevertheless, will be able to understand sufficient symbols to gain an overall impression of what is 'written'. For example, a pupil completing a geographical study may be given a sheet to record the work that has been done and the areas that have been covered. This sheet may be filed away and after a short time have little meaning to the pupil. The addition of symbols will allow the pupil to recall the work that they did during that theme, even some years later. In this way pupils can become actively involved in their own Records of Achievement.

Similarly the use of symbols can allow pupils to construct their own written material. Carpenter and Detheridge (1994) examine how the use of symbols, in conjunction with information technology, has enabled pupils who have learning problems to construct written material, and they describe the positive effect this has on the pupils cognitive skills.

An example of this is provided by a group of KS3 pupils with SLD who, as part of a theme on 'Dwellings', set up their own estate agency in which they displayed their own houses for sale. They used an overlay keyboard to construct their house specifications, selecting from a bank of appropriate words/symbols (e.g., The Rebus Symbol Collection from Widgit Software). They were able to think and then write about not only what features their own houses had but also the geographical location of their homes. The overlay encouraged them to make decisions about whether their homes were near the park, near the hospital or close to the town centre shops. When they found it hard to make a decision they were helped by studying a map of the town (cf. KS3, PoS, 12a:

Pupils should be taught the reasons for the location, growth and nature of individual settlements).

Resources for geography

There is a growing range of geographical resources. Books, including children's' stories not written for geographical purposes but that do, for example, involve journeys, are available and can be very relevant to pupils with learning difficulties. There are maps, including three dimensional maps, that will fulfil a variety of purposes. An increasing number of paper based resources are becoming available on CD-ROM and other forms of computer software, with the added facilities of sound and animation. There are simulation programs which allow the establishment of settlements with or without ensuing disaster. Video tapes of foreign countries and the coastline of the United Kingdom can enhance the geographical understanding of all pupils and virtual reality promises the opportunity to explore a variety of areas.

An electronic camera has the potential to greatly enhance geographical experiences and aid the acquisition of geographical skills. This piece of equipment allows 'photographs' to be recorded on trips out of school and then viewed immediately on return to school. The pictures can be transferred to a computer, accompanied by text and then displayed or used as the basis of a multimedia presentation.

The Internet provides a vast resource of information about the weather. The quotation at the beginning of this chapter was gathered via the World Wide Web and daily weather satellite images are also readily available. It is possible to gather real-time images from fixed cameras in different global locations, so it is possible to visually check the weather, for example, in Tromsø. Video conferencing facilities allow these cameras to be moved so as to take in the wider panoramic view and also to engage in conversations with people in different parts of the world.

Teaching geography

The following examples of activities concerned with teaching geography to pupils with a range of learning difficulties are offered, not as perfect examples but, in order to illustrate some ways in which geography has been approached and to highlight some issues about relevance and access.

During an integrated theme on 'Work', a group of pupils were driven around the local environment to identify places of work. The minibus stopped at each work place and the pupils were encouraged to talk about the location. They completed a work sheet accompanied by symbols which asked questions requiring a 'yes' or 'no' answer and an electronic photograph was taken at each location. On return to school the camera was connected to a television and the pupils were immediately able to discuss the journey and to recall facts about each of the work places they had visited as they reviewed the pictures. The pictures were transferred to a computer. The pupils inserted the pictures into a word-processing program and wrote about each site. The pictures were then used to illustrate a map of the town on a display board, which allowed the pupils to see the work places in relation to each other and to make judgements about why some of them were located in particular positions. For example, one pupil with SLD deduced why the factory which built submarines had to be so close to the sea, (cf. KS1, PoS, 5d: Pupils should be taught: how land and buildings, e.g., *farms, parks, factories, houses,* are used).

Another group of pupils were involved in making a computer-based multimedia presentation about the small town where they lived. The group gathered around the computer and were encouraged to think about what people might like to know about the town. One pupil suggested that it was important to say how many people live in the town. When questioned about how that information could be obtained, several suggestions were made, including standing outside Marks and Spencer and counting people as they went past. When it was pointed out that not everyone would be visiting the town centre at the same time, another pupil suggested counting the names in the telephone directory. When the observation was made that not every individual would be listed in the directory, another pupil suggested that a telephone call to the Town Hall would provide the answer and it did. (KS3, PoS, 2b: In investigating places and themes, pupils should be given opportunities to: identify the evidence required and collect, record and present it).

E-mail can be used to extend geographical knowledge. A group of pupils in a school for pupils with learning difficulties have access to e-mail. Membership of the Apple Global Education (AGE) project has enabled them to link with schools in other countries, gradually developing a global awareness and increasing the understanding of pupils and staff, of other cultures. The map of the world on the classroom wall became an important reference point and pupils were encouraged to find the countries from which the messages had originated. The countries were marked and a discussion took place about comparative distances, how long it would take to travel to each of the countries and what kind of transport might be used. The project gave rise to several interesting exchanges. For example the following unsolicited request arrived:

> Hello! My name is Corinne Byrum and I am in the Seventh Grade at the Upper Pittsgrove Middle School in Monroeville, New Jersey, United States of America. In our social studies class we are studying your country, Great Britain. We would like it if you would send us a flag of your country. It should be about 90 cm tall and 130 cm wide. If you send us a flag of Britain we will send you a flag of our country, the United States of America. Sincerely,
> Corinne Byrum and your friends in the United States of America. Upper Pittsgrove Middle School.

This request caused a discussion about how every classroom in the USA usually has a flag. There were several electronic exchanges as the school in the UK explained, with some embarrassment, that very few schools in this country have even one flag. This particular school had to undertake some research to discover a suitable flag before the swap took place. (cf. KS1, PoS, 1c: Pupils should be given opportunities to: become aware that the world extends beyond their own locality, both within and outside the United Kingdom). What is particularly inspiring about this exchange is that Corrine and her friends did not know, nor did they need to know, that the pupils they were writing to had learning difficulties. E-mail can be a cloak of anonymity providing everyone with equal opportunity on a global scale (NCET, 1995).

Another electronic exchange was with the pupils on the Norwegian island of Rovaer, which is the chosen contrasting location for the group of pupils who undertook a comparative study of the two islands. (KS1, PoS, 4: Two localities should be studied: the locality of the school and a locality, either in the United Kingdom or overseas, in which the physical and/or human features contrast with those in the locality of the school). The exchange began with a series of questions which in due course received the following reply:

Here come our answers to your questions! Sorry for the delay.

How big is your island? The island is 1,4 square kilometers. (!!!)

Do you have lots of boats? We have 2 big fishingboats on the island, about 15 other smaller fishingboats and our ferry.

How far away are you from the main land? About 10 kilometers.

How long does it take you to get to the main land? It takes 45 minutes by our ferry.

Does your island have some shops on it? Yes, the island has a small shop where you can buy the things you need.

Does your island have a swimming pool? No, we swim in the sea (in the summer, of course!).

Are your houses made out of wood or are they made out of

bricks? Most houses are made out of wood; but none are made out of bricks.

Do you have a golf course on your island? No, we don't have

any golf course. There is none in Haugesund, either.

Our weather has been very stormy lately. What is your weather like at the moment? At the moment we have a north-western storm with some rain and sleet.

(E-mail from Røvær Skole, Norway).

Although the exchange began with e-mail it soon required the services of 'snail mail' to deal with the packages of maps, leaflets and photographs which were collected and swapped. An added dimension to this was that although the two schools had been corresponding for over two years, this produced the first Norwegian stamp.

During a study of 'Weather', pupils were encouraged to make their own daily records of the weather. In order to add to the interest the weekly long-term forecast, shown on the BBC each Sunday, was recorded and played back to the pupils on Monday morning. A record was made of the daily forecast for the subsequent week. Each day before the pupils went home they referred to the weather predictions and decided whether or not it had been accurate. The pupils made their own weather maps, selecting the appropriate symbols for the weather that they predicted would occur in each of the countries in the British Isles. They were then recorded on video reading their forecasts. Not only did this activity enhance their awareness of the weather and extend their knowledge of weather symbols, it also helped to improve their knowledge of the relative positions and names of the countries in the British Isles, (KS1, PoS, 5c: Pupils should be taught: about the effects of weather on people and their surroundings).

During a study of 'Transport and travel' and in order to extend their knowledge of their own locality, some pupils in Barrow-in-Furness, Cumbria studied the A590, a trunk road which plays an important role in the economy of the region in which they live. The pupils went to Junction 36 of the M6 motorway where the road starts and then tracked it for over 30 miles to where it ends on Walney Island, close to the pupils' school. They were required to make notes of the towns and villages through which the road passes and any other important features. On another occasion the pupils went to a lay-by midway along the road and where a mobile snack van provides refreshment for commercial vehicle drivers. Under careful supervision the pupils questioned the drivers about where they had come from, where they were going and what, if anything, they were carrying in their vehicles. The pupils' level of motivation was greatly increased by being able to sample the bacon butties for which the snack van is renowned! (KS3, PoS, 12a: In investigating the characteristics of settlements... pupils should be taught: the reasons for the location, growth and nature of individual settlements).

Conclusion

If geography is more 'about the relationships between people and places' (Sebba, 1995) than the study of physical features, political boundaries and climatic processes, then it has relevance for all pupils. All pupils, including pupils with learning difficulties, have the right to be assisted to make sense of their surroundings and to develop an understanding about the interaction of people within their environment. When this is accomplished, all pupils can be recognized as the geographers they already are.

References

Bines, H. (1993) 'Whole school policies in the new era', *British Journal of Special Education,* 20, 3, 91–4.

Byers, R. (1994) 'The Dearing Review of the National Curriculum', *British Journal of Special Education,* 21, 3, 92–6.

Carpenter, B. and Detheridge, T. (1994) 'Writing with symbols', *Support for Learning,* 9, 1, 27–32.

DES (1986) *Geography from 5 to 16,* Curriculum Matters 7, London: HMSO.

DfE (1995) *Geography in the National Curriculum,* London: HMSO.

Halocha, J. and Roberts, M. (1995) 'Geography', in Ashcroft, K. and Palacio, D. (eds) *The Primary Teacher's Guide to the New National Curriculum,* London: Falmer Press.

NCET (1995) 'A sense of the world', *Extending Horizons,* Coventry: National Council for Educational Technology.

NFER (1995). *Small Steps of Progress in the National Curriculum: An executive summary,* Slough: NFER.

OFSTED (1995) *Guidance on the Inspection of Special Schools,* London: HMSO.

SCAA (1994) *The National Curriculum and its Assessment; Final report,* London: SCAA.

SCAA (1996) *Planning the Curriculum for Pupils with Profound and Multiple Learning Difficulties,* London: SCAA.

Sebba, J. (1995) *Geography for All,* London: David Fulton.

Sebba, J. and Clarke, J. (1991) 'Meeting the needs of pupils within history and geography', in Ashdown, R., Carpenter, B. and Bovair, K. (eds,.) *The Curriculum Challenge: Access to the National Curriculum for pupils with learning difficulties.* London: Falmer Press.

Stevens, C. (1995) 'News from SCAA', *British Journal of Special Education,* 22, 1, 30–31.

Ware, J. (1994) 'Implementing the 1988 Act with pupils with PMLDs', in Ware, J. (ed.) *Educating Children with Profound and Multiple Learning Difficulties,* London: David Fulton.

Resources

Widgit Software, 102 Radford Road, Leamington Spa, Warwickshire CV31 1LF (Tel.: 01926 885303).

Chapter 8

Art

Melanie Peter

The state of the art

The National Curriculum, with its aspirations for 'breadth and balance', has given status and recognition to art as a foundation subject in its own right – 'art for art's sake'. No longer is it sufficient for art activity solely to 'service' other areas of the curriculum, for example to illustrate topic work. In principle at least, the National Curriculum is committed to the notion of one 'art for all', with teachers answerable for the progress of *all* their pupils in understanding and using art as a form of expression and communication. Teachers have an obligation to ensure quality learning by pupils and that good standards are achieved in art, taking account of pupils' relative ability to record what they have seen, imagined or recalled.

Whilst teachers are required to plan for progression and continuity in the artistic development of all their pupils, guidance within the documentation is limited. The full scale of the complexity of the subject becomes apparent when teachers actually begin to draw up a curriculum map and schemes of work for their pupils, with increasingly challenging art experiences and with full regard to breadth and balance in the kind of activities planned. There would seem to be several aspects stated in the Programme of Study (PoS) for each Key Stage (KS) and both Attainment Targets (ATs), all of which need to be addressed developmentally. For example, progression and continuity in:

- the art elements – pattern and texture, colour, line and tone, shape, form and space;
- the strands that comprise investigating and making art (AT1):
    - recording responses
    - gathering resources
    - exploring and experimenting with media
    - reviewing and modifying work

- the strands that comprise knowing and understanding about art (AT2):
    - understanding the work of other artists
    - responding to the work of other artists

- the basic art practices – drawing, painting, collage, print-making and 3D work, including textiles in KS2.

Teachers of pupils with learning difficulties in particular may experience the tension of translating essentially process-based open-ended PoS, into teaching objectives with clearly-observable, realistic outcomes, by which they may assess their pupils' progress in sufficiently small steps. Issues relating to teaching methodology have been removed from National Curriculum documentation. Whilst this is in one sense liberating, the non-specialist, generalist class teacher may find it problematic to know where to begin planning sufficiently challenging, developmentally appropriate activities for groups with diverse needs. As noted in *Art for All 1 – The Framework* (Peter, 1996a), this all begs the question as to what actually constitutes progress. Is it being able to do things that are increasingly more complex? Or is it doing the same thing but better? Or the same thing, but with greater awareness and understanding of the process involved?

Developing 'art for art's sake'

At particular stages in children's development in art, certain characteristics tend to 'hang together'. Rate of progress may be affected by environmental factors, children's direct experiences and materials available. Particular disabling conditions and emotional stability may also be contributory factors. Teachers need to have an awareness of patterns of growth in art, and an ability to plan and implement developmentally appropriate activities, with a clear sense of direction regarding pupils' needs and how they may progress in the different forms of art-making, in two-dimensional and three-dimensional work. Only then can truly differentiated work be planned and implemented to meet the individual needs of pupils in all aspects of the subject of art.

A series of overlapping stages of artistic development may be identified and related to the characteristic attainments of average learners at KS1 to KS3. They are:

the stage of random *scribbling* (pre/lower KS1)
the *pre-schematic/symbolic* stage (upper KS1)
the *schematic/emerging analytic* stage (lower KS2)
the stage of *visual realism/analytic* stage (upper KS2 into KS3).

Children's artistic expression reflects the way they organize information and make sense of their world. Pupils with learning difficulties may pass through the same developmental stages as their peers, although the actual chronological timing will differ. Developmentally young children may engage initially in a stage of random *scribbling* (pre/lower KS1), which gradually becomes more controlled in a range of marks, with children possibly naming them and thereby attaching representational significance (a huge conceptual leap). As their symbolic development becomes consolidated (*pre-schematic/symbolic stage* – upper KS1), so they may draw or paint what they know and what has personal significance, not necessarily what they see; this growing ability to want to organize experience is paralleled in abstract work with a greater sense of arranging and rearranging marks or items. During the *schematic/emerging analytic stage* (lower KS2), children characteristically begin to attend to detail, and strive for a greater sense of order. They typically arrange images along base-lines in representational work, and achieve more complex arrangements of items and marks in abstract work. The *visual realism/analytic stage* (upper KS2 into KS3) reflects children's developing powers of observation and social awareness: a preoccupation with creating a sense of volume, depth and three-dimensionality in both representational and abstract work, and the potential for harnessing a range of artistic styles and techniques to express and communicate ideas, thoughts and feelings.

Development, however, should not just be considered as pupils' relative ability to recreate naturalistic images: as indicated above, children's progress in abstract work – exploration and use of the art elements for their own sake – may become equally sophisticated and refined. The teacher needs to be aware of features in the child's work that may be indicative of development towards a next stage, and be ready to point this out to the child. However, points of transition between stages of development are often fuzzy: children typically may take a long time to move into a new stage, and may even appear to regress for a while, preferring to express themselves in a way characteristic of an earlier stage. Many pupils with learning difficulties characteristically may have irregular developmental profiles in different aspects of art. For example, a blind child's grasp of colour may not be as advanced as his or her ability to work with shape and form in three-dimensional sculpture.

Children will need a *balance* of familiar art experiences in which they may express themselves confidently and improve their proficiency with techniques, and also new experiences in which they will be challenged to discover different and/or more complex approaches to art-making. Ultimately, the child should have 'ownership' of the piece of work, and make the final executive decisions in the last instance. It is our responsibility as teachers to ensure that choices are made from an informed basis, and to encourage children to become as independent as possible in organizing and executing work in a range of art practices, so that they may be able to select the most appropriate medium to achieve a desired intention.

Coming to terms with art

National Curriculum documentation contains terminology which, at first glance, may be bewildering if not deskilling for the non-specialist. For example, what actually is progress in the art elements? What does it look like? How can teachers recognize it and plan for the creative development of all their pupils? The development of certain art elements tends to be closely associated: pattern and texture, line and tone, and shape, form and space, in addition to colour. In reality the different art elements are used in combination and in support of one another. Particular art practices, however, may inherently emphasize certain elements: for example, pattern and texture in collage; colour in painting; line and tone in drawing; shape, form and space in sculpture/3D work. By offering a balanced diet of different art practices (drawing, painting, collage, print-making and sculpture/3D work), teachers may be confident that they will be fostering their pupils' all-round experience with the art elements. The following definitions are fairly crude, but hopefully demystifying:

- *pattern* – considered arrangements occurring in the natural or made environment (regular or irregular, random, ordered, overlapping, tessellating, etc.) and which may be created on a surface by impressing, embossing, and/or painting, drawing or printing on it
- *texture* – the quality of a surface (degree of roughness and smoothness), which may be real (e.g., thickly layered paint or raised pattern of collage items) or apparent (e.g., furriness suggested in a line and tonal drawing)
- *colour* – the *hue* is the generic name of a colour (e.g., red, brown, etc.), which may vary in *intensity* (e.g., bright, dull, etc.); colour may have an emotional impact and

sometimes symbolic significance – reactions to colour tend to be historically and culturally relative

- *line* – a range of possible marks of different lengths and thicknesses (straight, wavy, roving, continuous, broken, dense, loose, stippled, hatched or cross-hatched), which may be combined to make shapes, to suggest three-dimensionality, and to create pattern and suggest texture
- *tone* – shades of light and dark, which may be created through diluting fluids (e.g., paint, ink, etc.) for patches of different intensities, or by adjusting the pressure with sensitive, responsive graphic materials (e.g., pencil, charcoal, coloured pencils, wax crayons, etc.) and compacting marks to different densities
- *shape* – these may be regular, irregular, simple, complex, angular or curved, and created by enclosing lines (e.g., using pencil, paintbrush, threads, yarns, etc.), moulding malleable materials (e.g., dough, clay), carving or combining rigid ones (e.g., mosaic pieces, found sources, etc.) or manipulating semi-rigid ones (e.g., cutting, pleating or folding paper, fabric, etc.)
- *form* – three-dimensional shape and structure (e.g., volume, weight, etc.), and quality (e.g., solidity, hollowness, fragility, etc.) of natural and made features in the environment, which may be recreated or harnessed in both two- or three-dimensional work
- *space* – the position of imagery (abstract or representational) in relation to each other and with regard to spaces between images, and how they are placed selectively (randomly or ordered) and integrated within a two-dimensional or three-dimensional composition.

Teachers need to identify at which stage in their art development their pupils may be operating, and plan for *breadth*, to extend pupils in activities appropriate for that particular stage. This will enable them to harness, transfer and generalize their understanding and use of the art elements in different art practices, but in a way that is meaningful to the child. In planning for pupils' progress in their understanding and use of the art elements, it may be helpful initially to consider broad characterizing features of 'normal development' within KS1, 2 and into 3 (see the list below). Further differentiated planning will also be necessary, in order to embrace individual needs.

Pre/lower KS1 – the 'scribbling' stage

– awareness and exploration of the art elements in increasingly controlled mark-making

- *pattern and texture*: multi-sensory exploration of a range of materials; sorting materials for gross difference; making random, irregular arrangements
- *colour*: sorting fabrics and papers for increasingly finer difference; identifying and naming colours; discovering the behaviour of colour using fluid materials (e.g., paint) – lightening a colour using white;
- *line and tone*: discovering a range of possible marks of different lengths and thicknesses, and enclosing and combining them to make shapes and images of different sizes; discovering tones by observing fluid materials on wet and dry surfaces
- *shape, form and space*: manipulating and moulding rigid and malleable materials in the natural and made environments; applying items and cause-effect mark-making within a prescribed area in large- and small-scale work.

Upper KS1 – the 'symbolic'/pre-schematic stage

– basic understanding of the art elements with a developing sense of order in representational and abstract work

- *pattern and texture*: sorting, choosing and placing materials with finer discrimination, and/or making a range of marks to create ordered arrangements
- *colour:* discovering and learning to mix secondary colours (green, orange, purple) by combining controlled amounts of primary colours (red, yellow, blue)
- *line and tone:* combining lines to create abstract and/or representational images; experiencing tone by adjusting the pressure with sensitive drawing materials; creating shades and tints by lightening paint using white
- *shape, form and space:* making controlled marks with regard for space available and space between images; sorting, arranging and rearranging items within a prescribed area; combining and re-forming malleable and rigid materials to make abstract and/or representational forms.

Lower KS2 – the 'emerging analytic'/schematic stage

– refining subtlety and complexity of control over the art elements with greater attention to detail and placement of images

- *pattern and texture:* making alternating and repeating patterns of increasing complexity in a range of textured materials
- *colour:* mixing a range of secondary and tertiary colours (browns and greys) from a limited palette, and lightening and darkening to create associated tints and shades
- *line and tone:* versatile use of marks to create outlines and detail in large- and small-scale work; creating areas of light and dark, by shading using pressure-sensitive drawing materials, wiping areas with an eraser, and/or diluting fluid materials
- *shape, form and space:* ordering images within a composition (abstract and representational), with greater awareness of relative size and placement to one another.

Upper KS2/3 – the 'analytic' stage/stage of visual realism

– integrating the art elements to express ideas, thoughts and feelings in a range of possible media and artistic styles

- *pattern and texture:* using pattern and texture for a particular purpose (functional, decorative, etc.) in complex, intricate repeated designs, with attention to spaces between motifs
- *colour:* mixing desired colours to a required intensity, and using them to achieve a particular intention (e.g., muted, harmonizing, discordant, complementary)
- *line and tone:* using a range of lines to different densities and lengths, for detail or decoration; creating illusions of texture, volume and depth by shading and cross-hatching in a range of densities and pressures
- *shape, form and space:* integrating images within a composition, with attention to negative shapes (spaces between images), detail, proportion and scale, and relative distance and obscurity to give a sense of depth and perspective (e.g., overlapping images) and three-dimensionality.

Developing skills in art-making

AT1 (investigating and making art) identifies the experiences that comprise the actual process of art-making: *recording responses, gathering resources, exploring and experimenting with media,* and *reviewing and modifying work.* From the teachers' point of view, however, there is minimal indication of how to break down these strands into manageable steps, so that they may become learning objectives for their pupils.

Recording responses

Arguably the most significant strand to art-making is the way pupils *record responses* in art to aspects of their experience. Hence the importance of pupils being motivated in the first place by a stimulus – something to which to respond. In the case of certain pupils with learning difficulties, especially those at the *scribbling stage* (pre/lower KS1), the time-gap may need to be very short indeed between recalling a past experience and experimenting with memory in a creative way. Art materials need to be offered which will resonate with the stimulus – they may even be the stimulus itself, with which the pupil may interact and meanings change in the process. The gap may be gradually widened between a direct experience and following it up in art as pupils reach the *pre-schematic/symbolic stage* (upper KS1): pupils may be encouraged to work freely from memory and recall aspects of greatest personal significance, through repeated opportunities to work on favourite topics, shapes and forms (abstract and representational). By the time pupils have reached the *schematic/emerging analytic stage* (lower KS2) in their art development, they may be encouraged to develop their own skills in working from direct observation: looking carefully at what they can actually see, not just what they know – sketching 'in the field' and using reference material back in school, as well as returning to working directly from a stimulus in the classroom. Pupils at the *analytic stage of visual realism* (upper KS2 into KS3) may subsequently develop an ability to work from secondary reference material (photographs, reference books, etc.), to plan and research their work for specific details, and take inspiration from a range of approaches of other artists in developing their own style.

Gathering resources

Pupils need to be challenged to organize themselves as independently as possible, by *gathering resources* for their art-making. Developmentally young pupils (pre/lower KS1) may be actively involved in collecting items 'in the field' to be incorporated in their art-making and retrieving pre-selected resources from where they are stored; they may also need to consolidate their symbolic understanding, that experiences may be (literally) re-presented in art-making. Pupils may learn to be mindful of amassing resources for themselves to inspire and inform their art-making (upper KS1) – collecting souvenirs and 'found' sources, taking photographs as *aides-mémoire*, and beginning to develop the habit of sketching in the field. This process may become increasingly selective (lower KS2): sketching features for attention to detail, assembling a range of reference material to support art-making, and slowing down the art-making process to 'research' a piece of work. Pupils may learn to extend this wider (upper KS2 into KS3): using reference sources in the community for a specific purpose (e.g., libraries), and taking time to select, assemble and rearrange materials and resources (e.g., a still-life set-up, appropriately lit).

Exploring and experimenting with media

Pupils need to become aware of a range of options for expressing themselves in art, and become proficient in *exploring and experimenting with media* in two and three dimensions and on a variety of scales. Pupils' confidence and pleasure in art-making will develop through learning to control and use a limited range of tools and materials, rather than superficially experimenting with a bewildering array. The introduction of new equipment needs to be sensitively paced, with the range available gradually broadened, to enable pupils to work in open-ended tasks involving a suitable level of 'risk-taking'. Instruction needs to be succinctly presented, and clearly illustrated with visual aids. Teachers need to be aware of steps involved in art-making activities, in order to present pupils with procedures that are developmentally appropriate, with an awareness of how an activity may be 'revisited', and challenges gradually broadened and/or increased to extend and improve pupils' perception and practical skill.

Initially, developmentally young pupils (pre/lower KS1) may learn to recognize tools and materials by name, and develop an understanding of which tools and materials are associated with particular art practices (e.g., a felt pen for drawing), and learn to control them purposefully, accurately and safely. Pupils may learn to follow and implement basic art and craft techniques, with respect for the care and use of materials (upper KS1). 'Dry' techniques tend to be inherently less complicated and easier for pupils to learn to control: for instance, they may be encouraged to become more fluent in organizing themselves independently for a drawing activity (lower KS2), whilst perhaps still requiring support to execute a more complex procedure such as print-making using rollers, inks and stencils. In time (upper KS2 and KS3), they may become proficient in executing 'wet' procedures independently, including complex 'joining' techniques such as gluing and knotting, with appropriate attention to protecting themselves and the work space.

Reviewing and modifying work

Pupils also need to acquire an ability to *review and modify work*, both during the process and after its completion, with a view to future developments. They must be encouraged to develop, change and reorder their ideas, accepting or rejecting the opinions of others, and to identify and negotiate their learning needs. Whilst art-making may be a highly personal and private form of expression, art also makes an impression, and children need to be made aware of the impact of their work on others. This requires time and sensitivity on the part of supporting staff, regarding timing of comments, probing questions and intervention. Supporting staff need to develop a flexibility in their questioning skills in order to draw out pupils' creative responses. Even if pupils cannot express themselves verbally but are capable of indicating 'yes' or 'no', they may be empowered to make creative decisions, at very least regarding choice of tools and materials (e.g., 'Would you like to use this colour paint – yes or no?').

Developmentally young pupils (pre/lower KS1) may spend a matter of minutes on a piece of work, the satisfaction being in the immediacy of the process. They should be given maximum opportunity to make guided decisions regarding choice and placement of tools and materials, and should be encouraged to consider their work after its completion, with opportunity to follow up straightaway with another piece. As pupils spend longer on a piece of work (upper KS1), so they may be more receptive to considering their work in process, with supporting staff timing comments and offering suggestions when they pause momentarily. They may be encouraged to talk about their work afterwards, particularly regarding its content and distinctive features. As they become habituated to standing back from their work and more concerned with detail, so pupils may learn to slow down the art-making process (lower KS2); to reconsider their work in the light of their original intention; to research or practise a required technique for further development; also to explain how it was created as they reflect on their work afterwards. As pupils' knowledge of artistic styles and traditions expands, so they may be encouraged to develop a greater flexibility and open-mindedness to future developments, both in process and with regard to returning to their work at a future point (upper KS2 into KS3).

Becoming visually literate

Empowering pupils to 'read images' may offer them insight into different cultures and traditions and enjoyment of their artistic heritage, as well as inspiring and informing their own art-making. It may also prepare them to discern meanings (explicit and implicit) from the bombardment of visual imagery that they are likely to experience during their lifetime. Thus, art helps to foster pupils' spiritual, moral, social and cultural development. Art may also contribute to other foundation subjects across the curriculum. For example, aspects of social history may be revealed in the depiction of clothing, buildings, transport, occupations and landscape. Principles of 'breadth and balance' need to be applied rigorously: children may be very alert to 'pleasing teacher' and, therefore, care should be taken to present a range of works beyond one's own personal taste! They should be exposed to a range of both two- and three-dimensional works, large and small scale, abstract and naturalistic, from different cultures and historical times, and by both male and female artists. This should be reinforced through effective use of local artists, galleries and museums – at the very least, pupils may then discover that original works of art are not all the same size as a postcard reproduction!

Works of other artists should be presented that will support and reinforce pupils' own art-making. A work may provide a starting point – a stimulus – for pupils' own art-making, either thematically, or for developing a particular approach or technique. Pupils should be allowed time to react spontaneously to a work that is presented to them before they are engaged in more in-depth discussion in order to focus them on features of the work, to feed in information relating to the context in which it was created, and to raise awareness of the artist's intentions. This may then be followed up with a related art-making experience, in which pupils make their own interpretations, suitably inspired and informed. Alternatively, a work may be introduced after an art-making experience, by way of consolidating, reinforcing or extending pupils' own work. In this way, it is used to present an alternative interpretation, in order to validate and celebrate diversity in approaches.

Pupils' ability to relate to the work of other artists will reflect their own stage of development in art-making (their own mode of expression) and the way they perceive and organize information. It is important, therefore, that works are presented in a meaningful way which offers pupils an appropriate point of contact and which has a relevance to their own experience. Teachers need to be mindful of the kinds of information pupils may prioritize and wish to express (their interests and life experiences), and also of the pupils' ability to control media and realize their intentions. Developmentally young children may be able to relate to concrete objects and events common to human experience (e.g., themes like animals, the home, food, weather, etc.), and to certain uses of the art elements in more abstract work (e.g., colour, shape). Older pupils may be able to cope with more abstract themes (e.g., war), and the portrayal of feelings and emotions in naturalistic and abstract work. Follow-up art-making activities need to be pitched in a way that will challenge and extend pupils' own artistic expression, whilst illuminating their understanding of the work of others.

Understanding the work of other artists

Understanding the work of other artists has to be grounded in pupils' own direct experience and knowledge of artistic methods, tools and materials. Developmentally young pupils (pre/lower KS1) will need the opportunity to experience examples of work in the basic art practices (drawing, painting, collage, sculpture and print-making) in their immediate environment – a reproduction may not look like a real painting to the child! Ideally, they should have the opportunity to witness others involved in art-making, in order to generalize their understanding of practices, and be encouraged to emulate certain processes. In practice, certain techniques used by modern artists are accessible to children of all abilities (e.g., trailing paint in the abstract style of Jackson Pollock). As pupils' own symbolic development becomes more consolidated in their own visual representations (upper KS1), so they may be able to consider and emulate appealing or intriguing features in the work of others; for example the way an artist has used the elements of art to create distortions or distinctive features. As their awareness of different approaches broadens, so pupils may be able to consider the way different artists have treated similar themes, and make their own interpretations by harnessing a particular technique or preferred style (lower KS2). Pupils may be challenged to grasp something of the social, historical and cultural context of a work, and a particular artist's philosophy (upper KS2 and KS3); they may be encouraged to select from a range of styles and traditions, towards developing and consolidating their own personal form of expression in a preferred medium.

Responding to the work of other artists

Pupils of all abilities may be encouraged to respond to and evaluate art, although this may require imaginative presentation (e.g., projecting slides large, or 'hands on' for certain pupils), skilled questioning and sensitive interpretation of a pupil's reaction on the part of the teacher. Pupils should be encouraged to express their reactions, whether positive or negative, and to substantiate these according to their ability. For example, developmentally young pupils (pre/lower KS1) may respond non-verbally (e.g., grimacing, flinching, smiling, gasping), or be able to indicate 'yes' or 'no' in reply to a teacher's closed question (e.g., 'Do you like it – yes or no?'), and be able to notice certain features about the work (e.g., 'Can you show me the cat?'). Pupils may be encouraged to bring their own personal experiences and associations to the content and subject matter of a work (upper KS1), to describe it in simple terms and to offer their thoughts and feelings. As pupils become more preoccupied with detail in their own work (lower KS2), and as their own experience of art-making broadens, so they may be able to comment more systematically on how a work was created, as well as its content or subject matter. Pupils may be encouraged to use appropriate art, craft and design vocabulary and to draw on their knowledge (upper KS2 into KS3) to substantiate their ideas and opinions about a work and the context in which it was created (e.g., social, cultural and historical influences).

Art in practice

So how does all this translate into quality teaching and learning in the classroom? The classroom environment needs to be structured and orderly, to enable pupils of all abilities to negotiate their working space confidently and as independently as possible. Effective use must be made of designated areas. Pupils' imagination and inventiveness at all levels of ability may be promoted, enriched and challenged through displays of stimuli for art-making, pupils' work and that of other artists. There should be access to a range of art equipment, with pupils encouraged to use tools and materials judiciously and economically, and with respect. Tools and materials should be sufficiently varied and challenging, and of a suitable quality, to foster pupils' art-making and to develop their skills (in two- and three-dimensional work and in their use of information technology). There should also be access to a range of resources for teaching historical and critical aspects of art: collections of prints and reproductions, books and slides of western and world art. An ethos should be encouraged whereby everyone is mindful of the safety of others and takes responsibility for keeping the environment clean and tidy, with items replaced after use.

Planning should begin with the pupils' needs, not by the teacher arbitrarily plucking an 'idea for art'. As suggested in *Art for All 2 – The Practice* (Peter, 1996b), pupils may be grouped according to their general stage of artistic development, which will give a broad indication of the kind of art experiences which will be appropriate. However, the teacher needs to be aware of how to *differentiate* aspects of art within the basic art practices (drawing, painting, collage, print-making and sculpture/3D) to meet individual needs, and also how to cater for *progression* (i.e., how the same activity may be revisited, but with new challenges, in order to build on previous experiences). For example, an art activity in every teacher's repertoire will invariably include print-making with a potato 'block', but individuals should be challenged and extended according to their ability to:

- engage in experimental cause-effect mark-making using a prepared potato 'block' (pre/lower KS1)
- make ordered marks using a choice of 'blocks', with prints placed selectively in designated space available (upper KS1)
- make alternating or repeated patterns, including carving away the potato to make an original 'block' (lower KS2)
- make complex repeated patterns, including etching a design into the potato with a sharp tool (upper KS2 into KS3).

Practical consideration will need to be given to allocation of staffing, with appropriate briefing and training as necessary. Staff will need to be assigned to support individuals and groups of pupils, but sufficiently briefed to prevent them from dominating the activities. Pupils of all abilities should experience working at individual and collaborative pieces. The session will need to be paced to ensure it runs smoothly, with sufficient time for reflection and clearing up. Thought will need to be given to which materials will be prepared and how the room will be organized so that resources are readily available and retrievable by the pupils. Choice of tools and materials will need to be carefully structured so that pupils are not bewildered by a dazzling array, yet have sufficient scope to make informed selections.

A further consideration will be the amount of space required according to the scale on which pupils will be working, how many pupils will be engaged in art-making, and the nature of the art-making process(es) in which they will be engaged. 'Wet' activities tend to be more space- and time-consuming, and should involve the pupils in adequately protecting both themselves and their environment. Space will be required for pupils to handle visual and tactile resources and multi-sensory displays, to inspire and inform the art-making process; for example, natural objects, artefacts, walk-in environments and 'corners', and pictorial reference material – all well away from the sink or messy area. It may also be viable to arrange the space to include a dry 'containing' activity at which pupils may work independently whilst staff are absorbed 'hands on' elsewhere.

With regard to supervising pupils at their art-making, teachers will need to be aware of the kind of developmental changes to expect from their pupils with learning difficulties. Pupils should be encouraged to engage in divergent thinking and develop a sense of resourcefulness and individuality with regard to their art-making. The position of the teacher may shift, so that responsibility is placed on pupils to devise and research their own solutions to problems, to negotiate their own outcomes and learning needs. Staff will need to spend time observing and listening, as much as talking and intervening. Timing comments and intervention is a sensitive matter, as already indicated. Pupils may require a range of intervention strategies at different stages of a lesson:

- *looking and responding to a stimulus* – opportunity to return to a stimulus, to consolidate their original response to it;
- *explaining and demonstrating approaches and techniques* – opportunity to consider possible ways of responding to the stimulus;
- *exploring processes* – support in practising and experimenting with methods and procedures in structured exercises;
- *selecting and creating* – support in executing particular skills and techniques to rectify 'problems' emerging in their chosen approach in an open-ended piece of work.

Teachers need to cater for breadth and balance in art experiences. Within a lesson, this should include a balance between structured and unstructured elements, with opportunity for decision-making, experimentation and problem-solving. Over the school year, medium-term planning should cover experiences in a range of art practices and on a range of scales. Similarly, long-term planning should reflect a breadth and balance, with consideration of how art practices will be revisited across the phases, to challenge and extend pupils at different stages of their artistic development. Drawing and painting should not be compromised for the sake of working in other art practices, as they most readily facilitate self-expression of many pupils. It may be appropriate to consider pupils spending as much as one half of their time engaged in these practices, with the remaining time shared amongst print-making, collage, sculpture/3D and additional, more specialist practices (e.g., photography, weaving, jewellery, ceramics, using information technology, etc.).

Art for all

Regardless of how 'artistically challenged' the teacher may feel personally, from the pupils' point of view it is more important that a conducive atmosphere is established: not where there may be a 'right response', but where they may feel that they are collaborating in a shared venture, motivated and inspired by their teacher's commitment and enthusiasm! Equally however, teachers should be aware of their own professional development needs regarding art in education. Pupils should perceive art as having status and importance as a means for personal and cultural expression. Attitudes to art will be revealed explicitly and implicitly: through the way it is taught, how it is presented in the school environment, and evidenced in the sensitivity of pupils' responses. Pupils' work should be displayed thoughtfully, with pride and esteem set on the achievements of pupils of all abilities: responses should be regarded as valid statements in their own right, not as an inferior form of adult art.

There should be a vitality, vigour and excitement over art-making permeating the school environment, where teachers and pupils of all abilities enjoy art and relish the challenges the subject presents. Art is essentially concerned with the *aesthetic*. Whilst this has come to imply notions of taste and beauty, 'aesthetic' literally means a concern with *feeling* responses – knowing through the senses. Pupils of all abilities should be moved by their art experiences in school – it has to be our responsibility at very least to prevent them from experiencing art as *anaesthetic*!

References

Peter, M. J. (1996) *Art for All 1 – The Framework*. London: David Fulton.
Peter, M.J. (1996) *Art for All 2 – The Practice*. London: David Fulton.

Further reading

Atack, S. (1980) *Art Activities for the Handicapped,* London: Souvenir Press.
Barnes, R. (1987) *Teaching Art to Young Children 4–9,* London: Allen & Unwin.
Barnes, R. (1989) *Art, Design and Topic Work, 8–13,* London: Routledge.
Gentle, K. (1993) *Teaching Painting in the Primary School,* London: Cassell.
Lancaster, J. (1990) *Art in the Primary School,* London: Routledge.
Morgan, M. (ed.) (1991) *Art 4–11,* Hemel Hempstead: Simon & Schuster Education.
Taylor, R (1986) *Educating for Art,* London: Longmans.

Chapter 9

Music

Penny Lacey

Music is officially on the curriculum! For generations it has been a 'Cinderella' subject reliant on the existence of specialist teachers. Some schools have had a wonderful tradition of orchestras, choirs, shows, computer software and rock bands whereas others have had hardly a note sung or played. The inclusion of music as one of the foundation subjects of the National Curriculum means that this unevenness of practice is no longer acceptable. Many schools have a long uphill struggle to meet the requirements of the order but a report by the Office for Standards in Education (OFSTED) indicated that of the schools inspected during the year 1992–3, 'most of the primary schools responded promptly and generally effectively', although 'the response of the secondary schools was less immediate' (OFSTED, 1993). Much has been achieved already but there are still schools who need to 'review and revise their schemes of work in line with National Curriculum requirements', update their resources, make better use of Information Technology (IT) and 'consider more fully the assessment, recording and reporting of pupils' progress in music'.

In this chapter, I will be addressing some of these issues, particularly with pupils with special educational needs (SEN) in mind. First the order for music will be outlined, then planning and recording will be considered, followed by aspects of resources, teaching approaches and management strategies. The chapter concludes with a brief look at music across the curriculum.

The order

The original order which arose from the Music Working Party formed in 1990 is largely unchanged in the revised version of 1995. Wording has been clarified and examples have only been included where they aid this clarification, with the result that the present order has a conciseness congruent with providing a framework rather than a straitjacket. There is guidance (e.g. Thompson, 1995), but teaching music is very much in the hands of individual teachers and schools.

Although pupils with SEN were not much considered in the first set of orders for the National Curriculum, the Report of the Working Party for Music (DES, 1991) did include a section on this aspect. Music was one of the last subjects to be debated and the plea from the special education lobby to be included had been heeded, at least in part.

Our intention has been to make [the order] flexible enough to allow modifications to permit access without isolating pupils with special educational needs from their peers (DES, 1991, para. 6.16).

Each of the advisory bodies for the revised orders contained a member representing SEN and I was invited to serve on the music group. My views were taken very seriously and I felt that there was a genuine attempt by all concerned to ensure that pupils with SEN receive their entitlement. The inclusion of the general statements at each Key Stage, under the heading 'Pupils should be given opportunities to:' is one very positive move to include even children with the most profound of learning difficulties. The first of these, 'a) control sounds made by the voice and a range of tuned and untuned instruments' (PoS, 4a), can be interpreted in an infinite number of ways. It can range from learning to make a sound from bells strapped to the wrist to experimenting with the tonal qualities of a synthesizer whilst exploring subtle changes in the musical elements.

The specific Programmes of Study (PoS) at each Key Stage (KS) set out what pupils should be taught to do. (Interestingly, the wording 'pupils should learn' was rejected in favour of 'should be taught to' as it is so difficult to be sure what pupils have learned.) There are two attainment targets (ATs), one encompassing Performing and Composing and the other Listening and Appraising. There is no indication in the revised order concerning the weighting of these two but the fact that there are four aspects to AT1 and two for AT2 suggests that greater weight should be given to performing and composing than to listening and appraising. Certainly, the original Working Group felt that there are three ways in which we engage in music: composing it; performing it and listening critically to it, and that they are all equally important (Stephens, 1995). In conclusion, it can be assumed that spending two-thirds of the time on AT1 and one-third on AT2 will reflect their view.

It is the intention, though, that the two ATs should be taught together. OFSTED (1993) give an example of good practice at KS 3 where pupils listened to Saint Saëns 'Danse Macabre', discussed and analysed it and then applied similar methods to their own compositions. At an earlier stage an example of combining ATs might be where pupils are performing their own simple compositions to accompany others dancing.

The Key Stage-specific PoS contain the detail of what is to be taught. This is divided into 13 activities which can be found in all three Key Stages. Progression is built in. For example, the programme for recording compositions progresses in the following manner:

Pupils should be taught to:
KS1 – record their compositions using symbols, where appropriate (PoS, 5h)
KS2 – refine and record their compositions using notation(s), where appropriate (PoS, 5h)
KS3 – refine and complete composition using notation(s), including conventional staff notation and recording equipment, where appropriate (PoS, 5h).

Within this progression lies a clear indication of what is expected at each stage. For many pupils with SEN the full demands of KS3 will not be attainable but adaptations will enable most to experience making a permanent record of their compositions, however simple they may be. IT can offer much help in this area (see also the chapter by Tina Detheridge in this book).

The end of Key Stage descriptions are deliberately written to encourage teachers to assess pupils' achievements in an holistic way. They are meant as 'best fit' descriptions of attainment and teachers are specifically discouraged from breaking down the descriptions into checklists. Teachers of pupils with SEN whose attainments do not fit the descriptions could adapt the wording. For example, in trying to describe the work of pupils who are working on AT1 within KS1, the following wording might be used:

> Pupils join in a variety of songs and simple accompaniments with a growing awareness of pulse. They explore sounds and are beginning to respond to changes in dynamics, speed and volume.

This maintains the flavour of the end of Key Stage descriptions but adjusts it to fit the pupils in question.

Planning and recording

Planning and recording are essential aspects of ensuring effective learning and it can be helpful to conceive of this on four different levels: whole school, schemes of work, class lessons and individual objectives. The whole-school policy will contain the generalities of aims and how these will be met, issues such as equal opportunities, resources and participation in music within the community. There will also be reference to the way in which pupils will be assessed and their achievements reported.

It is unusual to plan at the level of individuals in mainstream schools, but for many pupils with SEN it is necessary to consider exactly what is intended to be the learning opportunity if there is to be any sense of progression. There will be occasions when the objectives for individuals will be of a more fundamental nature than is included in the subject music, but these will be worked on during a music lesson. For example, for a pupil with profound and multiple learning difficulties (PMLD), an objective may be: 'N will have the opportunity to show awareness of a sound source presented directly in front of her'. For another more able pupil in the same class, an objective might be more overtly musical: 'N will have the opportunity to discriminate between two very contrasting sounds by choosing the correct instrument to play in imitation of a demonstration behind a screen'.

Other children in the same class will be able to join in this simple game. Some may be able to discriminate between sounds closer in quality, others may be able to imitate specific rhythms played as a demonstration, and some may be able to take a turn playing the instruments behind the screen.

Planning at this level will originate from documents written for the whole school or department. The PoS offer the framework, but each school will have schemes of work through which these are translated and extended into specific learning opportunities. One school for pupils with learning difficulties has divided its scheme into the two ATs and six sections representing years 1–4, under-fives and pupils with PMLD. Progression can be seen across these six sections. For example:

> Pupils with PMLD – vocal response to sound
> Under-fives – learns actions and words to new songs
> Year 1 – chants words
> Year 2 – sings wide range of songs from memory
> Year 3 – sings wide variety of songs, varying pace and volume
> Year 4 – sings songs with several verses
> (Alexander Patterson School, 1995)

This progression is accompanied by advice for teaching and resources, which for singing includes ideas concerning suitable songs, accompaniment, breathing activities and learning aids such as props and flashcards.

Birmingham Curriculum Support Service (1992, p. 14) suggests that a scheme of work for music should contain:

- suggestions for activities
- notes on managing the activities in the classroom
- lists of appropriate resources and their location
- notes on formative and summative assessment
- notes on ways of recording pupils' progress
- information about how pupils' special needs can be met
- suggestions for the management of time for music education
- opportunities to 're-visit' musical skills and musical elements.

There are several publications which can help with planning at different levels specifically for pupils with SEN (see Resources).

Prior to the National Curriculum, detailed planning was unusual in music. It was often felt that the arts gave an opportunity for pupils to relax and enjoy themselves and thus could be ad hoc in nature. In special schools, especially, music was often a sing-song with drums and tambourines used to fill in moments between 'real work'. There was a feeling that singing could help to improve communication skills and give practice in counting but music was not taken very seriously as a subject in its own right. There is still a very strong case for using music to support other parts of the curriculum, and this will be explored later in this chapter, but there is no doubt that it has much to offer as a separate subject.

If planning has been unsatisfactory then assessment and recording have been almost non-existent. End of Key Stage descriptions have already been considered but this really only satisfies summative assessment. Formative records need more detail and progress week-by-week can be noted down briefly to aid planning. It was never intended that music should demand lengthy record-keeping, so a balance will need to be made between brevity and clarity. A note of class and group activities can be kept, as can any interesting responses from pupils. In the smaller classes of special schools, more detailed records can be kept of individual progress which may vary tremendously within one group of pupils. For pupils with severe/profound learning difficulties most of what happens in a music lesson may be recorded elsewhere. For example, achievements in social interaction, discrimination between sound sources and expressing choices may be part of the early section of the English curriculum rather than music. Music records may merely consist of the experiences offered and examples of responses.

Resources

One of the most important aspects of planning, implementing and assessing in music is the part that staff play in the process. Many teachers feel that they lack experience and expertise and thus are unable to teach it sufficiently well. It is the most feared subject in primary or special schools as people feel they cannot teach music if they cannot play an instrument themselves. There are, of course, a few people who are genuinely 'tone deaf' in that they cannot discriminate between sounds or they cannot hold a steady rhythm, but the majority of teachers have already got or can be given the basics of what they need to teach aspects of music effectively.

A specialist musician in a primary or special school is an undoubted advantage for helping to ensure that music is well taught. It can, however, be counterproductive to use that person to take sole responsibility for all the teaching. A judicious mix of specialist and generalist teaching gives pupils a balance and ensures that music is not relegated to half-an-hour if the specialist is not covering for a sick colleague. Where no one on the staff has musical knowledge, a visiting musician may be an alternative, though dwindling LEA Music Services has reduced the number of visiting musicians over the last few years.

One secondary special school had a visiting teacher who came for one afternoon per week. The staff pondered how best to use this resource. There were too many classes for him to teach them all every week so it was decided that he would arrange his timetable to spend time with two teachers and their classes each week, teaching a lead lesson and giving ideas for follow-ups. He built in as much training for staff as he could and once a term reorganized so that he could lead an in-service workshop after school. He also checked the instruments and made sure that the guitars and chord harps were tuned correctly. He found an interested teacher who was keen to learn how to do this herself and gradually trained her to manage basic tuning. Finally, with this teacher, he organized a week-long residency for a local pop group who ran workshops for the older pupils.

Teachers may wish to consider planning focused-music topics as 'blocked' work, in the manner advised by SCAA (1995; 1996). Finding imaginative ways of using staff, the most important resource, is very important for a subject such as music. Classroom staff in primary and special schools have a crucial part to play but they cannot do this without training. It is perfectly possible to teach music at KS1 and 2 without learning to read conventional notation, but there are many other aspects which present problems to non-musicians. Frequent workshops are necessary to help build confidence in teachers. It is probably better to teach the same thing several times, for example simple chord progression using three chords, demonstrating how this can be used in many different ways, than trying to cover a lot superficially.

There are, however, many aspects of music that can be taught with minimum specialist knowledge. Musical games are very useful and can supplement work done by specialists. There are many publications which give examples of games such as the following, from Birmingham Curriculum Support Service (1992):

Equipment: a variety of tuned and untuned percussion instruments
Activity: pupils seated in a circle
Teacher chooses three different instruments and taps out messages in 'code' e.g.: sit still (two sounds on claves); stand up quietly (five sounds on tambour); stretch (long ring on Indian Bells)
The children respond to each coded message played in random order.
The pupils can then make up message of their own and take turns to control what happens.

Training all class teachers to become competent music teachers is no small task. It is hoped that succeeding generations, who will have experienced National Curriculum music themselves, will be more capable than the present generation but this is a lengthy process.

Although competent teachers are a vital resource, choosing and maintaining instruments is also very important. It is always better to have a smaller number of good quality instruments than lots of poor quality. One orchestral-size cymbal on a strap will give a much more satisfying sound than six pairs of toy cymbals – often found in primary or special schools. Home-made instruments are rarely satisfying to play although much can be learned from making them. Finding sound-makers from unusual sources can also offer some interesting opportunities for learning and can perhaps be used to provide sound effects for stories. Many exciting percussion instruments have become available to schools over the last few years, such as the vibra-slap, the chocolo, the cabasa and sets of tongue drums. They are attractive to look at and give many opportunities to hear instruments with different timbres (sound qualities).

Some pupils with SEN will need adapted instruments, either because they have physical difficulties or because they find them too difficult to play satisfactorily. For example, hand chimes are useful for pupils who find the precision of hitting a chime bar with a beater hard; they have a beater attached and need only to be rung like a bell. Tuning three guitars one to each of the chords in a three-chord sequence can enable pupils to play to accompany folk songs without having to learn where to put their fingers on the fretboard. Each pupil plays only when their chord is needed in the song. Tuned percussion or keyboards can be colour-coded so that younger or less able pupils can follow a simple score.

A few books of songs and musical games have been written with pupils with SEN in mind and are listed under 'Resources' at the end of this chapter. There are, of course, many others which have been produced for mainstream primary schools which are very helpful for all abilities, particularly the A & C Black series. Some have accompanying cassettes which unconfident teachers will find invaluable. You will also find listed at the end of this chapter three primary music courses which are recommended for mainstream and can be adapted for pupils with SEN.

It is at this point that teachers of secondary-aged pupils with SEN sigh and say, 'There is never anything for teenagers'. They are right, of course. Very little has been written that combines simplicity with age-appropriate material. Teachers have to be very inventive, writing new words to well-known tunes and simplifying the words of pop songs. It might also be considered appropriate to move on with the kinds of instruments chosen for teenagers with learning difficulties. Keyboards, guitars, electronic drum machines, and a drum kit may offer a different challenge from primary percussion instruments which they have been playing for many years. Progression can be built in to the opportunities offered to pupils even if they do not make much progress musically. Listening to music can change a little too, though I do not subscribe to the feeling that teenagers with severe learning difficulties (SLD) should not be allowed to listen to nursery songs if that is what they like. I would encourage a wider repertoire but would not want to deny enjoyment of the familiar. Generally, my attitude to age-appropriateness is more connected with the way in which one treats and values people with learning difficulties. It has very little to do with taking teddy bears and children's songs away from them.

Teaching approaches

Music lends itself well to a whole variety of different strategies for teaching. Sometimes teachers will lead and direct closely what is happening, but there will be other occasions when they will stand back and encourage pupils, giving them advice and facilitating their efforts. Equally there will be times when pupils are working alone, in pairs, or small groups as well as the whole class together. Finding space for several small groups or pairs to work at once is very hard in some schools, especially those that are open-plan in design. If space is difficult then it may be necessary to stagger composition classes. Using headphones for keyboards is another possibility.

Infant classes have traditionally had the Music Corner where instruments and other sound-makers are available for experimentation, or tapes can be listened to, or simple work cards can be left to encourage practice of skills taught in lessons. Some special school classrooms would find this difficult to emulate because of the presence of a few pupils whose behaviour precludes leaving out expensive equipment. It might, however, be possible to provide this independence at particular times or in particular places, for example, through centralized resource/interactive display areas.

Many class teachers find it difficult to teach the use of tuned percussion instruments. Often they feel reasonably comfortable with untuned percussion but xylophones, glockenspiels and chime bars present considerable problems. This may be where music specialists can be best used so that class teachers can concentrate on practising skills already learned. However, there are many activities that are possible with minimal musical knowledge. Helping pupils to compose simple tunes using the five notes CDEFG or the pentatonic scale CDEGA, or even the whole octave C to C can be about what sounds 'right' or 'interesting', 'scary' or even 'terrible'. Everyone's view is valid. Tape-recording the results can provide a permanent record of the tune if pupils are not able to devise notation of their own.

Music is essentially a practical subject. There is knowledge to be gained concerning the musical elements, resources, musical character, styles and traditions, how music is communicated and how it reflects its historical and social context, but all these must be learned through experience rather than by didactic instruction (Stephens et al., 1995). Movement and dance are very useful for experiencing a variety of styles, traditions and cultures. Often pupils can express what they feel about a piece of music through their movements which they would find difficult to express in words. I will return to movement and dance in the final section of this chapter on the relationship of music to other parts of the curriculum.

It has often been said that class music is not primarily about performance and that producing school concerts is not time well spent. I both agree and disagree with the sentiment. Certainly, giving over the whole of the half term before Christmas to rehearsing for the nativity play may well put the balance of the curriculum into jeopardy, but judicious use of performance is essential in music. Some of this may be given over to pupils performing their own compositions to each other but some will be given to performing the work of others. The opportunity to rehearse and refine songs and pieces is a good discipline and will be echoed in other parts of the curriculum, especially in drafting and redrafting written work in English. Putting on a concert can be an excellent topic for any age and ability group. There are opportunities for English, mathematics, technology and art as well as music if the pupils are encouraged to engage in sending out invitations, painting posters, making props as well as composing and performing.

Performance is also about listening to others perform. Many community musicians, orchestras and bands have educational aspects to their work and are available to lead workshops and give concerts in schools. This is most effective when school staff can be involved in planning and follow-up work, meeting with professional musicians to decide on a focus, organizing concert visits, taking part in workshops with pupils in school and reinforcing what has been covered in subsequent music lessons.

One aspect of music associated with special education is music therapy. This should not be confused with classroom music, although I would claim that as a teacher of pupils with SLD I used music in a therapeutic manner. Music therapists, however, draw a clear distinction between teaching and therapy, maintaining that in therapy, they are using music to reach children's emotions, to arouse and engage them more effectively with the world around them. Music is the means through which communication is made but the intention is not to teach the children music skills. Often though, considerable musical progress is made as well as progress in communication. Music is chosen as the medium because it is claimed that the ability to appreciate and respond to music is inborn and is frequently unimpaired by disability, injury or illness (Association of Professional Music Therapists, 1988).

Music therapy training is open only to music graduates and it might be said that because of its exclusivity, it has become a much-desired service. There are not many therapists around the country and many teachers and parents feel somewhat cheated that their children cannot benefit from something which is so obviously 'a good thing'. There are a few LEAs which offer in-service training to teachers who are not music graduates so that they gain further understanding of the therapeutic uses of music and learn some techniques for practice (Mills, 1991). This is a welcome initiative and seems to be the most sensible way forward so that more pupils with SEN can benefit from what music therapy has to offer.

Managing sessions

Returning to music teaching, one of the most difficult aspects for staff who lack musical confidence is managing lessons. There is enormous potential for mayhem in terms of noise, and many teachers are wary of what might happen if they allow pupils to compose and perform freely. While this is quite understandable, it is important to find a way to organize sessions other than class singing and playing controlled by teachers. Encouraging pupils to work in pairs is a good place to begin. A lead lesson can be taught to the whole class and then pairs of pupils can work on their own response. Several pairs can work at once in different corners of the room and corridor. The rest of the class can be working on a different subject whilst they await their turn, which may not come for several days. A time can be arranged to share what they have been doing.

It is a little easier in special schools, where the classes are smaller, but certainly in schools for pupils with SLD there may be very difficult pupils who disrupt the class. Often, in these circumstances there are two or more members of staff in the class, in which case it is relatively easy for one to take a small group of pupils and support their efforts at exploring sounds and composing simple pieces. The pentatonic scale (CDEGA) mentioned earlier is very useful for pupils with learning difficulties as, even played randomly, pleasant sounds can be made. The teacher can accompany these sounds on, for example, just C and G, varying the rhythm to encourage awareness of differences.

Another problem facing the less confident teacher of music is how to manage whole-class percussion sessions. Everyone wants a turn and if rules are not made chaos can soon reign. Enabling the pupils to make their own rules is a good place to begin. How many do they think it would be sensible to have in the band? What is the fairest way to allocate places? How often should rotation happen? Pairing pupils can be helpful here too, so everyone knows to whom they are handing on their instrument. Try dividing the class into two, pairing everyone in the first half. They will be this week's players, taking half the playing each. The other half of the class are either critical listeners or singers, depending on the piece being performed. For the next lesson, the roles will be reversed.

Again, in the small classes of a special school this is less of a problem. With pupils with PMLD it may be necessary to work individually with each pupil as they have few skills for interacting with others. A large drum or cymbal are good instruments to encourage reactions even from these pupils. The cymbal is particularly good as it resonates for some time, enabling someone who may react very slowly, ample opportunity to respond. Another useful sound-maker for giving time for listening is a microphone attached to an electronic digital delay (e.g., Boss SE50 or RSD10). Every sound made into the microphone can be repeated several times. It can also be slowed down and speeded up, altering the pitch – useful not only to attract attention but for creating interesting sound effects for stories.

For pupils with moderate and severe learning difficulties, music can be very useful for encouraging social interaction. There are a wealth of activities aimed at this:

1. Sit in a circle. One person begins a simple rhythm such as 'fish fingers and chips' (with or without the words to help). He then 'throws' this rhythm across the circle to someone he can see, who 'catches' it and performs it herself. She then 'throws' this to another person across the circle and so on.
2. Sit in a circle. One person walks (or wheels) across the circle to play a cymbal to another person. She plays a 'message' to that person, perhaps indicating 'hello'. That person then takes the cymbal and greets someone else. He must find a different way to play the instrument from the first person. It can be different in dynamics, style, rhythm or speed. The game continues until the participants have run out of different ways to play it or all have been involved.
3. Sit opposite a partner. The pair has one instrument between them. They have a 'conversation' using the instrument to speak for them. They take it in turns to 'speak' using the instrument to represent their mood.
4. In pairs, using two instruments that are contrasting in timbre (sound quality), compose a short sequence of rhythms. This could be made more difficult by asking for contrasts in dynamics or speed.

Music and other subjects

From these activities it can be seen that although music has a valid life of its own, there are many ways in which it can be taught in combination with other subjects. Performance arts are probably the most natural to combine. Movement and dance have already been mentioned, but drama, puppetry, mime, poetry and prose all have moments when they can support and be supported by music. A simple example demonstrates how music and movement can influence each other.

A pair of pupils (A and B) has one instrument between them. A plays the instrument to control the way in which B moves. Alternatively, B leads and her movements influence A's playing of the instrument.

Adding sounds to a story can give opportunities to learn more of both music and stories. Teenagers with learning difficulties particularly enjoy bringing life to the picture book *Haunted House* by Jan Pienkowski (1979). This is a young children's book with doors to open and tabs to pull, all depicting horror scenes. There is no written story but much to imagine. The first page, for instance, has a staircase, a mouse, a pair of moving eyes, a door, a spider and a cat. Each one can be represented by a sound from an instrument, the voice, the body, or can be electronically concocted. The whole can be made into a musical piece by composing a suitable beginning, middle and end, and the performance can be led by a pupil who points to the different parts of the picture in turn. Other pages can follow depending upon the concentration span of the pupils involved. This could be developed further through moving away from the original picture stimulus into a specific horror story acted by a group of pupils, accompanied by the score.

Combining performance arts is not only sensible in today's crowded curriculum but it also gives many opportunities for pupils to experience and use a set of expressive tools which support each other naturally.

Music can also support other aspects of the curriculum, especially English and mathematics, as both language and patterns are integral parts. Music from different times and cultures relates easily to history, geography and modern foreign languages, and explorations of the properties of sound to science. Instrument-making contributes to design and technology and recording music demonstrates information technology capability. Music has enormous potential, especially in the topic work found in primary and special schools, although dragging it into every topic is not advisable. Merely singing a song which has words which fit into the theme may actually be a poor choice in terms of the musical ability of the class, and listening to music for its representation of the sea or Spring can mask the real musical aspects of the composition (Glover and Ward, 1993).

Personal and social education is another aspect of the curriculum that can be well served by music. Social skills have already been mentioned, especially learning the basics of social interaction. Music can be made alone but there are also plenty of opportunities to come together, share, take turns and listen to each other. This leads naturally into choir, band and orchestra work.

Building self-esteem through taking part in musical activities is another important aspect and teachers have often been aware of pupils' successes which are not necessarily reflected elsewhere in the curriculum. Those who have difficulties in basic reading and writing are not necessarily disadvantaged in the field of expressive arts, although equally, it must be remembered that not everyone finds them easy. Skilled teaching can ensure a measure of success for almost everyone; gone are the days when children are banished from singing groups because they 'growl' and spoil the sound. Everyone is encouraged to sing and, through practice, almost all can improve. Using the voice is like playing any other instrument: it needs technique, practice and regular use.

Conclusions

I have great faith in the boost given to music through its inclusion in the National Curriculum. The orders themselves provide a helpful framework for pupils whatever their ability. It is certainly not difficult to see ways in which even pupils with the most severe learning difficulties can enjoy and benefit from music.

Training every class teacher in primary and special schools to a level of competence is a demanding task, but perhaps no more difficult than training them in any of the other subjects. Most schools have a rolling timetable of development and music will undoubtedly come to the top of the pile sometime. In the meantime, a combination of specialist teaching with encouragement of class teachers to follow-up ideas seems to be the best way forward. There is a tradition of specialist teaching in secondary schools anyway, but one of the greatest difficulties there is finding someone to fill the music post. Achieving this does not, of course, guarantee good practice for pupils with SEN. Many music teachers are already consulting with their learning support team and an extension of this will undoubtedly encourage more appropriate practice. It is hoped, also, that the aspects of music discussed in this chapter and the activities and resources mentioned will serve to inspire and encourage all those who teach music in mainstream and special schools.

References

Alexander Patterson School (1995) '*Schemes of Work for Music*', (unpublished) Alexander Patterson School, Park Gate Road, Wolverley, Kidderminster, Worcs DY10 3PP.

Association of Professional Music Therapists (1988) *Music Therapy in the Education Service: A consultation document,* London: APMT.

Birmingham Curriculum Support Service (1992) *Implementing Music in the National Curriculum* (2nd edn), Birmingham: Birmingham City Council Education Department.

Department for Education (1995) *Music in the National Curriculum,* London: HMSO.

Department of Education and Science (1990) *National Curriculum, Music Working Group: Interim report,* London: DES.

Glover, J. and Ward, S. (1993) *Teaching Music in the Primary School,* London: Cassell.

Mills, J. (1991) *Music in the Primary School,* Cambridge: Cambridge University Press.

OFSTED (1993) *Music Key Stages 1,.2 and 3: First year 1992–3,* London: HMSO.

Pienkowski, J. (1979) *Haunted House,* Oxford: Heinemann.

SCAA (1995) *Planning the Curriculum at Key Stages 1 and 2,* London: SCAA.

SCAA (1996) *Planning the Curriculum for Pupils with Profound and Multiple Learning Difficulties,* London: SCAA.

Stephens, J. (1995) 'The National Curriculum for music', in Pratt, G. and Stephens, J. (eds) *Teaching Music in the National Curriculum,* Oxford: Heinemann.

Stephens, J., Adams, D., Adams, K., Brewer, M. and Read, L. (1995) 'Planning for music in the classroom', in Pratt, G. and Stephens, J. (eds) *Teaching Music in the National Curriculum,* Oxford: Heinemann.

Thompson, P. (1995) 'Music', in Ashcroft, K. and Palacio, D. (eds) *A Primary Teachers' Guide to the New National Curriculum,* London: Falmer Press.

Resources

Allen, A. and Coley, J. (1995–96) *Dance for All (Books 1–3),* London: David Fulton.

Levete, G. (1982) *No Handicap to Dance,* London: Souvenir Press.

NASEN *The Music Curriculum and Special Educational Needs,* Stratford-on-Avon: NASEN.

Perry, T.M., *Music Lessons for Children with Special .Needs,* London: Jessica Kingsley.

Streeter, E., *Making Music with the Young Child with Special Needs,* London: Jessica Kingsley.

Ward, D., *Sing a Rainbow,* Oxford: OUP.

Ward, D., *Hearts and Hands and Voices,*. Oxford: OUP.

Wills, P. and Peter, M. (1995) *Music for All,*. London: David Fulton.

Wood, M., *Music for People with Learning Disabilities,* London: Souvenir Press.

Song and musical games books

Baxter, K., *Fundamental Activities,* Nottingham: Fundamental Activities, PO Box 149, Nottingham NG3 5PU (includes video).

Bean, J. and Oldfield, A., *Pied Piper,* Cambridge: CUP.

Holdstock, J. and West, M., *Earwiggo 1–6,* North Yorks.: Ray Lovely Music, 17 Westgate, Tadcaster, North Yorks. LS24 9JB.

Lennard, C., *Body and Voice,* Wisbech: LDA (includes tapes).

Pearson, D., *Up, Up and Away,* Oxford: OUP.

Powell, H., *Games Songs with Prof. Dogg's Troupe,* London: A & C Black (includes tape).

Thompson, D. and Baxter, K., *Pompaleerie Jig,* London: Arnold/Wheaton.

Primary music courses

Chacksfield, M. and Binns, P., *Sound Ideas,* Oxford: OUP.
Clark, V., *Music through Topics,* Cambridge: CUP (includes tape).
Gilbert, J. and Davies, L., *Oxford Primary Music,* Oxford: OUP (includes tapes).

Tapes

Folk dance tapes from Dancing Circles (PO Box 26, Glastonbury, Somerset BA6 9YA) are a very good source of pieces written in different rhythms for a variety of instruments.

Chapter 10

Modern Foreign Languages

Keith Bovair and Brian Robbins

There are ways of minimising teacher effort while maximising possibilities. (Bovair, M., 1995)

In the mid-1980s the teaching of modern foreign languages to pupils with learning difficulties was a rare event. Often they were withdrawn from these lessons to deal with their first language difficulties. Gradually, evidence was being established that teaching another language was exciting and rewarding for the pupil with special educational needs (Bovair, M., 1995; Bovair and Bovair, 1992; Bovair *et al.*, 1992; Robbins, 1995). It required the understanding that pupils with learning difficulties need what all pupils need which is:

- to know what is expected of them
- to understand how to go about their work
- to achieve success
- to have opportunities for reinforcement
- to see and record progress. (Bovair, M., 1995, p.32)

Also, teaching modern foreign languages requires a particular style of teaching:

The teaching of modern languages lends itself to a multi-sensory approach, which suits the students we are discussing. This style of teaching will be familiar to all teachers of modern languages. This will typically include:

- visual – realia, flashcards, overhead projector (OHP), etc.
- aural – teacher, LSA [special support assistant], tapes, language masters, etc.
- oral – repetition, pairwork, songs, conversations, etc.
- kinetic – action, mime, plays, games, etc.' (Bovair, M., 1995, p.32)

Before all this was recognized as a means to establish access to a subject which was often exclusive, the confidence of teachers had to be established to enable them to develop appropriate differentiated materials. The debate about entitlement had to be won and the doors to experiential learning had to be opened to establish motivation to teach and to learn another language. And by learning another language, the European dimension in a pupil's life becomes more accessible. Robbins (1995 p.16) points out that:

Young people with special educational needs, like all other young people, are growing up in a world of instant communications, within an economy that crosses national and even continental boundaries. If education is truly preparation for life, we should not deny them knowledge of the world as it is today and will be tomorrow.

Each pupil has a right of entitlement to the curriculum, to life experiences, including speaking French, German, Spanish, etc., and to be able to visit these countries. It is an equal opportunity issue. The following anecdote illustrates the opportunities which should exist as a matter of course. In a school for moderate learning difficulties (MLD), the modern foreign language teacher set up a system by which she would give points every time she heard a pupil speak French. There was an award for the pupil with the highest number of points. At the same time a new pupil joined the school. Asked by the headteacher after the morning break (which was supervised by the modern foreign language teacher) how he was getting on, the new pupil quickly replied, 'Fine, but they all speak French here!'

In 1988 the Council of Education Ministers of the European Community passed a resolution to strengthen the European dimension in their respective school systems. It is not a subject but something that permeates the whole curriculum. It's purpose is to raise awareness of Europe's common historical and cultural heritage, to give pupils perspectives that stretch beyond national frontiers and to prepare them better for life in an interdependent Europe.

In this chapter, it is suggested that the European dimension may be subsumed into the modern foreign languages curriculum, although it is cross-curricular and has its place in other subjects. The authors (both working in two major cities in Great Britain – London and Birmingham) recognize that by introducing modern foreign languages in a relevant and meaningful way and by giving them contact with native speakers, their pupils gain a great deal and benefit from the experience.

How does the teacher with this curriculum responsibility set about establishing modern foreign languages in his or her school? In the following, the authors hope to provide a practical, accessible way into the teaching of a modern foreign language, along with examples of projects that can motivate the school population. The suggestions for content are taken from the Programmes of Study (PoS) of the modern foreign languages order (DfE, 1995) and curriculum documentation of Hallmoor School, Birmingham which is a special school for pupils with MLD aged 4 to 19 years. It should assist teachers by giving models for a policy, aims and PoS in the primary and secondary departments for special schools for pupils with MLD.

Policy

In the statutory order for modern foreign languages (DfE, 1995) there is no requirement to teach modern foreign languages at KS1 and 2. Nevertheless, as is the case at Hallmoor School, schools may wish their pupils to have the opportunity to learn about other countries.

Pupils in KS3 and KS4 should follow a combined PoS and should learn at least one target language which is one of the official languages of the European Community. The PoS for KS3 and 4 consists of two parts: 'Learning and using the target language' and 'Areas of experience'. The first part covers the opportunities to be given and the understanding and skills to be developed through the target language in terms of:

- communicating in the target language;
- language skills;
- language learning skills and knowledge of language;
- cultural awareness.

The second part lists broad topics that provide contexts for learning and using the target language. There is no requirement that all of these should be covered in depth and teachers are free to add to the list as they feel fit.

The requirement of the National Curriculum order that the two parts have to be taught together may need to be modified to allow the practice of having some discrete teaching in the target language and reinforcement in other areas of the curriculum. Our experience is that this dual approach is more relevant and meaningful for the pupils.

Pupils in KS4 at Hallmoor School may continue French and learn a basic vocabulary in any other appropriate language in preparation for visits to other European countries.

The target language should be taught as a discrete element and within a broader cross-curricular theme on the European community. Schemes of work should include a European dimension whenever appropriate. This should arise from the topic rather than be a 'bolt-on'. Examples of activities with this theme are given later and in Robbins (1995). Most areas of the curriculum have a potential for bringing in a European dimension. modern foreign languages is one area but there is scope in all National Curriculum subjects.

Pupils should have the opportunity to gain appropriate accreditation for their achievements in modern foreign languages (NFER, 1995).

Aims

It is suggested here that the aims of the modern foreign languages curriculum may be:

- to develop the pupils' self-esteem;
- to develop their ability to communicate in another language;
- to develop general language skills through a new learning experience leading to a positive achievement;
- to develop the pupils' capabilities in their own language;
- to provide intellectual stimulation and to promote skills of more general application;
- to learn about the countries where the target languages are spoken and to encourage positive attitudes towards different cultures;
- to ensure that all pupils achieve a degree of understanding that their village, town or city and the United Kingdom are part of the European Union;
- to give pupils the opportunity to appreciate similarities and differences in lifestyles and customs and to learn that differences and diversity are an asset rather than a threat to living as a community;
- to establish links with other European countries;
- to appreciate the implications for everyday life of the single European market;
- to play an active part in developing professional understanding and collaboration in the field of special education.

PoS for a primary department

The PoS should provide an introduction to the target languages through activities aimed at developing a positive attitude to other languages. The presence in the class of bilingual pupils can provide an opportunity to demonstrate the idea of communicating in more than one language.

The use of greetings in the target languages is to be encouraged. The words for the numbers 'one' to 'ten' and the days of the week and months of the year can be used and displayed in the classroom.

Areas of experience

As the statutory order for modern foreign languages does not prescribe a PoS for KS1 and 2, the following shows only those sections of the areas of experience for KS3 and 4 which may be accessed in age-appropriate ways:

a. Everyday activities

- the language of the classroom
- home life and school
- food, health and fitness.

b. Personal and social life

- self, family and personal relationships
- free time and social activities
- holidays and special occasions.

c. The world around us

- home town and local area
- the natural and made environment
- people, places and customs.

d. World of work

- language and communication in the workplace.

e. The international world

- life in other countries and communities.

Scheme of work

The primary department should provide a wide range of experiences in relation to other cultures both in the classroom and in school or departmental assemblies. These include songs, stories and dramatic presentations.

A useful experience is to hold a 'Euro week' during which each class can become a European country and the pupils can learn greeting words from the native language and sample the national cuisine. Also, the opportunities offered by any visitors from other countries in the school or local community should be utilized to the full.

The five areas of experience in the PoS may be visited within cross-curricular topics. Teachers should include them when appropriate in the context of their planned work on relevant topics.

PoS for a secondary department

The emphasis should be on understanding and using words in the target language and building a vocabulary through conversation and exercises involving word recognition and writing. There should be specific 'language learning' lessons as well as practical tasks for practising and reinforcing the pupils' developing vocabulary.

There should also be opportunities for the pupils to learn about the countries where the target languages are spoken. This work comes within the ambit of the European dimension but should be planned to support the teaching of the target languages by providing relevant activities.

Each pupil in the department should be given the opportunity to participate at least once in a residential visit to a country in the European Union. The programme for this visit should be designed to relate directly to the PoS for modern foreign languages and the European dimension.

The following are the requirements of the statutory order (DfE,1995) for pupils in KS3 and 4 to be given opportunities to participate in the target language.

Learning and using the target language

1. Communicating in the target language

Pupils should be given opportunities to use the target language for real purposes and to develop their understanding and skills through a range of language activities (e.g. games, role play, improvised drama, and investigations). There should be much emphasis upon using the target language in the context of imaginative and creative activities as well as everyday classroom events. Pupils should have access to books, videos and tapes in the target language for personal interest and enjoyment, as well as for information. A range of reading and writing activities should be available as well as a range of resources for communication, such as the telephone, e-mail, and the fax machine.

2. Language skills

The order also stresses the importance of a range of listening activities and activities that encourage pupils to ask and answer questions, learn correct pronunciation and intonation patterns, initiate and maintain conversations. Also, they should have practice in reading and analysing a variety of texts in the target language so that they become adept at recognizing main ideas and remembering details. In short, they should be able to use the target language in a variety of contexts and for different purposes.

3. Language-learning skills and knowledge of language

This part of the order details the kinds of skills and strategies that pupils should learn that will assist them in learning the target language and coping with situations where they encounter unfamiliar words and phrases (e.g., use of dictionaries, use of context and other clues to interpret meaning). In addition, pupils should learn the formal rules of the target language.

4. Cultural awareness

Most importantly, the order details the opportunities that pupils should have if they are going to achieve an understanding of the culture in the countries or communities where the target language is spoken. It stresses the importance of using authentic materials such as newspapers, magazines, books, films, radio and television from these countries or communities. Also, it recommends contact with native speakers of the language either in this country or, where possible, abroad. Finally, it requires that comparisons should be made between the pupils' own culture and these foreign cultures.

Areas of experience

As noted above, schools have a good deal of freedom to make professional judgements about which areas to cover in depth and what additions may be made. In KS3 at Hallmoor School, as required by the order, pupils study:

a. Everyday activities

- the language of the classroom
- home, life and school
- food, health and fitness.

b. Personal and social life

- self, family and personal relationships
- free time and social activities
- holidays and special occasions.

c. The world around us

- home town and local area
- the natural and made environment
- people, places and customs.

Scheme of work for Year 7

a. Everyday activities
The following gives an idea of the range of possible topics within some of the areas of experience:

- colours
- numbers
- food and mealtimes
- markets and shops
- making tomato salad
- visiting a supermarket
- cafe
- sport and games.

b. Personal and social life
Given that the emphasis is upon the pupils themselves, their families, etc., there is a range of possible activities and topics, such as:

- what is your name?
- special occasions
- festivals.

Obviously, the vocabulary to be taught must be carefully considered in the light of the pupils' daily living experiences and environments in and out of school. Typical French phrases are: *bonjour, je. m'appelle, comment t'appelles tu? ca va? ca va bien, j'ai...ans, j'habite...* or whatever is equivalent in other target languages.

Teachers must carefully consider the assessment opportunities that offer themselves. For instance, can pupils ask for and give their name, age and where they live?

c. The world around us
The sections suggest a range of possible topics, e.g., houses, buildings, shops, the countryside.

Scheme of work for Year 8

The following indicate some further developments of selected areas of experience for Year 8 pupils.

a. Everyday activities
- watching food programme
- markets
- design – packaging
- labelling in target languages
- using advertising leaflets – costing exercise
- cheese
- foods from around the world
- recipe development
- menus
- herbs and spices
- fruits and vegetables
- supermarket visits
- fish, shellfish
- mini-enterprise
- hot chocolate
- eating out
- passing food, table manners
- sending postcards home.

c. The world around us
- growing garlic and other herbs
- local geography
- weather and climate
- rivers and canals
- ports
- stories of famous people.

Scheme of work for Year 9

a. Everyday activities
- breakfast – hot chocolate, bread, coffee
- shopping from adverts
- food from regions around the world
- shopping in different situations
- money – coin recognition
- cafe
- crepes, garlic bread.

Again, consideration must be given to developing assessment opportunities which are related to the activities, such as asking for *le pain, une tomate, le chocolate chaud, un cafe.*

c. The world around us
- countries of the world
- capital cities.

As noted above, actual materials are required, e.g. realia for a food project. Teachers may have to develop their own worksheets but many local authorities have adapted, or helped, teachers to adapt, existing materials in order to make them more accessible and a number of publishers have begun to respond to the specific needs of pupils with special educational needs. Similarly, there must be careful consideration of the potential role of information technology (IT) and of the types of materials required to make the activities meaningful, e.g. Euro STILE, jigsaws, puzzles, photographs, atlases, maps, artefacts from other cultures, etc.

PoS for 14+ pupils

The language skills developed in the secondary department may be extended by further work on speaking, reading and writing in the target languages at KS4 and beyond.

The objectives for learning and using the target language would be as described above for younger pupils in the secondary department. but with age-appropriate activities However, somewhat different areas of experience are identifiable from the statutory order. In particular, students in their final years of compulsory schooling and post-16 students should study areas A, B and C in greater depth plus one or both of the following:

d. The world of work

- further education and training
- careers and employment
- language and communication in the workplace.

e. The international world

- tourism at home and abroad
- life in other countries and communities
- world events and issues.

Scheme of work

The scheme of work should prepare students for the imminent move from school into the field of further education and/or adult employment. For instance, the area of 'The world of work' might involve activities relating to money and working in tourism. The area of 'The international world' might involve learning experiences relating to the European Union, the work of travel agents, visitors from abroad, and forms of transport and communications (e.g., airports, roads, railways, canals).

Developing the areas of experience

Materials are becoming available through the various projects that are underway in this country and other European countries, such as the Eurotech Project in Birmingham (see Robbins, 1995). At Hallmoor School, staff are collating materials from a variety of sources as school resources for particular areas of experience. The following is an indication of the range of 'topics' for which schools might develop resources.

a. Everyday activities

- family mealtimes
- markets and shops
- food
- sport
- school.

b. Personal and social life

- people's names
- special occasions.

c. The world around us

- houses
- weather and climate
- rivers and canals
- ports
- stories of famous people.

d. The world of work

- money
- working in tourism
- where things are made
- transportation of goods.

e. The international world

- the European Union
- travel agents
- visitors from abroad
- ferries.

Keeping up the motivation

The Rauzet Restoration Project – Durants School, Enfield, North London

This project had been set up to restore the fine romanesque Church of Rauzet in the village of Rozet, France. A main task was the restoration of a mediaeval fishpond within the grounds. In this experience the skills of learning a new language, self-sufficiency, practical problem-solving, enterprise, team-building skills, work experience, community/school links and extension of the National Curriculum occurred.

In 1993, Durants School was invited to join an existing work experience and community project in France. The project had been established the year before between White Hart Lane School, Le Lycee de L'image et du Son in France, the Craswell Grandmontine Society and the local community of Rozet.

Essentially, the project focused on the restoration of the Priory at Rozet. Durants School was invited to work on the site, restoring part of the grounds. This built on an established programme of pre-work experience skills based at Durants School and Capel Manor College in Enfield. The programme had been identified and established at Durants School to answer pupils' needs in helping them cope with emerging independence, practical problem-solving and the successful transference of skills into different work settings.

The work at Rozet was a) an extension of this, and b) designed to complement the archaeological work undertaken by the other groups. Durants School staff developed wider objectives for their students, encompassing a European awareness programme and self-sufficiency. These included a European food project, funded by North London Training and Enterprise Council. Initially the work was planned and coordinated between White Hart Lane School (who liaised with the Lycee in France) and Durants School. All three schools liaised with the Grandmontine Society.

Outcomes of the project could be seen in the growth of pupils' self-esteem. This in turn helped them to develop many skills towards becoming independent young adults and extended their confidence in their academic learning.

The project supported curriculum development in French, European awareness, mathematics, technology, history, geography and art.

Team Enterprise

Team Enterprise allows pupils to experience setting up a business. The skills of management, accounting, product design and selling are learnt through the framework of this area.

Pupils from Durants School, with assistance from the Enfield Chamber of Commerce and Safeways Supermarkets, set up an English market stall in and around Nantes, France. They spent a whole week in the region, learning a variety of skills, in French, to make the work a success. This success was due to the experience of the previous project and the skill and confidence of the staff who saw, along with the pupils, the benefit of learning another language. Thus, Team Enterprise, which is a 'mainstream' educational opportunity, was enhanced by relocation to France.

The Birmingham Eurotech Project – Hallmoor School, Birmingham

The Eurotech Project 1995 was a technology-based project within Key Stage 3. It was developed over two terms. In the autumn term pupils were asked to:

- investigate signs in the community, such as shop signs, road signs, everyday signs;
- investigate information found on packaging such as weight, number of units, serving suggestions, country of origin, manufacturers, price, nutritional information and shape of packaging and materials;
- compare home packaging to foreign packaging to see if the same information could be gathered despite language barriers;
- look at how packaging is put together by dismantling and assembling different types
- explore different shapes and packages and their suitability for a range of foods;
- visit local shops and a variety of markets;
- research pricing, availability;
- design an item which was small and cost less than 25 pence, and a quick-to-eat snack given a design brief;
- design packaging for their snack food, market it and sell it.

During the spring term links were made with nine schools in Europe and a joint food project was initiated. The countries involved were Germany, Denmark, Northern Ireland, Holland and England. This involved pupils recording their daily food intake on a specific day and recording the types of shops that they purchased in and the prices they paid. They then sent the information to the other schools and exchanged examples of packaging with each other. Those schools that had a fax were able to exchange information rapidly. They produced a video of the snack food which they had designed in the Autumn term. The pupils then set up a mini-enterprise scheme to raise money to sponsor some pupils for a residential visit to France. They had to develop the following skills:

- survey techniques within the school;
- safe food-handling procedures;
- recipe development;
- food tasting;
- recording and handling data;
- evaluation skills.

The two terms' work culminated in a residential visit to France continuing the theme of communication and marketing. Overall the impact on the curriculum of this project can be seen in Figure 10.1.

Other projects and trips to the continent have occurred in both authors' schools. For instance, at Hallmoor School, exchange visits of pupils and staff from link schools in Germany and amongst its local primary and secondary schools have enhanced and extended the curriculum.

The experiences of both schools can be summarized in the following:

> To watch one of our girls who is normally very shy helping one of the boys to buy an ice-cream at Mont St Michel was an object lesson in the growth of self-confidence...
>
> With their growing confidence we have seen improvements in other areas of the curriculum. The progress shown by pupils in reading and writing English is due in no small measure to their increased awareness of signs, interpreting another language and taking notice of written information in their environment. (Robbins, 1995, p.16)

Teaching pupils with severe learning difficulties

There has been much scepticism about introducing a modern foreign language to pupils with severe learning difficulties (SLD). Typically, the argument goes something like this: we should not be teaching a foreign language to these pupils when they still have significant language deficits in their own language. Although it is understandable that teachers may show caution, some schools have had a positive experience of teaching a foreign language and have found that it has the potential to be interesting, enriching and a great deal of fun. Moreover, it provides a new and effective experience of learning language skills (which are common to all languages) untainted by past failure, and students can be delighted to find that they are studying a subject studied by their brothers and sisters at their schools.

At George Hastwell School, Cumbria, the introduction of a French week was so successful that French now occupies a regular weekly position on the timetable for secondary-aged pupils. Throughout the French week, lessons were planned with a French focus; in mathematics they learned to count up to ten in French and to compare

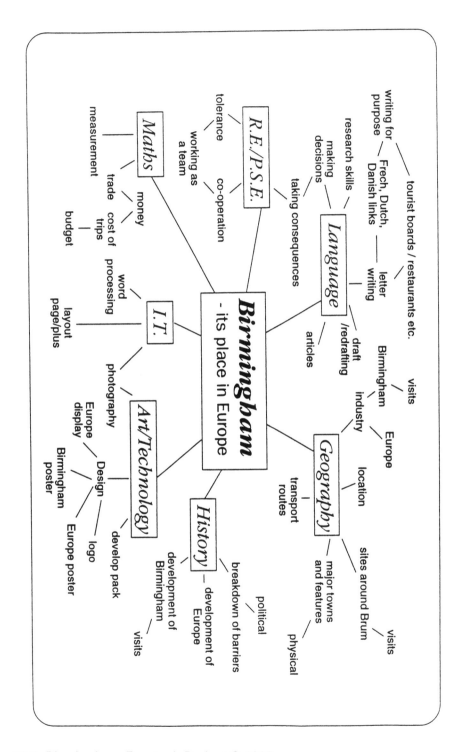

Figure 10.1 Birmingham Eurotech Project © 1995

French and British money; in geography they looked at books and maps of France; in physical education they played boules; in music they listened to the work of French composers; in art they painted French flags and produced posters; in design and technology they planned typically French meals, compiled menus and searched for French food at the supermarkets. The highlight of the week was the conversion of one classroom into a French cafe which displayed their work and allowed visitors to select drinks and snacks made by the pupils.

In particular, the use of IT has been a major factor in making the modern foreign languages curriculum accessible at George Hastwell School (McKeown, 1993). Communication devices which can digitize and store sounds have been programmed with simple French phrases which pupils with communication problems or less confident pupils can produce by touching the appropriate part of the overlay of pictorial symbols on the keyboard. The overlays may be changed depending on the lesson content and may contain, say, pictures of food or clothes, or symbols which represent common phrases (see Figure 10.2 for an example of symbols for basic phrases).

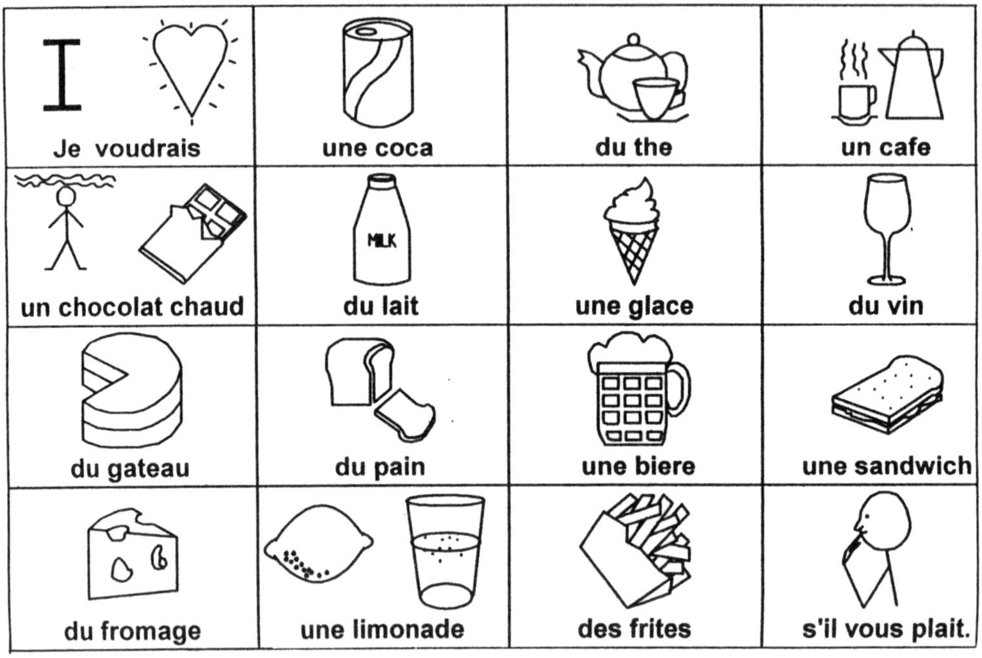

Figure 10.2 Symbol overlay for basic phrases

Individualized work sheets may be prepared using symbols from, say, the *Rebus Symbol Collection* from Widgit Software (see resources list at the end of this chapter) and may be associated with general topic areas. Using this software and an overlay keyboard, pupils may produce pieces of their own French writing accompanied by the appropriate symbols (see Figure 10.3).

Computers can also be set up with a number of programs which may help pupils practise their French vocabulary. For instance, pupils may have access to slide shows created using Kid Pix Companion, which is a program which allows pictures, including digitized images, to be placed in a sequence and accompanied by the sound of

Figure 10.3 Writing in French with Symbol Software

somebody labelling the image. At George Hastwell School, a popular slide show contained digitized photographs of each pupil accompanied by his or her voice announcing '*Je m'appelle...*'. And of course, when a pupil could not speak, the rest of the group recorded the greeting '*Bonjour...*' for when his or her picture appears.

Dignity in education

The curriculum challenge for these schools has been to meet the decry, 'Why teach these pupils modern foreign languages? They can hardly speak English'. Yet, this chapter has provided the evidence that this may be done appropriately and to the benefit of the pupils.

The only 'disabling' condition that our pupils have are low expectations and assumptions made by adults. As Pablo Casals is quoted as saying in one of his master classes: 'Children should be dignified by their learning'. It is our responsibility as educators to make the opportunities for this to happen.

Acknowledgements

The authors wish to acknowledge the contribution of the staffs at Durants School and Hallmoor School to the development of the curriculum described here and the material supplied by Clare Martin of George Hastwell School.

References

Bovair, K., Carpenter, B. and Upton, G. (1992) *Special Curricula Needs*, London: David Fulton.
Bovair, M. (1995) 'Only the top sets did French', *Special*, 4, 1, 31–2.
Bovair, M. and Bovair, K. (1992) *Modern Languages for All*, London: Kogan Page.
DfE (1995) *Modern Foreign Languages in the National Curriculum*, London: HMSO.
McKeown, S. (1993) 'French connections', in the pull-out supplement 'Key Issues and Key Stages; Keeping track of the National Curriculum', *Times Educational Supplement*, 30 April.
NFER (1995) *Small Steps of Progress in the National Curriculum; Executive summary*, Slough: NFER.
Robbins, B. (1995) 'Links across Europe', *Special*, 4, 1, 15–17.

Further reading

Kenning, M. (1994) 'Foreign languages and special needs: implications for teacher support', *British Journal of Special Education*, 21, 4, 152–6.
Lucas, S. (no date) *Communication in French: A Package Developed for Use with Students with Severe Learning Difficulties*, Metropolitan Borough of Wigan Education Department.
National Curriculum Council (1993) *Modern Foreign Languages and Special Educational Needs: A new commitment*, York: NCC.
Nichols, R. and Thomas, G. (1992) 'Introduction of a foreign language into the special school curriculum', in Bovair, K., Carpenter, B. and Upton, G. (1992) *Special Curricula Needs*, London: David Fulton.

Resources

Information sheets on activities and materials are available from the Centre for Information on Language Teaching and Research, 20 Bedfordbury, London WC2 4LB.
Widgit Software, 102 Radford Road, Leamington Spa, Warwickshire CV31 1LF.

Chapter 11

Design and Technology

Helen Mount

The delivery of technology is a subject which continues to generate passions and controversy among professionals. This chapter aims to unravel some of the perceived mysteries and assist those teachers who may be experiencing difficulties. It should also provide clarification for those teachers who have attempted to deliver a broad, balanced and relevant design and technology curriculum to pupils who have learning difficulties through topic-based/thematic or modular approaches (Byers, 1990; Mount and Ackerman, 1991; Rose *et al.*, 1994). It is neither necessary nor particularly relevant to spend time examining the detail of the first requirements for technology when the National Curriculum was in its infancy but a brief overview of the original statutory requirements, the nature of the subject and some of the problems encountered will provide the background to the current changes. The main requirements of the current orders will be discussed in more detail and practical suggestions for delivering the design and technology capability within this framework will then be offered.

Background

In the first version of the National Curriculum five formerly discrete subjects were amalgamated under the subject of technology. These were design and technology, craft, business education, home economics and information technology (IT). Technology comprised two profile components – design and technology and IT (DES 1990). The four attainment targets (ATs) – identifying needs and opportunities; generating a design; planning and making; and evaluating – were not seen as separate entities but part of an AT, and pupils should have been encouraged to develop their capability through an iterative spiral which promoted reflection and action. Design and technology was, and to a great extent still is, an extremely wide-ranging subject containing a complex web of cross-curricular links. It encompasses practical and theoretical elements, is essentially processed-based and may be summarized as:

> The purposeful and practical response to perceived needs or opportunities, that must be worked out in particular contexts and against particular values. It is about being practically but intelligently capable – of doing, making, of knowing how (Pring, 1989).

From the beginning of its introduction as a 'new' foundation subject in the National Curriculum, the delivery of technology caused anxiety among some non-specialist teachers in mainstream primary and special schools (Lever, 1990). The nature and design of many all-age schools for pupils with learning difficulties, especially those with severe learning difficulties (SLD), created particular problems. Most of these schools lacked specialist teachers in many subject areas. In addition, they lacked facilities for pupils of secondary age who had limited if any access to laboratories, workshops and home economics rooms. In the current climate of economic constraints it is unlikely that much has changed and teachers in these schools still have to adapt and be resourceful in their approach.

It was also apparent from early Her Majesty's Inspectorate (HMI) reports that some teachers lacked confidence and possibly skills in tackling the breadth and balance in design and technology. They therefore tended to concentrate on those areas with which they were familiar and experienced, like home economics – an area of the curriculum which has been well established in most special schools for many years. In reports on two schools, paragraphs on technology show significant emphasis on preparation and cooking of meals despite some more positive references to producing artefacts using paper, fabric and card in one of the schools. Recent OFSTED reports have also expressed concern about the lack of breadth and balance in design and technology in some special schools (HMI, 1992; 1993). This traditional emphasis on food technology and the limited way in which it has been interpreted in some quarters provides only a very narrow, restricted and potentially prescriptive element of design and technology. Delivering technology with this emphasis created an imbalance in the experiences offered to pupils in special schools. It did not fulfil the requirements then nor does it fulfil the requirements of the current orders. Technology offers tremendous scope for increasing pupils' independence by developing their confidence and ability in problem-solving, testing, evaluating, reflecting, and making aesthetic, technical and social judgements. This can be achieved by blending practical and theoretical experiences. Although the orders for the subject have been modified and the language simplified, the underlying objectives and processes remain similar and some previous publications still contain much information that will be helpful to those teachers who are having difficulty with the delivery of design and technology, albeit with some modifications to bring it up to date (Mount and Ackerman, 1991; Ort Trust, 1993; Tearle, 1991).

Successful learning outcomes for pupils with (or without) learning difficulties in design and technology depend considerably on the approaches of those teaching them. Teachers do not enhance the design and technology capability of their pupils by providing templates or cardboard cut-outs at the start of the lesson. As Sebba *et al.* (1995) point out, this approach eliminates the 'essential problem-solving feature of the subject'. It is only through their interaction with pupils, through skilful and discrete intervention (which does not prescribe what pupils are going to make today, but asks them to find out about or try doing something together), that teachers and support staff can guide them to develop their capability, knowledge and understanding. This is one of the most challenging aspects of design and technology, particularly for those teachers of pupils who have SLD or profound and multiple learning difficulties (PMLD). What will enhance learning, is appropriate, balanced and meaningful has to be the decision of the class/subject teacher concerned. Offering pupils breadth and balance should not result in tokenism, and some of the concepts involved, especially at higher Key Stages, have questionable validity for pupils who are functioning at a very early developmental level. However, there is much in the orders that can be made accessible, and giving pupils more responsibility for their own learning is essential if design and technology programmes of study are applied appropriately.

The current position

In the current version of the National Curriculum, IT has become a discrete element with its own statutory orders and far-reaching cross-curricular implications. The revised design and technology curriculum was presented in a more straightforward way with a considerable reduction in the volume of information and prescription. Despite being an apparently slimmer version, however, it remains a subject with considerable scope and opportunity which should develop pupils' capabilities of invention, imagination, reasoning, problem-solving and quality control, together with practical skills and understanding of working safely with a variety of materials and tools. In recognition of the cross-curricular links between design and technology and other subjects, the Programmes of Study (PoS) contain cross-references to the science, maths and art orders, but there is not much information to help class teachers deliver.

The revised order for design and technology in the National Curriculum states that:

> Pupils should be taught to develop their design and technology capability through combining their designing and making skills with knowledge and understanding in order to design and make products. (DfE 1995)

In England the PoS for Key Stages (KSs) 1– 4 are compulsory, but in Wales there are no statutory requirements at K4. There are eight level descriptions that provide information relating to types and range of pupils' performance. Level eight is available for 'very able pupils' and there is a further level to help teachers differentiate 'exceptional performance' at KS3. The common requirements of the order for design and technology do not contain any additional points with regard to access statements, use of language, IT, etc. It is assumed that the reader is familiar with these, as they are similar for all National Curriculum subjects and do not, in my opinion, provide teachers of pupils with learning difficulties with anything they were not already modifying in support of their pupils. What is important to note is that the new requirements have been written in as non-prescriptive a way as possible. For some teachers this is a welcome statement and challenge which offers maximum opportunity for taking advantage of their own expertise, interests and local resources. For others with less confidence and experience of the subject, the lack of prescription may raise concerns about what to teach, when, where and how to teach it, what resources to use and how to ensure breadth and balance. By now, however it should be clear that design and technology by its very nature cannot be prescriptive and this should become more apparent as the main issues and practical implications are discussed further.

There are now two ATs – AT1 Designing and AT2 Making. This reduction and simplification should be welcomed, although those who considered food and textiles as significant elements of the old orders may be disappointed. It should also be noted that the programmes of study for food and control do not appear until KS2. There are two core sections of the PoS which are interrelated – one on designing and making, the other on knowledge and understanding. There are also supporting sub-sections of the PoS outlining the knowledge and understanding required. These are:

- materials and components (at KS1 these are in the opportunities section)
- mechanisms and control

- structures
- products and applications
- quality
- health and safety
- vocabulary.

Delivery of the core and supporting sections of the PoS can be achieved in three related areas. First, there is the introduction of designing and making assignments in which pupils design and make products. Second, there are focused practical tasks in which pupils experience a range of techniques and practice new or particular skills, developing their knowledge and understanding. Third, pupils are to be given opportunities to investigate, disassemble and evaluate simple products which will also add to their knowledge, repertoire of skills and their understanding. It is expected that these three related areas will provide the principal focus for delivery and occupy a substantial proportion of teaching time.

The former requirement to make three different types of products in five different contexts at each Key Stage, using at least five different materials, has been dropped, as it was recognized that this was practically impossible to achieve, particularly at the early Key Stages. It was also recognized that the former AT1 – 'Identifying needs and opportunities' – presented difficulties for young pupils; this could also be applied to pupils who have learning difficulties. This unrealistic goal has been modified to 'investigating and clarifying a task' to make it more practical and applicable at KS1 and 2, although the initial rigour of this has been retained at KS3 and 4. Another significant modification to the original orders stems from the acknowledgement that categorization of artefacts, systems and environments (and the boundaries between them) was imprecise, and these categories have therefore been removed. From this has developed the recommendation that pupils should be required to 'make a manageable range of good quality products' (Design and Technology Association, 1993).

Despite the slimming down, modification and clarification that has occurred in the current orders for design and technology, it is clear that there are several issues that concern those teachers attempting to deliver the design and technology curriculum to pupils with a range of learning difficulties. There remains an obvious demand for further in-service in this subject area as questions are raised about certain aspects of delivery, especially the precise nature of what constitutes a design and making assignment and the length of time that should be spent on it. There are also issues relating to the use of materials, the potential blurring of boundaries between focused practical tasks and investigating, disassembling and evaluating materials and, finally, the need to incorporate progression and differentiation into schemes of work.

Planning and practical applications

In recognition of some of the difficulties faced by many teachers SCAA has produced two publications outlining the new requirements for design and technology (SCAA, 1995a; 1995b). The first of these covers KS1 and 2 and the second, KS3. Both contain illustrative examples describing how current practice can meet the statutory requirements. A wide range of examples is provided in order to show how the requirements can be achieved through many different activities, and it includes cross-curricular links relating to different subject areas. In the KS1 and 2 publication there is progression through the activities from KS1 to the upper end of KS2, although it is stated that most of the activities described are suitable for use with children of any age. The same publications should offer some clarification for teachers with coverage of the following aspects of design and technology:

- design and technology capability
- the structure of the order
- design and technology in practice
- designing and making skills
- knowledge and understanding
- planning in practice.

In attempting to offer some practical applications of the current orders it is not possible to please all of the people all of the time as each school has its own whole curriculum including the National Curriculum. It is also impossible to write a design and technology curriculum or offer more than a snapshot of activities in the space available, but it is hoped that the illustrations provided can be applied in schools for pupils with a range of learning difficulties. This should be equally relevant whether schools take a thematic/topic-based, modular, or subject-based approach.

Design and technology can provide many experiences which address the serious issues of equal access for girls as well as boys, equal access for pupils with different abilities and equal access for children from different cultures. Cross-cultural links can be embedded into all thematic work and topics that are rich in these include food, ourselves, clothes and celebrations/festivals, among others. Other considerations which should be made are the inclusion in displays of published materials, books and posters showing alternative life styles, languages and customs, visits to and from religious and cultural centres as well as visits from relatives and friends of pupils from ethnic groups. Shops and markets in multicultural areas offer a wide variety of foods, clothes, jewellery and other artefacts and some cultural centres or individuals may have items which can be borrowed such as instruments, cooking utensils, ornaments or clothes (Manchester Primary Science Team, undated).

Using a thematic approach should generate a wealth of ideas and information that form the basis for activities and may be blended with individual and group objectives. The main features of this approach may be summarized thus:

- the whole school staff or class staff meet to agree a topic/theme and 'brainstorm' ideas. This leads to the development of a topic web comprising a variety of sub-themes or activities
- activities may then be related to the whole curriculum including the National Curriculum incorporating cross-curricular links
- where the whole school has planned together, individual classes take one aspect of the web and develop it further. The activities should then be differentiated at this point to make them accessible and suitable for pupils of different ages and with different abilities. This should ensure that pupils have different experiences of the same theme/topic at different times as they progress through the school and, careful planning is needed at this stage to ensure progression (Byers, 1990).

An illustration of the first part of this process is provided in Figure 11.1 where the web has been generated by 'brainstorming' areas that relate to the topic/theme of 'Materials'. This is, however, only one way of viewing 'Materials' within a thematic approach and another method could be adopted. For example, individual classes could explore and

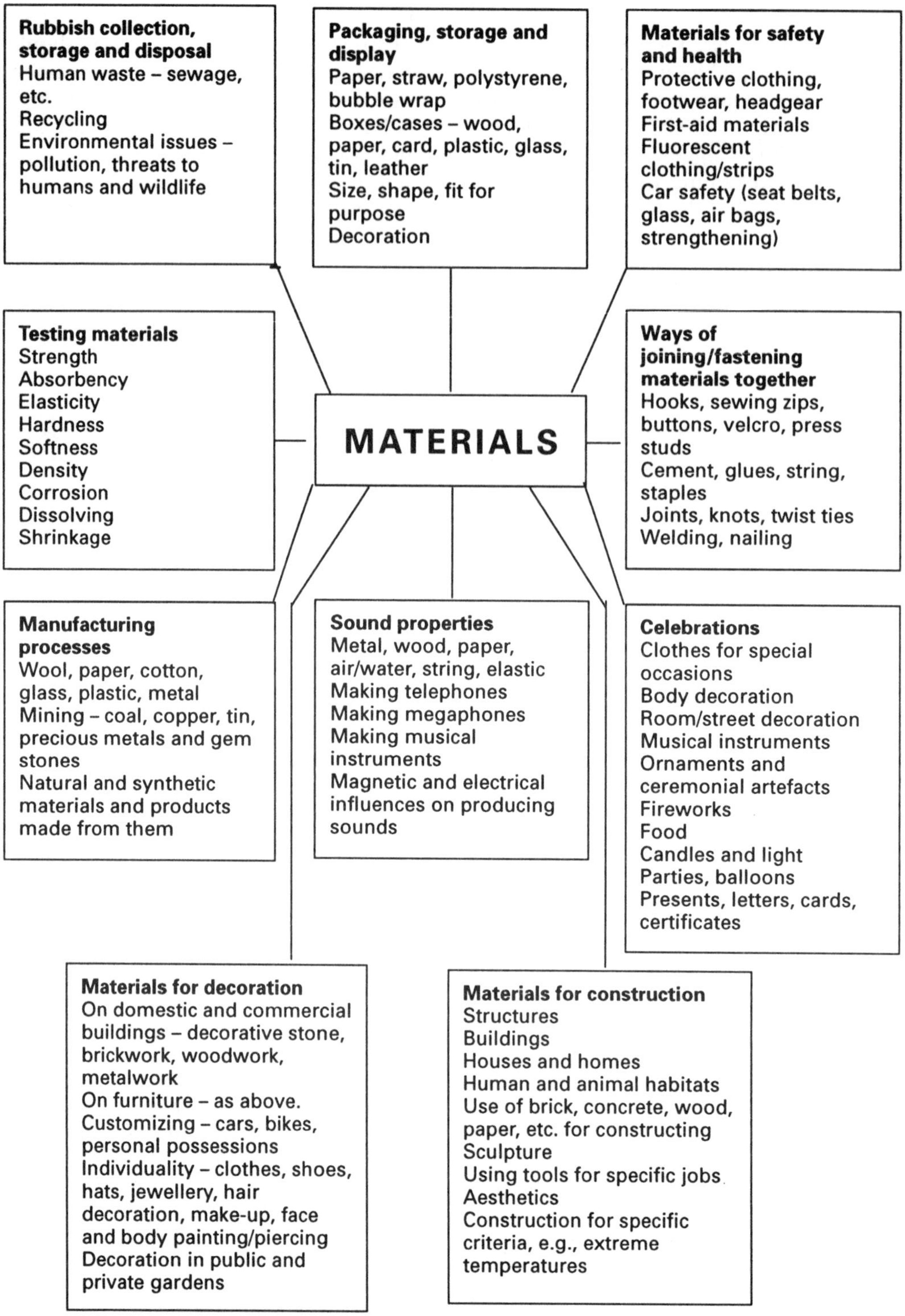

Rubbish collection, storage and disposal
Human waste – sewage, etc.
Recycling
Environmental issues – pollution, threats to humans and wildlife

Packaging, storage and display
Paper, straw, polystyrene, bubble wrap
Boxes/cases – wood, paper, card, plastic, glass, tin, leather
Size, shape, fit for purpose
Decoration

Materials for safety and health
Protective clothing, footwear, headgear
First-aid materials
Fluorescent clothing/strips
Car safety (seat belts, glass, air bags, strengthening)

Testing materials
Strength
Absorbency
Elasticity
Hardness
Softness
Density
Corrosion
Dissolving
Shrinkage

MATERIALS

Ways of joining/fastening materials together
Hooks, sewing zips, buttons, velcro, press studs
Cement, glues, string, staples
Joints, knots, twist ties
Welding, nailing

Manufacturing processes
Wool, paper, cotton, glass, plastic, metal
Mining – coal, copper, tin, precious metals and gem stones
Natural and synthetic materials and products made from them

Sound properties
Metal, wood, paper, air/water, string, elastic
Making telephones
Making megaphones
Making musical instruments
Magnetic and electrical influences on producing sounds

Celebrations
Clothes for special occasions
Body decoration
Room/street decoration
Musical instruments
Ornaments and ceremonial artefacts
Fireworks
Food
Candles and light
Parties, balloons
Presents, letters, cards, certificates

Materials for decoration
On domestic and commercial buildings – decorative stone, brickwork, woodwork, metalwork
On furniture – as above.
Customizing – cars, bikes, personal possessions
Individuality – clothes, shoes, hats, jewellery, hair decoration, make-up, face and body painting/piercing
Decoration in public and private gardens

Materials for construction
Structures
Buildings
Houses and homes
Human and animal habitats
Use of brick, concrete, wood, paper, etc. for constructing
Sculpture
Using tools for specific jobs
Aesthetics
Construction for specific criteria, e.g., extreme temperatures

Figure 11.1 Topic web for some aspects of materials

investigate one single material each, e.g., class 1– paper, class 2– wood, class 3 – clay, class 4 – fabric, class 5 – metal, class 6 – glass, and so on. This alternative method should be equally acceptable and capable of offering breadth and balance as well as relevance. A range of activities across different curriculum areas including design and technology should be easy to identify by brainstorming as before or, in this case, by adapting and expanding those suggested in Figure 11.1 It should not be necessary to illustrate this in every detail, repeating the activities and experiences provided in Figure 11.1, as the reader will wish to do this in relation to their own pupils' needs. What is illustrated in Figure 11.2 is an example of how one of the materials (paper) may be approached. Most of the same headings could be used for the other materials but there will need to be some additions and deletions appropriate for each material.

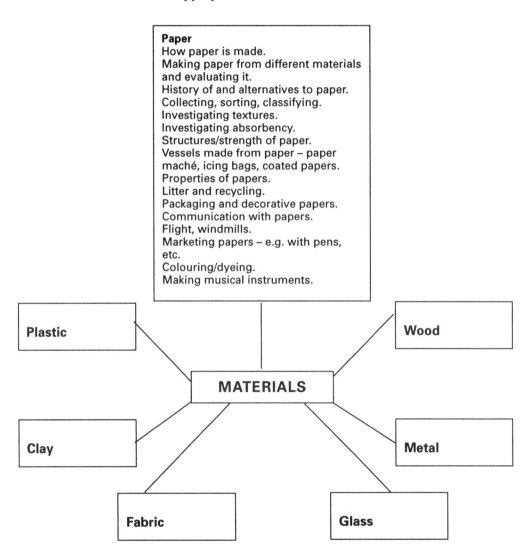

Figure 11.2 Alternative approach to developing a topic web

Once the framework is in place, design and technology, along with other subject areas, has to be identified. Using topic webs as the starting point it is possible to list some suggestions for activities (general and specific) that relate to the PoS for subjects of the National Curriculum and religious education. As with Figures 11.1 and 11.2, the suggestions are not meant to be the definitive list but memory joggers and starting points which can be adapted, developed and applied in a variety of ways. Some suggestions for different subject areas are listed below and cross-curricular links should be apparent. Focusing on the aspect of Figure 11.2 that has already been expanded (i.e. paper as part of a 'Materials' theme), the following activities are suggested for different subjects:

English
Using a story or poem as a stimulus to generate ideas for pupils to write a story about the characters and put on a show or present it at assembly.
Making a variety of books – zigzag, pop-up, shaped, etc.
Writing with a variety of implements.
Imaginary play with a library or book shop/stationers.
Using shopping lists, displays, labelling as a focus.
Exploring newspapers, magazines, other publications.
Writing about visits, recording results, sequencing with storyboards.
Examining different forms of writing and scripts including codes and musical notation.
Reading and writing as a form of communication.
Writing greetings cards, invitations, captions, slogans.

Mathematics
Exploring 2D and 3D shapes and pattern (tangrams, origami, tessellation).
Exploring structures.
Weighing and measuring.
Sorting, classifying, matching.
Handling data and problem-solving.
Exploring similarities and differences, opposites.
Using computers to create and transfer shapes.

Science
Trees – growth, needs, similarities and differences, recognition of parts of a plant.
Absorbency testing.
Testing strength.
Colouring with inks and dyes.
Relating structure to strength, e.g., folding, rolling, bending, joining.
Effect of elements on papers.
Light-sensitive papers.
Effect of forces on materials.
Exploring texture.
Animals/minibeasts using paper for nests and other habitats.
Exploring the sound-making properties of paper.

Technology
The manufacturing of papers.
Designing and making kites, windmills.
Investigating papers for specific purposes.
Designing and making greetings cards.
Designing and making puppets.
Designing and making musical instruments.
Investigating packaging in particular contexts.
Making and using templates.
Making and evaluating models and mock-ups.

Using tools appropriately and safely.
Evaluating quality and recording information.
Investigating moving joints for paper and card.
Disassembling a range of paper products including greetings cards.
Investigating decoration and applying a range of finishing techniques.
Investigating and evaluating failure of some structures.
Using construction kits.
Testing products against set criteria.

Information technology
Recording results and storing information.
Using IT in the design process, exploring new techniques, editing work, displaying and printing.
Retrieving information.
Using IT to model, e.g., design for greetings card or verse inside.

History
History of paper (handling and using artefacts).
Alternatives to paper through the ages.
Paper-making through the ages.
Illuminated scripts and changes in presentation.
Development of communications (history of printing, books, important people in relation to development).
Local history in relation to communications and print.
Women as authors, composers, etc.

Geography
Where paper is made.
Climate for growing appropriate trees.
Availability and uses of paper in different geographical areas.
Mapping where trees for paper are grown in the locality, England, in Europe, in the world.
Management of different environments for growing trees for paper.

Art
Decorative papers – wrapping paper, decorations.
Exploring colour and contrast using different papers and paints.
Paper curling, folding, cutting, tearing to produce 3D effects.
Paper sculpture, shape and form.
Applying finishes to paper puppets, musical instruments, kites, etc. using a variety of stimuli.
Applying pattern and texture from experiences.
Opportunities to recognize similarities and differences in art and craft from different times and places.

Music
Exploration of sound making with paper.
Making instruments with paper/card using a variety of means to produce sound.
Performing with instruments made and evaluating their qualities.
Composing for instruments made using specific symbols for each instrument.

Modern foreign languages have not been considered for this topic.

Physical education
Moving like gyros, windmills, paper kites, darts (using paper as the stimulus).
Exploring moods and feelings, using suitable music to identify with 'paper' movements.
Using paper lariats in dance to explore movement.

Religious education
Using the bible as a focus.
The story of Moses.
Using religious festivals and artefacts.

A further alternative could be to take a modular approach as described by Rose (1994). This whole-school approach to curriculum planning resulted in one special school developing a series of modules which are effectively short courses designed for specific groups of pupils. While the development of documentation for each module is initially time-consuming, the resulting sharing of good practices, the avoidance of unnecessary repetition, the positive management of time and resources, differentiation, cross-curricular coverage and recording make this a worthwhile alternative to consider. Each module lasts for either half a term or a term (approximately) and uses the same standard format outlining the progression from previous work as appropriate, suggested activities for the lesson, equipment needed and cross-reference to other curriculum areas. Relating this approach to the thematic approach should not be difficult and it should be possible to develop modules covering the different aspects of materials already identified in Figure 11.1 and consider differentiated activities for pupils of different ages and abilities.

Either Figures 11.1 or 11.2 could provide the basis for a modular approach addressing the needs of particular pupils. Further illustration of the planning and practical applications of the modular approach is not possible here; for a more detailed description see Rose (1994). The SCAA publication on the new requirements for KS1 and KS2 of design and technology also contains useful information on design and technology capability by planning and delivering via 'units of work'. These are similar to a modular approach and ensure that existing activities relating to design and technology are built on and that the requirements of the National Curriculum are fulfilled (SCAA, 1995a).

Continuing to use paper as the focal point of our theme, design and technology capability needs to be examined further. The whole process began with a wide-angle view, brainstorming as many ideas and links as possible. This was followed by zooming in on specific aspects until a close-up picture containing more detail was developed. The next step therefore is to examine which PoS can be covered using the activities already suggested and applying them to KS1. Figure 11.3 illustrates how using one designing and making assignment (making a greetings card for Mothers' Day) can fulfil the requirements in the PoS.

The left- and right-hand columns show all the PoS for KS1, although some of those in the right hand column have been abbreviated. The suggested activities are listed in the central column and if pupils are actively engaged in these over half a term the requirements for the subject should be fulfilled. The designing and making of a greetings card for a particular context (Mothers' Day) is a designing and making assignment covering PoS 1a in this example. Focused practical tasks (PoS 1b) include investigating a variety of joints to create movement, practising ways of joining paper and card together, using appropriate tools, and making templates, among others. Investigating, disassembling and evaluating simple products (PoS 1c) may be achieved through giving pupils opportunities to take apart a range of commercially-produced greetings cards, investigate how they are made, the effectiveness of the design for the purpose, what they like or dislike about particular cards and giving reasons for their comments.

These are just a few example from Figure 11.3 that help to illustrate the relationship between the activities and the programmes of study but, together, all the activities cover designing, making and the development of skills, knowledge and understanding. The teacher's role in the planning and delivery of the activities is critical. Not only do they guide their pupils' learning by careful questions and intervention but they also gain information which they can use to record the level of knowledge and understanding their pupils have gained.

Programme of study	Activity	Programmes of study (cont.)
1) Pupils should be given opportunities to develop their design and technology capability through: a) assignments in which they design and make products b) focused practical tasks c) activities in which they investigate, disassemble and evaluate simple products	Designg and making greetings cards	
	Investigating papers and card for specific purposes	
	Making and using templates	
2) Pupils should be given opportunities to: a) work with a range of materials and components, including sheet materials, items that can be assembled to make products, e.g., reclaimed material, textiles, food and construction kits b) investigate how the working characteristics of materials can be changed to suit different purposes c) apply skills, knowledge and understanding from the PoS of other subjects, where appropriate, including, art, maths and science	Making and evaluating models and mock-ups Using tools appropriately and safely Evaluating quality and recording information Investigating moving joints for paper and card and other ways of introducing 3D aspects	5) Knowledge and understanding Activities include all the sub-sections from the PoS: a) mechanisms b) structures
3) Designing skills; pupils should be taught to: a) draw on their own experience to help generate ideas b) clarify their ideas through discussion c) develop their ideas through shaping, assembling and rearranging materials and components d) develop and communicate their design ideas by making freehand drawings, and by modelling their ideas in other ways, e.g., by using actual materials and components with temporary fixings e) make suggestions about how to proceed f) consider their design ideas as these develop, and identify strengths and weaknesses	Disassembling a range of products, including greetings cards Investigating decoration and applying a range of finishing techniques Investigating and evaluating failure of some structures Using construction kits Testing products against set criteria and evaluating quality Making suggestions for Mother's Day cards for women in different age groups	c) and d) products and applications e) quality f) health and safety g) vocabulary
4) Making skills; pupils should be taught to: a) select materials, tools and techniques b) measure, mark out, cut and shape a range of materials c) assemble, join and combine materials and components d) apply simple finishing techniques, e.g., painting. e) make suggestions about how to proceed f) evaluate their products as these are developed, identifying strengths and weaknesses	Cutting and joining paper with an awareness of safety issues Expanding range of vocabulary through discussion and expanding knowledge and under-standing through practical application of skills Using the computer to generate all or part of the design and/or greeting Collecting reference material to produce a selection of patterns	

Figure 11.3 Design and technology capability at KS1. Paper using the theme of 'Materials' with PoS references

Recording

Products and/or photographs of objects are a common method of recording in many schools. Examples of types of recording sheets for individual and group objectives are illustrated in Mount and Ackerman (1991). Figure 11.3 could be adapted by leaving the central column blank so that a range of activities for different topics and different aspects of technology could be written in, giving a quick visual check as to the aspects of the programmes of study that are covered.

Writing down or taping what children say in the context of their design and technology activities is crucial for the teacher who can use the information as evidence of pupil progress. Models and mock-ups of design are an additional source that can be used, and a photographic sequence of various stages of development of a product, together with relevant written information about what the pupil said and did at each stage, should provide an extremely informative assessment tool and record. The pupils' own recording and other written evidence should also be used. Although there are no specific references to ways of recording in the SCAA publications (SCAA, 1995a; 1995b), they do provide helpful suggestions to guide teachers on the sorts of questions they could ask at particular stages of the design process and in the various programmes of study. These will help teachers not only to develop pupils' capability, but also provide them with responses that can be recorded in order to assess their learning.

Conclusion

While there have been changes to the volume and presentation of the design and technology requirements since the Dearing Review, there is much to be gained from examining and reviewing what is currently being delivered in school. In the publication on KS3 design and technology (SCAA, 1995a), one of the sections that drew my attention was a description of the way in which one school that had little experience of long-term planning in design and technology approached the challenge. Not surprisingly, they started by looking at what they were doing already and built on those experiences. That is the most useful advice that can be offered to any school and it is likely that many are fulfilling at least some of the new requirements with the curriculum that they are already offering. For those schools that have further to go it is hoped that this chapter has offered some assistance along the way.

References

Byers, R. (1990) 'From myths to objectives', *British Journal of Special Education*, 17, 3.

DES (1990) *Technology in the National Curriculum*, London, HMSO.

DfE (1995) *The National Curriculum*, London, HMSO.

Design and Technology Association (1993) *Design and Technology Teaching*, 25, 2, 4–8.

HMI (1992) *A Report by HMI – Dee Banks Special School, Cheshire*, London: HMSO.

HMI (1993) *A Report by HMI – Tye Green School, Essex*, London: HMSO.

Lever, C. (1990) *National Curriculum Design and Technology for Key Stages 1, 2 and 3*, Stoke-on-Trent: Trentham Books.

Manchester Primary Science Team (undated) *Me and My World*, Manchester City Council Education Department.

Mount, H. and Ackerman, D. (1991) *Technology for All*, London: David Fulton.

Ort Trust (1993) *Design and Technology in Special Education,* London: Ort Trust.

Pring, R. (1989) *The New Curriculum,* London: Cassell Education.

Rose, R. (1994) 'A modular approach to the curriculum for pupils with learning difficulties, in Rose, R., Ferguson, A., Coles, C., Byers, R. and Banes, D. (eds) *Implementing the Whole Curriculum for Pupils with Learning Difficulties,* London: David Fulton.

Rose, R., Ferguson, A., Coles, C., Byers, R. and Banes, D. (eds) (1994) *Implementing the Whole Curriculum for Pupils with Learning Difficulties,* London: David Fulton.

SCAA (1995a) *Key Stages 1 and 2, Design and Technology – The new requirements,* London: SCAA.

SCAA (1995b) *Key Stage 3, Design and Technology – The new requirements,* London: SCAA.

Sebba, J., Byers, R. and Rose, R. (1995) *Redefining the Whole Curriculum for Pupils with Learning Difficulties* (2nd edn), London: David Fulton.

Tearle, A. (1991) 'Dimensions of design and technology, in Ashdown, R., Carpenter, B. and Bovair, K. (1991) *The Curriculum Challenge,* London: Falmer Press.

Further reading

Bell, P. (1990) *Practical Topics for the Primary School. Part 1 – Science and technology,* Fulwood, Preston: Topical Resources.

Browne, N. (ed.) (1991) *Science and Technology in the Early Years,* Buckingham: Open University Press.

Burton, P. (1995) 'A one-hop centre for toolbox safety', *Times Educational Supplement: Curriculum Update,* 29 September, 16.

Chadwick, E. (1990) *Collins Primary Technology – Teachers' guide for Key Stage 1,* London: Collins Educational.

DES (1987) *Craft, Design and Technology from 5–16.* Curriculum Matters 9, London: HMSO.

Lancashire County Council (1990) *Design and Technology – A practical approach for primary schools* (pre-publication version), Lancashire Primary Schools Design and Technology Working Group: Lancashire County Council.

NCC (1990) *Non Statutory Guidance: Design and technology capability,* York: NCC.

Schools Examination and Assessment Council (1990) *Learning Through Design and Technology,* The APU Model, Leaflet No.1, London: SEAC.

Schools Examination and Assessment Council (1991) *Negotiating Tasks in Design and Technology,* Leaflet No.2, London: SEAC.

Schools Examination and Assessment Council (1991) *Structuring Activities in Design and Technology,* Leaflet No.3, London: SEAC.

Chapter 12

Information Technology

Tina Detheridge

This chapter begins by setting the context for the educational uses of information technology (IT) for pupils with special educational needs (SEN). It will discuss the requirements and recommendations of developing IT capability in the National Curriculum as far as it affects pupils with learning difficulties and disabilities. It will look particularly at the role of IT in providing access to learning. This will be illustrated by a number of examples where IT has made a significant contribution to a pupil's achievements. It will finally discuss some of the issues facing schools on identifying solutions and effective implementation.. Readers who are interested in the historical development of IT and SEN will gain useful information from Hawkridge and Vincent (1992), HMI (1990), Hope (1987), and Roberts (1991).

Why is IT important?

That IT forms a significant part of life in the late twentieth century is undeniable. It is essential to our communications systems, to industry and also to many of the services that individuals require. Recent radical developments in technology "are so fundamental that they will alter our work, our culture and our educational systems," (Brown and Howlett, 1994). At a personal level IT is also taking an increasingly important role. The use of personal computers for private, educational and social purposes is bringing IT within the realms of most people in society. For this reason, the development of the skills to use and manage IT is essential for employment and personal benefit.

For many of us who grew up before the firm establishment of IT, it has seemed a difficult and daunting task to develop these skills. This will, or should, not be the case for children currently passing through the educational system. The aim of the IT capability strand of the National Curriculum is to develop skills and confidence in the use of IT so that, as they mature, students can take their place in all aspects of society.

One of the benefits of IT is that it can simplify and automate many processes. This is changing the nature of education and the particular skills that are needed. It may no longer be necessary to develop fine handwriting skills, since most formal writing will be increasingly done on a word-processor. This is not to say that handwriting is redundant, but its principal purpose will be for personal use. It is no longer necessary to have a great facility in long multiplication or long division because the calculator can accomplish this more quickly and accurately than most people. What is necessary, however, is to acquire higher order skills of estimation, understanding number and logical thinking, so that the right calculations are made. In this way the user develops an intuitive understanding of the necessary processes and can apply their knowledge in generalized situations. Access to large information sources through CD-ROM, on-line databases and through the Internet are bringing personal research skills within the reach of everybody. Children exploring topics at school will no longer be restricted by the resources of the financially pressed school library. The new technologies will 'enrich curriculum content by improved access to resources' (DfE, 1995a). The pupils will need to develop skills to assess the quality of information they find, to analyse and discuss their findings.

These same features, offered by IT to everybody, have particular benefits to those with different special needs. IT can facilitate access to learning for those with physical or sensory impairments. It can also provide a range of mechanisms that simplify processes for those with learning difficulties. With the support of various technologies many of the difficulties experienced by those with learning disabilities or difficulties can be overcome, putting them on a more equal footing with their peers and providing the means to engage in the same educational, work, social and personal opportunities as everybody else. For this reason it is even more important that pupils with learning disabilities or difficulties are given access to, and training in, the use of IT in schools.

IT capability and the National Curriculum

The Programme of Study (PoS) for IT at Key Stage 1 states that 'Pupils should be taught to use IT equipment and software confidently and purposefully to communicate and handle information, and to support their problem solving, recording and expressive work.' (DfE, 1995b, p.14). This may appear to be a hard target for some pupils with learning difficulties, and the Attainment Target (AT) level descriptors are helpful in making this seem more accessible. These descriptors provide clues as to how this can be accessible to some of the younger and less able pupils. In *IT for All*, Banes and Coles (1995) provide a clear insight into what these strands mean for pupils with severe or profound learning difficulties, and how they may be accessed. In particular they emphasize the expressive, communicative aspects. There has been a tendency in the past for the use of IT for pupils who cannot read text to use IT in a passive, receptive manner with less attention to its role in supporting communication and creativity. The advent of software that allows pupils to receive information and to communicate using pictures, symbols and sounds has created new opportunities for access for pupils who have not reached the stage of using standard orthography.

It is also very clear in the National Curriculum that the development of IT capability should be practical and useful. There is reference to the use of IT across the subject range. It is intended that much of this capability will be gained whilst following the normal curricula. This intention provides the link between the two roles of IT, capability and access, as they affect pupils with SEN.

Access technology and the Code of Practice

The Code of Practice (DfE, 1994) recognizes the important role that IT can play in assisting access to learning. It is particularly clear when discussing special education provision for pupils at Stage 3 of the process. For example, the LEA is guided to ask whether, in addressing a child's learning difficulty, 'the school has explored the possible benefits, and where practical secured access to, appropriate information technology' (ibid., p.56, 3:58 iii). This query is raised with respect to each area of special need, together with some examples of the types of technologies that could be particularly appropriate. These examples can provide useful suggestions, not just for pupils at Stage 3: they could also be valuable at earlier stages. The Code of Practice suggests that 'The answers to these questions may indicate immediate remedies which would mean that a statutory assessment was not necessary' (ibid., p.54). The emphasis, because of its use across the curriculum, has been on tools for communication: word-processing, spell checkers, painting and drawing packages, and the use of a range of alternative input devices such as overlay keyboards, which can simplify the process. To explore the benefits, the school will need to take time with the pupil to assess his or her response to a range of strategies. This may rely on the specialized knowledge of an IT or SEN coordinator. Clearly not all schools will be in a position to have the required breadth of expertise amongst their staff, and strategies have to be found to address this. This issue is discussed in later in the section on identifying solutions.

Securing access presents the school with a number of questions of management, of prioritizing the availability of resources between different children and different classes. Wherever possible, it is desirable that the solutions should be found through the management of the same resources as are available to other pupils. Where the same piece of software can be used by all pupils, through its in-built flexibility or through the use of additional utilities, such as an on-screen selection grid (see below), the pupils are gaining in two ways. It facilitates equality and integration and may allow the teacher to differentiate activities more easily.

The guidance in the Code of Practice also questions whether there has been training in the use of the technology 'for the child, his or her parents and staff, so that the child is able to use that technology across the curriculum and, wherever appropriate, at home.' (DfE, 1994, 3:58 iii). If the child, teacher and any supporting adults 'are not able to use the equipment effectively, then the advantages of an IT solution are lost' (Day,1995). This has implications to the policy and management of IT, which and discussed later.

In discussing access technology, Day (1995) identifies three types of access: physical, cognitive and supportive. Physical access "is technology at its most dramatic, liberating the pupil from the physical barriers to learning." (p.4). Cognitive access is aided where the IT is used to present the curriculum in a variety of ways that may make it more accessible to pupils with special needs, such as presenting information in small steps. Supportive access is where the technology can assist the pupil with tasks and skills that are difficult. For example, the pupil with poor handwriting who becomes demotivated by his or her presentation skills, or the pupil with spelling difficulties who, by hearing his or her own writing read back may be helped to identify and correct mistakes.

Across each of these types of access there will be a continuum of need. At one extreme the technology will be a lifeline. Without it the pupil is unable to communicate or engage in the learning process. For example, the pupil without speech may use a communication aid with the help of switches. At the other extreme the technology will act as a facilitator. In these cases it will not be essential for the pupil, but will make the process easier or help to raise the pupil's motivation and self-esteem.

To identify the need, as required under the Code of Practice, teachers need to be able to identify the type of access and where on the continuum of need the pupil's use of technology lies. Chapter 2 in *Access Technology* (Day, 1995) provides a useful checklist to help teachers in this process. In the checklist teachers are led to consider the context and purpose behind the intended use of technology, the resourcing, support implications and then to consider the expectations, by the learner as well as staff and parents, and it raises questions of management, monitoring and transition.

Examples of the IT used to enhance access to learning

This section presents a number of examples where IT has been used to provide or enhance access to learning. Its purpose is not to provide a training manual, but to illustrate the variety of approaches and at the same time building the different strands of IT capability. The majority of the illustrations are concerned with communicating ideas. This reflects the importance of communication for pupils with SEN. Without the means to communicate pupils are unable to demonstrate their understanding or receive recognition for their capabilities (Kiernan *et al.*, 1987). There are many pupils across the spectrum of learning abilities who have understanding, but are unable to demonstrate this through the normal channels. IT has been shown to provide such a means for some pupils with profound and multiple learning difficulties (PMLD) (Detheridge, 1996). Other pupils, with emotional and behavioural difficulties may find that IT provides some of the necessary conditions to motivate and enhance concentration so that they are able to learn and to express their ideas (Howard, 1991). Although Day (1995) identified three separate types of access, in practice many pupils will require support of more than one type. The child who, because of his or her physical disability has missed many of the play opportunities to explore and manipulate objects may require cognitive support as well as physical support, such as when working in areas of mathematics involving shape and space. For clarity, the examples below have been put under the dominant heading.

Physical access

Veronica has cerebral palsy, no speech and severe physical disabilities. For her first few years at school she used a wooden communication board with symbols which she selected by pointing with her fist. This gave her access to some 60 symbols and phrases at any one time. The symbols were chosen for her by a speech and language therapist to meet her most immediate needs. Interaction in class was mainly through a facilitator who read the symbols indicated and interpreted other gestural signals that Veronica made. Her means of communication now relies heavily on IT. She uses a communication aid that gives her access to over 1,000 words and phrases. The flexibility means that she is no longer dependent to the same extent by the vocabulary that has been considered appropriate – she can choose her own. She can also type words, so theoretically she is gaining access to unlimited communication. An integrated system that will bring speech communication, writing and mobility control into one device will soon give her a freedom that was unthinkable without IT.

Ben is in a nursery class. He has no sight, minimal physical movement and makes very few sounds. These disabilities made it very difficult for him to join in with group activities in the classroom and to play and make friends. He has been given a small device that can record several seconds of sound which can be activated by a single press. As soon as he was given this very simple communication aid he showed that he understood cause and effect and that he could participate in a game with his teacher. Ben works with a small group of pupils to play a version of 'Simon Says'. When he hits his switch it says, 'Clap your hands'; a friend has one that says, 'Wave your hands'. Although neither of these pupils can physically respond to these commands, they can perceive the rest of the group doing it. This is clearly seen by their facial gestures and body language. Ben has shown that he can understand a game, take turns but more importantly is learning to be assertive, to make his presence felt.

Martha also has cerebral palsy which, whilst not severe, makes writing and manipulating objects difficult. Many of the play activities in her reception class involve manipulating objects, doing puzzles, sorting and building. She uses a computer program, which allows her to move shapes on the computer. She can do this easily with the help of a roller ball. She can move the object slowly to the area where she wants it and then press a button to put it in the right place, something she could not do with her hands. Given this tool Martha has shown that she understands many mathematical concepts and, because this is a tool used by all of the class, is not being singled out in any way.

Cognitive access

There are three major ways that IT can enhance cognitive access to learning, and to communication in particular: through simplifying the writing process, allowing pupils to explore ideas and try things out before committing themselves to a final outcome, and by presenting information in small assimilable quantities.

Children, who are full of ideas and excitement, can be prevented or deterred from writing stories or expressing their own ideas because they have not acquired adequate writing skills. Overlay keyboards and on-screen grids, can be used to give the pupil lists of words that they can use directly in their texts without having to learn to spell them first. It can give whole words and phrases as well as providing clearly defined topic lists or subsets of information, making selection and choosing much quicker and easier. Figure 12.1 shows the use of an on-screen grid set up so that the pupil can write with symbols as well as words. The content of the grid is easily set up by the teacher. Clearly the pupils will be developing the finer skills in parallel, but will be practising creative writing at the same time.

James, who is 17 and has severe learning difficulties, is unlikely to acquire a high level of reading using standard orthography and uses pictorial symbols as an alternative and support for words. With software that allows him to write in symbols, James can record his experiences and what he has learned. His class teacher is confident that by writing his ideas down James has been helped to structure his thoughts. It has improved his thinking skills as well as helping him to show the extent of his ideas in a way that can be recorded. Carpenter and Detheridge (1994) show how this approach can create new opportunities, enhance self-esteem and promote autonomy.

Hawkridge and Vincent (1992) illustrate many ways in which children across the spectrum of learning difficulties can be helped to write and communicate their ideas. In particular the facility offered by a word-processor for writers to draft and redraft their work gives the chance to explore ideas and to develop thinking in the process at whatever pace they are able to work.

Talking books and multimedia CD-ROMs can provide material that is accessible to learners who have difficulty reading large amounts of material at a time. Information is presented in small chunks, often supported by pictures or moving images and with sound support. Like a book it can be browsed, and need not be followed in a strictly linear fashion, unlike video and audio tape. This can encourage pupils to search and develop information-handling skills at the same time as presenting material in ways that

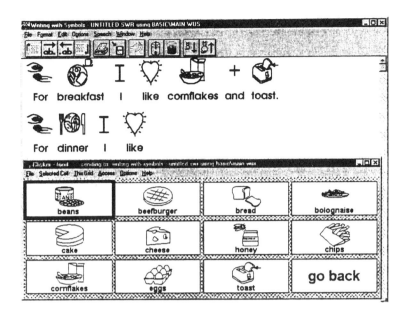

Figure 12.1 Writing in a word- or symbol-processor using an on-screen grid such as Clicker or Point

they can easily assimilate. McKeown and Thomas (1995) give many examples where multimedia has provided motivation and the right environment for pupils to maintain concentration for much longer periods than is their norm. The multi-sensory delivery makes information accessible to pupils with a range of difficulties, making it a particularly suitable medium for supporting differentiation in the classroom. Software that allows pupils to create their own multimedia presentations encourages collaboration, interaction and communication between peers. A group of deaf children in a first school created stories developed from previous reading. The IT helped them to work together and to express their ideas in media that they could share with their hearing friends.

Supportive access

Speech output either from pre-recorded speech or through speech synthesis, is one of the major ways in which the newer technologies can support cognitive access to learning. Pupils who find difficulty spelling and reading can gain reinforcement from their work by hearing it read. As well as the motivational effect, it can help pupils develop their own strategies for overcoming difficulties (Day, 1993; Miles, 1994). Kate, who has severe spelling and reading difficulties, used a computer with a spell checker to help her gain some independence in her writing. After a while using this she was able to cope well with a hand-held spell checker which she could keep in her pencil case. This was important to Kate because she, like Mark, did not want to be seen as different from her peers, as well as wanting a device that she could use in class and at home. The thesaurus facility on the spell checker helps her find the meanings of words when she is reading. She finds using a dictionary for so many words slows her reading, but the thesaurus, by suggesting similar words that she might know, helps to keep up the momentum of the text.

A major role of IT is its motivational effect. This can particularly be seen in the facilities offered for high quality presentation of work (Zvacek, 1992). Jo, who had poor handwriting and found it difficult to concentrate for long periods of time, was demotivated at school because however hard he tried, his work did not look as good as that of many of his peers. Using different layouts and effects and printing it from a good quality printer, inspired Jo to take care with his work and to persevere to improve its quality. He used graphic images from Clip Art sources to illustrate his writing and began to make the appearance reflect the topic being covered, clearly showing his sense of audience. Abbott (1995) describes many similar examples of the way in which IT can provide support to learning for pupils who have difficulties with basic literacy and numeracy skills.

Identifying solutions

To be able to identify appropriate solutions to meeting individual need the teacher has to be aware of the types of solution and strategies available, and requires training in their implementation. This has to be set in a context of limited budgets and realistic time-frames. The starting point must, however, be the identification of the pupil's learning needs and objectives. It is only when these have been clarified that particular strategies, including those involving IT, can be evaluated and proposed.

IT solutions

The section above gave a number of illustrations of the use of IT to facilitate access to learning. Hopefully a picture has emerged of the enormous range of solutions that may exist, many of which serve to develop IT capability and to enhance learning for all pupils, not only those with special needs. Although some pupils will require specialized equipment, resources or strategies to give them the necessary access to learning, it is very desirable, as far as possible, for them to use generic tools which are used by everybody. By finding a means of accessing standard, commonly used equipment and software, pupils with particular needs can participate in the same activities as their peers. It facilitates inclusion and, importantly, gives them the tools required for use in further education and in the workplace.

In the early days of IT, specialist software was written so that pupils who could not manage a keyboard could write using switch-operated word-processors. Much of the early learning software was designed specifically with this type of user in mind. Although useful, it encouraged separate provision. The trend has changed through two types of development. The first is that specialist software developers are creating products that are of much more general applicability. Typically these programs have a range of options that can be selected by the teacher or user to give the necessary facilities to the individual. The second type of development is through mainstream product development. Software developers and hardware manufacturers have perceived that the special needs market is not so small as they first thought, and are including some additional facilities in their products, for example options for text to be spoken, or for the operational mechanisms to be simplified.

The most significant developments for pupils with severe disabilities has come about through the interaction between these two types of development. This is where a program which is used by the majority of pupils can be made accessible to pupils with learning difficulties through the use of an additional, specialist device or software application. For example the use of an overlay keyboard or, more flexibly, an on-screen grid, allows much simpler input to the main program by presenting symbols, words or phrases that the pupil can select rather than by typing in the individual characters. In this way pupils can write and express their knowledge and ideas independently of their handwriting or reading difficulties. Software that allows teachers to present information through the use of symbols and pictures brings reading to pupils like James, who was discussed above. The use of an on-screen grid gives him the chance to write for himself using these graphical alternatives to text. The technology has created new opportunities for expression, leading to enhanced self-esteem, independence and autonomy for pupils at all stages of the continuum of learning difficulties. *Access to Words and Images* (Rahamim, 1993) provides an overview of these approaches.

As computer software becomes more sophisticated and its costs rise, use of generic types of solution, as far as possible, makes sense from a school management point of view and for the pupil. As well as describing a continuum of need, Day (1995) discusses a continuum of provision across the pupil range. The needs of the majority of pupils will be met through the good use of existing resources which are available to all pupils in a mainstream class. At the other end of this continuum a pupil may, as a result of a Statement of Special Educational Needs, be provided with specified equipment for their sole use. It is likely, in making such a recommendation, that the school will need to consult specialists. As the severity of need becomes more acute, so the strategies, such as selection of appropriate devices, the positioning of the pupil and switches, becomes crucial.

Training

Whichever type of provision is made, for it to be most effective the pupil and anyone working with him or her needs to be trained in its use. The Code of Practice (DfE, 1994, 3.58.iii) specifically includes parents in this aspect, so that the equipment can be used wherever it is needed. Part of costing any solution must, therefore, include recognition of this. The costing may imply arranging time for training, but in some cases it may require particular events. There have been too many examples of IT equipment being under-used, or worse, not being used because the initial person trained is no longer available. Ensuring that all participants are given the opportunity to become familiar with resources will go some way to ensuring continued effectiveness. It is also worth considering who needs what type of training. A classroom assistant working extensively with a pupil may require greater familiarity with specific equipment than the class teacher, whilst the SEN and IT coordinators will require a greater understanding of the purposes and objectives behind each provision.

Review

Finding an appropriate access solution is not a one-off event. Not only do curriculum needs change, but also individual capability develops. There needs, therefore, to be a continuous process of evaluation and review. Monitoring progress fulfills the audit requirements and also gives detailed background information to identifying future provision. One of the hesitations behind review is concern that expensive equipment will have to be replaced. The school will require, as part of its IT and SEN policies, to develop mechanisms whereby equipment can be re-channelled to new pupils.

It is particularly important to review provision and training requirements at points of transition. Moving from one class to another will make one set of training demands on staff; transition between schools will make another. What might have been appropriate in one context may need revision in another set. For example, access to a classroom computer may have given adequate support to a pupil with learning difficulties in a primary classroom, but the mobile life in a secondary school may suggest access to a portable computer.

Access to information and professional development

Historically many steps have been taken, under DES/DfE initiatives, to develop expertise in the different aspects of IT and special needs, which have offered training and advice to school and LEA advisory staff. The teachers thus trained not only developed particular strengths of their own but, through the network built up, had access to other teachers who could offer compliementary knowledge. Various initiatives have attempted to maintain the expertise, but changing practice in local education authorities, the delegation of budgets and the focus of cost-centred services has had a significant impact on this network and it has become difficult for the majority of schools to tap into it. New approaches to training and strategies for accessing information are required by teachers in this changing situation. There are many sources of specialized information through various charitable and educational organizations, the IT and special needs press, and increasingly through both IT and special needs exhibitions, but the most interesting new approach to sharing information and expertise has come about through electronic communications.

Electronic communications

Electronic communication, although still fairly new, has shown itself to be a very valuable source of information. As well as the peer support, many organizations are seeing the Internet, the world-wide network of electronic information, as a means of providing their materials to customers just as and when they are needed. Teachers are required to become discriminating because they have to be the judges of the value of material which is no longer mediated by advisory or support services and INSET providers
   Another area in which electronic communications is likely to grow in importance for teachers is in their professional development and training. Current trends have made it increasingly difficult for teachers to be released for postgraduate training. Electronic communications have long been used to provide tutor support to students at the Open University, and it is likely that distance learning and distance supported training will eventually become the norm. But for the moment, its role in supporting teachers in school to address individual pupil needs simply by making information accessible is of paramount importance.
   There are many sources of information available through the Internet. As well as contact with individuals and organizations through e-mail, there are news groups and forums on a vast range of topics. Individual users can subscribe to these special interest groups, sharing ideas and information. Many organizations, large and small, are also setting up pages of information that are easily accessible. The difficulty for most users will be finding the most relevant material quickly and easily. Two strategies exist for this. The search tools available through Internet service providers help to narrow the enquiry field to a certain extent, but the most useful is likely to be through providers who gather

and summarize material as part of their service. At the time of writing the two most useful points of contact for information on special educational needs are NCET and SENSOR.

Conclusion

Information technology is an important medium for the whole of society. It provides powerful tools for expression, presentation, for exploring ideas and gathering information. On its own, however, it cannot do any of these things. The resources and equipment have to be chosen to meet the need of the individual as well as the group. It is not a cheap option, and so school policies need to reflect matters of resource purchase, management, training and development. The most important factor in the successful use of IT to meet individual need will be the knowledge and sensitivity of the staff working with the pupils: sensitivity to when intervention and help is needed; when to leave the individual to face challenges alone; and when it is more appropriate for pupils to work together. For pupils with learning difficulties, careful selection of resources can facilitate peer interaction as well as individual learning in ways that would not otherwise be possible. Teachers are not going to acquire all of these skills easily or quickly, and plans need to be made for them to network with colleagues and to have access to specialist advice. There is, however, sufficient evidence to show that the use of IT can facilitate access to learning when used appropriately to support other tried and tested educational strategies.

References

Abbott, C. (1995) *IT Helps,* Coventry: NCET.

Banes, D. and Coles, C., (1995) *IT for All,* London: David Fulton.

Brown, J. and Howlett, F. (1994) *IT Works,* Coventry. The National Council for Educational Technology.

Carpenter, B. and Detheridge, T. (1994) 'Writing with symbols', *Support for Learning,* 9 1, 27–32.

Day, J., (1995) *Access Technology: Making the right choice* (Second Edition,) Coventry: NCET.

Day, J., (1994) *A software Guide for Specific Learning Difficulties,* Coventry: NCET.

Detheridge, T., (1996) 'The role of information technology in bridging the production/competence gap in severely disabled students', (unpublished MPhil thesis) Warwick University.

DfE (1994) *Code of Practice on the Identification and assessment of Special Educational Needs,* London: HMSO.

DfE (1995a). *Superhighways in Education,* London: HMSO.

DfE (1995b) *The National Curriculum,* London: HMSO.

Hawkridge, D. and Vincent, T. (1992) *Learning Difficulties and Computers,* London: Jessica Kingsley.

HMI (1990) *Education Observed: special needs issues,* London: HMSO.

Hope, M., (1987) *Micros for Children with Special Needs,* London: Souvenir Press.

Kiernan, C. Reid, B and Goldbart, J. (1987) *The Foundations of Communication and Language,* Manchester: Manchester.University Press.

Howard, W., (1991) *IT across the Curriculum: Supporting learners who display challenging behaviour,* Coventry: NCET.

McKeown, S. and Thomas, M. (1995) *Special Edition,* Coventry: NCET.

Miles, M. (1994) 'The Somerset talking computer project', in Singleton, C. (ed.) *Computers and Dyslexia,* University of Hull, Dyslexia Computer Resource Centre.

NCET (1993) *Opening up the Library for Visually Impaired Learners*, Coventry: NCET.

Roberts, P. (1991) 'Cross-curricular approaches to information Technology', in Ashdown, R., Carpenter, B., and Bovair, K. (eds.) *The Curriculum Challenge*, London: Falmer Press.

Rahamim, L. (1993) *Access to Words and Images*, Coventry: NCET.

Wedell, K. and Detheridge T., (1995) *Electronic Communications to Support Special Needs Co-ordinators*, Coventry: NCET.

Zvacek, S. (1992) 'Word Processing and the teaching of Writing', in Hartley (ed.) *Technology and Writing*, London: Jessica Kingsley.

Electronic Sources of Information

Internet for Learning, Research Machines, New Mill House, 183 Milton Park, Abingdon, Oxfordshire OX14 4SE
Internet Address: http://www.rmplc.co.uk

SENCO Electronic Communications Project, NCET – The National Council for Educational Technology, Millburn Hill Road, Science Park, Coventry CV4 7JJ
Email address Enquiry_Desk@ncet.org.uk
Internet address http://ncet.csv.warwick.ac.uk/WWW/senco/index.html

SENSOR - 1 Whitecroft Street, Watersheddings, Oldham
Email address : sensor@campus.bt.com

Part II:
Access and Entitlement to the Whole Curriculum

Chapter 13

Religious Education

Erica Brown

The principal aim for the whole school curriculum as set out in the Education Reform Act (1988) (ERA) is to promote the:

> spiritual, moral, cultural, mental and physical development of pupils and of society, and prepare pupils for the opportunities, responsibilities and experiences of adult life. (Clause 1. 2.b)

The ERA reaffirmed many of the statutory requirements of the 1944 Education Act for religious education whilst also amending and introducing new requirements for LEAs and schools.

Religious education is a statutory part of the basic curriculum although, unlike the National Curriculum, it is administered at a local rather than a national level. It has equal standing in relation to the core and other foundation subjects although it is not subject to nationally prescribed attainment targets (ATs) and assessment procedures.

The stated aim for religious education in DfE Circular 1/94, which was published to clarify the 1988, 1992 and 1993 legislation on religious education and collective worship, is as follows:

> RE in schools should seek to develop pupils' knowledge, understanding and awareness of Christianity, as the predominant religion in Great Britain, and the other principal religions represented in the country; to encourage respect for those holding different beliefs; and to help promote pupil's spiritual, moral, cultural and mental development. (para. 16)

Religious education is primarily concerned with three main areas namely: spiritual development; a knowledge of the belief and practice of religion; and opportunities to explore religious perspectives on human experience. This understanding of religious education involves the whole personality. There is knowledge to be learned and skills to be developed; there are attitudes to be encouraged and emotions to be explored; there is self-understanding to be nurtured and developed and an identity to be fashioned; there are personal beliefs to be formed (Brown, 1996)

Statutory requirements

The Education (Schools) Act 1992 requires HM Chief Inspector of schools to keep the Secretary of State for Education informed about religious education and the spiritual, moral, social and cultural development of pupils via the four-yearly inspection of schools. The requirements are as follows:

- Religious education must be provided for all registered pupils.
- The term 'religious instruction' used in the 1944 Education Act is replaced by 'religious education'.
- Parents retain the right to withdraw their child from religious education.
- Religious education must be taught according to a locally agreed syllabus prepared by an Agreed Syllabus Conference made up of representatives from the LEA, teachers, the Church of England (not in Wales) and other Christian denominations, and members of other world religions present in the area. Representatives of grant maintained schools in the area may also be included.
- Religious education must not be denominational, although teaching about denominational differences is permitted.
- Any new locally agreed syllabus must reflect the fact that the religious traditions in Great Britain are in the main Christian, whilst taking account of the teaching and practices of other principal religions represented in the country.

Pupils in special schools are referred to in the Education Act 1993, which states:

> Every pupil attending a special school will, so far as is practicable, attend collective worship and receive religious education unless the child's parents have expressed a wish to the contrary. It is for the schools to decide what is practicable but, in general terms, the Secretary of State would expect the question of practicability to relate to the special educational needs of the pupils and not to problems of staffing or premises. (Paragraph 44)

Model syllabuses for religious education

In 1994 the School Curriculum and Assessment Authority (SCAA) published two *Model Syllabuses for Religious Education*. Although these documents are not statutory and they are intended to provide guidance to Agreed Syllabus Conferences and to the Standing Advisory Councils on Religious Education (SACREs) rather than schools, many new syllabuses reflect the content of the models, including Programmes of Study (PoS) based on the beliefs and practices of Christianity and the other principal religions.

The principal world religions

Although legislation does not define which principal religions should be taught, it has come to be accepted that all principal religions in Great Britain should be included and children should learn about and from the religions studied. Traditionally, there are six major world religions: Christianity, Islam, Hinduism, Buddhism, Sikhism and Judaism.

What is the place of religious education for pupils with special educational needs?

In spite of the lengthy deliberations which took place when the Education Reform Bill (1987/8) was going through Parliament, and the many responses to the ERA legislation by Agreed Syllabus Conferences, SACREs, SCAA and members of world faith communities, the matter of religious education which is accessible to all pupils has not been documented in detail. Some agreed syllabuses produced after ERA offer a very few lines of guidance, such as:

> Special schools will be expected to implement the Programmes of Study and assessment arrangements of this Agreed Syllabus so far as is practicable. (The Agreed Syllabus for Religious Education in Avon, 1993)

Other agreed syllabuses are more helpful:

> Religious Education provides opportunities for imaginative, flexible and sensitive teaching of pupils of all abilities. In mainstream school teachers need to be aware of the particular needs of the pupils with special educational needs and should develop strategies and resources to provide support for such pupils. Teachers and schools need to address the issue of differentiation and accessibility of materials and their presentation. (The Agreed Syllabus for Religious Education in the London Borough of Hounslow, 1992)

Most agreed syllabuses for religious education are united in the view that, in the early years of pupils' religious and spiritual development, teaching should be relevant to children's life experiences whilst also encouraging an awareness and understanding of the belief and practice of religion.

Among the few educationalists who have written about religious education for all children is Flo Longhorn. Referring to pupils whom she calls 'very special', she says special schools provide a relevant environment in which children can stretch, reach and attain their full individual potential (Longhorn, 1993).

Dowell and Nutt (1995) building on the work of Brown (1991; 1993), have emphasized the importance of helping children in special schools towards a greater awareness of themselves and other people. They believe this can be encouraged through activities 'in class, in the whole school and in the wider community'. Goss (1995) shares this view and he charges teachers of pupils with profound and multiple learning difficulties (PMLD), 'to attempt to recognize emotional, and spiritual needs within the curricular and social experiences provided'.

A differentiated approach to learning

A differentiated approach to learning which treats pupils as individuals should apply in religious education. It should allow the teacher to provide appropriate teaching strategies for groups of pupils.

The *Code of Practice for the Identification and Assessment of Special Educational Needs* (DfE, 1994) requires Individual Education Plans (IEPs) to be used in the planning, implementation and review of pupils' learning in order that they are able to achieve at the highest levels of which they are able. In religious education this will include:

- the delivery of carefully structured teaching approaches
- providing imaginative learning experiences which arouse and sustain children's interest

- supporting the learning which takes place in religious education by what is taught in other curriculum areas.

The spiritual dimension of religious education

The National Curriculum Council discussion paper on spiritual and moral development (NCC, 1993) argues that spiritual development is 'fundamental to other areas of learning'. In the context of religion this may include beliefs and a sense of awe, or transcendence. But spirituality is also concerned with the very essence of what it means to be human and in this sense it includes self-understanding and self-worth, creativity, emotional responses, a personal quest for meaning and purpose, and forming relationships.

All agreed syllabuses produced since the ERA charge teachers to introduce experiences which give pupils opportunities to respond with awe and wonderment. But they seldom suggest how this might take place within a busy classroom.

> Recently I joined a group of children with moderate learning difficulties as they explored the theme of 'New Beginnings and Springtime'. A large vase of daffodils on the table caught their attention. Selecting one of the flowers from the vase, Richie began to explore the frilled trumpet with his forefinger and then put the bloom to his face. The tip of his nose became covered in pollen. Ruth, who was sitting next to him, giggled and, selecting a flower for herself, she carefully pushed the entire length of her little finger into its centre. Withdrawing it she admired the yellow dust and turned to her teacher and said, 'The bee collects that and then the Mummy and Daddy bee do a miracle. They go to the bee house and they make the dust into jam'. 'No they don't', replied Richie, 'God does that for them and then he turns it into honey'.

These children have discovered something for themselves. They have brought their past learning experiences to the present time in an effort to make sense of what they are encountering. On one count we could argue that their understanding of bees is incorrect, but on another we can allow them to ponder on the wonderment of creation.

Religious perspectives on human experience

Whilst in the early stages of pupils' religious education, study units may contain little which is explicitly religious at all, children's own life experiences provide an essential framework for understanding religion. All children come to school with experiences of relationships with those people who care for them. Within the school family they will need encouragement to respond to their learning in a way which nurtures positive attitudes towards themselves and towards other people.

Knowledge and understanding of religious belief and practice

For children to begin to understand something about the belief which lies at the heart of religious practice they will need to learn about religion as well as learning from religion. Although many children may come from homes where religion is not a way of life, others will learn about faith and practice in their families through such things as the clothes they wear, the food they eat or the objects and symbols which surround them.

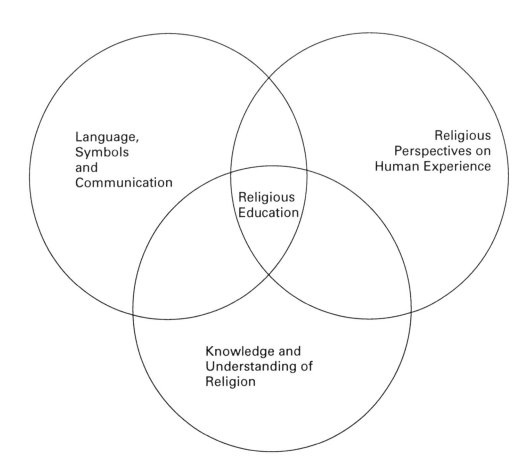

Understanding religion demands that children learn 'about' and 'from' the beliefs, values and customs which underpin the faiths studied. The scheme of work and framework of assessment uses the two Attainment Targets. 'Knowledge and Understanding of Religion' and 'Human Perspectives on Religious Experience'. The two Attainment Targets may be achieved through the learning experiences provided which are underpinned by nine study units. Language, symbols and communication play an important part in helping pupils to understand how religious belief and practice are expressed.

Figure 13.1 Dimensions of religious education

IN FAMILIES CHILDREN LEARN ABOUT RELIGIOUS PERSPECTIVES ON HUMAN EXPERIENCE AS THEY:

GO SHOPPING

DRESS FOR THE DAY

VISIT PLACES OF WORSHIP

WATCH RITUALS AND CEREMONIES

SHARE IN FESTIVALS AND CELEBRATIONS

SEE RELIGIOUS OBJECTS AND SYMBOLS

ATTEND CHILDREN'S GROUPS

LISTEN TO FAMILIAR SOUNDS

ASK QUESTIONS

HEAR STORIES

Figure 13.2

Foundation experiences

In the very early stages of children's religious and spiritual development it is necessary to provide a foundation on which to build an increasing awareness of themselves as individuals and of relationships with other people. This is particularly important for children with PMLD. Helping pupils to respond to different environments and giving them a wide range of opportunities to experience sensory learning will provide a framework for developing attitudes such as delight or curiosity, or skills such as reflection. Children should learn through using their senses and share experiences which enable them to become aware that people, objects, symbols, places, food, and occasions have special importance.

A sensory approach to learning

All babies and children use their senses to learn. A sensory approach is appropriate to all children's learning in religious education. The following list is not a definitive one; rather it gives some examples for learning experiences which might be incorporated into schemes of work or study units, using the sense of smell.

Objectives
Develop an awareness of different forms of religious expression.
Develop confidence in responding freely and appropriately.
Explore and share experiences and feelings.
Participate as a member of a group.
Develop preferences.

Christianity
Visit a church decorated for a special occasion and smell the perfume of the flowers.
Smell the musty smell of an old hymn book or Bible.
Smell the heavy smell of incense from a thurible.
Smell altar candles after they have been snuffed out.
Smell the palm of palm crosses.
Smell the spicy warmth of hot-cross buns.

Judaism
Smell cinnamon, nutmeg and cloves in a spice box.
Smell warm challah bread.
Smell Shabbat and havdalah candles.
Smell the leather of phylacteries.

Hinduism
Smell spices used for the puja ceremony (e.g., saffron, cumin, haldi, turmeric).
Smell warm ghee used in cooking.
Smell ghee as divas burn.
Smell joss sticks and incense.

Sikhism
Smell the distinctive smell of dye used on a turban length or a sari fabric.
Smell divas and joss sticks burning.
Smell warm karah parshad.

Islam
Smell the wood of a Qu'ran stand.
Smell the fabric of a prayer carpet.
Smell Muslim festival food.

Key Stage 1

At KS1 religious education should strive to build on children's understanding of themselves and their experiences of family life and relationships. It is important teachers take the variety of children's experience into account when planning schemes of work. All pupils should learn from the attitudes which they encounter in school that they are personally valued, whilst also beginning to discover the contribution which other people make. They should become increasingly aware of things which are special and important to themselves and other people.

Children will benefit from opportunities to develop their awareness of the local environment through journeys and visits and by having a chance to experience awe and wonderment in the natural world. They should be introduced to symbolism in religion and hear stories about the lives of key figures and religious leaders.

Pupils should be encouraged to celebrate their own achievements and milestones as well as joining in a variety of occasions when people meet together for worship and festivals. Some children will find it very difficult to enter imaginatively into the

Figure 13.3 My moth falls down when I'm not sewre

experience of other people and they may need help in order to be aware of the needs and desires of their peers and their teachers.

Key Stage 2

KS2 should enhance the opportunities and experiences which pupils have already encountered in order that they may build on their knowledge and understanding of religion and increase their spiritual and moral development.

Children should be developing a greater understanding of themselves and an awareness of the needs and feelings of other people from a variety of faiths and cultures. They should be given an opportunity to interact with the natural world and the local environment. By the end of KS2 pupils should have been helped to explore a range of religious ideas and themes, including how these are communicated through sacred writings and symbols. They should have heard stories about the life and teaching of Jesus and other religious figures and have been given opportunities to consider their own questions and concerns arising from the PoS. Their knowledge of religious belief and practice will grow through activities such as visiting places of worship and meeting people from religious communities.

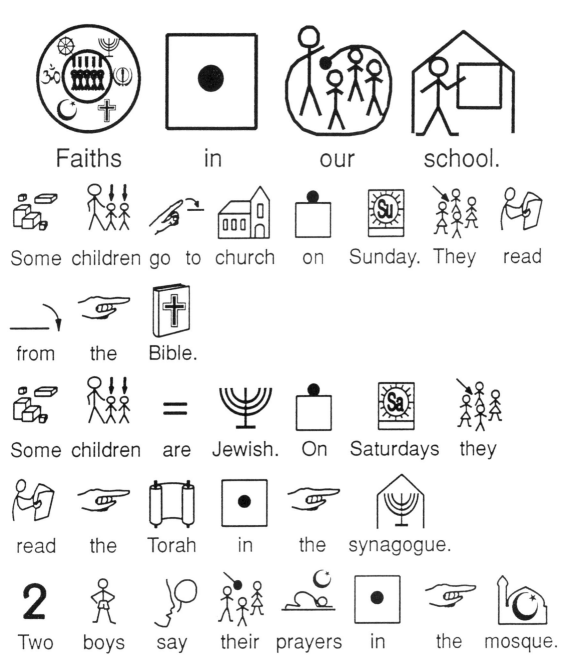

Faiths in our school.

Some children go to church on Sunday. They read from the Bible.

Some children are Jewish. On Saturdays they read the Torah in the synagogue.

Two boys say their prayers in the mosque.

Figure 13.4

Areas of learning or study units

In order that children are given a broad and balanced curriculum study units are suggested which develop the three dimensions of religion.

- Human Experience ⎫
  ⎬ including lifestyles
- The World Around ⎭
- Special People/Key Figures and Leaders
- Special Books/Sacred Writings
- Special Buildings/Places of Worship
- Festivals and Celebrations
- Special Times/Rites of Passage
- Special Journeys/Pilgrimage
- Language, Symbol and Communication.

The first two areas, which are concerned with 'Religious Perspectives on Human Experience', lay the foundation for beginning to explore other dimensions of religion. The remainder of the study units are concerned with 'Knowledge and Understanding of Religious Belief and Practice'.

The scheme of work for religious education

In order that the religious education taught in a school reflects a curriculum which is broad and balanced, whilst also being relevant to the life experiences and individual learning needs of pupils, the content will need to be planned carefully. This cannot happen unless teachers are prepared to stand alongside their pupils and to meet them at their point of learning. A scheme of work is an essential tool in the planning process, but if it is to meet the specific needs of individual children it will have to be interpreted and implemented creatively through the opportunities for learning which are provided.

The content of the school's scheme of work should be clearly identified and documented. Although special schools do not have to follow an agreed syllabus for religious education, it is important that what is taught contributes to a broad and balanced curriculum. A broad and balanced religious education curriculum will include the range of beliefs and practices of Christianity and other principal world faiths.

Recording pupil achievement

Understanding religion demands that children learn 'about' and 'from' the beliefs, values and customs which underpin the faiths studied. In the current National Curriculum, Statements of Attainment have been replaced with Level Descriptions. However, Statements of Achievement are suggested here as well since they have value as progressive statements of competence for pupils to develop (see below).

The use of ATs, Statements of Achievement and Level Descriptions will provide an important tool in enabling teachers to:

- plan future work, setting tasks and providing learning experiences appropriate to pupils' ability and development;

- provide objectives for pupils' learning;
- build on learning experiences provided ensuring continuity and progression to the next stage.

The framework of assessment uses the two ATs: 'Knowledge and understanding of religion' and 'Religious perspectives on human experience'. The ATs define the knowledge, skills and understanding which pupils of different abilities and maturities are expected to have gained by the end of each key stage. The first AT, 'Knowledge and understanding of religion', should include helping pupils to understand about beliefs, practices and lifestyles at each key stage and throughout each topic or theme. Both ATs are underpinned by the nine study units which have been interwoven throughout the PoS illustrated in the charts.

In addition, Level Descriptions have been selected in order that the achievements of all pupils may be recorded. They may be used as a guide to both the current performance of an individual pupil and as an indicator of how future progress may be made. They also indicate individual pupil reactions to the learning encounters provided through:

- experiencing the activity
- awareness of the activity
- participation in the activity
- involvement in the activity

Teachers will need to show how pupils have demonstrated the Statements of Achievement. In many cases this will be supported by the Level Descriptions which describe the pupil involvement in the learning experiences provided. For example, the achievement of a pupil at the foundation for religious education within the study unit 'The world around', might be recorded as: 'Responds to the natural world', with the comment, '...has shown an awareness of the beauty and shape of a flower as she explored the trumpet of the daffodil with her fingers'.

PUPIL RECORD

Name: Darren Lewis   *Half Term Ending:* Oct 96

Key Stage: 2

Topic or Theme: Sikhism

KNOWLEDGE OF RELIGIOUS BELIEF AND PRACTICE

Special People/Key Figures and Leaders
* Is becoming aware of the importance of key figures and religious leaders eg. Guru Nanak, through hearing stories.
Language, Symbol and Communication
* Begins to understand the importance of artefacts as a focus of attention or as an aid an aid during prayer.
* Begins to use appropriate symbols for artefacts.
Learning Experiences
Darren has selected Sikh artefacts and printed the correct symbols from the computer programme to match the artefacts he has selected.
Statement of Achievement (including level)
Darren was involved in selecting symbols from the computer programme and he has completed the task he was set.
He participated in the acting of the story of Guru Nanak and the Needle.

RELIGIOUS PERSPECTIVES ON HUMAN EXPERIENCE

* Is encouraged to talk about people who are special to him.
* Makes a collection of objects which are important to himself and to his peer group.
* Reflects on special ceremonies and occasions in his own life.
Learning Experiences
Darren has joined in role-play in the home corner using Sikh cooking utensils and dressing up in Sikh clothes. He has made a card for Guru Nanak's birthday and listened to Indian music.
Statement of Achievement
Darren was actively involved in the celebration of Guru Nanak's birthday and he chose some symbols to express how he felt joining in with other pupils.

the five Ks   Kachera   Kirpan   Kara   Kangha   Kesh

Shrine   holy book

Figure 13.5

Foundation for religious education – Statements of Achievement

Human experience

- Is beginning to develop an awareness of self
- Is beginning to develop an awareness of other people
- Is beginning to develop an awareness of belonging to a group
- Is beginning to develop self-control
- Hears a range of stories about human experience themes.

The world around

- Experiences the natural world
- Responds to the natural world
- Responds to different environments
- Experiences situations which may evoke a sense of awe and wonderment, e.g. raindrops rolling down the window pane, watching baby chicks hatch, feeling the wind blow on face and through hair.

Special people/key figures and leaders

- Recognizes special people in own family
- Recognizes familiar people in school environment
- Recognizes familiar people in the local community.

Special books/sacred writings

- Enjoys the tactile qualities of a book
- Shares a story book with an adult
- Listens to a favourite story about everyday experience
- Recognize favourite stories/books

- Begins to show an awareness of books which are special to other people.

Special buildings/places of worship

- Responds to the atmosphere in different environments within school
- Recognizes familiar environments
- Experiences a variety of different religious buildings in the local community.

Festivals and celebrations

- Experiences sights, colours, smells, tastes, sounds associated with celebrations at home and at school
- Encounters a variety of religious celebrations.

Special times/rites of passage

- Shares photographs of special occasions in own life with an adult
- Responds to a milestone or special occasion celebrated in own life.

Special journeys/pilgrimage

- Responds to own experience of journeys and travelling
- Participates in a special journey.

Language, symbol and communication

- Experiences signs and symbols in everyday life
- Begins to show an awareness of symbols in everyday life
- Recognizes some symbols associated with religious festivals and celebrations.

End of KS1 – Statements of Achievement

Human experience

- Is developing an awareness of self in relation to others
- Is beginning to develop healthy self-esteem
- Is aware of the contribution they make as part of a group
- Demonstrates a degree of self-control
- Is beginning to demonstrate emotional responses to happenings in their own life, e.g., happiness/sadness
- Demonstrates an awareness of other peoples' emotions
- Listens to a range of stories with human experience themes (e.g., families; friendship; loss and change) and is able to relate these to own experience.

The world around

- Is able to identify different environments
- Expresses curiosity and interest at the world around
- Is beginning to be aware of how people care for living things and the local environment
- Has heard several creation stories.

Special people/key figures and leaders

- Meets members of faith communities
- Is aware that some people follow a religious way of life
- Identifies the key figures from a Bible story and a story from one other sacred book
- Is aware some people believe God to be important.

Special books/sacred writings

- Is aware that a story may be told for a specific purpose
- Is able to identify a story from the life or teaching of Jesus
- Is beginning to develop an awareness that holy books should be respected and handled carefully
- Can identify a Bible and knows the book comprises the Old and New Testaments.

Special buildings/places of worship

- Understands there are special places where people go to worship
- Has been introduced to some of the key points in a place of worship e.g., altar, pulpit, font; quiblah, minbar; ark; shrine; langar
- Begins to demonstrate an awareness of the distinctive atmosphere of a religious place
- Begins to demonstrate respectful behaviour when visiting a place of worship
- Has encountered a variety of sensory experiences in places of worship e.g., heard music; touched different materials from which buildings are constructed; smelt incense; watched candles/sacred lights burning; looked at and touched fabrics and embroidery

Festivals and celebrations

- Is beginning to recognize there are times which have special significance for some people
- Helps to prepare and tastes a variety of foods associated with festivals from the religions studied

- Begins to recognize the importance of preparing for a festival or celebration
- Begins to show an awareness of the pattern of religious festivals for Christians and one other religion.

Special times/rites of passage

- Begins to show an awareness of special events and milestones within own life e.g., staying away from home for the night; starting school; losing a tooth
- Begins to show an awareness of special events within family life e.g., birth/initiation ceremonies; coming of age; weddings
- Is helped to make a pictorial chart of special times in own life from birth to the present day.

Special journeys/pilgrimage

- Experiences some different kinds of journeys and begins to recognize some of the reasons and motivations for these journeys
- Hears a first-hand account from someone who has been on a special journey or pilgrimage
- Brings to school a souvenir or memento of a special journey or a visit and explains to peer group the significance of the item.

Language, symbol and communication

- Is beginning to develop a sensitivity towards the special meaning conveyed by some religious symbols e.g., dress; food
- Is able to recognize symbols representative of the religious group to which they belong.

End of KS2 – Statements of Achievement

Human experience

- Has increased knowledge of self
- Is able to reflect on own sense of uniqueness
- Is able to make choices
- Demonstrates an empathy towards key characters in stories with human experience themes
- Shows empathy towards the needs and feelings of people from a variety of faiths and cultures
- Shows sensitivity towards the lifestyles of other people within the school family and the local community.

The world around

- Demonstrates a sense of responsibility towards living things and the environment
- Participates in learning experiences which relate to environmental issues
- Begins to develop a concept of the interdependence of humankind and the created order
- Begins to recognize the commitment which religions have to the world in which we live
- Begins to appreciate the pain and beauty of the natural world
- Is beginning to reflect on existential questions of meaning and purpose.

Special people/key figures and leaders

- Is becoming aware of the importance of key figures and religious leaders e.g., Jesus, Moses, Muhammad, Guru Nanak, Siddartha Gautama, through hearing stories and increasing knowledge of religious belief and practice
- Meets and interacts with leaders from the Christian community and two other religions.

Special books and sacred writings

- Can identify and name some holy books and recognizes a story from the Christian Bible and one other story from another faith
- Shows awareness of the importance of religious books and sacred writings to some people
- Is able to identify and name holy books from the religions studied
- Is able to name some of the books of the Old and New Testaments in the Bible.

Special buildings/places of worship

- Has had opportunities to explore space within religious buildings
- Has visited a variety of local places of worship from the Christian tradition and other religions studied
- Demonstrates an ability for quiet reflection when visiting a place of worship
- Is able to identify some of the key points in a place of worship and to sign/explain why they are of significance to worshippers.

Festivals and celebrations

- Begins to explore the significance of shared meals and special foods e.g., Pesach; the Eucharist
- Knows that Sunday is a special day for Christians and recognizes the importance of a daily/weekly time of worship/reflection for some people
- Is able to retell through words/pictures/signs/symbols the Easter and Christmas stories as recorded in the Gospel narratives
- Is able to explain the significance of Easter for Christians.

Special times/rites of passage

- Has watched a video or experienced first-hand a baptism and wedding within the Christian tradition, and a wedding and an initiation ceremony from one other religion studied
- Is able to talk about/sign or to explain in symbols the importance of family photographs, visual reminders and accounts as reminders of rites of passage
- Begins to understand the importance of ritual and symbol in rites of passage e.g., water in baptism; the exchange of rings during the marriage service; sacred thread; sharing special food; flowers and memorials at funerals.

Special journeys/pilgrimage

- Is able to identify several different reasons for making a journey
- Begins to understand the significance of artefacts and mementoes as reminders of a special journey
- Has visited a place of pilgrimage or a place which has special meaning for an individual or for a faith community e.g., a cathedral, tomb or burial place
- Is helped to find in an atlas or on a globe significant places of pilgrimage from religions studied.

Language, symbol and communication

- Has explored the symbol of the cross within Christianity and has encountered a variety of different crosses/crucifixes
- Begins to understand the importance of artefacts as a focus of attention or as an aid during prayer
- Is able to identify artefacts from own religious tradition (if appropriate) or the religions studied and is able to show how they might be used by a member of the faith tradition
- Has experienced first-hand or through audio-visual aids a variety of forms of worship from the religions studied
- Begins to use appropriate language/signs/symbols for artefacts.

JESUS

A woman had ten pieces of silver.

The woman lost one piece of silver.

and was sweeping up and in the dust was the lost coin.

and then had a friend round to tea.

Figure 13.6

Guru Nanak's birthday: learning experiences to develop the scheme of work

Background

Guru Nanak was the founder of Sikhism. The name Guru means 'disciple'. Guru Nanak was born a Hindu but he rejected the caste system and idolatry and he taught that only one God should be worshipped. Guru Nanak is deeply admired by Sikhs as an example of piety and holiness. He is regarded as a man who was chosen by God to reveal His message.

Objectives

- To help pupils reflect on celebrations and occasions which occur annually
- To develop an awareness of how religious beliefs and lifestyles are expressed through symbolism
- To increase pupils' knowledge and experience of stories about key figures and leaders in religion.

Resources

- A large brightly coloured circular tablecloth
- A collection of Sikh artefacts including a framed picture of Guru Nanak and the five Ks
- A Sikh garland used for decoration
- Divas or night lights contained in brightly coloured holders
- Examples of symbols, badges, special clothes which are familiar to the pupils and representative of groups to which they belong.

Setting the scene

Invite several pupils to help put the tablecloth on the floor. Seat the group around the edge of the empty cloth. Have examples of symbols and badges which are familiar to the pupils and a box of carefully wrapped Sikh artefacts close to hand.

The activity

Talk about the symbols, badges, clothing, etc. which belong to the pupils, emphasizing how important they are because they are representative of special places, groups, etc. Invite pupils to place their symbols on one half of the cloth.

Introduce the five Ks by very carefully unwrapping them and explaining they are symbols which Sikh people use to show they belong to the faith. Allow pupils to try on the kara and to feel the tactile quality of the wooden comb.

Display the five Ks on the other half of the cloth and once again draw the attention of group members to their symbols.

Carefully unwrap the picture of Guru Nanak and talk about 'special' people and leaders within the pupils' experience. Explain Guru Nanak is a special person for Sikh people and place the picture on the cloth close to the five Ks.

Ask how the pupils celebrate their birthdays. Encourage discussion about cakes and shared meals with families and friends.

Tell the Needle Story (see Brown, 1995) and explain how Sikh people celebrate Guru Nanak's birthday. Invite a pupil to decorate the picture of Guru Nanak with the garland.

SIKHISM

KNOWLEDGE AND UNDERSTANDING OF SIKHISM
(including belief and practice)

There is one God who is Creator.
All humans are equal before God.
Ceremonies: e.g. naming, marriage, turban-tying.
Celebrations: e.g. birthdays of Guru Nanak, Guru Gobind
   Singh; Baisakhi.
The lives of the Gurus.
The Guru Granth Sahib – its care in the Gurdwara.
Worship – led by the Granthi. Consists of: kirtan;
   ardas; langar.

LEARNING EXPERIENCES

Pupils could:
Hear Sikhs talking about themselves and their faith.
Listen to stories about Guru Nanak and other Gurus.
Observe a Sikh tying his turban.
Find out about the birthday of Guru Nanak and how it is
   celebrated.
Look at pictures or a video of the Golden Temple and find out
   where Amritsar is on a map.
Listen to the story of Baisakhi.
Share ideas about the importance of names and look up their
   own names in a dictionary of first names.
Visit a Gurdwara and identify expressions of Sikh belief and
   practice.
Make a poster explaining the 5 Ks.
Design their own symbol(s) to express something about themselves.

RELIGIOUS PERSPECTIVES
ON HUMAN EXPERIENCE

Pupils should be encouraged to think about:
Times when it is easy to share and times when it is difficult.
Their own families and the activities which they enjoy.
Signs of belonging, e.g. uniforms, badges, symbols.
   Ways in which people demonstrate respect, and how it
      feels to be respected.
   Feelings which are evoked when visiting a place
      of worship.
   The importance of community meals – meals
      which are special.
   Books which are special to them.

SYMBOLS

   The 5 Ks: kachera; kangha; kara; kesh; kirpan.
   Karah parshad.
   Khanda.
Nishan Sahib.

Figure 13.7

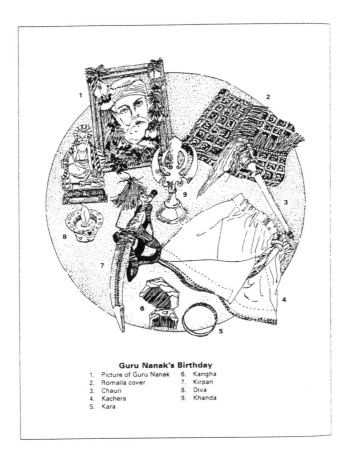

Guru Nanak's Birthday

1. Picture of Guru Nanak
2. Romalla cover
3. Chauri
4. Kachera
5. Kara
6. Kangha
7. Kirpan
8. Diva
9. Khanda

Figure 13.8

GURU NANAK'S BIRTHDAY

KNOWLEDGE AND UNDERSTANDING OF SIKHISM
(including belief and practice)

There is one God who is Creator.
Equality of humankind before God.
Truth revealed by the Gurus and the Guru Granth Sahib.
The community as a family.
The Gurdwara as a place of worship and a place for sharing.
Stories of the lives of the Gurus.
Worship in the Gurdwara – led by Granthi. Consists
    of: kirtan; ardas; langar.

LEARNING EXPERIENCES

Pupils could:
Dress dolls in 5 Ks.
Role play in home corner, using Sikh cooking
    utensils and dressing up in Sikh clothes.
Cook and taste karah parshad and Indian foods.
Experience different ways of celebrating birthdays.
Make cards for Guru Nanak's birthday.
Experience Indian music.
Visit a Gurdwara.
Make a class book about the life of Guru Nanak.
Bring to school/talk about things which are special to them.
Listen to stories about Guru Nanak.
Act out a story from the life of Guru Nanak.

RELIGIOUS PERSPECTIVES
ON HUMAN EXPERIENCE

Pupils should be encouraged to think about:
How and why we share with each other.
How and why visitors are welcome to home and to school.
The importance of family life.
    Books which are special to us.
    People who are special to us.
        How we show concern for each other.
        Symbols in everyday life.
            Special clothes.
            Special ceremonies for special occasions.
            When and why people pray.

SYMBOLS

Sikh appearance – the 5 Ks: kachera; kangha;
    kara; kesh; kirpan.
Karah parshad.
Khanda.
Nishan Sahib.

Figure 13.9

Place a lighted diva on the cloth, emphasizing how important candles and light are for festivals and celebrations.

At the end of the activity, pack the Sikh artefacts away, reminding pupils of the importance of looking after 'special' objects.

Sensory learning experiences

Using the display described in the activities for Guru Nanak's birthday, pupils might be encouraged to explore Sikh artefacts:

- Trace the shape of the khanda with your fingers.
- Touch the course yak hair of the chauri.
- Feel the tactile qualities of the wooden kangha.
- Put the garland over your head and look at your image in a mirror.
- Wear the kara. Feel the coolness of the steel and its weight on your wrist.
- Smell warm karah parshad.
- Smell the candle wax of the diva.
- Watch the curving diva flame.
- Taste warm karah parshad.
- Look at the rich embroidery on the romalla cover.
- Feel the fringes of the romalla cover against your face.

Concluding remarks

It is a sobering fact that a child's view of what happens in the classroom is sometimes quite different from that of the teacher. As a profession we often think that we are providing learning opportunities which are within the grasp of children, yet their reactions reveal this is not so. However we choose to teach religious education, we should set ourselves high standards in order that we provide signposts to children's learning which will help them to reach milestones along the way.

References

Brown, E. (1991) *Opening Children's Eyes to Worship*, London: The National Society (Church of England) for Promoting Religious Education.

Brown, E. (1993) *Mixed Blessings – The Special Child in Your School*, London: The National Society (Church of England) for Promoting Religious Education.

Brown, E. (1995) 'Circles of growth', *PMLD Link*, 22.

Brown, E. (1996) *RE for All*, London: David Fulton.

DfE (1994) *Code of Practice on the Identification and Assessment of Special Educational Needs*, London: Department for Education and the Welsh Office.

DfE (1994) Circular 1/94 *Religious Education and Collective Worship*, London: Department for Education.

Dowell, J. and Nutt, M. (1995) 'An approach to Religious Education at Piper Hill School, *PMLD Link*, 22.

Goss, P. (1995) 'Opening up: the inner lives of individuals with PMLD', *PMLD Link*, 22.

Longhorn, F. (1993) *Religious Education for Very Special Children*, Isle of Man: ORCA Publications.

NCC (1993) *Spiritual and Moral Development – A discussion document*, London: National Curriculum Council.

SCAA (1994) *Model Syllabuses for Religious Education*, London: Schools Curriculum and Assessment Authority.

Further reading

The Special Religious Education Network publishes a termly journal, *Respect*, edited by Erica Brown. Details from: Erica Brown, 7 Elyham, Purley-on-Thames, Berkshire RG8 8EN.

Chapter 14

Coordinating the Whole Curriculum

Robert Ashdown

Introduction

The focus of this chapter is upon the principles which underpin sound approaches to curriculum planning. It does not deal with the actual content of the whole curriculum which is a matter for individual schools to determine in the light of their particular circumstances, the age and ability range of the pupils, the policies of the local education authority (LEA) and the requirements of national legislation. Although there is still room for much debate about desirable curriculum content, the requirements to deliver a curriculum which has 'breadth and balance' and which is relevant to the pupils' needs are well established.

The Office for Standards in Education (OFSTED) has produced *Guidance on the Inspection of Special Schools* (OFSTED, 1995a) which makes plain the expectation that each school must deliver a curriculum which meets the legal requirements and which clearly supports the school's published statements about aims and values. The handbook emphasizes the need for a structure and organization to the school curriculum which is efficient, and for unambiguous policy statements and schemes of work for each curriculum area (whether these be National Curriculum subjects, religious education or other aspects of the whole curriculum). It also requires close scrutiny of the effectiveness of those teachers who have special responsibilities for coordinating the development of specific aspects of the curriculum as well as the strategies for monitoring and supporting curriculum development used by the headteacher and the other senior teachers who constitute the school management team (SMT). Reviews of the content of reports of OFSTED inspections of special schools suggest that many schools have yet to establish an approach to curriculum planning which is rigorous and which has agreed formats for monitoring, review and evaluation of policies as well as actual policy setting (Sebba, Clarke and Emery, 1995; Tobin, 1994).

The planning cycle

The School Curriculum and Assessment Authority has now produced non-statutory guidance on planning the whole curriculum for teachers of pupils in ordinary primary schools (SCAA, 1995a) and teachers of pupils with profound and multiple learning difficulties (PMLD) (SCAA, 1996). In addition, Byers and Rose (1996) have produced their own guidance on approaches to curriculum planning which contains helpful examples of policy documents, planning activities and record forms which are relevant to schools teaching pupils with a whole range of special educational needs. Readers are strongly recommended to read all three booklets because each has its strengths as well as its limitations; a synopsis is offered here.

The whole-school curriculum

The first task for schools which are initiating this recommended process of curriculum planning is to review and discuss the school's aims, objectives, policies and priorities in the curriculum. Consensus and clarity at this level of planning is essential since the taught curriculum should directly reflect the aims and policies. The result should be a written policy statement defining the content of the whole curriculum and clarifying the role which the National Curriculum subjects, religious education, personal, social and health education (PSHE), the various therapies and the cross-curricular elements play in it. This document could also show how the school ensures that pupils are enabled to access the whole curriculum; Byers and Rose (1996) and SCAA (1996) provide models for access and enablement statements. This written policy document could also be the place to set out for each curriculum area a brief overview of the school's work which makes plain general teaching aims, philosophy and other principles and shows how these determine what is taught and how it is taught.

Long-term planning

The next task is to produce a formal document which describes the school's long-term curriculum plans in terms of a cycle or rolling programme of units of work across a key stage or key stages, as appropriate. As a first step towards producing this documentation, schools are recommended to consider how the content of the whole-school curriculum may be organized into manageable teaching units. The suggested method is that schools should identify all of the proposed units of work and divide them into two broad categories of *continuing* and *blocked* work. Continuing work requires regular and frequent teaching throughout each school year, whereas blocked work can be taught within a specific amount of time, usually not exceeding a school term. In the case of statemented pupils, schools must ensure that the planned units of work will meet the objectives specified in every pupil's statement and elaborated in his or her individual education plan (IEP).

This documentation could also identify the school's assessment policy for the various curriculum areas; the OFSTED handbook (1995a) clarifies expectations about assessment practice and the SCAA has provided advice about the content of an assessment policy in *Consistency in Teacher Assessment: Guidance for Schools* (SCAA, 1995b), which is the first in a series of booklets on consistency in teacher assessment.

Each school needs to decide which aspects of the curriculum are best treated in depth and which are to be treated in outline only. One example of this decision-making relates to the aspect of the Key Stage 4 programmes of study (PoS) for science and concerns the effects of alcohol, drugs and tobacco. Obviously, a degree of knowledge about these will be important to teach to some pupils but a decision may need to be taken to teach this in outline only on the grounds that they may not be able to assimilate all of the relevant knowledge and understanding as easily as their age peers.

Schools are also recommended to consider the potential advantages, in terms of curriculum coherence and effectiveness, that may accrue from formally linking together specific units of work from different aspects of the curriculum. This should not be done simply to save time, and there is no value in devising links that are contrived or artificial. It should also be remembered that OFSTED (1994) has counselled that *topic work* tends to be more effective when it has a single-subject bias. There are limits to the number of curriculum areas which may be linked through topic work without affecting the ability of staff to keep work focused and ensure that intended progression within curriculum areas is achieved and easily monitored. Although examples of all-embracing topic work still abound in the literature, there has been a move towards developing modules of work which have a single subject bias in special schools. Rose (1994) has described the development of focused modules of work in at least one special school. Teachers will be aware, however, that a single-subject focus in all modules may not be beneficial or feasible with all pupils: for instance, a module on 'My family', which is focused solely on history, may be unduly limiting for pupils with PMLD because relevant aspects of science and geography might be more appropriate to their needs and offer more obvious opportunities for enriching experiences.

SCAA (1996) also recommends that, in all aspects of their planning, assessing, teaching, recording and reporting, teachers of pupils with PMLD must be careful to distinguish between activities which are *experienced* by pupils and learning outcomes which are actually *achieved*. Jones et al. (1993) discuss this distinction in relation to assessment of progress against *milestones* in science: following their example, *experienced* may be used by to refer to the fact that a pupil has participated in a particular area of learning, reacting to the experiences and opportunities offered; *achieved* denotes a consistent achievement in this area in a variety of situations; and *studied* may be used to show that a pupil has spent time working in a particular area in a variety of situations but is not consistent in his or her achievement. Jones and his colleagues also recommend use of a simple form for recording coverage of topics and subjects during each academic year of a pupil's school career. This degree of formal planning and recording is necessary to monitor breadth and balance in the curriculum, document pupils' responses, and avoid unnecessary repetition of activities for individual pupils.

Each school is expected to give guidance to teachers on time allocation to the various areas of the curriculum as a means of ensuring breadth and balance for all pupils, even those who are not of compulsory school age. This guidance should be regularly reviewed as part of the whole-school curriculum plan and in relation to the SMT's strategy for monitoring time allocation by class teachers. The non-statutory guidance for primary schools (SCAA, 1995a) offers a model for deciding precise time allocation which may be appropriate in many special school settings. However, this model will be very difficult to use where the curriculum does not have a subject orientation and many units of work do not have a specific subject-focus. In fact, the non-statutory guidance for teachers of pupils with PMLD recognizes that it may be impractical to precisely allocate hours and minutes in a year to each subject because of the nature of the teaching activities and other essential demands on teacher time (SCAA, 1996).

Nevertheless, time allocation poses a dilemma for schools. On the one hand, the legal requirement for breadth in the school curriculum means that the appropriate National Curriculum subjects together with religious education and other age-appropriate aspects of the whole curriculum should be covered during the course of each year or, possibly, each Key Stage and that this coverage should be documented. Moreover, the balance of the curriculum can be ensured only by some description of the amounts of time to be allocated to each curriculum area and a school requirement that teachers work within this framework. On the other hand, there are the daily demands on teacher time by children who, say, present severely challenging behaviours or require special health and welfare care routines. For such reasons, it may make little sense in some schools to specify average percentages of time allocation for subjects and curriculum areas. One possible strategy that may serve as a guarantee of breadth and balance is to give each class teacher specific guidance on time allocation which is appropriate to his or her assigned class, and which reflects the ages and specific educational needs of the pupils in the class. Most importantly, this guidance would require regular review on an annual basis at least. It should allow teachers scope to plan to use the available teaching time with due regard to the priority teaching objectives for individual pupils. It should also allow for the fact that teaching time will be reduced by the amount of time that must be spent in transition from one activity to another (e.g., clearing away, setting out equipment, settling teaching groups, minibus travel to the swimming pool, etc.) and in care and other routines. Of course, the guidance cannot allow for certain kinds of disruptions which inevitably will occur (e.g., episodes of incontinence, epileptic seizures, seriously challenging behaviours, unexpected visitors).

Medium-term planning

The next task is to produce a series of formal documents which specify the details of each unit of work and finalize the sequence of work to be covered during each term by each year group, Key Stage or all of the pupils in the school, as appropriate. These schemes of work should identify the learning outcomes for notional groups of pupils at different age stages in the school, showing how these relate to the statutory PoS wherever possible. Aside from the content of skills, knowledge and understanding to be taught, these schemes of work should also include descriptions of general teaching methods and assessment opportunities, indicating any changes in emphasis for different age groups. Other helpful information for staff might include likely differentiation strategies, planned cross-curricular links, available resources, and methods for recording pupils' responses.

Medium-term planning also needs to focus on the individual pupil. As regards each pupil's IEP, the relevance of last year's objectives and the effectiveness of past teaching strategies should be considered at each formal annual review of his or her statement. This will also be the occasion when new objectives and strategies will be identified and recorded. As a result of the introduction of the *Code of Practice for the Identification and Assessment of Special Educational Needs* (DfE, 1994), the expectation is that there should be a clear relationship between the identified targets and strategies described in annual review reports and the objectives and strategies specified in the pupil's statement.

Short-term planning

Schools will also have their own system for more frequent, informal reviews of progress and setting of objectives which meet the requirements of the *Code of Practice* and long-established good practice in the field of special education. Typically, the result of this review process is that a teacher will set, probably once or twice per term at least, new short-term targets for individual pupils which are immediate priorities for their further learning and development and which will lead to the identified longer-term objectives. The onus is on the individual teacher to make short-term curriculum plans for sessions or lessons which may include descriptions of activities, differentiation strategies, classroom management, pupil groupings and staff deployment, as appropriate. These should be designed to meet the specific objectives for each pupil during the term or a shorter period. Significantly, SCAA does not give restrictive specifications about desirable practice in short-term planning and recognizes that much of it will be ephemeral and that documentation, where it exists, will be short-lived working tabletop materials. However, SCAA strongly recommends that schools should develop resource banks of short-term plans in each curriculum area because these may be useful to other teachers in the school and will provide a focus for staff discussion about future curriculum development (SCAA, 1996). Obviously, schools must develop a consistent approach for two reasons: first, to ensure continuity and progression in learning; and second, to facilitate the development of a system for monitoring and improving the quality of education available in each class group. Readers looking for possible models for short-term planning may find the books by Byers and Rose (1996) and Lawson (1992) helpful.

Assessment and recording

It is essential that schools establish a policy about recording pupils' responses to teaching activities. Monitoring and recording of pupils' responses have typically been done in order to provide the evidence needed for reporting pupil progress and reviewing IEPs. However, SCAA (1996) stresses that this evidence can be used for the review of school curriculum plans as well. This process demands time for reflection; teachers need to evaluate whether planned outcomes of work are being realized. This raises the problem of deciding what to record, because clearly it is impossible and unprofitable to record every pupil response to every teaching activity. Each school will have to determine its own system for recording significant pupil responses, and deciding what constitutes a significant response. Schools tend to have well-developed record systems in relation to priority objectives, but may need to consider whether these records can demonstrate coverage of the curriculum for each pupil during each year and usefully inform any curriculum audits. Again, guidance may be found in the books by Byers and Rose (1996) and Lawson (1992).

Review and evaluation

The final task in the planning cycle is to decide systems for monitoring, review and evaluation. Schools with statemented pupils will already be used to reviewing IEPs and this process could achieve impact on curriculum development if progress and new targets are explicitly documented. In addition, schools should ensure that they periodically review and evaluate policy, long-term plans, schemes of work and short-term plans in relation to each curriculum area as part of a rolling programme. Schools should consider whether they have adequate formal systems for ensuring that these reviews take place in a planned and coherent fashion. A successful system of review will require frequent curriculum audits which can be used to inform school development planning, and Byers and Rose (1996) specifically address the question of how to conduct curriculum audits.

Coordinators' responsibilities

The non-statutory guidance from SCAA (1995a; 1996) and the handbook for the inspection of special schools (OFSTED, 1995a) stress that there should be sound management of the planning process by the headteacher and other members of the SMT. Successful curriculum planning requires strong and enthusiastic leadership, good coordination and close support for individual teachers. School inspection teams also look for clear evidence that target-setting is integrated into development planning and that schools have strategies for monitoring and evaluation . The curriculum planning cycle also demands that all staff must be involved in the process. Ideally, one tangible result should be that all staff feel that they have ownership of the school curriculum. The other beneficial outcome should be that staff achieve a collective understanding of the implications for their practice in the classroom of current legislation about the curriculum, the policies of the LEA, and the school's own curriculum policies. Schools should have mechanisms for consultation with staff as part of the school development planning process; hopefully, as a result of proper consultation, staff will feel that they exercise greater control over the school curriculum rather than that they are at the mercy of every new curriculum initiative.

Curriculum planning would be an impossible task without each individual teacher having his or her share of the administrative and managerial responsibilities. The introduction of the National Curriculum forced the rapid development of curriculum coordinator roles for all teachers, not just a few senior teachers. It is now commonplace for all teachers to be given a substantive curriculum responsibility for actively promoting the development of a negotiated area or areas of the school curriculum. The precise curriculum responsibilities may change from year to year to meet new targets in the school development plan, but they are likely to include as a minimum:

- making a regular (perhaps annual) audit of the available teaching resources throughout the school, the professional development targets for staff, and any requirements for policy development;
- summarizing this information and making recommendations about development needs in a written report which will serve to inform governors, the headteacher and other staff about the state of curriculum development and suggest future targets for the school development plan;
- maintaining centralized teaching resources and ordering new materials to restock or extend these as and when funds are made available;
- managing a delegated budget for meeting development targets;
- liaising with appropriate advisers, advisory teachers of the LEA and coordinators in other schools and attending professional development activities which may contribute to the development of this aspect of the school curriculum;
- developing a good level of personal knowledge of any relevant National Curriculum orders and non-statutory guidance, and keeping up to date with new developments in teaching methods and resources.

Coordinators will require job definitions, clear targets and guidance from the SMT so that they meet these responsibilities. The informal contacts which they have with their teaching colleagues will often serve to determine what is going on in their curriculum area or areas in the rest of the school. However, formal procedures will also be necessary for effective curriculum planning. In particular, regular curriculum audits are essential because they identify what a school has achieved, future development targets, and the strategies and resources required for achieving these targets. The term 'curriculum audit' has been used to denote a variety of pupil shadowing activities described in non-statutory guidance (NCC, 1992) and by Galloway and Banes (1994). However, other types of curriculum audit are possible. For instance, coordinators need to ask whether the written documentation is adequate and whether there are any obvious omissions. Does it need to be made more user-friendly? Are there clear guidelines on assessment? Does it make plain what pupils should be taught at a particular age or Key Stage? Does it meet the legal requirements? Is there explicit cross-referencing to the National Curriculum PoS? Also, they must consider whether the whole-school resources and classroom resources are adequate, including the information technology which is available. What are the professional development needs of individual staff and staff groups? An accurate audit may depend on collating the results from formal questionnaires circulated among staff or, if non-contact time can be provided for pupil shadowing, observations of teaching activities in other classes could be very informative.

In many schools, coordinators are given specific responsibilities for advising teachers about planning, teaching, recording and assessment. In relation to their assigned curriculum area(s) they may be asked to:

- give direction to school-based professional development activities and reviews by curriculum working groups;
- comment on specific aspects of pupils' IEPs and teachers' short-term planning and recording;
- provide training or demonstrate good practice by teaching alongside colleagues who have identified weaknesses;
- introduce a curriculum initiative and evaluate its impact throughout the school.

These types of responsibilities may pose considerable difficulties for coordinators; although some colleagues may welcome guidance and feedback about their performance, coordinators may encounter inertia, hostility or apathy instead of active cooperation. Therefore, it is important that this kind of responsibility should only be given to successful teachers who have considerable credibility with their colleagues. They must also perceive the need for change, be well-rewarded for their efforts and have healthy ways of combating stress. They will need opportunities for careful planning with members of the SMT; there must be clear targets for the intervention and a realistic timescale for achieving them. There is also value in developing mutually supportive teams of teachers who have similar ideas and attitudes rather than expecting lone coordinators to work in isolation in stressful circumstances. Also, it is important to work initially with those staff in the school who would be supportive of change or at least willing to give it a fair trial. Ultimately, the SMT will have to address the difficult problem of bringing into line those teachers who are weak, defensive or resistant to change. However, these are not the people on whom to spend energies unduly when setting up the momentum for change.

The whole-school curriculum coordinator will have a crucial role in providing moral and practical support to other coordinators when the going gets tough. This senior teacher will also be responsible for coordinating and directing the work of the coordinators so that curriculum audits and planned curriculum developments take place coherently and according to the timescale indicated in the school development plan. This teacher must be capable of motivating colleagues to meet their assigned targets in time and should be one of the key players in monitoring whether classroom practice reflects school policies and whether the quality of teaching is sound in all its aspects. The whole-school curriculum coordinator will have overall responsibility for producing each year the whole-school curriculum development plan which will set out the targets, strategies and timescales. These are compelling reasons for giving this role to a member of the SMT who is a good strategist and planner and who has proven leadership qualities;

inevitably, in many smaller schools this role will fall to the headteacher or deputy head. The role of any coordinator will only have impact if he or she is equipped to do the job. Coordinators will need material resources and opportunities for professional development. Ideally, they should have timetabled non-contact time or, at the very least, be released from teaching responsibilities at times when their workload is exceptionally high due to the planning, implementation and monitoring of agreed development work. The SMT must determine the cost of the physical and other resources required. The management of this part of the school 's financial resources may then be delegated to the whole-school curriculum development coordinator and other coordinators, as appropriate, in order to give them the budgetary control that they require to implement the strategies needed to meet their targets.

Purposes of monitoring

As noted above, SCAA and OFSTED expect that schools will have in place their own formal systems for monitoring the work that goes on in classrooms in order to determine its quality and whether it reflects school policies. This can be only achieved if identified members of the SMT, particularly the headteacher and the whole-school curriculum coordinator, can plan to spend sufficient time in classrooms. If they can do this, the members of the SMT should be able to give teachers explicit feedback about:

- whether classroom practice reflects school policy
- teaching methods
- lesson planning
- recording and reporting of progress by pupils
- management of physical resources
- deployment and briefing of staff
- the quality of the learning environment.

In addition, monitoring strategies should result in the identification of resources that are lacking, possible solutions to teaching problems, and the professional development needs of staff. Almost certainly, they will also make it possible to identify any practical problems inherent in school policies or schemes of work. Finally, they make it possible to explicitly recognize good teaching work and celebrate this.

All staff need to be involved in the creation of a system which will support them in their work rather than serve as a mere check on their practice. The rationale for monitoring strategies must be developed in consultation with all staff. It is most important that the developmental goals of monitoring are stressed, because there are dangers in having a lop-sided emphasis on making purely summative judgements about the quality of education available in each classroom. For these reasons, it would be a mistake to regard the headteacher and other members of the SMT just as 'inspectors in residence'; they have an equally important role as potential mentors. Unlike the formal school inspection process, the school's system for monitoring should be explicitly related to a supportive, mentoring processes like those which have been developed for newly qualified teachers and new headteachers. Nevertheless, there must be an element of performance management, and the OFSTED framework for school inspection does offer useful models for developing monitoring strategies. The guidance on recording inspection evidence (OFSTED, 1995b) shows the various forms that information collection might take:

- observation of actual teaching activities including a range of one-to-one and small-group work as well as whole-class teaching;
- scrutiny of documentary evidence (e.g., pupils' work, individual pupil portfolios, pupils progress records, IEPs, lesson plans, etc.);
- interaction with pupils to get evidence of educational standards (e.g., hearing them read or talking with them about current activities);
- observation of a range of other activities beyond the classroom (e.g., assemblies, extra-curricular activities, mealtimes, play times, etc.).

The person carrying out the monitoring clearly does not want to disrupt normal classroom activities in any way, but staff and pupils will have to get used to his or her presence in the classroom. The observer may need to remain on the edge of activities to avoid influencing the course of these, but unlike an OFSTED inspector, the school-based observer can gain a lot by becoming fully involved in them.

The OFSTED inspection materials lay down objective criteria for making judgements and also provide an observation form (OFSTED, 1995b). Of course, schools may wish to develop the criteria to suit their circumstances and devise their own forms for recording. Indeed, schools may have very good reasons for not using the system of grading that must be employed by inspectors; for instance, it may be considered too crude a measure or too judgmental. Also, it is a matter for each school to decide whether any records of observations should be kept but, obviously, the feedback to the teacher will be more explicit if the observer can provide concise written notes that describe the evidence that has been used to arrive at a judgement. As a matter of courtesy and in order to develop a mentoring process, the class teacher should be given the opportunity to discuss this evidence and these judgements. Therefore, these opportunities for dialogue between professionals might best occur in the context of semi-formal or formal meetings between the individual teacher and the appropriate member of the SMT. One outcome of such meetings should be the clear identification of targets that should be achieved by either the teacher or the school.

A decision will have to be made about the amount of time to be spent making observations to get a realistic impression of what is going on in the classroom. School inspectors aim to spend at least 60 per cent of the time that a school is in session on observations of lessons, sampling pupils' work and talking to pupils (OFSTED, 1995a). During the course of an inspection of a medium-sized special school, a team may make about one hundred such observations. Therefore, school-based observers from the SMT may feel obliged to make at least as many observations of, say, 45 minutes duration as a minimum in order to get a good picture of what is going on in school. The allocation of yet more precious time for monitoring strategies will pose difficulties for the SMT, but the team does not have to do its work within the confines of one week as inspection teams do. It may help if a cycle of visits for observations is timed to coincide with the introduction of, say, a new curriculum policy or work on a particular topic throughout the school. Also, the SMT can take a whole term or year to balance out the observations between classes and curriculum areas.

Concluding remarks

The Education Reform Act of 1988 introduced a period of rapid curriculum innovation in all schools and, unfortunately, it often seemed that every new initiative was accompanied by uncertainties about its relevance for pupils with significant learning difficulties. The situation was often not helped by confused or contradictory messages within the accompanying documentation. However, schools have been promised a period of relative stability and the model for a curriculum planning cycle which has gradually emerged can be applied with confidence that it is appropriate and flexible enough to meet the idiosyncratic needs of each school. Schools still face an enormous task, but the mechanisms for phased curriculum development and the best strategies for monitoring, review and evaluation of policy and practice are now more certain.

References

Byers, R. and Rose, R. (1996) *Planning the Curriculum for Pupils with Special Educational Needs: A practical guide*, London: David Fulton.

DfE (1994) *Code of Practice for the Identification and Assessment of Special Educational Needs*, London: HMSO.

Jones, L., Skelton, S., Fagg, S., Aherne, P. and Thornber, A. (1993) *Science for All* (2nd edn), London: David Fulton.

Galloway, S. and Banes, D. (1994) 'Beyond the simple audit', in Rose, R., Fergusson, A., Coles, C. Byers, R. and Banes, D. (eds) *Implementing the Whole Curriculum for Pupils with Learning Difficulties*, London: David Fulton.

Lawson, H. (1992) *Practical Record Keeping for Special Schools*, London: David Fulton.

NCC (1992) *Curriculum Guidance 9: The National Curriculum and Pupils with Severe Learning Difficulties*, York: NCC.

OFSTED (1994) *Primary Matters: A Discussion on Teaching and Learning in Primary Schools*, London: OFSTED.

OFSTED (1995a) *Guidance on the Inspection of Special Schools*, London: HMSO.

OFSTED (1995b) *Inspection Resource Pack*, London: HMSO.

Rose, R. (1994) 'A modular approach to the curriculum for pupils with learning difficulties', in Rose, R., Fergusson, A., Coles, C., Byers, R. and Banes, D. (eds) *Implementing the Whole Curriculum for Pupils with Learning Difficulties*, London: David Fulton.

SCAA (1995a) *Planning the Curriculum at Key Stages 1 and 2*, London: SCAA.

SCAA (1995b) *Consistency in Teacher Assessment: Guidance for Schools*, London: SCAA.

SCAA (1996) *Planning the Curriculum for Pupils with Profound and Multiple Learning Difficulties*, London: SCAA.

Sebba, J., Byers, R. and Rose, R. (1995) *Redefining the Whole Curriculum for Pupils with Learning Difficulties*, London: David Fulton.

Sebba, J., Clarke, J. and Emery, B. (1995) 'How can the inspection process enhance improvement in special schools?', paper presented to the Fourth International Special Education Conference, Birmingham, 10–13 April.

Tobin, D. (1994) 'The inspection of special schools for pupils with severe learning difficulties: validation or valediction?', *The SLD Experience*, 10, 1–4.

Chapter 15

Classroom Processes

Richard Byers

Introduction

In *The Curriculum Challenge*, Ashdown *et al.* (1991) brought together a collection of chapters which raised a host of issues in response to the implementation of the original National Curriculum in special schools in 1990. Much has happened since. Most schools moved swiftly through a phase of shock and hostility into a period of development, testing out the hypothesis of the first set of orders against the reality of classroom experience. Although this may have resulted in the National Curriculum monopolizing the energies of practitioners and policy-makers alike for a period, while some people concentrated on mobilizing an anti-National Curriculum backlash, the tendency of all upheavals is to move inexorably towards balance. Schools experiencing an unaccustomed sense of relative calm should not allow themselves to become complacent, however. While some of the issues raised for debate in books, articles, professional development centres and staffroom discussions since 1990 have been resolved, many others, like the heads of the hydra, arise in their place to prompt fresh debate and reinvigorated development. This is a process to be welcomed. The school that stops and congratulates itself on having arrived is a school that is in danger of dying on its feet.

This chapter sets out to explore some of the issues, with their origins in classroom practice, which continue to provoke debate and prompt development. It is in the classroom, after all, at the interface between teacher and learner, that real development begins and ends. Outside influences will impinge upon these processes. All members of the school community – governors, parents, staff and pupils – will have their say in the creation and ratification of policy. Committees and working parties will watch over the budget and the refurbishment of buildings. But in the end schools are really all about teachers and learners and the curriculum which is an expression of the work that they do together.

In examining classroom processes, this chapter will discuss:

- whole-curriculum issues;
- individual priorities;
- sharing purpose and intention;
- providing appropriate tasks and activities;

- teaching approaches and learning styles;
- access, support and resources;
- interaction; and
- reflection and review.

In the spirit of perpetual development which informs this chapter, no attempts will be made to reach cosy conclusions. Staff in schools are only too aware of the complexity of many issues which continue to challenge and to create real tensions. The following sections will, however, bring together some of the ideas that inform curriculum development and set out some of the implications of those ideas for classroom practice.

Whole-curriculum issues

Two of the central themes of Sir Ron Dearings review of the National Curriculum were to 'identify the essential elements of knowledge, understanding and skill within each subject' and to provide, for school staff, 'significantly greater scope for the exercise of professional judgement' (Dearing, 1993). The subject review teams set about slimming down the curriculum to 'the essential statutory core' by reducing the number of attainment targets in many subjects; removing 'unhelpful areas of overlap', and stripping out, for the most part, references to teaching methodology (Byers, 1994a; SCAA, 1994). The revised National Curriculum 'sets out a flexible framework which enables schools to plan their whole curriculum within a statement of minimum entitlement' (Stevens, 1995a). It describes that material which 'by law must be taught' while opening up 'opportunities for debate' (Tate, 1994) which had been inhibited by the original overloaded and over-prescriptive National Curriculum. This new flexibility, and the increase in matters which are to be left to the discretion of members of school communities, is, of course, broadly to be welcomed, not least by those working among pupils with special educational needs (SEN). There is little doubt that the uncoupling of chronological age from Key Stage, without the requirement to modify statements of special educational need (DfE, 1995), constitutes a major step forward. Similarly, the move, in the revised National Curriculum, away from statements of attainment, mechanical rules and checklists (SCAA, 1994) and towards the use of level descriptions which entail 'professional judgements' being made about the whole of a pupil's performance in a range of contexts and across time must be seen as positive (Byers and Rose, 1994).

Although this more flexible framework, with its focus upon the programmes of study (PoS) rather than structures for assessment; upon professional judgement and discretion at the classroom level; and upon a vision of the curriculum being created, owned and maintained by school communities, has many benefits, it also has at least one major potential drawback. One impact of the original National Curriculum legislation upon schools catering for pupils with SEN was to force an increase in curricular breadth (Sebba and Byers, 1992; Sebba and Fergusson, 1991; Sebba *et al.*, 1995). In part, this increased breadth concerned subjects and subject content. It required schools to take account of scientific discovery and technological innovation as well as teaching life skills and survival cookery. It enabled pupils to engage with story, verse and drama as well as acquiring a social sight vocabulary. It entailed learning about historical, geographical and cultural contexts as well as knowing how to use the bus route from school to the town library. All of these changes must be seen as bringing breadth and richness to a curriculum which had begun to be seen as narrow and impoverished.

If schools are to build honestly and productively upon the tradition of curriculum development over recent years, however, then breadth in the curriculum must mean something more than simply 'extra subjects'. The National Curriculum Council's seminal work of guidance on whole-curriculum planning (NCC, 1990) established a sound working definition of a whole curriculum which includes:

- the subjects of the 'basic curriculum', with their associated assessment procedures;
- cross-curricular elements, including key skills, cross-curricular themes and pupils' personal and social development in a range of dimensions;
- extra-curricular activities;
- the spirit and ethos of each school community, which contribute to the intangible, or hidden, curriculum;
- strategies for the management of the school and its curriculum; and
- 'the most effective teaching methods'.

The document goes on to suggest that. '...the wide range of skills which pupils must acquire must be reflected in an equally wide variety of approaches to teaching' (NCC, 1990, p.7) and that the responsibility for selecting those teaching methods which will ensure equality of opportunity for all pupils must remain with school staff. It may be seen as appropriate, therefore, that the revised National Curriculum does not prescribe teaching methods; that messages about how to teach have largely been removed from the PoS. The danger is that this revision of prescriptive language is seen as a justification for a return to a narrow range of classroom experiences for pupils with SEN. It is not simply the content of the whole curriculum which needs to be broad, balanced and relevant. With the review of the National Curriculum, there is even more of a requirement upon school staff to ensure that approaches to teaching, and the range of ways in which pupils are encouraged to learn, continue to evolve and develop in response to the changing needs of pupils.

As has been said before, 'it is not possible to implement the subject content of the National Curriculum without entering into the methodological debate' (Byers, 1994b). The National Curriculum entitles pupils to experience learning in a new variety of styles as well as opening up new areas of subject content. This is, in part at least, why the attitudes of the *E Qual S* movement seem to be so depressingly outmoded. No one is suggesting that 'everything that pupils with SLD need' (Humphreys, 1995) can be drawn from the National Curriculum. No one, in fact, is suggesting that everything that *any* pupil needs can be met solely by providing access to the core and other foundation subjects.

Individual priorities

It can be argued, however, that the National Curriculum has led to a broadening of the whole curriculum for pupils with SEN, both in terms of knowledge, skills and understanding and in terms of learning processes themselves. Do school communities wish to return to times when pupils with learning difficulties were trained to plug in a kettle safely without any attempt being made to help them to understand the uses and dangers of electricity from a scientific point of view? Would it serve the interests of pupils with SEN if schools excluded them from active participation in historical site visits and geographical fieldwork in peer groupings in order to revert to systems of one-to-one teaching and 'withdrawal for support'? What can a 'complementary curriculum that is taught without reference to the National Curriculum' (Humphreys, 1995) offer that cannot be encompassed within a well-rounded and inclusive whole curriculum which provides access to the subjects and learning processes of the National Curriculum even as it also addresses the needs of the whole pupil? Carpenter (1995) eloquently describes the ways in which pupils' varying individual needs can be met within inclusive activities which offer access to National Curriculum subject content. The School Curriculum and Assessment Authority (SCAA) proposes a vision of a whole curriculum which is indivisible, promoting learning for pupils in key areas of their personal and social development even as they encounter experiences founded in the subjects of the National Curriculum (SCAA, 1996).

There is no suggestion here that the National Curriculum is complete and sufficient as a whole curriculum. As has been shown above, the National Curriculum was only ever intended to constitute part of the basic curriculum, within a far broader whole curriculum, for all pupils. For many pupils with learning difficulties, the task of addressing, as a priority, those particular targets and objectives which are expressed in individual education plans (DfE, 1994) will mean working towards communication skills, interpersonal interactions or physical competences which are not explicitly described in the PoS for any subject within the National Curriculum. This chapter argues that priorities such as these fall within National Curriculum Council's definition of the whole curriculum (NCC, 1990) and do not need to be addressed through the development of a separate curriculum. Indeed, the range of learning experiences inevitably provided in any honest attempt to implement the National Curriculum will also offer meaningful contexts in which to pursue pupils' individual priorities (Byers, 1994c).

The OFSTED Handbook: Guidance on the inspection of special schools (OFSTED, 1995), also suggests that classroom staff should employ a range of teaching methods in seeking to meet the curricular requirements. Thus pupils should sometimes experience whole-class teaching which may involve listening to explanations, answering questions or participating in discussions. At other times and in other situations, staff may encourage smaller groups of pupils to work together on shared tasks or set up individual activities. Whatever organizational strategies are selected, and there is no suggestion here that any particular methods are to be prescribed for any particular occasions, staff are encouraged to consider:

whether the objectives are best achieved by pupils working alone, in pairs or small groups, or all together;
• whether the form of organisation allows the teacher to interact with pupils positively and economically. (OFSTED, 1995, p.72)

In OFSTED's view, effective teaching has many facets and pupils should be encouraged to learn in a variety of ways which match:

• the nature of the curricular objectives being pursued; and
• what pupils know, understand and can do, and what they need to learn next. (OFSTED, 1995, p.72)

The UNESCO resource pack, *Special Needs in the Classroom* (UNESCO, 1993) also emphasizes that all pupils can be helped to learn when:

• school staff know pupils well and, through continuous assessment and evaluation processes, have a clear idea of what has already been achieved;
• pupils are helped to understand what they are learning and, through the negotiation of objectives (cf DfE, 1994), why it is significant for them;

- classrooms are organized and support deployed in such a way so that all pupils are purposefully occupied for as much of the time as possible.

Building upon these principles and the OFSTED model, the following sections will explore some of the classroom processes which can help to promote effective learning.

Sharing purpose and intention

The UNESCO pack (1993) stresses the significance of ensuring that learning activities are meaningful for pupils. Bennett (1991) notes that there may often be a mismatch between the intentions of school staff and the reality of classroom tasks experienced by pupils. Frequently, Bennett proposes, the intention to challenge is reduced, in the transfer from teacher to learner, to the repetitive practice of established skills. Part of the solution to this problem lies in the accurate assessment of pupils' prior achievements and experiences (see below) but the deliberate sharing of purpose and intention between teacher and learner can also play an important role. Byers (1994c) argues that the meaning of activities should, where possible, be accessible to pupils from the outset, so that they are 'cued into the activity'. This may be achieved, in some situations, by a clear verbal explanation given to the whole class. The UNESCO pack (1993) describes a dynamic relationship between teacher and learner whereby clear demonstration of the task at hand leads to opportunities for pupils to engage actively in practical learning activities – food technology sessions may often begin in this way, with staff demonstrating the techniques which pupils will later use themselves. In other situations, it may be difficult to share the purpose of activities with whole class groups. Discussion of tasks with small groups of pupils may lead to clarity of intent, while the negotiation of shared objectives with individuals will assist staff in meeting the requirements of the *Code of Practice* (DfE, 1994) with regard to partnership with pupils. Fergusson (1994) gives a host of examples of strategies which staff can use to establish 'anticipation or intention' with pupils for whom the written or spoken word is problematic. These include the use of signs, symbols, objects of reference (Ockelford, 1993) and tactile cues (Ouvry, 1987).

   Maintaining meaning and purpose for learners during classroom activity is likely to be as important as establishing shared intention at the outset. The provision of appropriate levels of support, together with carefully judged interventions, can keep pupils focused as well as guiding them towards new challenges. Staff may need to check pupils when they begin to 'drift', reminding them of previously established codes of conduct or shared performance criteria. Questions may be used to review, reaffirm or redirect activity. Options or points of decision which evolve during learning can be identified and discussed. Harris *et al.* (1996) suggest that the clarification of choices for pupils may have a positive impact upon behaviours which interfere with learning, as well as promoting self-esteem and self-reliance. Again, encouragement, guidance, negotiation and ongoing feedback during tasks can be non-verbal as well as verbal.

Providing appropriate tasks and activities

Well-focused learning opportunities are likely to be those which build upon pupils' previous skills, interests, experiences and aptitudes. Bennett (1991) and OFSTED (1995) stress the significance of the relationship between curricular intent, the reinforcement of previous achievements and fresh challenge. Accurate assessment of pupils' prior learning is clearly of fundamental importance here and it is suggested that this is, once again, an aspect of classroom process which can, and should, meaningfully involve pupils (Fletcher-Campbell and Lee, 1995; Lawson, 1992).

Designing and selecting tasks so that they provide pupils with challenge at an appropriate level is part of the differentiation process whereby educational experiences are adapted to take account of the differing needs, interests, aptitudes and previous experiences of different children. As Hart (1992) points out, differentiation must not become so extreme (constantly withdrawing individuals with particular learning difficulties for 'special programmes', for example) that pupils are marginalized; denied access to a broad range of curricular experiences; segregated from their peers. Viewed from the outset as pathways to access, inclusion and enhanced learning for *all* pupils, differentiation strategies of various kinds (Lewis, 1992) can help staff to tailor class or group activities, focused upon the curriculum, in order to provide opportunities to address individual priorities.

In many instances, this will simply mean planning consolidation or enrichment activity for some pupils while allowing learning to proceed at a slower pace for other members of the group. For other pupils, it may mean conceptualizing a meaningful distinction between experience and achievement. Curriculum-related group experiences can offer relevant, purposeful contexts in which achievements are possible in terms of particular individual objectives. A modern foreign language lesson, for example, may provide opportunities for individual pupils to consolidate their communication skills in interaction with their peers, even though they could not be said to be learning French.

Brown (1996) argues that the notion of experience itself can be differentiated. On one level, a pupil may simply be present during an activity and may be said to have encountered a learning opportunity without any discernible outcome. For some pupils, of course, the willingness to tolerate shared activity may, in itself, be significant. At another level, it may be possible to note that a pupil is aware of, attending to, or focused upon an experience. For some pupils, again, this may constitute an important step on the road towards responding to experiences in positive ways. Smiles; enthusiasm communicated through body language; visual or aural attention redirected when activity shifts location, or even signs of frustration or dissatisfaction, may all express early reactions worthy of note. These sorts of responses may, in turn, lead towards supported involvement and perhaps active participation in group experiences. As has been suggested, outcomes such as turn-taking, communicating or reaching and grasping in new contexts may themselves constitute very significant individual achievements for particular pupils.

The relationship between experience and achievement is therefore complex, but guidance from SCAA (1996) suggests that consideration of issues such as these will form a productive part of the process of designing well–differentiated activity. The recognition of the value of experience can help to promote meaningful involvement in group activity for all pupils, including those with profound and multiple learning difficulties (PMLD). Indeed, Dearing (1995), Tate (1994) and Stevens (1995b) take this debate further. They emphasize that curriculum plans may themselves be differentiated so that some aspects of subjects are treated in depth while others are offered in outline only. This means that pupils, by design, may encounter parts of the curriculum as experiences rather than as opportunities to gain knowledge, understanding or skills in depth. Pupils with moderate learning difficulties (MLD) studying English in Key Stage 3, for example, may explore a

Shakespeare play in depth, reading scenes aloud together in the original language; watching video interpretations; visiting the theatre for a life performance; learning about the historical context. They may, in contrast, experience the narrative skills of Dickens and Hardy in outline only, by watching costume adaptations on video and listening to passages read aloud. In a similar spirit, the programmes of study for history in Key Stage 2 may be implemented in a school for pupils with severe learning difficulties (SLD) by treating the study units concerning 'local history', 'a past non-European society' and 'Victorian Britain' in depth, as topics taught over extended time-scales. The remaining study units may then be treated 'with a lighter touch' (Dearing, 1995), offering broadening and enriching experiences through site visits, museum trips, stories, drama and video. Curriculum planners will arrive at decisions about which aspects of subjects to treat in depth and which to cover in outline in the light of considerations about their relevance to pupils, their accessibility, and the need to maintain breadth and balance in the whole curriculum.

Teaching approaches and learning styles

It is appropriate for teams of teachers, with the support of subject coordinators and senior managers, to come to corporate decisions about curricular intentions at the strategic, long-term planning stage (SCAA, 1995). Individual classroom practitioners will, however, continue to shape those plans in response to the particular needs of particular pupils, and in the light of their own interests and talents, in the short term. Making learning interesting, exciting and engaging for all participants, staff and pupils alike, will remain a primary task for classroom staff. However well-planned the curriculum – however successfully the big issues of progression, continuity, breadth and balance are addressed in schemes of work (Byers and Rose, 1996) – pupils' experiences and achievements will be diminished by classroom activities which are dull, unimaginative, plodding and pedestrian.

In debating the task of 'mapping individual learning routes' through 'meaningful, relevant group activity', Sebba *et al.* (1993) stress intrinsic motivation. They describe ways in which pupils may be encouraged to pursue their individual learning targets by the creation of purposeful contexts within fresh, new experiences. These experiences, relating to well-founded curriculum plans which include the National Curriculum, may stand in contrast to the narrow, utilitarian programmes of one-to-one training in essential skills which have, in the past, characterized schooling for pupils with learning difficulties. The UNESCO pack (UNESCO, 1993) emphasizes the role of choice in providing classroom experiences which offer pupils a stimulating variety of learning opportunities. This is not to argue for an extreme form of *laissez-faire* education in which pupils 'do what they want', but to suggest that involving pupils in the direction which their own learning takes, with the planned generation of points of decision, or options, will be likely both to promote involvement and motivation and to teach young people to become self-managing, self-directing, self-responsible learners. This, surely, is what we ought to mean when we speak of an education for independence.

As has been shown above, OFSTED (1995) indicates that a range of teaching approaches will encourage a similar diversity of learning styles. No teacher in a mainstream setting would argue that pupils should undertake all their learning through a single means of accessing information – solely through reading, for example, only by attending to 'chalk and talk', or always by practical investigation. A well-rounded education will provide all pupils with opportunities to learn in a variety of ways. Ouvry (1987) argues that 'free exploration, trial and error, modelling and imitation, shaping, backward and forward chaining, or a combination'. of such styles will also provide 'effective routes to learning' for pupils with the most profound difficulties. Byers (1994c) discusses the notion of 'whole pupil engagement' in learning opportunities which are relevant, purposeful – and fun. The contention here is that active participation and meaningful involvement can be positively encouraged through styles of learning which involve exploration, pupil initiation and problem-solving. Of course, passive, though attentive, watching, listening or experiencing, may also constitute appropriate ways to learn for most pupils on certain occasions and effective teachers will wish to take account of this variety in making decisions about their approaches to teaching a range of aspects of the whole curriculum.

The significance here of the notion of the match between methodology and curricular intent cannot be over-emphasized. *The OFSTED Handbook* (1995) lists 'exposition, explanation, demonstration, discussion, practical activity, investigation, testing and problem-solving' as potentially useful teaching methods and notes that the 'use of questions' should probe pupils' knowledge and understanding and challenge their thinking. It will be apparent here that these methods cannot all be used at once. The value of a problem-solving activity will be destroyed by prior demonstration and explanation. Exposition may follow practical activity but is likely to be an inappropriate way to support pupils' learning during an investigation. However, these examples give some idea of the range of approaches which can be employed, in balance, over time.

Access, support and resources

The revised National Curriculum (DfE, 1995) also encourages classroom staff to provide for pupils a range of adapted modes of access to learning activities. The common requirements in the PoS for all subjects suggest that pupils may need to use augmentative means of communication, involving signs, symbols or information technology, for instance, as well as adapted equipment and resources. While the lists of potential modes of access are not exhaustive, the message is clear. As well as supplementing worksheets with symbols or transferring writing tasks onto the computer, educators should feel free to adapt, extend, augment and interpret the PoS for National Curriculum subjects in any way in order to promote access for pupils to the concepts, knowledge, skills and understandings which lie behind the language of the orders. It is also worth noting here that decisions about the availability to pupils of resources and equipment can have a significant impact upon their development as independent learners. While there are obviously some items of school equipment which, for safety reasons, will only be operated under supervision, it is possible to promote active participation, initiation and self-directed learning by opening up access for pupils to an increasing range of resources. On one level this may simply mean keeping items like paper, crayons and glue in trays or on shelves at an appropriate height and accepting that pupils will only learn to become responsible resource users through experience. For many pupils, however, the ready availability of personal computers, tape recorders and communication aids may be of fundamental importance. These should not be items which are shut away for supervised use at certain times of the week but considered, in many instances, as integral parts of general classroom activity.

If it is appropriate to adopt this flexible attitude to the use of resources, it is also important to consider the role of support staff. Ware (1994a), in her discussion of classroom organization, draws attention to the need to plan for the targeting of support time in order to promote equality of opportunity for all pupils. This may not mean that all pupils receive the same amount of support. It does mean that the time which is available is directed equitably towards those pupils for whom adult support in particular learning situations is appropriate and productive. Balshaw (1991) and Fletcher-Campbell (1992) argue that the effective use of classroom support is founded upon whole-school policy for team work and cooperation, and in particular upon:

- shared understandings about pupils' needs and difficulties;
- shared intentions about curricular aims, priorities for individual pupils, classroom management issues and teaching approaches;
- shared development of skills, interests, awareness, expertise and collaborative attitudes between all members of staff;
- shared interpretations of professional roles, responsibilities and lines of management.

Steel (1991) notes the significant role that monitoring, evaluation and review by senior staff can play in securing progress towards the kind of collaborative approaches elaborated by Lacey and Lomas (1993). All parties agree that effective partnership between professionals is founded upon shared planning. Hornby (1994) and Gascoigne (1995) remind us that parents should also be seen as partners in the kind of 'social network system' (Appleton and Minchom, 1991) model of collaboration since championed by the *Code of Practice* (DfE, 1994).

Interaction

It is beyond the scope of this chapter to survey, in any kind of appropriate detail, work in the major field of communication and interaction. It may be worth noting, however, that experience in schools and during development programmes indicates that staff in schools for pupils with learning difficulties are pursuing, with vigour, interest and commitment, the kinds of interactive strategies described by Dunne and Bennett (1990), Rose (1991), Sebba *et al.* (1995) and Byers and Rose (1996). Expertise in planning sessions involving cooperative and collaborative groupings of pupils with MLD and SLD is acknowledged by many teachers as part of their repertoire of class and group management strategies. Pupils who are not yet ready for the challenge of working in a larger group may be given experience of paired learning as part of a process of development towards the team approach. Peer coaching, where pupils revisit, refocus and extend their understandings and achievements by supporting partners who are working at a slower pace, is seen as a useful method of promoting and consolidating learning for all concerned.

Planning group activities which meaningfully involve pupils with PMLD presents a greater challenge. Here the role of staff in finding non-directive, empathic modes of interaction with pupils in order to facilitate contact, cooperation and communication between young people and their peers is crucial. Nind and Hewett's work (1994) on intensive interaction illuminates the territory in instructive detail. Although the authors suggest that many young people with very severe learning difficulties may never become 'sophisticated and subtle enough in their interactive abilities to learn to socialise and play together', and adhere to a position of 'tasklessness' in which interaction is an end in itself, many practitioners are finding that the techniques of intensive interaction can open young people up to the possibilities of contact with their peers and participation in the curriculum. Watson (1994) describes pupils who are 'relating better to other pupils', 'more involved socially' and making progress in terms of language and interpersonal behaviour after a programme of intensive interaction. Ware (1994b) notes that pupils who are encouraged to respond to adults within the classroom environment become more likely to initiate interactions themselves. This would bear out Nind and Hewett's evidence of 'students beginning to enter dialogue-like exchanges' and becoming less isolated after experiencing intensive interaction.

If staff are to play a part in developing young people's experiences of one another, they will be forced to consider subtle shifts of persona. The task of becoming a surrogate peer may not co-exist comfortably with the roles of teacher, curriculum manager or disciplinarian. Just as staff who seek to become advocates on behalf of their clients experience a potential conflict of interest, so empathic interactors may feel uneasy slipping back into more traditional roles within the classroom. Adopting intensive interaction as another teaching technique may propel staff towards a profound review of the complex matrix of roles, rules, routines and responsibilities within the classroom.

Reflection and review

This sort of review of methodology will be familiar to the practitioner who has learned to become professionally reflective. Skrtic (1991, p.35) argues that,

> the invention of new programs for unfamiliar contingencies through divergent thinking and inductive reasoning on the part of multidisciplinary teams of professionals engaged in a reflective discourse,

is an inevitable and welcome part of life in a 'problem-solving organization' such as a school catering for a diversity of pupils. SCAA (1996) and Byers and Rose (1996) emphasize the significance of monitoring, review and evaluation in all phases of the work of schools. Thus the review of short-term pupil priorities drives the process of revising long-term goals; pupil progress and achievement are used as measures in evaluating the effectiveness of schemes of work in terms of method as well as content; reshaping curriculum plans will lead to the revision of policy and the consideration of new strategies for the ongoing development of the school as a community endeavour. Whatever the future of the OFSTED inspection process, the creation of a culture of school self-evaluation and self-review, driven by a celebration of pupil diversity as a positive force, has to be seen as very healthy.

If schools are to move forward in this spirit, then the task of arriving, through assessment and diagnosis, at a view of the needs of individual pupils remains central (SCAA, 1996). The design of appropriate tasks and activities, as discussed earlier in this chapter, is founded upon accurate assessment, for example. If schools are also to meet the requirements of the *Code of Practice* (DfE, 1994) and the mood of a revitalized National Record of Achievement, then the involvement of pupils themselves in this process will be pivotal (Tilstone, 1991). Shining examples of imaginative and effective strategies for pupil self-recording can be found in most schools for pupils with learning difficulties. The task of further promoting self-assessment and self-review appears on many development plans for improving policy and practice in assessment, recording and reporting. Creating routes of increased access for pupils to these reflective aspects of the learning process is one thing. Moving steadily towards pupils taking on increased responsibility for their own learning is another.

Mitchell (1994) describes a number of initiatives in which pupils and students of various ages are encouraged to become involved in sharing target-setting and negotiating performance criteria as well as actively participating in review and assessment. These ways of working, Mitchell suggests, 'allow pupils to take a degree of control over their learning – and thereby, their lives' on an individual basis, just as the creation of student councils or committees (Winup, 1994) can provide pupils with routes whereby their views can contribute to the generation of curricular options and whole-school development (Fletcher and Gordon, 1994; Tyne, 1994).

Summary

It is the contention of this chapter that careful consideration of classroom processes must be seen as part of whole-curriculum planning for all pupils. Certainly, pupils with special educational needs will benefit from the levels of planning detail proposed here. What is suggested by the research (Ainscow and Muncey, 1989) is that schools which provide effective teaching for those pupils who experience learning difficulties will be likely to be effective schools in general. Of course, good teaching and effective learning do not occur in isolation. Ainscow (1991) notes the importance of:

- leaders committed to addressing the needs of all;
- staff who have confidence in their own abilities to meet a diversity of needs;
- an ethos in which all pupils are expected to achieve;
- structures which provide support for individual members of staff;
- whole-school commitment to curricular breadth, balance and access for all;
- systems for monitoring and reviewing progress.

Best (1989), in advocating a whole-curriculum model for pupils' personal and social development, emphasizes the role of school managers in providing inspiration, leadership and appreciative support, as well as opportunities for professional development, adequate resources and constructive appraisal. In times when criticism of school staff in general, and the identification of 'failing teachers' in particular, seem to be a requirement of any person commenting upon educational quality, it is important to reflect upon the lot of the many enthusiastic and committed teachers who become disillusioned, disenchanted and disaffected under poor leaders and inadequate managers. If school staff are to devote the energy, forethought, intelligence, cooperation and effort which effective classroom processes inevitably entail, then they have a right to expect their work to be valued and supported in equal measure.

References

Ainscow, M. (1991) 'Effective schools for all: an alternative approach to special needs in education', in Ainscow, M. (ed.) *Effective Schools for All*, London: David Fulton.
Ainscow, M. and Muncey, J. (1989) *Meeting Individual Needs in the Primary School*, London: David Fulton.
Appleton, P. and Minchom, P. (1991) 'Models of parent partnership and child development centres', *Child Care, Health and Development*, 17, 1, 27–37.

Ashdown, R., Carpenter, B. and Bovair, K. (1991) *The Curriculum Challenge,* London: Falmer Press.

Balshaw, M. (1991) *Help in the Classroom,* London: David Fulton.

Bennett, N. (1991) 'The quality of classroom learning experiences for children with special educational needs', in Ainscow, M. (ed.) *Effective Schools for All,* London: David Fulton.

Best, R. (1989) 'Pastoral care: some reflections and a re-statement', *Pastoral Care,* 7, 4, 7–13.

Brown, E. (1996) *Religious Education for All,* London: David Fulton.

Byers, R. (1994a) 'The Dearing Review of the National Curriculum', *British Journal of Special Education,* 21, 3, 92–96.

Byers, R. (1994b) 'Teaching as dialogue: teaching approaches and learning styles in schools for pupils with learning difficulties', in Coupe O'Kane, J. and Smith, B. (eds) *Taking Control: enabling people with learning difficulties,* London: David Fulton.

Byers, R. (1994c) 'Providing opportunities for effective learning', in Rose, R., Fergusson, A., Coles, C., Byers, R. and Banes, D. (eds) *Implementing the Whole Curriculum for Pupils with Learning Difficulties,* London: David Fulton.

Byers, R. and Rose, R. (1996) *Planning the Curriculum for Pupils with Special Educational Needs – A practical guide,* London: David Fulton.

Carpenter, B. (1995) 'Building an inclusive curriculum', in Ashcroft, K. and Palacio, D. (eds) *The Primary Teachers Guide to the New National Curriculum,* London: Falmer Press.

Dearing, R. (1993) *The National Curriculum and its Assessment – Interim report,* York: NCC/SEAC.

Dearing, R. (1995) 'Foreword', in SCAA *Planning the Curriculum at Key Stages 1 and 2,* London: SCAA.

Department for Education (1994) *Code of Practice on the Identification and Assessment of Special Educational Needs,* London: HMSO.

Department for Education (1995) *The National Curriculum,* London: HMSO.

Dunne, E. and Bennett, N. (1990) *Talking and Learning in Groups,* London: Macmillan.

Fergusson, A. (1994) 'Planning for communication', in Rose, R., Fergusson, A., Coles, C., Byers, R. and Banes, D. (eds) *Implementing the Whole Curriculum for Pupils with Learning Difficulties,* London: David Fulton.

Fletcher, W. and Gordon, J. (1994) 'Personal and social education in a school for pupils with severe learning difficulties', in Rose, R., Fergusson, A., Coles, C., Byers, R. and Banes, D. (eds) *Implementing the Whole Curriculum for Pupils with Learning Difficulties,* London: David Fulton.

Fletcher-Campbell, F. (1992) 'How can we use an extra pair of hands?', *British Journal of Special Education,* 19, 4, 141–3.

Fletcher-Campbell, F. and Lee, B. (1995) *Small Steps of Progress in the National Curriculum – Final report,* Slough: NFER.

Gascoigne, E. (1995) *Working with Parents as Partners in SEN – Home and school: a working alliance,* London: David Fulton.

Harris, J., Cook, M. and Upton, G. (1996) *Pupils with Severe Learning Disabilities who Present Challenging Behaviours: A whole school approach to assessment and intervention,* Kidderminster: BILD.

Hart, S. (1992) 'Differentiation – way forward or retreat?', *British Journal of Special Education,* 19, 1, 10–12.

Hornby, G. (1994) *Counselling in Child Disability – Skills for working with parents,* London: Chapman and Hall.

Humphreys, K. (1995) 'Facing up to whose reality? Major Throng to Ground Control', open letter to *E.Qual.S.* members, The University of Northumbria: Special Educational Needs Resource Centre.

Lacey, P. and Lomas, J. (1993) *Support Services and the Curriculum,* London: David Fulton.

Lawson, H. (1992) *Practical Record Keeping for Special Schools – Resource material for staff development,* London: David Fulton.

Lewis, A. (1992) 'From planning to practice', *British Journal of Special Education,* 19, 1, 24–7.

Mitchell, S. (1994) 'Some implications of the High/Scope curriculum and the education of children with learning difficulties', in Coupe O'Kane, J. and Smith, B. (eds) *Taking Control – Enabling people with learning difficulties,* London: David Fulton.

National Curriculum Council (1990) *Curriculum Guidance 3: The whole curriculum,* York: NCC.

Nind, M. and Hewett, D. (1994) *Access to Communication: Developing the basics of communication with people with severe learning difficulties through intensive interaction,* London: David Fulton.

Ockelford, A. (1993) *Objects of Reference,* London: RNIB.

OFSTED (1995) *The OFSTED Handbook: Guidance on the inspection of special schools,* London: HMSO.

Ouvry, C. (1987) *Educating Children with Profound Handicaps,* Kidderminster: BIMH.

Rose, R. (1991) 'A jigsaw approach to group work', *British Journal of Special Education,* 18, 2, 54–7.

SCAA (1994) *Consultation on the National Curriculum – An introduction,* London: SCAA.

SCAA (1995) *Planning the Curriculum at Key Stages 1 and 2,* London: SCAA.

SCAA (1996) *Planning the Curriculum for Pupils with Profound and Multiple Learning Difficulties,* London: SCAA.

Sebba, J. and Byers, R. (1992) 'The National Curriculum: control or liberation for pupils with learning difficulties?', *The Curriculum Journal,* 3, 2, 143–60.

Sebba, J. and Fergusson, A. (1991) 'Reducing the marginalisation of pupils with severe learning difficulties through curricular initiatives', in Ainscow, M. (ed.) *Effective Schools for All,* London: David Fulton.

Sebba, J., Byers, R. and Rose, R. (1995) *Redefining the Whole Curriculum for Pupils with Learning Difficulties* (2nd edn), London: David Fulton.

Skrtic, T (1991) 'Students with special educational needs: artifacts of the traditional curriculum' in Ainscow, M. (ed.) *Effective Schools for All,* London: David Fulton.

Steel, F. (1991) 'Working collaboratively within a multi-disciplinary framework', in Tilstone, C. (ed.) *Teaching Pupils with Severe Learning Difficulties,* London: David Fulton.

Stevens, C. (1995a) 'Foreword', in Byers, R. and Rose, R. (eds) *Planning the Curriculum for Pupils with Special Educational Needs,* London: David Fulton.

Stevens, C. (1995b) 'News from SCAA', *British Journal of Special Education,* 22, 1, 30–31.

Tate, N. (1994) 'Target vision', *Times Educational Supplement,* 2 December.

Tilstone, C. (1991) 'Pupils' views', in Tilstone, C. (ed.) *Teaching Pupils with Severe Learning Difficulties – Practical approaches,* London: David Fulton.

Tyne, J. (1994) 'Advocacy: not just another subject', in Rose, R., Fergusson, A., Coles, C., Byers, R. and Banes, D. (eds) *Implementing the Whole Curriculum for Pupils with Learning Difficulties,* London: David Fulton.

UNESCO (1993) *Special Needs in the Classroom – Student materials,* Paris: UNESCO.

Ware, J. (1994a) 'Classroom organisation', in Ware, J. (ed.) *Educating Children with Profound and Multiple Learning Difficulties,* London: David Fulton.

Ware, J. (1994b) 'Using interaction in the education of pupils with PMLDs (i). Creating contingency sensitive environments', in Ware, J. (ed.) *Educating Children with Profound and Multiple Learning Difficulties,* London: David Fulton.

Watson, J. (1994) 'Using interaction in the education of pupils with PMLDs (ii). Intensive interaction: two case studies', in Ware, J. (ed.) *Educating Children with Profound and Multiple Learning Difficulties,* London: David Fulton.

Winup, K. (1994) 'The role of a student committee in promotion of independence among school leavers', in Coupe O'Kane, J. and Smith, B. (eds) *Taking Control: Enabling people with learning difficulties,* London: David Fulton.

Chapter 16

Assessment

Ann Lewis

It is a truism that learning must start from the point at which the pupil is; how could it be otherwise? What is harder to achieve in practice is that teaching begins from where the pupil is or, to put it another way, that teaching matches the pupil's learning needs. This stance is endorsed in the *Code of Practice on the Identification and Assessment of Special Educational Needs* (DfE, 1994) which states that 'At the heart of every school and every class lies a cycle of planning, teaching and assessing' (2:1). The same point is made very strongly in the School Curriculum and Assessment Authority's (SCAA) 1996 document in relation to planning the curriculum for pupils with profound and multiple learning difficulties (PMLD). That document explicitly links short-term planning with ongoing teacher assessment and, in turn, such assessment with record-keeping. A discussion of record-keeping is beyond the scope of this chapter (cf. Byers and Rose, 1996; Lawson, 1992) but effective assessment procedures will need to link with records of children's learning and experiences.

The Task Group on Assessment and Testing (TGAT) produced a report (DES/WO, 1988) which described assessment as being at the heart of promoting children's learning. It emphasised the potential breadth of assessment instruments and noted that these might encompass interviews, various tasks and quizzes. One should add 'observation' as a key assessment tool in relation to pupils with special needs. The common goal of these various approaches is to obtain valid information about a pupil's attainments. Importantly, the TGAT Report stressed that the assessment process 'is the servant, not the master, of the curriculum' (para 4). It is worth reiterating the TGAT Report's stance:

> The assessment process ... should not be a bolt-on addition at the end. Rather, it should be an integral part of the educational process, continually providing both 'feedback' and 'feed forward' (para 4).

In many ways the TGAT Report's vision of the nature of National Curriculum linked assessment has been lost or forgotten. However, although the details are now different, the principles remain valid.

The National Curriculum can be seen as one way of fostering, through assessment, a matching of pupil and curriculum. Early documentation about end of Key Stage assessment emphasized the links between teaching, learning and assessment (SEAC, 1990). Later announcements and materials (for example, Shephard, 1994) have made a stronger distinction between continuous teacher assessment, to be linked to teaching (i.e.

formative assessment), and summative assessments, made at the ends of Key Stages, explicitly for reporting purposes.

Gipps (1994) has drawn attention to the differences between 'ta' (non-moderated teacher assessment, used for formative purposes, or just within the classroom), 'TA' (moderated teacher assessment used for reporting purposes outside the classroom) and external tests. One might add, in relation to pupils with statements of special educational needs (SEN), a fourth type of assessment – that linked with statutory assessments. This chapter focuses on the first of these four types of assessment of pupils' learning: continuous formative assessment (see Lewis 1995a, 1996 for discussion of standard tests and tasks in relation to pupils with special educational needs).

The National Foundation for Educational Research produced a report (NFER, 1995; Fletcher Campbell, 1996; see also SCAA, 1996) on the assessment and recording of small steps of progress in the National Curriculum which identified some questions about assessment that schools might consider. These are summarized below:

- Is assessment sufficiently accurate and focused to inform future teaching and enable the setting of goals?
- Are assessment opportunities and activities built into schemes of work/programmes of learning?
- Do records include details of pupils' experiences or achievements and, if appropriate, the extent of support provided?
- Is assessment used to monitor progression towards short- and long-term goals?
- Is assessment used as a way of recognising and valuing all achievements and progress, however small, in all aspects of the curriculum and in whatever contexts?
- Is pupils' participation in self-assessment and recording actively promoted?
- What evidence is kept and collated to support teachers' assessments?

These questions provide a broad framework within which the ideas in this chapter can be located. Further discussion of these questions, particularly ways of responding to each question, can be found in SCAA's examination of the curriculum for pupils with PMLD (SCAA, 1996).

The NFER project has also supplied helpful evidence about what teachers look for in assessment approaches. Suggestions made in relation to accreditation of learning at Key Stage (KS) 4 for pupils with special needs have relevance for other age groups (Fletcher-Campbell, 1996). These features tie in with the questions posed above and highlight some particular characteristics teachers were seeking in accreditation of learning for pupils with SEN. As teachers were looking for these features in externally derived assessment procedures, it is reasonable to suppose that they would also look for them in their own assessment procedures. Some of the key points were:

- a small steps approach linked with regular and frequent reviews and target-setting
- recognition of the use of the same skill in various contexts
- recognition of experience as well as attainment
- use of a variety of means of assessment
- flexibility of content and approach so that assessment methods suited pupils with various learning styles, interests and ages
- focus on achievement
- maximum pupil involvement in self-assessment.

These points are implicit in the following discussion.

Monitoring and review cycle

The *Code of Practice* (DfE, 1994) sets out five stages through which the assessment of a pupil thought to have special educational needs may move. The stages are not compulsory, but the Code describes each stage as a guide to help schools monitor such pupils' needs and progress. The features that have been found to be associated with perceived usefulness of the Code, such as Special Educational Needs Coordinator (SENCO) involvement in senior management, collaboration between teachers and a situation that fosters close monitoring of individual pupils across subjects) (Lewis *et al.*, 1996) are likely to be found in special schools. Thus special schools are likely to find stages 1-3 in the Code a useful framework even though these have been put forward as 'pre-statement' guidelines. In this chapter relevant aspects of these are extrapolated as a guideline for the assessment of pupils attending special schools or for teacher assessments of pupils with statements of SEN in mainstream schools.

In a special school, it would be reasonable to adapt stages 1 to 3 of the Code as a baseline position applicable to all pupils. The 'home' teacher will be continually gathering relevant information, consulting the parents and taking action to prevent difficulties from arising or escalating. The Code lists the types of information relevant at stage 1; adapted for pupils in special schools or pupils with statements in mainstream schools, these might include:

- contextual school and class information highlighting ways in which classroom organization may be inadvertently exacerbating a pupil's difficulties
- class records
- National Curriculum attainments
- standardized test results or profiles
- records of achievement
- reports on the pupil in school settings
- observations about the pupil's behaviour
- parental views on the pupil's health and development
- parental perceptions of the pupil's progress and behaviour
- parental views about possible factors contributing to the pupil's difficulties (see Hughes and Carpenter 1991)
- parental views about action the school might take
- the pupil's perceptions of his or her difficulties
- the pupil's views about how difficulties might be addressed
- relevant information from other sources, such as medical or health services
- reports supporting the statement
- information gleaned from annual reviews
- links with mainstream – nature, frequency, duration, purpose, monitoring arrangements, perceptions (see Lewis, 1995b)
- links with external support agencies, including evaluation of these links for individual pupils
- re-evaluation of the need for a statement and/or special school placement.

Information may also be sought, with the parents' consent, from the pupil's GP. It is likely that individual education plans (IEPs) (see DfE 1994 pp. 26–29) will be an appropriate way to monitor progress.

Assessments through classroom observation

Observation of pupils is a vital first step in planning how their learning can be fostered. Observation can take many forms, structured or unstructured, involving the teacher working with the pupil or remaining distanced. When and how teachers observe pupils will depend both on the aims of that observation and on what is realistic in a busy classroom. While teachers recognize that watching how pupils are learning is an important part of teaching, it requires careful planning to incorporate such activity into everyday classroom life.

Teachers may make time for observing pupils by doing more collaborative teaching. A variety of occasions arising unexpectedly (for example, in the playground) may provide the opportunity for informal observational assessments. Adults, other than the teacher, might also carry out the observations if given clear and detailed training about how to do this. I have worked with nursery nurses in primary schools who, using structured observation schedules, have monitored the integration of pupils from special schools (see Lewis, 1995b). Similar work is described in accounts of Sunnyside Primary School's experiences of integration (Bell and Colbeck, 1989). This type of work can generate valuable data about whether or not pupils with difficulties in learning are isolated in mainstream school classes and about the types of activities in which they are engaged.

The following discussion considers various approaches to continuous teacher assessments of pupils' development and learning, from relatively informal approaches to more formal and pupil-specific methods. Although they are of general relevance, they are particularly important in the planning of teaching and learning.

General classroom observations

A variety of general observations helps the teacher to get to know individual pupils. They are also important in order to avoid unwarranted assumptions about apparent deficits needing to be taught specifically. Campione (1989) has referred to this as the 'leap to instruction'.

- In which kinds of activity does the pupil concentrate better or less well? What are typical periods of concentration for the pupil on particular activities?
- Which kinds of activity seem to be most meaningful for the pupil?
- In which kinds of activity is the pupil most confident?
- Does the pupil have a preference for certain kinds of materials (for example, micro-computer based or linked with a particular piece of equipment such as a synchrofax or *Language Master* machine; trackerball, mouse, on-screen clicker or touch screen when working on a computer)?
- Does the pupil work better at certain times of the day (for example, always tired in the first part of the morning or regularly livelier after the midday break)?
- Are there particular classroom friends with whom the pupil works well or poorly?
- What motivates the pupil to learn?
- What special interests does the pupil have?
- In which kinds of classroom grouping does the pupil work better or less well?
- Does the pupil prefer a noisy or quiet working environment?
- How does the pupil respond if given scope for developing his or her own ideas?

All these things relate to getting to know the pupil and, once identified, they can be built on constructively so that classroom experiences foster learning. In the longer term, pupils who favour a particular learning style (for example, using computer-based materials) will need to have experience in using other approaches also.

The importance of motivation in influencing what pupils are apparently capable of is illustrated in the following account. A 7-year-old, Sarah, seemed unable to write even a sentence towards a story or 'news'. However, one day Sarah received a party invitation from a friend, Marie, in another class. She took the invitation home and showed it to her father, who wrote a reply saying that Sarah could come to the party. Sarah lost this note on her way to school the next day and became very upset about this. Her class teacher reassured her, saying that it would be all right as she would pass on the message to Marie's teacher for her to give to Marie. However, later that day Sarah handed her teacher a carefully written note saying: 'To Marie, I am coming to your party. From Sarah.' Sarah had written the note and may have had help from other pupils with spellings but, highly anxious not to miss the party, she had been prompted to write a message. The message had a real purpose and brought out her writing abilities.

These general observations may alert the teacher to possible hearing, visual or motor impairments in a pupil (see Lewis, 1995a for further guidelines concerning these areas). If evidence about suspected difficulties is collected by care-givers and teachers, then health professionals have a useful supplement to medical diagnosis. This broader picture may help to rule out non-medical factors influencing behaviour. For example, a pupil may show fear in physical education (PE) activities in school. If this goes alongside coordination problems at school and at home then resultant action will differ from that in which this does not happen, and fearfulness in school PE seems more related to a lack of self-confidence.

Teachers of children with learning difficulties may also have to respond to a range of pupils' medical problems, notably asthma, epilepsy and diabetes. A recent asthma awareness campaign has suggested that teachers should not, as has apparently been common practice in many schools, keep inhalers in a 'safe place' which is inaccessible to the pupils. Instead pupils who may need inhalers should have ready access to these at all times. Work by Bannon *et al.* (1992) showed that few teachers had received information about childhood epilepsy and they lacked confidence in dealing with it. However, the teachers had a good general knowledge of this condition and adequate awareness of the likely difficulties experienced by a pupil with epilepsy. The authors concluded that local health authorities have an important role to play in providing appropriate training packages for teachers. There are a number of publications outlining the implications for teachers of pupils' medical conditions (for example, ATL, 1994; Webster *et al.*, 1994).

Systematic observation

It may be appropriate to carry out some systematic observations of pupils, using structured observation schedules. Roffey *et al.*, (1994) identify four means of structuring classroom observations. These strategies are: making a tally, taking field notes, using a checklist, or monitoring behaviour at timed intervals. The latter involves recording pupils's activities, using a schedule based on prespecified lists or categories of observed behaviours, often monitored over regular time periods (for example, every 30 seconds). The use of these schedules was noted earlier in relation to using different adults to make classroom observations. Systematic schedules are particularly useful for monitoring social behaviour. They can also be useful when monitoring a group of pupils in order to ascertain, for example, which pupils in the group contribute most to the conversation.

The following approach (adapted from Sylva *et al.*, 1980) was used by staff in several schools who were monitoring the kinds of classroom interaction in which pupils with severe learning difficulties in primary schools were involved. A similar, but more tightly structured, example of this approach was used in the PACE project which investigated the impact of the National Curriculum at Key Stage (KS) 1 (see Pollard *et al.*, 1994). The approach could be adapted for a variety of situations and aims (discussed more fully in Lewis 1995a).

There are both strengths and disadvantages in using structured, systematic observation schedules within a classroom. If the schedule is clearly structured and appropriate for the aims then it can supply useful information. It can show whether or not a teacher's impression is justified, for example, that a particular pupil habitually concentrates much better on oral than on written activities, or that two pupils work more productively together than separately. However, a structured observation schedule may be difficult to use effectively. Pupils may interrupt or behave differently because they are aware of being monitored. The use of structured observation schedules also requires at least two adults to be present, one to carry out the observations and one to work with the class. Several detailed accounts of formal observational methods (for example, Croll, 1986; Sylva and Neill, 1990; Wragg, 1993) expand on their use in classrooms.

Observational methods are useful ways in which teachers can build judgements about individual pupils and the dynamics of the classroom. They may also point to features of the classroom which the teacher could improve, such as making certain types of resources more accessible or changing the location of some materials so that withdrawn pupils become more involved with other pupils. So far in this chapter, identifying the point reached by a pupil has focused on observations of pupils's general development and behaviour. Observational methods need to be supplemented with assessments which focus on curricular tasks.

Pupil-adult conferences

It is useful if the teacher can observe a pupil both working alone on a particular activity and working alongside the teacher. This is important because it enables the teacher to assess, first, the processes of learning and not just the end-products and, second, what the pupil can do alone compared with what he or she can do with some guidance. This kind of activity is described in the TGAT report (DES/WO, 1988) and in National Curriculum-linked assessment materials (SEAC, 1990).

The National Curriculum Council (NCC, 1992a; 1992b) and Byers and Rose (1996) give examples of starting points for assessment activities which could be used as part of pupil-adult conferences. For example, a pupil could be given 2D or 3D shapes for sorting. On what basis does the pupil sort the shapes when asked to sort them into 'the shapes that go together'? What does the pupil do when given a prompt (e.g. 'look at the colours')? Does he/she use this prompt or treat it as an irrelevant cue? If the latter, does this seem to be because the word 'colour' has not been understood? How does the pupil explain his or her sorting pattern? This apparently straightforward example can generate information about the pupil's hearing, vision, colour blindness, vocabulary (receptive and expressive), manipulative skills, attention and distractability and motivation, as well as the mathematical understanding being targetted. By talking through with the pupil (or communicating through sign) the adult may gain information about these diverse areas, rather than assuming that completion or otherwise of the task reflects strength/limitations specifically and exclusively in the targetted area of understanding.

Organizing pupil-adult conferences
- Acknowledge that it will be done relatively infrequently but in some detail for individual pupils.
- Acknowledge that some pupils will need this more frequently than do other pupils.
- Discourage other pupils from interrupting the activity.
- Avoid handing over this task to other adults in the classroom unless they fully understand its purpose and how to carry it out.
- Making time for pupil–adult conferences may (depending on pupil–adult ratios) require that teachers make more use of techniques in which pupils work without direct teacher involvement (e.g., collaborative work with classmates and self-checking games).
- It may be useful to tape-record or video the conference so that it can be analysed later. The tape will also provide evidence about the pupil's learning which could be kept as a record. Pupils often like to hear such tapes replayed and to comment on their learning and interaction with the teacher.
- Capitalize on occasions when the pupil is highly motivated and has a good relationship with the teacher, especially if this happens infrequently.

Key questions
- Can the pupil explain why he or she is carrying out an activity in a certain way?
- What can the pupil do alone, compared with prompting? This is also very important for identifying able pupils who are doing work well below that of which they are capable.
- What can the pupil do already on his or her own? (Teaching should extend not duplicate this.)
- Has the pupil retained earlier steps in learning? For example, a pupil who has difficulty in completing tens and units sums involving carrying might have forgotten the 'base 10' concept underlying the activity.
- Can the pupil complete a given task in one context and transfer it to another (e.g., add numbers using beads on a string and using a number line)?
- Can the pupil apply knowledge and skills in a new context (e.g. multiply numbers in a maths game and use multiplication facts to work out the numbers of rulers needed by groups of pupils in an art activity)?
- Can the pupil respond to a variety of question types (e.g. questions requiring recall, evaluation, speculation, problem-solving)? (For example, after a science activity: what happened when we...? Could it have been done in a better way...? What might happen if we...? How did you feel about...?)
- Does the pupil understand what he or she is being asked to do? For example, does he or she understand the vocabulary of the teacher's question?

Swann (1988) gives a good example which illustrates this last point. He describes talking to a 5-year-old girl during her first week at school. The girl was drawing around flat, plastic shapes. He asked her, in the course of the conversation, how many sides the square had and in response the girl laid out, side-by-side, three other squares. He put them back and asked the girl to show him a side of a square. She pointed to the centre of the top surface of one square. He goes on to discuss the various and ambiguous contexts in which the girl may have come across the word 'side' (sides of a team, sitting side-by-side, the side of a cupboard, etc.) and conjectures that the girl's responses reflected her thinking through different meanings of 'side'. He concludes that the pupil's 'difficulty' with the task was largely illusory and that the real problem was a failure of communication on his part, and not the pupil's.

The ambiguity of teachers' talk, particularly when pupils may not have become socialized into, or do not recognize, school procedures and expectations, has been documented by Cleave *et al.* (1982) and by Willes (1983). Both sets of research provide salutary reading, as they indicate the potential for misunderstandings in classrooms. Examples include a pupil who interpreted the teacher's instruction, 'Would you like to join the story group now', as an invitation ('no thank you') and pupils being confused by the ambiguities of the teacher's request for them to 'line up'. Similarly, a friend was recently asked by her daughter for some sweets. My friend replied 'You want some sweets... what's the magic word?' Her daughter paused thoughtfully then said, 'abracadabra?' Pupils who find school learning difficult may be slower than other pupils to tune into the specific language conventions of the classroom.

Diagnostic assessment
There is a relatively strong tradition of pupil–adult conferences, in special needs contexts, for diagnostic purposes. This is illustrated in various approaches to assessing and helping pupils with reading difficulties. Pupil–adult conferences are widely supported in this context, although there are differing views about the best focus of the conference. Two contrasting foci have been strongly advocated. One focus, developed from formal testing of 'sub-skills', has been on the psychological sub-skills believed to underlie particular tasks, notably reading. Thus, for example, many 'reading readiness' tests have included assessments of the pupil's visual sequencing (for example, identifying the next letter(s) in a regular sequence), auditory sequencing (for example, recalling aural sequences of letters or numbers) and visual memory (for example, drawing from memory a shape shown briefly). The rationale was that reading was composed of discrete and identifiable sub-skills which could be isolated and measured. It then seemed logical to identify and remedy, by specific teaching, any weak sub-skills. Unfortunately, there was generally little transfer from resultant proficiency in the sub-skill(s) to facility in reading (see Adams, 1990).

A different focus in pupil–adult conferences has been on analyses of pupils' errors in a particular activity. Systematic analyses of errors (or 'miscues') can provide useful clues for teaching. For example, there are different implications for teaching in the case of James, who repeatedly makes phonic errors in spellings (for example, 'storiz' for 'stories'), compared with Toni, who fails to apply a common spelling rule (for example, she writes 'storys' for 'stories', 'worrys' for 'worries', etc.). How the teacher chooses on which errors to focus and how these are analysed will reflect his or her theories (possibly implicit) about the nature of the knowledge/skills and the processes of acquiring these.

Communication between pupils can provide a valuable and unique basis from which to assess competence in various domains, particularly linguistic. The task of tutoring another pupil can push the child tutor into explaining a task and so articulating thought processes. Thus the tutoring process can draw out social, cognitive and linguistic skills which may not otherwise be revealed. Pupils with severe learning difficulties placed in the position of tutoring non-disabled children have been found to produce unexpectedly complex linguistic structures and a variety of social skills (Lewis, 1995b). If diagnostic procedures include pupil-pupil interaction as well as pupil-teacher interaction, then there is a much broader base to the assessments.

Statutory end of Key Stage teacher assessments and tasks

This chapter has been concerned with formative teacher assessments of pupils with special educational needs. These feed into teacher assessments of pupils at the ends of the Key Stages. Pupils with special needs may take statutory tests but are more likely to take the statutory tasks. In addition, they will, like other pupils, be involved in summative teacher assessments.

Reports from SCAA on end of Key Stage assessments have shown that teachers at KS1 were more well-disposed to tasks than to tests (SCAA, 1995a). This may be because the tasks were closer in style to the types of teacher assessment routinely carried out in classrooms. The support for the assessment tasks can be interpreted as showing that teachers were retaining, or increasing, confidence in their assessment skills. There have been indications that the DfEE is considering making the tasks optional at KS2 and KS3 (DfEE, 1996). This would lead to considerable savings (approximately £1,000,000 per year) which, it is suggested, could be used to support teacher assessment at KS2. Such a move would reflect increased support for teacher assessment and would change the target from special needs groups (lower and higher ability) to more generic teacher assessment skills.

The emphasis given by SCAA (1995b) on the equality of status between tests and teacher assessments has been generally welcomed by teachers. The stance has also been endorsed by the Secretary of State (DfEE, 1996). It is likely that statutory teacher assessments in the non-core subjects will be brought in at KS3 in 1997 (DfEE, 1996). This too can be seen as a re-emphasis on the place of teacher assessment.

Conclusion

This chapter has examined the importance of trying to identify where pupils are in their learning. Several possible foci and some ways of carrying out individual assessments have been discussed. Identifying pupils' starting points is the first step in planning teaching.

Curriculum-based assessment is, in the contexts of the *Code of Practice*, the National Curriculum and past work in relation to pupils with special needs, part of a continuous cycle of teaching and assessment. The approaches emerging provide reassurance for those who, like Rouse (1991), were concerned that,

> Whatever proposals eventually emerge from government… we must not be allowed to be overwhelmed by systems designed to compare schools and which are only capable of saying that some of our students are still working at level 1…. When the current storm of uncertainty has settled, we may be able to look back and say, some good came out of it after all. (p.309)

Concerns remain about league tables and the uses to which such information may be put but, alongside these, a useful development of teachers' assessment skills is taking place. This is shaped through procedures being evolved by teachers independently as well as through the sort of guidance being explored by NFER and SCAA. This guidance is both influenced by, and an influence on, classroom pedagogy.

NOTE
This chapter draws on material published in Primary Special Needs and The National Curriculum (2nd edn, 1995, London: Routledge).

Acknowledgements

My thanks to Felicity Fletcher-Campbell and Chris Stevens for discussion of materials relevant to this chapter.

References

Adams, M.J. (1990) *Beginning to Read: Thinking and learning about print*, Cambridge, Mass: MIT Press.

ATL (Association of Teachers and Lecturers) (1994) *Achievement for All*, London: ATL.

Bannon, M., Wildig, C. and Jones, P.W. (1992) 'Teachers' perceptions of epilepsy', *Archives of Disease in Childhood*, 67 1467–71.

Bell, G.H. and Colbeck, B. (1989) *Experiencing Integration: The Sunnyside action enquiry project*, London: Falmer Press.

Byers, R. and Rose, R. (1996) *Planning the Curriculum for Pupils with Special Educational Needs*, London: David Fulton.

Campione, J. (1989) 'Assisted assessment: A taxonomy of approaches and an outline of strengths and weaknesses', *Journal of Learning Disabilities*, 22, 3, 151–65.

Cleave, S., Jowett, S. and Bate, M. (1982) *And So to School*, Windsor: NFER/Nelson.

Croll, P. (1986) *Systematic Classroom Observation*, London: Falmer Press.

DES/WO (1988) *National Curriculum: Task Group on Assessment and Testing* (TGAT Report), London: HMSO.

DfE (1994) *Code of Practice on the Identification and Assessment of Special Educational Needs*, London: DfE.

DfEE (1996) *Review of Assessment and Testing*, consultation paper, London: DfEE.

Fletcher-Campbell, F. (1996)' Just another piece of paper? Key Stage 4 accreditation for pupils with learning difficulties', *British Journal of Special Education* 23, 1, 15–18.

Gipps, C.(1994) 'Teacher assessment and teacher development in primary schools', address to annual conference of the Association for the Study of Primary Education (ASPE) Hertfordshire, September.

Hughes, N. and Carpenter, B. (1991) 'An active partnership', in Ashdown, R., Carpenter, B. and Bovair, K. (eds) (1991) *The Curriculum Challenge: Access to the National Curriculum for pupils with learning difficulties*, London: Falmer Press.

Lawson, H. (1992) *Practical Record Keeping for Special Schools*, London: David Fulton.

Lewis, A. (1995a) *Primary Special Needs and the National Curriculum* (2nd edn), London: Routledge.

Lewis, A. (1995b) *Children's Understanding of Disability*, London: Routledge.

Lewis, A. (1996) 'Summative National Curriculum assessments of primary aged children with special needs', *British Journal of Special Education*, 23, 1, 9–14.

Lewis, A., Neill S.J. and Campbell, R.J. (1996) *The Implementation of the Code of Practice in Primary and Secondary Schools*, London: NUT.

McIntosh, A. (1978) 'Some subtractions: What do you think you are doing?', *Mathematics Teacher*, 83, 17–19.

NCC (1992a) *Teaching Science to Pupils with Special Educational Needs*, Curriculum Guidance 10, York: NCC.

NCC (1992b) *The National Curriculum and Pupils with Severe Learning Difficulties*, York: NCC.

NFER (1995) *Small Steps of Progress in the National Curriculum*, Slough: NFER.

Pollard, A., Broadfoot, P., Croll, P., Osborn, M. and Abbott, D. (1994) *Changing English Primary Schools?*, London: Cassell.

Roffey, S., Tarrant, T. and Majors, K. (1994) *Young Friends: Schools and friendship*, London: Cassell.

Rouse, M. (1991) 'Assessment, the National Curriculum and special educational needs: confusion or consensus?', in Ashdown, R., Carpenter, B. and Bovair, K. (eds) *The Curriculum Challenge*, pp.

293–314, London: Falmer Press.

SCAA (1995a) *A Report on the 1995 Key Stage 1 Tests and Tasks in English and Mathematics*, London: SCAA.

SCAA (1995b) *Review of Assessment and Testing*, London: SCAA.

SCAA (1996) *Planning the Curriculum for Pupils with Profound and Multiple Learning Difficulties*, London: SCAA.

SEAC (1990) *A Guide to Teacher Assessment*, Packs A, B and C, London: SEAC/Heinemann.

Shephard, G. (1994) Statement by Secretary of State for Education on Assessment and Testing Arrangements 1995, 5 September. London: DfE.

Swann, W. (1988) 'Learning difficulties and curriculum reform: integration or differentiation', in Thomas, G. and Feiler, A. (eds) *Planning for Special Needs: A whole school approach*, pp. 85107, Oxford: Blackwell.

Sylva, K. and Neill, S. (1990) 'Assessing through direct observation', Unit 2, Warwick University Early Years Team, *Developing your Whole School Approach to Assessment Policy*, Windsor: NFER/Nelson.

Sylva, K., Roy, C. and Painter, M. (1980) *Childwatching at Playgroup and Nursery School*, London: Grant McIntyre.

Ware, J. (ed.) (1995) *Educating Children with Profound and Multiple Learning Difficulties*, London: David Fulton.

Webster, A. and Webster, V. with Moon, C. and Warwick, A. (1994) *Supporting Learning in the Primary School*, Bristol: Avec.

Willes, M. (1983) *Children into Pupils*, London: Routledge and Kegan Paul.

Wragg, E.C. (1993) *An Introduction to Classroom Observation*, London: Routledge.

Chapter 17

Pupils with Profound and Multiple Learning Difficulties

Carol Ouvry and Suzanne Saunders

Introduction

Although the term profound and multiple learning difficulties (PMLD) has now been in use for many years, it is still necessary to define what is meant by it for a particular purpose or document. In many schools for pupils with severe learning difficulties (SLD), the proportion of pupils with PMLD has increased in relation to the total school roll (Male, 1996). Over time, the criteria for placing pupils into this category may have changed. On the one hand, advances in medical science ensure the survival of children with very extensive disabilities, thereby increasing the number of profoundly disabled pupils in schools (Carpenter, 1994a). Some pupils who would, in the past, have been regarded as having PMLD, are now perceived to be more intellectually able in comparison with other pupils. They may be regarded as having multiple disabilities but *not* profound intellectual impairment. Consequently, the pupils who are now referred to as having PMLD may well be more disabled than would have been the case in previous decades. If this is the case, the task for teachers of pupils with PMLD is now even more challenging.

Ware (1994) defines PMLD as 'having two or more severe impairments, one of which is profound learning difficulties'. She supports this definition by referring to research published in the 1980s which showed that comparatively few people with profound learning disabilities had no other severe impairments. However, this small number of pupils who have profound learning disabilities but do not appear to have additional impairments can be the most challenging to teach as there is no obvious focus to provide a starting point for the teaching process.

The School Curriculum and Assessment Authority has produced non-statutory guidance, *Planning the Curriculum for pupils with profound and multiple learning difficulties* (SCAA, 1996), in which a clear description is given of the pupils whose difficulties are the focus of the document. They are:

> pupils with profound and multiple learning difficulties who, in some respects appear to be functioning at the earliest levels of development and who, additionally have physical or sensory impairments. Some of these pupils may be ambulant and may also behave in ways that either challenge staff and other pupils or result in their isolation making it difficult to involve them in positive educational experiences. Most experience difficulties with communication. (p.8)

The curriculum for pupils with PMLD

All of these barriers to learning have to be addressed in the curriculum for pupils with PMLD and, prior to the introduction of the National Curriculum, the developmental curriculum provided the structure for creating an individual education plan (IEP) for each pupil (see Ouvry, 1987). The introduction of the National Curriculum changed the focus of curriculum development towards issues of entitlement and access across all curriculum subjects for all pupils. However, in spite of the work that has been undertaken to develop extended Programmes of Study (PoS) by individual schools and working groups of teachers throughout the country, and the changes which have been made since the National Curriculum was first introduced (SCAA, 1994), many practitioners who work with pupils with PMLD are still striving to achieve a satisfactory synthesis between the subject-led National Curriculum and the developmental and learning needs of these pupils.

Figure 17.1 (from Ouvry, 1991) shows a model of the whole curriculum which includes the developmental curriculum, the additional curriculum and the National Curriculum. This demonstrates the overlap and interrelationship of these three aspects of the whole curriculum. This model has been modified (Sebba and Byers, 1992; Sebba *et al.*, 1995) by changing the relative size of the circles to indicate the different emphasis which can be placed on the various aspects of the curriculum for each individual pupil or group of pupils.

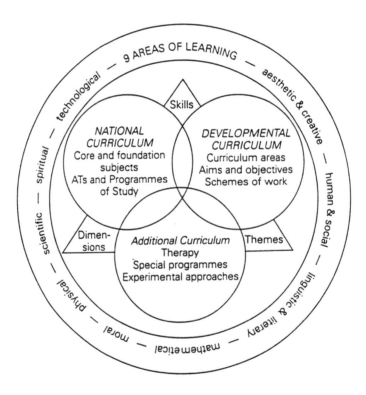

Figure 17.1 The whole curriculum for pupils with PMLD

It demonstrates that the National Curriculum subjects alone cannot provide the whole breadth necessary for pupils with PMLD who will need additional and very specific activities to cater for their individual needs. The Dearing Report states that,

> A slimmer statutory National Curriculum will, by providing time for use at the teacher's discretion, go a long way towards giving teachers the scope necessary to provide all pupils with a meaningful entitlement to a broad, balance and relevant curriculum. (SCAA, 1994, para 6.3)

The intention is clearly to release time for additional work on priority areas within the National Curriculum (Boyd and Lloyd, 1995) but for pupils with PMLD, the entitlement to balance and relevance would clearly indicate the need for time to be spent on elements of the developmental and additional curricula which are not easily embedded into work derived from the National Curriculum. In spite of this additional flexibility, the challenge still remains of entitlement and of providing useful and meaningful, rather than tokenistic, access to the National Curriculum subjects for pupils with PMLD (Kent TVEI, 1995).

Rather than viewing the whole curriculum as a conflict between the subject-led National Curriculum and the needs-led developmental and additional curricula, we can regard them as having parallel and interrelated strands, all of which merge in the pupils' IEPs. Indeed the stated purpose of the SCAA document is 'to show how all the priorities for pupils' learning can be planned for, both *through* and *alongside* the revised National Curriculum orders' (SCAA, 1996, p.1, emphasis added). Figure 17.2 shows how one school has conceptualized the interrelationship between the three main aspects of the whole curriculum.

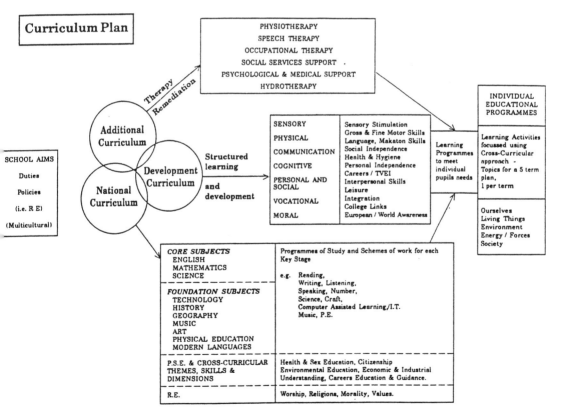

Figure 17.2 The three strands of the whole curriculum in parallel

Many of the priorities in IEPs for pupils with PMLD are likely to involve the acquisition of basic and fundamental skills which are not amenable to categorization into subject-related knowledge, skills and concepts (Coupe O'Kane et al., 1995). Nevertheless, for pupils with PMLD the National Curriculum PoS can provide a structure and context for teaching activities which offer opportunities for working on individual priorities. The SCAA document states that, 'Subject-specific contexts can be provided to teach skills identified in a pupil's individual targets, whether these are directly related to the subject or not' (SCAA, 1996, p.12).

In this case the pupil is not learning *about* the subject, but learning *through* the subject. Just as the National Curriculum can be a vehicle for general learning, other aspects of the whole curriculum (whether it is additional subjects which are traditionally regarded as part of the developmental curriculum, or alternative activities, such as the therapies, remedial and innovative work) can be a vehicle for subject related learning. Figure 17.3, adapted from Ouvry (1994), shows in a schematic way how both focus on individual learning priorities and breadth of experience can be addressed through activities which are derived from different elements of the whole curriculum.

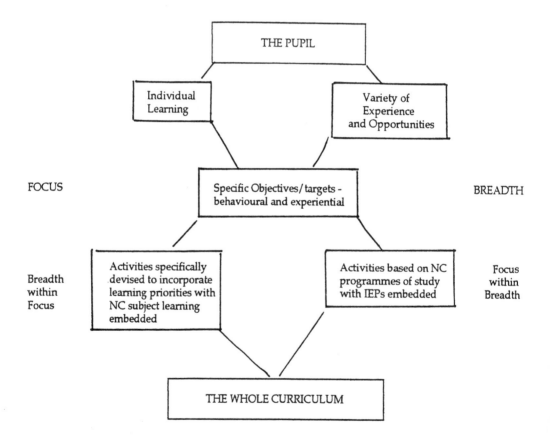

Figure 17.3 Focus and breadth in the curriculum

The SCAA document gives a number of examples of working on individual objectives within the context of a subject-based activity (SCAA, 1996, pp.10, 17), and in doing so it validates this as an approach which can offer both relevance and breadth of experience. However, it would be a mistake to assume that subjects can only be used with pupils with PMLD as vehicles for learning basic and undifferentiated skills, the 'continuing work, comprising skills and processes that might permeate all learning experiences for pupils with profound and multiple learning difficulties' described in the SCAA document (SCAA, 1996, p.32). Each subject can be seen as providing a *learning continuum*, starting with the general basic concepts and skills acquired during the early stages of learning which are the foundations for all future learning, and progressing, through the teaching activities, towards subject-specific concepts, knowledge, skills and understanding. At some point along the learning continuum the pupil will begin to grasp the subject-specific elements and the subject, as well as the activity to which it has given rise, will then have meaning for the pupil. We are all of us at some point along this learning continuum, which extends to the farthest limits of human understanding; a point which very few of us indeed will ever achieve. Figure 17.4 illustrates this learning continuum from basic general concepts and skills to highly specific subject-related skills, knowledge and understanding.

It is not possible to predict when or whether a pupil with PMLD (or indeed a young child, or a pupil with SLD) will reach a stage when the learning changes from general to subject-specific. However, the use of subjects as vehicles for general basic learning ensures that no pupil is denied the possibility of making this transition, and if it does not occur, ensures breadth and variety of experience while still focusing on learning priorities. A pupil can be said to be learning through the subject – the subject is part of the method rather than the content.

The SCAA document gives an example in which pupils with PMLD were involved in a maths activity with their class group. The subject content was estimation and measurement of distance, but the individual content for the pupils with PMLD was physical release of grip on a car and visual tracking as it rolled down a slope. All the pupils in the group would be at their own individual levels of understanding and achievement of the subject-related content. It is interesting to speculate how far along the continuum each pupil with PMLD might be, and whether the positioning of the pupils allowed opportunities to access both general and subject-related content. It is important to realize that pupils will only be able to achieve the more specific subject-related learning if the opportunities for this are made available and accessible.

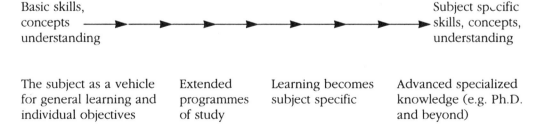

Figure 17.4 The learning continuum

In some areas the developmental curriculum sits easily within the National Curriculum framework and forms part of, or extends the subject content. The core subjects, and those with more concrete and practical elements, may require ingenuity on the part of the teacher, but no longer pose major problems in planning for access, and pupils with PMLD can justifiably be said to be learning some of the subject-specific skills and concepts. It is the subjects which involve concepts which are more abstract and more distant from the 'here and now' of the world of pupils with PMLD, such as the humanities, which still create difficulties in linking content with the learning needs for pupils with PMLD.

In *Teaching Humanities to Pupils with Special Educational Needs* (Coupe O'Kane *et al.*, 1995), the history section has not avoided the challenge of access for pupils with PMLD. In 'History with meaning' the fundamental concepts of *sequences* ('the knowledge of the connections between repeated events that otherwise have no natural connection') and *causality* ('understanding the consequences of actions') are identified. These are general and fundamental concepts which do not relate only to history, but they move a little further towards subject-specific concepts in identifying these, and other general concepts such as anticipation, developing preferences, change and understanding of the causes of change, as contributing to the beginning of a 'sense of history'. In 'Steps through history', early historical concepts are linked with these fundamental concepts and provide extended PoS to lead into the National Curriculum orders.

The sensory approach

The sensory approach is widely used as a point of access to a wide range of subjects and experiences (Bowe, 1994; Longhorn, 1994) but there is a danger that this level of access may be accepted as sufficient in itself. Many teachers are concerned that sensory experiences alone are not enough because they do not necessarily have any meaning for the pupil. It is only when they have an intrinsic meaning of their own, or are part of an experience which itself has meaning, that they will provide the opportunity for meaningful involvement in the learning process and the development of concepts leading to more subject-specific understanding. As well as providing a broad range of sensory stimuli and facilitating the acquisition of perceptual skills, sensory experiences should also provide opportunities for conceptual learning and greater understanding of the surroundings and the activities and experiences of everyday life (Carpenter, 1994b).

The sensory approach can be used in a number of ways (Moss, 1994; Sims, 1994). First, the traditional approach, which is rooted in the developmental curriculum, is used to 'stimulate' the senses in order to:

- increase awareness of change in the surroundings
- improve acuity
- develop perceptual skills to gather information from the environment.

Activities are devised to provide sensory experiences which are usually based on stages of sensory development and the acquisition of basic skills identified as priorities in the pupils' IEPs. The equipment and materials used are frequently specialized and often have no inherent meaning of their own, or they are used in a way which is quite different from that for which they were made. Activities using this type of equipment are often carried out in situations which do not provide a meaningful context.

This approach is useful for assessment and training of sensory skills, for providing motivating experiences in which a pupil at the earliest stages of learning can engage, for encouraging the use of the senses to promote quality of life (Sanderson, 1994), and for providing a starting point for the functional use of the senses. However, it has limitations as a long-term teaching technique.

Second, sensory experiences may be incorporated into activities which have their own structure and meaning, but which have been devised to provide opportunities for sensory work within the sequence of the activity. The sensory experiences will still be based upon individual priorities, and focus on the development and use of perceptual skills. Drama games, music, art massage, and many other activities are used in this way, and there is an increasing number of 'packages' which are commercially available, such as 'Galaxies' and 'Tac Pac' (see 'Resources' at the end of this chapter) which focus on sensory experiences within a structured activity.

Third, sensory experiences are used as an access route to subject-based activities which have their own body of concepts, knowledge, skills and understanding, some of which may be accessible to pupils with PMLD (Moss, 1994). The activity has its own meaning and also offers opportunities for sensory experiences which may or may not have meaning for a pupils with PMLD. The difficulty here is that the sensory experiences may seem quite random and meaningless to the pupil with PMLD when provided through a subject whose meaning is outside the understanding of the pupil.

The challenge facing teachers is how to create a meaningful sensory experience for pupils in all teaching contexts and one which provides the opportunity to progress beyond experience to understanding. The sensory experience has to be invested with its own meaning for those pupils who are currently learning at that level, in addition to any meaning it may have in relation to the subject which forms the context for the activity. This applies equally to activities which are not specifically National Curriculum focused. The experiences must provide opportunities for conceptual learning, as well as providing sensory experiences. There are a number of ways in which this can be achieved.

A sensory experience can acquire meaning in relation to different aspects of any given situation or activity. Figure 17.5 shows how the different aspects of an activity provide ever-widening possibilities for creating meaning from sensory experiences.

The sensory experience

Some of the youngest pupils and a small number of older pupils with PMLD, will be at the earliest stages of learning, when the sensory properties are the focus of learning. McInnes and Treffry (1982) have called this the 'TRY' stage, and describe it as providing the child with the motivation to reach outside himself and to initiate interaction between himself and the environment (p.19). Engagement and interaction with the materials leads to the earliest meanings with the development of preferences, and of early concepts of object permanence, cause and effect and means-end relationships, with the ability to control events.

However, the sensory experiences can also contain conceptual elements such as similarity and difference, or specific concepts relating to the particular sense. For example, the sense of touch is used in many activities to explore artefacts related to the subject or used in the activity. In addition to the sensory properties of the materials used, concepts can be introduced through carefully chosen experiences which demonstrate similarity and difference; contrasts of temperature, texture, weight, etc.; and the identification of objects relating to the activity

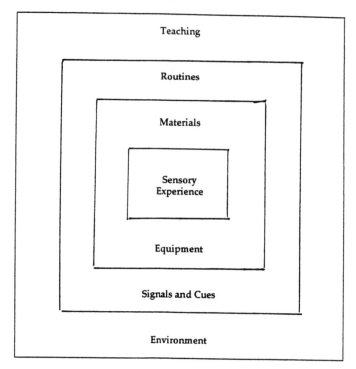

Figure 17.5 Aspects of an activity which provide meaning to sensory experiences

Materials and equipment

Materials and equipment can acquire meaning by association with familiar activities; for example, items related to personal welfare, eating and drinking, food technology, design and technology, and information technology. Regular appropriate and specific use of objects can be built into the scheme of work, and this may enable objects of reference to be used to identify the activity in advance and prepare the pupil for participation.

Progress can be seen in terms of:

- recognition of objects/materials used regularly
- noticing absence of objects/materials used regularly
- expression of likes and dislikes, and ability to make considered choices between different materials
- differentiation of actions used in relation to materials
- functional understanding of a range of materials/equipment
- complexity of equipment/materials and their functions and properties
- appropriate use of familiar objects/materials in other settings
- using a range of actions with new materials in new activities.

In the history section, 'Recollecting experiences' in *Teaching Humanities to Pupils with Special Educational Needs* (Coupe O'Kane *et al.*, 1995), there is an example of using objects which have a very personal meaning to the pupils, such as outgrown boots, or armbands for swimming, which are no longer used. By evoking a sense of personal history in pupils with PMLD, the opportunity is taken to introduce subject-related concepts such as the passing of time.

Routines, signals and cues

Familiarity with routines and sequences of events which form a regular part of an activity can also invest the sensory experiences with meaning as they become signals and cues for what is going to happen. The meaning is derived from the structure of the activity.

Routines, signals and cues can be built into all teaching activities, whether personal welfare, classroom tasks, thematic experiences, or subject-focused activities. Routines will allow recognition of the sensory elements of the activity, anticipation of what is coming next and the opportunity for active participation. Within the routine, pupils can be given choices based on the sensory experiences or their meaning for the pupil. They can be given space for initiatives within the known routine, e.g. what comes next, what shall we use next, or this is not the usual way. Distinct start and finish routines can give information on what the activity is about, the sequence of experiences within the activity, and what is going to happen next.

Progress can be seen in terms of:

- active engagement in the activity
- demonstrating anticipation of the sequence of events
- ability to initiate within the routine
- ability to participate in the routine at any point in the sequence
- ability to recognize the routine in a different environment
- increasing number of routines in which the pupil can take an active part.

The teaching environment

The surroundings will also invest the sensory experiences with meaning. Pupils learn how to 'read' the environment using their senses and learning the familiar landmarks, signals and clues which tell them about the place and the activity or event. There is a need for a variety of environments to be provided, particularly as pupils move towards adulthood, including off-site and community environments, so that they can use their skills in reading the environment and become familiar with a variety of different places.

Progress can be seen in terms of:

- familiarity with learning environments
- anticipation of the learning event/activity
- increased number and complexity of environments which are familiar
- ability to function and participate in an increasingly greater number of environments.

The history section in *Teaching Humanities to Pupils with Special Educational Needs* (Coupe O'Kane *et al.*, 1995) includes a number of examples which show how sequences of events and consequences of action can lead to a concept of time passing or change. These examples illustrate many of these ways of using sensory experiences and making them meaningful. They show the way in which the regular association of experiences can create meaning – the linking of a person with a particular experience, a symbol with a regularly occurring event, activities within the sequence of events, a place with a regular event, culminating in the sense of a personal history by the use of articles with a very personal meaning to each pupil such as outgrown boots, or armbands which are no longer used. One object or experience on its own has no meaning, but in association with others it acquires meaning.

The following detailed example of the planning and carrying out of a project in design and technology will show how an activity generated by the National Curriculum can provide a context for learning at a number of levels, and for creating meaning from sensory experiences.

Design and technology for pupils with PMLD

As with all the National Curriculum subjects, design and technology can be used as a context for learning fundamental skills and concepts and working on individual objectives. However, subject-specific skills, concepts and knowledge can also be made accessible for pupils with PMLD.

The current orders for design and technology describe ways in which pupils develop their design and technology capability through the process of perceiving a problem, designing something that will solve or alleviate the problem, making the article, and evaluating the finished product. In KS1, pupils are working with a wide range of materials to make products; experiencing elements of construction by assembling and disassembling products; and seeing how the characteristics of materials can be altered and used to suit different purposes. They are also generating ideas about what to make and how to make it, designing, making and modifying products, reflecting on the process and finished product and evaluating strengths and weaknesses. Throughout the process they are expanding their technological vocabulary and understanding and are beginning to develop their thinking in a technological way. As they move through the subsequent Key Stages, pupils are engaged in a similar process of designing, building and evaluating but are developing more complex practical skills and engaging in technological debate at a higher level.

In thinking about how pupils with PMLD may be given access to design and technology, as with many of the other subjects of the National Curriculum, we must first consider the essence of the subject and discover what, at its most fundamental level, it is all about. We can then go on to consider how we may convey this essence to our pupils and give them experiences which will help them to extend their experience and develop their understanding of it. Design and technology is, at its heart, about finding solutions to problems, and about fulfilling a certain type of need in the best possible way. When we think of the subject in this way it is easier to see how we can begin to encourage the development of technological thought in our pupils.

To a large extent we, as teachers, are responsible for the environment in which our pupils learn, the ways in which staff relate to children, the activities and tasks that pupils engage in, and their experience of daily living. Our pupils will begin to think in a technological way and to develop their thinking from the general to the more subject-specific over time if we can teach them to recognize the following: that problems exist but that they can be solved; that they have the power to change things and make them different either through action or communication; and that they can express an opinion about how something should be and then experience the consequences of their decisions.

The roots of design lie in choice, and it is only when we can perceive the different ways that something might be, or might be used, that we can begin to think of the best or most suitable way to make them. By encouraging our pupils to express opinions and make choices in all areas of the curriculum and all aspects of the life of the classroom, they can be said to be beginning to design. This can be practised in activities such as art or craft, where pupils can easily be given free choice about the outcome of a piece of work, and it can be developed in one-to-one teaching sessions to encourage the pupils to make choices in order to bring about a desired or favoured outcome. Choices may be expressed through a range of communicative acts (e.g., eye-pointing, blinking, facial expression, smiling, head-turning, etc.). All of these communication indicators carry meaning: it is a skilled teacher who can receive that message, interpret it and respond appropriately.

Similarly, evaluation at its most simple involves expressing an opinion about something and asking pupils for opinions or noting likes and dislikes, all of which is fundamental to our teaching. If this can be extended by allowing pupils to experience the results of technological efforts; encouraging them to experience successful and unsuccessful outcomes; trying different ways of doing things; expressing opinions about them, even if this is only at the level of acceptance or rejection, then they are having opportunities for evaluation, and are beginning to make evaluative judgements.

In these ways we can begin to enable our pupils with PMLD to have access to design and technology by helping them to develop the beginnings of technological thinking and by using general skills and concepts in a technological context. We can do this by providing opportunities for problem-solving, designing and evaluating, and these opportunities and skills can be practised in all curriculum areas and in many of the daily tasks that are carried out in the classroom. In this way all subjects can be seen as vehicles for developing technological capability, and design and technology can also be used as a vehicle for reinforcing many of the specific objectives set for individual pupils that enable them to become more active participants in their world and to learn how they can affect their environment and control their lives.

However, this is by no means the full extent of the ways in which children with PMLD may participate in the curriculum for design and technology, and whilst we can view the development of technological thought as a non-subject-specific process which is highly relevant to the personal development of the pupils, the specific elements of the technology curriculum can be used to extend the breadth of experiences that we offer pupils with PMLD.

Elements of the PoS that lend themselves to the programme of a child with PMLD include:

- working with a wide range of materials including textiles, food, and recycled materials;
- investigating how the characteristics of materials can be changed to suit different purposes;
- assembling and disassembling products;
- joining and combining materials;
- testing finished products.

They can also experience, with or without help, skills traditionally employed in making objects or products, such as cutting, planing, sawing, tearing, sticking, nailing, etc.

All these elements offer plenty of opportunity for sensory exploration, but they can also provide opportunities to lead pupils on from the purely sensory experiences to the development of skills and concepts. For example, feeling and handling different materials can lead on to the development of concepts such as hard and soft, rigid and pliable, rough and smooth, etc., whilst the experiences of sawing, breaking, tearing and nailing, sticking and sewing can lead to concepts of apart and together, changing and assembling objects.

The following example shows how design and technology can be included within a topic to give pupils unique experiences which extend the range of contexts in which they work, and encourage conceptual development as well as the development of specific skills.

Whilst it is accepted that a large number of pupils with PMLD will be learning within classes that span a wide range of ability, for the purposes of this example we will concentrate on the needs of a group of pupils with PMLD.

A design and technology project

The broad topic is movement, and much work has been undertaken in different curricular areas to explore a variety of aspects of movement. A design and technology component can provide a different context in which to work towards individual objectives, but it can also provide unique opportunities for exploring new or different environments and materials, practising new skills and introducing new activities and ideas.

Aims for the whole group might be:

- To experience moving a variety of objects in a variety of different ways.
- To experience and use a variety of woodworking tools and materials in an appropriate way.
- To experience a new subject-related environment with its own atmosphere and stimuli.
- To practise the skills of grasping, rubbing, sanding, hammering, screwing, etc. in a meaningful context.
- To participate in the making of a product to be used in daily life.
- To evaluate the product through their responses and expressions of emotion.

Problem
There is frequently a need to move items of equipment from one area of the school to another. The equipment can often be heavy and/or bulky, and take one or more people quite a long time to carry or drag.

Explor   o
Pupils experience moving different types of objects, e.g.:

heavy and light objects –	bricks, encyclopaedias, bag of feathers, polystyrene blocks
large and small objects –	bag of marbles, person, dice, spoons
long objects –	metal chain, garden cane, hosepipe
wheeled objects –	toy cars etc. wheelchair, standing frame.

They explore different ways of moving things such as pushing, pulling, carrying in hands, carrying on lap, throwing, sliding, rolling, tying to wheelchair and towing.

For some pupils, this stage of sensory exploration will provide opportunities to experience the different properties of materials and the contrasts between them. Some of the objects will already have meaning for the pupils because they are familiar everyday objects. The purely sensory experiences are extended by acting upon the objects in various ways. For other pupils the technology-related concepts such as fitness for purpose lead to the discovery that objects that are difficult to move can be moved more easily if they are given wheels or put onto a wheeled base.

Solution/task

To build a trolley that can be used to transport objects from room to room (and perhaps people for short distances).

At its simplest, the trolley could be a piece of medium density fibre board with castors attached to each corner. At its most complex it could include sides, handles, brakes, etc. The complexity of the task would be determined by the skills of those involved, but it is possible that, if the combined skills of the classroom staff were not adequate, that a school caretaker, another staff member, or a volunteer could be co-opted to provide some support.

Design

This is a potentially difficult area in which to involve pupils with PMLD, but by taking part in choices through the building process and seeing the results or consequences of their decisions, even if they lead to a temporarily unsuccessful product, they will be involved in the design process. For example, they could discover that a trolley with three wheels will not run, or that objects fall off if the board is too small.

The pupils should be given the opportunity to see and experience the consequences of faulty judgements or wrong decisions, as much can be learnt from mistakes.

Building and making

The project is ideal for pupils with PMLD as the potential for sensory experience is vast. The sounds, sights, smells and tactile experiences involved in handling woodworking tools and carrying out or being helped to carry out the tasks of sawing, planing, sanding, drilling, screwing, hammering, etc. are immense, and very different from other everyday life experiences. These sensory experiences have meaning beyond their properties because of the environment, they way they relate to the activity, and the way in which they are used.

Ideally, the making of the trolley could be done in a specific woodworking area within the school, such as a handyman's workshop, or garage converted for the purpose. Moving to the specific area with its atmosphere, smells, sounds, etc. helps the pupils to cue into the activity and to place it within an environmental context. Similarly, using materials and equipment specific to these sessions will help the pupils to recognize and anticipate the activities that are to follow.

Enabling pupils to handle tools, wood, nails, castors and use them in as productive a way as possible for each child should be a priority for these sessions, making the most of the sensory opportunities but also encouraging pupils to consider the design and development of the final product as far as possible. Issues of safety and good practice should never be forgotten.

Through the sensory activities, concept development and subject-specific information can be introduced which may be understood at a variety of different levels by individual pupils.

Evaluation

The pupils should be involved in using the trolley to move a variety of objects and may also be able to experience movement in it themselves either alone or whilst held by an adult. Their expressions of enjoyment or otherwise at riding in the trolley themselves, or being helped to move it manually or with their wheelchair, should be noted. Ongoing use of the trolley to transport personal items of equipment with the pupils in attendance will provide opportunities for the pupils to make the association between the product they have made and its ultimate usefulness. It will also provide opportunities for ongoing adaptation of the trolley to make it more effective, for example by adding a handle and harness that could be attached to a wheelchair to enable a child to tow it. As the trolley becomes a familiar and well-used item in the classroom, the pupils' responses to it may develop.

Example of individual objectives pursued through the project

Asad's IEP shows that he needs to work on fundamental skills such as turn-taking, placing, choice, appropriate use of objects, physical control and sitting balance. These can be addressed through the technology sessions and he will work on both behavioural and experiential objectives:

- Asad will participate in a reciprocal game of pushing different objects to and fro across a table with a known adult.
- Asad will place objects in a variety of wheeled vehicles when requested
- Asad will choose which tools he wishes to use by touching a picture when presented with three pictures, each depicting one tool.
- Asad will be helped to use a sandpaper block to smooth a piece of wood unaided.
- Asad will sit on the completed trolley with physical assistance from an adult, and be pulled the length of the corridor, at different speeds.
- Asad will experience and become familiar with a new environment and the activity which takes place there.
- Asad will experience the use of a variety of tools and materials.
- Asad will use an object in everyday settings to which he has contributed.

This example shows how pupils with PMLD can access the curriculum for design and technology and how it can be used as a vehicle for individual objectives relating to areas of personal development such as communication, socialization, choice and decision-making, as well as the development of hand and functional skills. However, it also shows that the specific content of the design and technology curriculum can be used with children with PMLD and that it can offer them unique sensory experiences which can lead to the development of fundamental and subject specific concepts through 'one-off' and ongoing experiences that they might otherwise not receive. These experiences expand the breadth of the curriculum that they are offered in ways which are useful, stimulating and enjoyable.

Finally, we can also see that design and technology offers opportunities for teachers to move pupils through sensory experiences to cognitive development as pupils are encouraged to develop their conceptual skills with regard to the properties of materials and tools; to follow an activity through many stages to its completion; appreciate that many parts can be assembled to form a whole, and to see that products can be used and adapted to fulfil a purpose. Such a valuable subject certainly deserves a place in the curriculum of every child with PMLD.

Record-keeping

The keeping of records in an appropriate way is an important element of the teaching process as it enables the teacher to maintain an ongoing awareness of the child's current abilities and level of skills so that future planning and teaching can be better focused and more effective. Figure 17.6 shows the stages in this process.

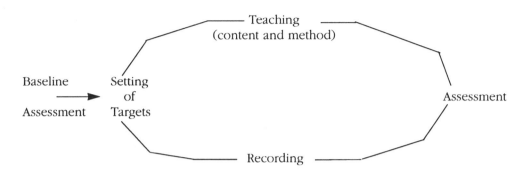

Figure 17.6 Stages in the assessment and recording process

Recording also meets the esteem and motivation needs of pupils, teaching staff and parents, who can see that the child is progressing. When, as with most children with PMLD, progress is slow and the steps made are small, effective record-keeping is even more important to show achievements. However, devising an effective record-keeping system is not an easy task and as Byers and Rose (1996) point out, many schools are still struggling to develop a format which is usable, manageable and also meets the needs of all pupils and teachers in a school.

It is important that a school has a coordinated approach to record-keeping with common systems and formats, but it is also essential that any system is flexible enough to meet the needs of a wide variety of pupils in a school.

There are many characteristics of a good record-keeping system, but when we are considering recording for children with PMLD the following features are particularly important. The record-keeping system should:

- allow for the recording of experiences given as well as responses or achievements made
- be able to be completed by a variety of staff, not just the teaching staff
- relate directly to the child's individual educational programme
- be able to take account of a wide variety of pupil responses to a situation
- record achievement in subject-specific understanding and individual priorities
- be capable of recording responses in whole-class and small-group sessions as well as in individual sessions
- allow for the recording of process as well as final result
- be simple to complete and analyse, leading directly to the assessment of progress and the planning of future work
- lead directly to the production of reports for a variety of interested parties.

A record-keeping system can easily become unwieldy and result in the production of volumes of paper which may never be looked at again. The teacher becomes a slave to the system, spending far too long filling in record sheets, leaving too little time to consider and analyse what the records show about the child's learning. *Planning the Curriculum for Pupils with Profound and Multiple Learning Difficulties* (SCAA, 1996) stresses that what is required is a system that enables pupils' responses to be recorded *if and when they are significant*.

It is crucial, therefore, that the teacher decides what *not* to record, as well as what is significant to an individual and therefore should be recorded. Using the child's IEP as a guide as to what to include can be a good starting point. Surprising or unusual responses, when the pupil acts in an uncharacteristic or markedly different way, should always be noted and the reasons for the change considered.

The SCAA document also emphasizes the need to record the child's experiences, as well as achievements. It is necessary to ensure that pupils have adequate coverage of the range of curriculum subjects and of the subject matter within these. However, showing evidence of curricular coverage need not involve the teacher in vast amounts of recording, as general schemes of work with an indication of whether the child was present for the session or not, may suffice. Of greater importance, and where teachers should concentrate their efforts, are the records that show significant individual responses in relation to the priorities highlighted in the child's IEP. These records should lead the teacher to consider the pupil's achievements, possible regression, lack of, patchy, or inconsistent progress, apparent difficulties, need for support, learning style and personal interests. All of these help the teacher to plan further work and to use teaching strategies best suited to each pupil's learning style.

It is also necessary to remember that, for pupils with PMLD, progress or achievement may not always equate with moving up a hierarchy of achievement, which describes an ever-increasing level of skill or knowledge. Whilst we are always working towards higher skill levels, we are also looking to increase understanding of experiences, to provide breadth and enable the pupil to carry out existing skills in different circumstances. Figure 17.7 illustrates these two dimensions of progress.

It is important that record-keeping systems are able to illustrate progress in both of these dimensions. In this respect, the shortcomings of the checklist system of recording are apparent as, all too often, these are designed to record progress on the vertical axis only, so that the child who has not developed new competences but has experiences, become tolerant of, and shown increasing ability to participate in a variety of situations is not given the recognition that he or she deserves. For pupils with PMLD, this dimension of progress may be the most achievable.

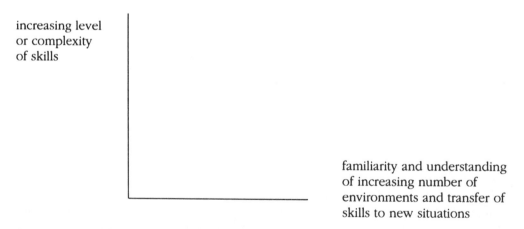

increasing level
or complexity
of skills

familiarity and understanding
of increasing number of
environments and transfer of
skills to new situations

Figure 17.7 Two dimensions of progress

References

Boyd, C. and Lloyd, P. (1995) 'The school context for curriculum change', in Ashcroft, K and Palacio, D. (eds) *The Primary Teacher's Guide to the New National Curriculum,* London: Falmer Press

Bowe, A. (1994) 'The evaluation of the sensory curriculum for meeting the needs of pupils with PMLD', *PMLD Link,* 20, 7–9.

Byers, R. and Rose, R. (1996) *Planning the Curriculum for Pupils with Special Educational Needs,* London: David Fulton.

Carpenter, B (1994a) 'Facing the future: the challenge of educating learners with PMLD', *Westminster Studies in Education,* 17, 37–43.

Carpenter, B. (1994b) 'Finding a home for the sensory curriculum', *PMLD Link,* 19, 2–3.

Coupe O'Kane, J., Wild, P. and Baker, P. (eds) (1995) *Teaching Humanities to Pupils with Special Educational Needs: A practical resource,* Telford: Ergent Publications.

Kent TVEI (1995) *Crossing the Bridge: Access to the National Curriculum for pupils with profound and complex learning difficulties,* Canterbury: South East Information Network.

Lee, B. and Fletcher-Campbell, F. (1995) *Small Steps of Progress in the National Curriculum. Final report: executive summary,* Windsor: NFER.

Longhorn, F. (1993) *Prerequisites for Learning for Very Special People,* Isle of Man: Orca.

Longhorn, F. (1994) 'Noses in action', *PMLD Link,* 20, 7–9.

Male, D. (1996) 'Who goes to MLD schools?', *British Journal of Special Education,* 23, 1, 35–41.

McInnes, J.M. and Treffry, J.A. (1982) *Deaf-blind Infants and Children,* Buckingham: Open University Press.

Moss, N (1994) 'Assessment, recording and reporting of the sensory curriculum', *PMLD Link,* 20, 10–12.

Ouvry, C. (1987) *Educating Children with Profound Handicaps,* Kidderminster: BIMH Publications.

Ouvry, C. (1991) 'Access for pupils with profound and multiple learning difficulties', in Ashdown, R., Carpenter, B. and Bovair, K. (eds) *The Curriculum Challenge: Access to the National Curriculum for pupils with learning difficulties,* London: Falmer Press.

Ouvry, C. (1994) 'Approaches to intervention', unit in *EDSE 35 – Strategies for Working with People with Profound and Multiple Learning Disabilities,* Edgbaston: The University of Birmingham.

Sanderson, H. (1994) 'A personal view of sensory approaches', *PMLD Link,* 20, 24–6.

SCAA (1994) *The National Curriculum and its Assessment,* London: SCAA.

SCAA (1996) *Planning the Curriculum for Pupils with Profound and Multiple Learning Difficulties,* London: SCAA.

Sebba, J. and Byers, R. (1992) 'The National Curriculum: control or liberation for pupils with learning difficulties', *The Curriculum Journal,* 3, 1, 143–60.

Sebba, J., Byers, R. and Rose, R. (1995) (eds) *Redefining the Whole Curriculum for Pupils with Learning Difficulties* (2nd edn), London: David Fulton.

Sims, J. (1994) 'Reflecting on the sensory curriculum', *PMLD Link,* 20, 4–5.

Ware, J. (1994) *Introduction to Working with People with Profound and Multiple Learning Difficulties – Unit 1: People with profound and multiple learning difficulties Part A: The population,* Birmingham: The University of Birmingham.

Resources

Ergent Publications, 26 Lower Wood, The Rock, Telford TF3 5DN.

'Galaxies' is available from Learning Development Aids, Duke Street, Wisbech, Cambridgeshire PE13 2AE.

'Tac Pac' is available from Bobbie Stormont, Newdigate, Church Hill, Harefield, Middx UB9 6DX.

PMLD Link is available from Carol Ouvry, The Old Rectory, Hope Mansell, Ross-on-Wye, Herefordshire HR9 5TL.

Chapter 18

Teachers Researching the Curriculum

Sally Beveridge

This chapter is concerned with the ways in which teachers can undertake research into the curriculum for children with learning difficulties. The idea of teachers researching the curriculum may appear rather peripheral, given the range of pressing and competing demands which schools face in the current educational climate. It is important, therefore, to begin by addressing the question of *why* teachers can find it both relevant and useful to adopt a research role. The answer lies in part within the notion of the teacher as a reflective practitioner.

The teacher as reflective practitioner

When students entering the profession are asked why they wish to become teachers, two reasons they frequently give are:

- that they find children's development fascinating, and want to be involved in enhancing their learning;
- that they think teaching will not be dull or unchanging, but will provide them with a range of varying challenges.

These reasons relate directly to two major interacting facets of the teaching role: the promotion of children's learning and the extension of teachers' own professional practice in ways most likely to facilitate this. It is central to teachers' work that they seek to ensure that the quality of the provision they make is as effective as possible in promoting children's learning. This requires that they become reflective practitioners, who evaluate the impact of what they do both at the level of individual classroom practice, and also at the level of whole-school policies.

At classroom level practice, teachers need to experiment with and evaluate many different aspects of their teaching. These might include, for example, modes of explanation and feedback, organizational strategies, physical arrangements, different teaching materials, the involvement of other children as a learning resource, and so on. They are also likely to include assessment, evaluation and record-keeping practices. It can be argued that there are a number of reasons why such experimental teaching becomes even more important when working with children who have significant learning difficulties. First, children with learning difficulties require an approach which is as responsive as possible to their diverse, complex and possibly idiosyncratic patterns of needs. Second, because they can sometimes appear to 'get stuck' on plateaus of learning, they require inventive and creative help from their teachers if they are to maintain motivation and make progress. Further, wherever progress is slow or uneven, both the children and their teachers need strategies which emphasize forms of monitoring and evaluation which are sufficiently detailed to promote a sense of achievement. Finally, children with the most complex learning difficulties may be particularly vulnerable to the fads and fashions which Robson (1993) argues that education is prone to. If this is so, then it is essential that their teachers should assess the impact of new methods and materials as carefully as possible.

Reflection upon their own practice can help teachers to extend the development of their professional skills, knowledge and understanding. While much of their evaluation must focus on what goes on at an individual classroom level, they can also work in cooperation with colleagues to monitor and appraise practices across the school. The focus of investigation at a whole-school level might include, for example, the channels of communication which exist among staff in school, and between school and parents and/or professional support agencies, and the ways in which these affect the curriculum.

Whether they engage in exploration of classroom-based or of school-based issues, when teachers seek to follow *more systematic approaches* in their investigations, they are extending their reflective practice to incorporate an element of research.

Research as an extension of professional skills

What is research? A dictionary definition of the verb 'to research' includes: to search into (a matter or subject); to investigate or study closely (*The Shorter Oxford English Dictionary*, 1973). Synonyms include: to investigate, explore, delve into, dig into, enquire and to examine, study, inspect (*The Oxford Thesaurus*, 1991). Robson (1993) has described the personal qualities needed by researchers as follows: 'having an *open and enquiring mind*, being a "*good listener*", general *sensitivity* and *responsiveness to contradictory evidence*' (p162).

It can be argued therefore that the term 'research' embraces a range of exploratory and evaluative activity which is directly associated with teachers' reflective practice; and also that it involves attributes and skills which should be central to their work. It would be misleading to conclude though, that this means that research is always an integral part of teaching. It involves a more rigorous approach than is usual in teachers' practice, and the use of systematic methods of enquiry. Accordingly, the research role is best seen as an *extension* of professional skills. Teachers are most likely to see a need to take on this extended role in order to:

- increase their understanding and awareness of their own practice and that of the school as a whole;
- gather relevant evidence about the effectiveness of their practice;
- enhance their confidence and skill for experimenting with new ways of working.

Whether teachers engage in individual or collaborative study with colleagues, they benefit from having someone who can play the part of a 'critical friend' (Lomax, 1991) to support them in their research role. By acting as a sounding board and by putting forward alternative perspectives, 'critical friends' can help researchers to articulate and clarify their thinking.

The role of teacher-researcher

Teachers have a number of advantages over outside researchers when it comes to the investigation of practice in their own school settings. For example, they have a wealth of background knowledge and experience of the context for their study. They are not only familiar with school policies and procedures, but have usually also built up relationships of trust with those who may be involved in the research. As a result, they should be in a good position to ensure that the study is developed in ways which are sensitive to the perspectives of the pupils, staff and parents concerned.

However, there are also disadvantages which can arise from knowing the setting so well. Teachers may need to 'fight familiarity' (Vulliamy and Webb, 1992), if they are to remain open to fresh perspectives, alternative interpretations and new insights into school-based practice. It is important to recognize too that teachers status in relation to pupils, parents and colleagues may well influence the research role that they are able to adopt. A teacher may find it hard, for example, to sit back and take a non-directive classroom role in the same way that an outside researcher might. It is therefore necessary for teachers to give thought to the nature of the research role they aim to adopt, and to communicate this clearly to others. In doing so, it is helpful to bear in mind the different sets of expectations which can be associated with teaching and research. Cooper (1995) suggests that while teachers are expected to make judgements and provide an active lead, researchers are required to be impartial and non-judgmental, following the lead of their subjects. Perhaps what is most significant here is the point that researchers need to try to see things from a range of different viewpoints, rather than only those which fit with the teacher perspective.

The role of teacher-researcher brings with it certain ethical considerations. First, wherever the subject of evaluative research goes beyond one's own practice to that of other people, it is evident that teachers must be alert to the potential sensitivities that can be involved. Those who are to be affected by the evaluation need both information and the opportunity to discuss the purposes and motivation for the research; the ways in which research evidence will be gathered; and the use to which findings will be put. For example, if the research aims to promote some change in school practice, then colleagues need to feel that they will have some involvement in the decisions which are made.

Further, there are some well-established principles in research which require careful consideration by teachers who wish to conduct investigations in their own school context. Depending on the nature of the research study, these can apply not only to colleagues, but also to pupils and their parents. They relate to the protection of anonymity and of confidentiality, which can sometimes be difficult to ensure within a small and close staff group (Robson, 1993). They also concern the extent to which the 'subjects' of the study have real choice about their participation (Clough and Barton, 1995). As a general principle, researchers should seek to ensure that all participants are clear about the purposes of the investigation and that they are willing to be involved. There are issues here when pupils are the focus of study. These arise both from their understanding and also from their relationship to teachers at school (Burgess, 1995). The issues become more complex among children and young people who have significant learning difficulties, and it is certainly likely to be important to communicate with their parents about their participation.

Purposes and approaches in teacher research

The focus of teacher research must clearly be the curriculum in its broadest sense, and the aim must be to ensure that the curriculum experienced by the pupils is as effective as possible in promoting their learning and development. Table 18.1 illustrates the sorts of topics which teachers of children with learning difficulties might seek to investigate. The table includes some examples focused on individual children and class groups, and others which are concerned with whole-school policy and practice. Teacher research can also address wider issues, such as the way in which the curriculum might be enhanced by communication with parents, support agencies, other schools and colleges, the local community and so on. Research topics may be identified as a result of factors outside school. For example, they may follow on from local or national government initiatives, or from attendance at a course which has stimulated staff interest in particular issues. On the whole though, the impetus for undertaking an investigation will tend to be teacher concern that there are aspects of current practice which may be in need of change. The intention then is to explore current practice, identify possible changes and, where these are implemented, monitor their effects. That is, the research is frequently of an evaluative and problem-solving nature.

Topic	Individual children and class group examples	Whole-school examples
Range and quality of planned learning experiences	curriculum audit; access to National Curriculum; specific teaching approaches; specific learning programmes; cross-curricular links; use of technology; etc.	process of curriculum planning, development and review; curriculum coordinator role; specific policy development; etc.
Processes of to development and learning	generalization of skills; problem-solving; aspects of communication; self-evaluation; self-advocacy; classroom-based assessment; etc.	whole-school approaches assessment, recording and reporting; the involvement of speech, physio- and other therapists; etc.
Classroom relationships and management	cooperative learning; peer interactions; behaviour management; room management; etc.	staff roles and responsibilities; working with support assistants; channels of communication; integration of pupils with complex needs; etc.

Table 18.1 Teachers researching the curriculum: some examples of research topics

Having identified a topic for research, the next step is to clarify what is to be investigated and why. Teachers can usefully develop their thinking about the specific research questions they wish to address in discussion with colleagues. They also need to seek out relevant sources of information, such as practitioner journals and professional contacts. It may well be that aims and intentions are only refined as the investigation gets underway, for example through the use of a pilot phase or a period of 'progressive focusing' (Corrie and Zaklukiewicz, 1985), in which research questions become more distinct as a result of the information which is gathered. However, it is essential for the overall sense of direction that sufficient time is given to ensure that purposes are as clearly stated as possible at the outset. The range of purposes may include:

- exploration, experimentation and evaluation of particular teaching strategies and procedures;
- the enhancement of teacher awareness and understanding, for example of the perspectives of pupils, parents and colleagues from other disciplines;
- the development of one_s own professional skills, for example in observational assessment, cooperative learning, the use of new technology, and so on.

Once the research questions and purposes are reasonably clear, it is possible to make decisions about the sort of research approach through which they might practicably be addressed. Robson (1993) has distinguished two main research approaches of particular relevance to teachers. When the research questions require a broad overview of evidence gathered in standard form from a number of different people, then a *survey approach* can be appropriate. For example, perspectives might be sought from teachers within the local area who have a responsibility for coordinating Information Technology across the curriculum; or from the music therapists who have links with the region's special schools; or from the mainstream pupils who have experience of a particular integration link scheme.

Frequently though, teachers' research questions require an approach which offers less wide-ranging but more detailed evidence. A *case study approach* allows an in-depth investigation, with for example an individual child or group of children, a group of school staff, an interdisciplinary team, or a single school, as the focus. One particular form of case study approach, referred to as 'action research', is often recommended for school-based problem-solving. This involves a cyclical process through which schools can continually modify and refine their practice. Adelman (1985) has described four stages of the process, in which school staff:

- identify their concerns and collect research evidence which will help them clarify what, if anything, needs changing;
- propose some changes which, on the basis of the evidence, provide possible solutions to their concerns;
- develop an action plan to implement those changes;
- monitor and evaluate their effects.

It is important to note that the choice between survey and case study does not have to be of an either/or nature, because for some evaluative studies it is helpful to combine the two approaches. For example, teachers can use a preliminary survey as a basis for identifying significant issues or examples of practice which they then go on to investigate at greater depth through case studies.

Contexts and methods of investigation

When the purposes and general research approach have been identified, then decisions need to be made about *who* is to be studied, in which *settings or contexts*, and in what sorts of *activities*, in order best to answer the specific research questions. Taking each of these in turn, the study may, for example:

● focus on individuals, groups or classes of children, and/or their parents and staff;
● take place in classrooms, staff rooms, playgrounds, homes, clinics, the local environment, or some combination of these;
● highlight particular sorts of events and activities, more or less structured learning opportunities, processes or products of interaction, and so on.

There are a number of texts which teachers can find useful in the detailed guidance they provide on research methods (e.g., Bell, 1993; Cohen and Manion, 1989; Robson, 1993). The following discussion offers a brief overview of issues in the use of the three main types of methods of investigation which can be chosen. They involve the researcher in observing behaviour; in asking people for information and for their views, feelings and perspectives; and in collecting written documents or visual records. These are not mutually exclusive approaches, and particularly in case studies, it is appropriate to consider combining a range of different strategies.

Observation

Direct observation allows the researcher to gather evidence about overt behaviour. The behaviour might be that of children, for example, in interaction with their teachers, with other children or with particular curricular materials; or it might be that of adults, for example, in parent-teacher consultations or in curriculum planning meetings.

Any observer brings a set of attitudes, expectations and experiences to the act of observing, which must influence both what they notice and how they interpret it. Accordingly, it is particularly important that researchers try to guard against bias, in the form of selective sensitivity to particular behaviours or types of behaviour. Helpful strategies include:

● aiming for precision in observational records;
● making clear distinctions between evidence (what exactly was observed) and interpretation (what was inferred);
● explicit reflection upon alternative possible interpretations.

Wherever possible, it is invaluable to share observations with others, to check whether they see the same behaviours and interpret them in the same ways. It is also important to ask colleagues and, where appropriate, parents, about the extent to which the picture that emerges from the observations corresponds with their experience.

There are a number of related questions which need to be considered when planning to use observational methods. These concern the observer role, the form of the evidence which is collected, and the length of time over which observations should take place. Researchers can act as participant or non-participant observers. As discussed earlier, it can be difficult for teacher researchers to take on the non-participant role if their investigation is focused on their own work contexts. However, the greater the degree of participation in events and activities, the harder it can be to gather detailed evidence at the same time. Participant observers may also find it difficult to retain sufficient detachment to allow them to keep an overview of what is going on. If practicable, it is worth considering the use of audio- or video-recordings to support the observation process. Although it takes time to transcribe information from such records, it can be helpful in providing a more complete picture than might otherwise be achieved.

When thinking about the form of the observational evidence which they wish to collect, researchers need to consider whether they want to try to observe and record everything that happens within a given time period or if they only interested in sampling certain aspects, such as the frequency or duration of particular types of behaviour. The first of these options is more open-ended, and may potentially offer richer insights, but it poses obvious practical difficulties as far as accuracy and detail are concerned. The second option requires a more structured approach, perhaps using prepared schedules such as those described by Croll (1986). It may lend itself to more objective and accurate information-gathering, but can only portray certain predefined aspects of behaviour. The extent to which researchers structure their observations to focus on specific aspects of behaviour has to be guided by the questions which they seek to address, but it must also be affected by practical considerations of how much can be noted down consistently and accurately within their research settings.

Whatever form their observations take, researchers need to feel confident that they have gathered a representative picture of what usually happens. This means that they have to make decisions about the length of time over which they should continue to gather evidence. Their own presence in an observer role can affect what takes place and this may be particularly apparent if they use an audio- or video-recorder with children or adults who are not used to this. It is important, therefore, to plan sufficient time within each observation period as well as a sufficient number of observation sessions overall, to provide a sound evidence base for the research.

Interviews and questionnaires

Interviews and questionnaires allow researchers to ask people directly for information. The information may be of a factual, knowledge-based kind, or it may also include feelings, attitudes and perceptions. For example, case study research into the effectiveness of school policy on managing difficult behaviour or on the integration of therapy within the curriculum, might involve asking staff, pupils and parents questions which are designed to elicit their understanding and feelings about the policy in action as they experience it.

The relationship between researchers and the people they ask for information can, of course, have an effect on the answers they get to questions of a less factual nature. This is likely to be the case when teacher researchers seek information from their colleagues, but it raises particular issues concerning parents and pupils, who may wish to give the responses they think are expected of them. When planning interviews or questionnaires, it is important, therefore, to give consideration to how best they can be introduced and their purposes explained in ways that will encourage openness in the expression of personal views; and how leading questions can be avoided.

It is only comparatively recently that researchers have attempted to access the views of children and young people with significant learning difficulties directly, rather than relying on the perceptions of their parents and teachers. A number of studies have been reported which address some of the methodological issues concerned (e.g. Beveridge, 1996; Lewis, 1995; Lloyd-Smith and Dwyfor Davies, 1995; Minkes *et al.*, 1995; Wade and Moore, 1993). The strategies which they consider include the use of visual aids to help responding, and ways of synthesising interviews or questionnaires with direct observation in order to build up as complete a picture of pupil experiences as possible.

Decisions about whether to use an interview or a questionnaire procedure are likely to be based primarily on the type of information which the researcher wants to gather and the numbers of people who are to be approached. Sometimes both may be used: for example, unstructured interviews with a small number of people may provide the material to draw up a questionnaire for a wider survey of opinion; or, more frequently, a broader questionnaire survey may reveal issues to follow up in greater depth through interviews with a sub-group.

Interviews usually involve individual face-to-face discussion, although there are advantages sometimes in a paired or small group context and, out of necessity, some teacher-researcher interviews may be conducted on the telephone. They can take the form of open-ended, unstructured discussions around the focus of the research concern, or they can have more structured formats. For most purposes, teacher-researchers tend to opt for a semi-structured approach in which they identify the main questions for discussion in advance, but vary the sequence of these, as well as their use of prompts and requests for elaboration, in response to the way that the individual interview develops. At its most tightly structured, an interview schedule begins to resemble a questionnaire to the extent that it has a standard sequence and wording of questions.

The greater the degree of structure, the more thought needs to be given to the wording of the questions to ensure that they are clear and, that, while they are not leading questions, they do relate constructively to the research focus. The design of a questionnaire, particularly one which is to be completed in the absence of the researcher, takes time and effort to get right: there are issues involved in layout, sequencing and response conventions which affect the likelihood that people will complete it, and that they will do so in the ways hoped for (see, for example, Robson, 1993).

Written documentation and visual records

Written documentation can provide a very important source of information in school-based research. A range of forms of written material is likely to be generally available in schools, and others might be specifically generated for the purposes of a particular study. Material can include formal documentation, for example, the school prospectus, written policies, curriculum plans and records, Individual Educational Plans, statements and annual reviews. It can also include less formal records such as home-school books or other correspondence with parents, teacher and pupil diaries, and so on. Photographs provide a form of visual record whose potential, for example when compiling pupils_ Records of Achievement, has been recognized by many schools for some time. More recently, researchers have begun to report on the use of photographs as a source of evidence in their investigations (e.g., Burgess, 1995; Walker, 1993).

It is important that the evidence from documentary sources, just like that from observations, interviews and questionnaires, is linked very clearly to the focus and purposes of the investigation, and therefore the ways in which written or visual records are used will vary from study to study. For example, written documents might be examined for their reference to pupil and parental involvement in decision-making processes, or for evidence of cross-curricular links in staff planning of programmes of study. Photographic records might be analysed for reference to individual therapy objectives within particular curricular activities, or for evidence of the relationship between physical organization and interactions in the classroom.

Stage	Example
Identify the research focus	A teacher has concerns about the extent to which cooperative learning approaches feature in the National Curriculum
Clarify research questions and purposes (consult relevant reading and professional contacts; discuss with colleagues)	She wants to evaluate the effectiveness of cooperative learning approaches for the pupils with SLD with whom she works, and provide structures that help her to develop cooperative learning within the classroom; develop her own skills in (i) the use of cooperative learning approaches, and (ii) classroom-based research
Decide on a research approach (e.g., survey, case study)	She chooses a case study approach with an action research element: her investigation will be shaped as it goes on by the information she gathers
Decide on the context: who is to be studied, in what setting(s) and in what sort of activities	The study will involve the senior group of pupils with SLD with whom she works most frequently, herself and 2 support staff. It will take place in the classroom, on a series of weekly sessions structured round cooperative learning tasks.
Decide on the methods (e.g., observation, interview, questionnaire, written documentation, visual records)	She needs to use a combination of methods. Participant ongoing *observations* of the pupils by all three staff (also audio-recorded) – frequency of their requests for staff help, comments to staff, comments to other pupils, negotiation, conflict; duration of their on-task behaviour. *Interviews* – structured feedback sessions with pupils; weekly discussion with support staff. Written *documentation* – teacher researcher diary – reflections on pupil responses to inform weekly planning; reflections on own practice

Table 18.2 A summary of stages in the planning of research

Planning into action

This chapter has focused primarily on the planning and preparation which teacher researchers need to consider prior to beginning their investigations. Table 18.2 summarizes the stages involved. It also incorporates an example which illustrates the way in which a case study approach can appropriately draw upon a combination of research methods.

When moving into the implementation of their research plans, teachers can usefully think about beginning with a preliminary exploratory or pilot phase, in which they:

- try out the practicalities of their chosen methods of investigation;
- check that the information they derive from their chosen method/s is what they actually need in order to address their research questions;
- undertake any fine tuning to their plans and methods that seems necessary.

It is particularly important that researchers pay attention to the reliability, or what Robson (1993) refers to as the 'trustworthiness', of the information they gather during their studies. They need to have procedures in place which allow them, and others, to feel confident about its accuracy and its representativeness. Joint information-gathering with colleagues, for example in direct observation or from audio- or video-records, is a very helpful strategy, but it is not always possible or appropriate. Self-reflection and regular discussion with other staff should always be practicable. They can have a useful monitoring function when they are structured to help researchers consider whether they are:

- being as consistent and rigorous as possible in the way they collect evidence;
- remaining open to alternative perspectives;
- demonstrating convincing evidence to support their interpretations and judgements.

The way in which teachers are able to use the results of their research will clearly vary according to its initial purpose and intentions. Most teacher-researchers undertake relatively small-scale studies within the contexts of their own classes or schools, and therefore it is important to be cautious about the extent to which their findings can be generalized more widely. Where the findings make sense, seem relevant and resonate with other teachers' experience and knowledge, then the research can communicate with and have an impact on a wider professional network. However, its main impact is always likely to be on the teacher-researchers' own practice. This may operate at a number of different levels, for example, on their:

- attitudes and understanding of differing perspectives;
- observational, listening and recording skills;
- analytical and informed approach to problem-solving;
- confidence and skill in experimenting with different teaching approaches.

It might be argued that professional development of this kind can only be to the benefit of the children and young people they teach.

References

Adelman, C. (1985) 'Action research'. In S. Hegarty and P. Evans (eds) *Research and Evaluation Methods in Special Education*. Windsor: NFER-Nelson.

Bell, J. (1993) *Doing Your Research Project. 2nd edition*. Buckingham: Open University Press.

Beveridge, S. (1996) 'Experiences of an Integration Link Scheme: the perspectives of pupils with severe learning difficulties and their mainstream peers'. *British Journal of Learning Disabilities*.

Burgess, R.G. (1995) 'Gaining access to pupil perspectives.' In M. Lloyd-Smith and J. Dwyfor Davies (eds) *On the Margins: The Educational Experience of 'Problem' Pupils*. Stoke-on-Trent: Trentham Books.

Clough, P. and Barton, L. (eds) (1995) *Making Difficulties: Research and the construction of SEN*, London: Paul Chapman.

Cohen, L. and Manion, L. (1989) *Research Methods in Education. 3rd edition*. London: Routledge.

Cooper, P. (1995) 'When segregation works: pupils' experience of residential special provision' In M. Lloyd-Smith and J. Dwyfor Davies (eds) *On the Margins: The Educational Experience of 'Problem' Pupils*. Stoke-on-Trent: Trentham Books.

Corrie, M. and Zaklukiewicz, S. (1985) 'Qualitative research and case-study approaches: an introduction." In S. Hegarty and P. Evans (eds) *Research and Evaluation Methods in Special Education*. Windsor: NFER-Nelson.

Croll, P. (1986) *Systematic Classroom Observation*. Lewes: Falmer Press.

Lewis, A. (1995) *Children's Understanding of Disability*. London: Routledge.

Lloyd-Smith, M. and Dwyfor Davies J. (eds) (1995) *On the Margins: The Educational Experience of 'Problem' Pupils*. Stoke-on-Trent: Trentham Books.

Lomax, P. (1991) 'Peer review and action research.' In P. Lomax (ed) *Managing Better Schools and Colleges: an Action Research Way*. Clevedon: Multilingual Matters.

Minkes, J., Townsley, R., Weston, C. and Williams, C. (1995) _Having a voice: involving people with learning difficulties in research.' *British Journal of Learning Disabilities, 23*, 94-97.

Robson, C. (1993) *Real World Research*, Oxford: Blackwell.

Vulliamy, G. and Webb, R. (eds) (1993) *Teacher Research and Special Educational Needs*. London: David Fulton Publishers.

Wade, B. and Moore, M. (1993) *Experiencing Special Education*. Buckingham: Open University Press.

Walker, R. (1993) 'Finding a silent voice for the research: using photographs in evaluation and research.' In M. Schratz (ed) *Qualitative Voices in Educational Research*. London: Falmer Press.

Part III:
The Context for the Whole Curriculum

Chapter 19

Enabling Partnership: Families and Schools

Barry Carpenter

> Parents and teachers are both there for one interest – the child's interest. (Father at a parent-partnership workshop, February 1996)

'Partnership with parents' (a well-rehearsed phrase) has developed something of a hollow ring. How do we give it back its meaning? How do we breathe life back into this concept which is so crucial to our work in schools? Maybe the time is right for us to reconceptualize partnership, to rediscover its true meaning. We could abandon it as yet another lost educational cause, but would that bring any real benefit to children, their parents, their teachers and our schools?

By redirecting our focus, we may enable partnership to become a reality once more. Many schools have established excellent working relationships with parents, gently nurtured over many years, but in the recent past our major efforts have been towards the implementation of the National Curriculum and the raft of legislation that has hit schools over the last decade. If we are truthful, has 'working with parents' been given sufficient in-depth attention in our policy, planning and practice? Only in the last two years has there been a resurgence of texts that discuss parents and their children with special educational needs (Dale, 1996; Gascoigne, 1995; Hornby, 1995; Mittler and Mittler, 1994).

Indeed 'parent-partnership' has now become the theme of a Grant for Education, Support and Training (GEST 24) specifically for the 'development of the SEN Parent Partnership Scheme'. The scheme is intended to enable local authorities to: support parents whose children are being formally assessed under Section 167 of the 1993 Education Act; compile a register of 'named persons'; develop links between schools and health and social services; and provide information on special educational needs for parents.

Legislation is the driving force of this initiative (but has caused 'parent-partnership' to be used even more glibly). The Code of Practice states that:

> The relationship between parents and school has a crucial bearing in the child's educational progress and effectiveness of any school based action. (DfE, 1994, Section 2:28, pp. 12–13)

It is certainly right in its assertion that:

Children's progress will be diminished if their parents are not seen as partners in the education process with unique knowledge and information to impart. (DfE, 1994, Section 2:28, pp. 12–13)

It is in relation to the child as a learner that parents enter into a dialogue with the Local Education Authority (LEA) and/or schools. They share their holistic insights of their child's development, and thus the ground is established for the ongoing interaction between school and parents. In the context of a school, the child's learning is set within the curriculum. That learning is supported by teachers, special support assistants, peers and associated professionals (speech therapist, physiotherapist, educational psychologist, etc.). In the home it is the parents, siblings, grandparents, relatives and 'significant others' (i.e. friends, neighbours, etc.) who nurture the development of the child. The shared focus for both environments – home and school – is the child; the common language is based upon the child's needs, and the common goal is to enable the child to develop through quality learning experiences. The ground is set for families and schools to share in the child's learning – to share the curriculum.

Sally smiles at her mother as they engage in a physiotherapy routine. Today, the motivation for her to stretch her arms is the bright purple Koosh ball she has brought home from school in her 'sensory bag'. Sally's parents have always received and valued the home diary from school, but never felt that they had much to share in return. This latest innovation – the sensory bag – in which Sally brings home a piece of equipment she is using to support her in-class learning, has meant that, at last, there is an activity which can be blended into the home routine. Sally's mum even intends to send into school the new aromatherapy oil she has found so effective in relaxing Sally when her leg muscles spasm and cause her distress.

Sally has profound and multiple learning difficulties (PMLD). She is 8 years old. Her parents, whilst happy with Sally's school, felt that because she could not speak or walk, there was little that they could do to help the work of the school. The recent development within Sally's school of using sensory approaches on a permeated, cross-curricular skills basis has meant that Sally is experiencing a range of sensory materials throughout her day. Her teacher has discussed this approach with Sally's parents who felt that at long last here was something tangible they could follow up at home. Their confidence has grown. They have found many opportunities in the home to transfer the learning approaches Sally uses in school. They feel that they are sharing the curriculum – their daughter's learning. The *Code of Practice* reminds us:

Professional help can seldom be wholly effective unless it builds upon parents' capacity to be involved, and unless parents consider the professionals have taken account of what they say and treat their views and anxieties as intrinsically important. (DfE, 1994, Section 2:28, pp. 12–13)

The child through the eyes of the family

The most important thing that happens when a child is born with disabilities is that a child is born. The most important thing that happens when a couple become parents of a child with disabilities is that the couple become parents. (Ferguson and Asch, 1989, p. 24)

Two American writers, Philip Ferguson (a parent) and Adrienne Asch (who is disabled) offer this powerful thought. They are affirming what is often not the case at all. Parents become 'Down's parents'; babies become 'deaf babies'; the child becomes 'the blind child'; the family becomes 'the disabled family'; and a completely different pattern to the family history is assumed. It is not what was hoped for or expected. Suddenly, in the eyes of some professionals and areas of society, that family is no longer an 'ordinary' family. However, whilst the journey may follow a different route to that which was anticipated, the destination is the same. It is the child, not the disability that should be uppermost in people's minds. But this is not always so, as Rod Wills, a parent, reminds us:

> Some of the roles assigned to parents cause great pain. What is imposed on parents is often based on mistaken belief, historical prejudice and myths. Negative attitudes towards disability have strongly shaped what we do to people who are disabled, how it is done, and the consequences for their family. (Wills, 1994, p.249)

Some professionals perpetuate these myths. Kimpton (1990), also a parent, reminds professionals and other experienced parents to think carefully about the language they use (cf. Chapter 22 of this book). Disability-related terminology that trips off the tongue may only add to the parents' feelings of confusion and inadequacy. Many parents report that in the early days of being with their child with a disability they felt rejection, isolation and a lack of empathy from professionals. They report that this led them to see their relationship with them in terms of dependency, alienation and manipulation (Clench, 1994).

There are now some powerful examples of how families have nurtured the development of the child with special educational needs (Hebden, 1985; Johnson and Crowder, 1994). The introduction to Pat Fitton's excellent book, *Listen to Me* (1994), illustrates how, through the eyes of a parent, the child is seen first and foremost as a child. Pat Fitton describes her daughter, Cathy. She contrasts how, if doctors were talking about Cathy, they would focus upon her severe learning difficulties and cerebral palsy, the range of medical conditions she had acquired during her years – the epilepsy, the rheumatoid arthritis, chest infections. If Cathy's friends and family were to tell you about her, they would talk about her personality, her likes and dislikes – music, travel, clothes. They would tell you about her humour, her love of swimming, her patient attempts to communicate with those unable to understand her.

Schools need to appreciate this perspective in working with families of children with special educational needs. There is, naturally, a range of emotions within families which may influence how they engage with a school. There is much debate around some of these theories (Dale, 1996), but it would be true to say that some parents in any school population where there are children with learning difficulties will display some of the characteristics associated with grief or sorrow. Indeed, other family members may also display such tendencies. Some reports have suggested that many grandparents have difficulty adapting to the situation and attempt to deny their child's disability, and thus offer low levels of support to the family (George, 1988; Hornby and Ashworth, 1994; Mirfin-Veitch et al., 1996). Other studies have expressed concerns about siblings and their perceptions of their brother or sister's disability, or their own interrelationship with their parents (Powell and Ogle, 1992).

Some parents claim that they accept their child, but never come to accept the disability completely (Russell, 1983). This bereavement response may remain with some parents for many years and tinge their interactions with the school. They may never seem to share fully the joy of their child's achievements, always grieving for that lost normalcy. Whilst many writers (Cunningham and Sloper, 1977) have attributed these feelings of grief and mourning to the early traumatic period following the disclosure of diagnosis shortly after the birth of a baby with a disability, experience has also shown me that a grief response is possible during the school years when parents are told that there is a possibility their child has some learning difficulty. Usually the confirmation of this comes in the form of a Statement of Special Educational Need, and again the shock of this may traumatize some parents in a similar way that a bereavement would, or it may affirm their own suspicions about their child's difficulties and they mourn. For as one mother of a child with specific learning difficulties said: 'In realizing his academic limitations I realized the loss of my own dream for his future' (Parent workshop, June 1994).

However much professionals may reassure, guide or offer support, these feelings cannot always be rationalized. We are far too dismissive of emotional responses; we need to acknowledge that they are an important feature of the adjustment process. If a child with learning difficulties is to be accepted as a full family member, then each family member must come in their own way to value and appreciate the many and diverse talents of the child and, moreover, to acknowledge the child as a person in their own right. Some parents leave grief behind (if ever a bereavement response was a reality for them), but they may have periods of recurring distress. One explanation for this is the 'chronic sorrow model' (Olshanksy, 1962). This model has had various phases of popularity, and both in the 1980s and 1990s it was the subject of some debate (Gabba, 1994; Wikler, 1984). Again, for some parents there may be some identification with this pattern of response. It is argued that parents may experience periods of grieving at later stages in their child's life without being poorly adjusted to their child. The parent who continues to feel sadness about a child's disability can still be confident and caring. The parent who is experiencing sorrow, however, may reflect this state of mind in the way they deal with their child's education.

Through working with parents of children with special educational needs over some 20 years, I have come to realize that vulnerability is particularly pronounced in many of them. This may manifest itself in hypersensitivity, short temper and an inability to cope with criticism of their child or themselves. For the parent, it may be symptomatic of the dread of further unanticipated bad news, the desire to protect their child in the face of a social structure whose capacity to care for that child is being continually eroded, an over-protectiveness or a desire to compensate. This may not be too far away from how any parent feels about their child; however, for the parent of a child with special educational needs, it is more accentuated.

Lessons from early intervention

With other families, there were interests in common other than our children, and time spent with these families was for the same reasons one might spend time with any set of friends. What is unique about friendship with other families [of children with special needs] is the depth of understanding: they are more than the sincere, empathetic professional. They have been there too – through the endless hospital appointments, the perplexing behaviour patterns, the unanswered questions. This in no way diminishes the invaluable contribution of professionals, but to live with a child with a disability 24 hours a day, brings lessons that no professional course of training can ever hope to teach. (A father, quoted in Carpenter and Herbert, 1995)

Developments in the field of early intervention, and a knowledge of how it has moved to more family-based approaches of service delivery, may inform our thinking about how we can construct our partnerships between schools and families. In the past, early intervention programmes tended to focus upon the child with special educational needs in particular areas of skill development. The nature of the programme may have become disorientating to the family; often little attention was given to the quality of relationships being established between the child and the family members. This could actually have had an adverse effect on the child/family relationship, with an unhelpful emphasis upon the provision of parents 'with teacher skills instead of strategies for communicating with their child in an optimal manner' (Basil, 1994).

More recently the move has been towards family-focused models of service delivery. Many researchers and practitioners feel that family-centred models are more humane and dignifying to the child and their family, although this is not to diminish the qualities that professionals working in the early intervention phase should possess. Such approaches acknowledge the child's context, for children do not develop separately from this context, but are always informed by their environment. Sue Buckley and Gillian Bird, in their recent guidance to parents on early intervention, emphasize that 'the most important gift parents can give their baby... is to ensure that he or she is a much-loved member of a stable family group' (Buckley and Bird, 1995, p.1).

The early intervention team which has the family at its centre, even in times of uncertainty and anxiety, should be self-supporting and self-sustaining. Such approaches also increase the capacity of families to provide resources to other families to assist in solving problems. Hornby (1989; 1995) has written extensively on parent-to-parent schemes which illustrate this particular approach. Sensitive interaction within the early intervention team will enable a family to change its contribution over a period of time. The dimensions of family involvement may increase or decrease depending on how the family may be feeling at a particular time. As with any child-rearing process there are problem patches. What we must acknowledge is that families of children with special educational needs are first and foremost families. Whilst being positive in our focus, there should be space for and acceptance of the full range of emotions experienced by any families and their implications for the dynamics within the team.

Family-centred approaches in early intervention have been strengthened in the USA through legislation. Public Law 99/457 formally requires an Individualized Family Service Program (IFSP) to be prepared. This is now the subject of much debate regarding family inclusion, parent participation and professional role definition (Bailey et al., 1990). Ideally, the IFSP is designed by parents and includes areas of emphasis that reflect parent resources, concerns and priorities for themselves and their children. The IFSP in the United States marks a shift away from the Individualized Education Programme (IEP), which was professionally driven and developed on the basis of a process whereby professionals share with parents evaluation information and divide goals and objectives. This shift is bringing with it considerable need to present information in 'parent language' as opposed to professional jargon (Campbell *et al.*, 1992).

In Europe, family-centred approaches to early intervention have been the subject of considerable research. Peterander (1995) writes that: 'holistic, family-orientated approaches... require close collaboration between the range of professionals in the fields of pedagogy, psychology, social sciences and medicine'. In Finland, Mattus (1994) and Maki (1994) have both stressed that family-centred intervention is to empower families. They go on to recommend an 'ecological' approach in which the involvement of the family is pivotal. The purpose of this approach is to gather information about the children's lives: their activities, interactions, experiences and peer contacts in natural environments.

It can be seen from the overview above that the contexts of early intervention have come under close scrutiny. The particular benefit to families of recent approaches is that it puts them in a position of control, whereby they can access services, rather than waiting in a dependent fashion for things to be done to them by the various service deliverers.

What constitutes the family?

> Professionals in families can work to eliminate the physical, cultural and social barriers that prevent families from attaining the best possible quality of life. (Seligman and Darling,1989, p.237)

So, what constitutes a family? Is the traditional nuclear interpretation valid? What of reconstituted families or families with different cultural traditions or faith backgrounds? And what of the extended family? Our definition of an extended family could be quite crucial to helping schools interact with families. If we include only blood-relatives, then we may be excluding other people who have a deep bond with the family and offer quality support at a variety of levels – social, emotional, psychological or practical.

In the Māori culture of New Zealand, they have a helpful concept known as a Whānau. A Whānau is a family social structure incorporating all age ranges, interests and experiences (Ballard, 1994). It constitutes an extended family in many respects. It incorporates a range of significant people who take a genuine and shared interest in each other's lives, and who will advocate for each other. Ought we to allow families to self-define their supporting social system?

With the increased use of 'named persons' in the United Kingdom following the implementation of the *Code of Practice*, many parents may choose a close friend, neighbour or representative from a voluntary organization to accompany them to review meetings in schools (Brown and Carpenter, 1995). The traditional family may be at the core of activity, but their social system of support may extend far more widely.

It is worth considering the current thinking about the roles of the key family members surrounding a child with special educational needs. Airi Hautamäki (1995) has produced findings from a cross-Nordic study where she contrasted over a thousand mothers of children with Down's Syndrome with mothers of non-disabled children. She found that these mothers had increased care-taking responsibility, had often amended their 'life project' goals, had more restricted leisure activities and different work patterns, and when they did work there were high levels of leave from work due to illness.

In the case of fathers, Herbert and Carpenter (1994) wrote that if we are to include those whom McConkey (1994) has described as the 'hard-to-reach' parents, then there needs to be greater coordination of services with the life-patterns of fathers to offer them an increased accessibility to information and support, opportunities for the father to network with other fathers and to address his needs for information and emotional support within the family. To achieve this, greater training and awareness amongst professionals is a necessary innovation.

Traditionally, it has been thought that siblings of children with learning difficulties suffered particular problems related to isolation, guilt or resentment. As with fathers, it is important that specific consideration is given to the needs of these family members, as a recent study by Newson and Davis (1994) has demonstrated. Their workshop materials for supporting brothers and sisters of children with autism led to some considerable adjustment in the siblings who were part of that group, leading to comments such as:

> Before I didn't know much about him. Now, I know quite a lot – why he behaves in the way he does. (Sibling, age 10; p.261)

Or

> I had all these feelings inside me, and I had to spill them out, [and in the group] I was able to. (Sibling, age 10; p.261)

Glynne-Rule (1995), whilst finding in her Cornish survey that a few siblings experienced bullying and teasing, also found that after the parents, the siblings of the child with special educational needs were the main relatives providing help, care and education.

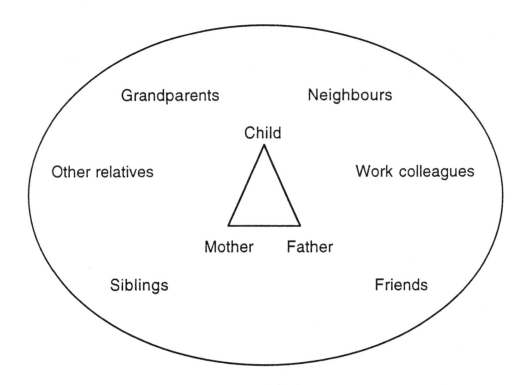

Figure 19.1 An extended family support network

The impetus for partnership

> ...the knowledge, views and experiences of parents are vital. Effective assessment and provision will be secured where there is the greatest possible degree of partnership between parents and their children and schools, LEAs and other agencies. (DfE, 1994, Section 1.2, p.2)

Since 1980, there has been a considerable amount of legislation which has influenced parental rights. Significantly there have been a series of Education Acts – 1981, 1986, 1988, 1992, 1993 – all of which have addressed parents, and also parents of children with special educational needs. The Children Act 1989 not only stressed the partnership with parents, but the importance of families and of the views of those families and children themselves.

All schools desire to be effective schools. The OFSTED (1995) *Framework for the Inspection of Schools* actively seeks to solicit the opinions of parents as to the effectiveness of a school. Good communication and collaboration with parents is one of the hallmarks of an 'effective school'.

Another indicator of an effective school is differentiation. Here, through partnership with families, schools can genuinely engage in meeting the individual needs of their pupils. As will be mentioned later in this chapter, there are many ways in which schools and families can achieve an active dialogue, but what is without doubt is the capacity of many families to spend considerable periods of time with their child, bringing relevance to a learning experience which teachers may not be able to ensure during the course of a busy school day.

This is not to say that working with the curriculum is an easy task for parents. As one parent, referring to the National Curriculum, commented recently: 'I don't know all these targets. How can I be involved?' It is quite probable that the language of the National Curriculum, which has become very public, has disenfranchised some parents. They perceive the common ground slipping away. The once-familiar curriculum terminology that was more understandable (social education, self-help skills, etc.) has been eroded in favour of subject-led terminology – history, geography, science, etc. Some parents' own experience of these subjects within school may lead them to believe that they are irrelevant to their children with special educational needs. Whilst teachers of children with learning difficulties know that all of these traditional and subject elements coexist, this needs to be reaffirmed and explored with parents.

There will always be opposing viewpoints from parents about their own levels of involvement. Take the following two quotations from a parent-partnership workshop held on the same day:

> I am not interfering with the curriculum. It's not my role. If I could do it as well as the teachers, then I may as well keep him at home. (Parent 1)
> Because I am with A so much I felt that I had the right to have a voice. This led me to dominate the situation. I have had to learn the hard way that the teacher does have a point of view, and that I can trust their opinion and skills. (Parent 2)

What is important is that we strive to build an inclusive curriculum (Carpenter, 1995) that includes any family member by whatever definition, at whatever level they wish to be engaged. For some this will be an extensive and active involvement; for others it will be possibly at a distance. What should be clear for all families is the range of opportunities they have to be involved in the learning experiences of their child with learning difficulties. Broad statements such as 'We have an "open door" policy' may mean nothing to some families; 'open doors' can be very draughty! And the often-heard comment of 'Drop into school at any time,' can be equally meaningless; any time is no time. Brown (1994) states: 'Schools need to recognise parent potential'. This could be extended to: 'Schools need to recognize the potential of families as partners in learning'.

Jim is keen to read. He sees his big sister with her homework and wants some for himself. Jim finds ordinary text too difficult, and other than his name he cannot read any words.

He is highly motivated by 'Thomas the Tank Engine' books. His teacher used this as a starting point for introducing symbols into his reading programme. She cut up a copy of *Thomas the Tank Engine* and wrote some simplified text. She then made a symbol card to support each key word. These are kept in a pocket at the back of the book, and can be placed above words in the story to clue Jim into the meaning of the word.

Jim finds symbols much easier to learn. He took his book home to show his parents. He sat his mum and dad either side of him on the settee, and this time he read them the 'Thomas' story. They were astonished. Jim has begun to teach his family some symbols!

Jim is 6 years old and has Down's Syndrome. So motivated were his parents by the above experience that they offered to buy some more 'Thomas' books and make up simpler story lines for him. They asked the teacher for help with the symbols. She told them about the computer program, 'Writing with Symbols' (Detheridge, 1995) that she uses to prepare Jim's symbols. Jim's big sister said the program was compatible with her computer, and so one weekend she borrowed the copy from the school resources library and prepared the symbols to support the text. Jim's stories go to and from school every day. After six weeks, he already knows ten words without symbols. His teacher hopes soon to interest him in some other reading material.

What do we know about partnership?

Children learn more when parents, teachers, and/or therapists work together. (McConkey, 1985)

There have been various phases in the growth of the parent/professional relationship. For many years, parents of children with special needs were left largely unsupported and received little help from professionals. Then the 'professional as expert' became an accepted way of working with parents of children with special needs. In this approach, the professional used their position and expertise to make judgements and take control of what needed doing. This approach was based on some unfortunate common attitudes to parents: that they were problems, adversaries, in need of treatment, causal, or needed to be kept at a professional distance (Hornby, 1995). Many teachers would claim that they are not comfortable with the role of expert, but it is acknowledged that some parents push teachers into that role. As one parent said recently in her child's annual review: 'I am most comfortable with the notion of you [the teacher] as an expert'. Naturally, she deserves to have this viewpoint respected.

The transplant model of parental involvement emerged in the early 1970s where the home was acknowledged as a potentially important learning setting, but one in which professionals could transplant their skills and expertise on parents. Workshops for parents to train them to use professional techniques was a common feature of this approach, particularly in relation to behaviour modification. Whilst the parent is valued in this approach for their interactive role, it is a professionally-led approach, with the professional transmitting skills to the parent, rather than the parent ever taking a lead for themselves. It clearly does not bear out Wolfendale's (1989) definition of 'equivalent expertise'.

The consumer model developed by Cunningham and Davis (1985) marks the beginning of true partnership. There was a shift in power from the professional to the parent, with the parent exercising control over the selection of services for their child. At a recent parent workshop, 'mutual respect' was the phrase used time and time again to express the key principle that should inform the working practices between schools and families. This is very much a feature of the consumer model which went some considerable way to achieving what Warnock described as 'a partnership, and ideally an equal one'.

The consumer approach requires professionals to display genuineness, respect and empathy towards parents. The working relationship between parents and professionals can be characterized as:

- a shared sense of purpose
- a willingness to negotiate
- sharing of information
- shared responsibility
- joint decision-making and accountability.

In the late 1980s, the rights of parents came to the fore. Networking was one thing parent groups of the time learnt to do well. A formidable array of contacts was systematically built up in key areas. Thus empowered as a group rather than as a series of individuals, parents began to assert their rights as well as those of their child. Ferrell (1989) lists these rights as:

- the right to feel angry
- the right to seek another opinion
- the right to privacy
- the right to keep trying
- the right to stop trying
- the right to set limits
- the right to be a parent
- the right to be unenthusiastic
- the right to be annoyed with your child
- the right to time off
- the right to be expert in charge
- the right to dignity.

From the background of this thinking, and the development in professional working practices, three significant models of working with parents and families emerged. The work of Hornby in this area (1989; 1995) has had a significant impact, and has been adapted by other authors (Carpenter and Herbert, 1994). Many schools have used the Hornby model as the framework for planning their policy for working with parents. The empowerment model (Appleton and Minchcom, 1991) gives us a strong indication of how the emphasis is beginning to shift from parents to families. The key points of this model can be summarized as:

- the rights of parents as consumers
- choice of service and level of engagement
- recognition of the family as a system
- recognition of the family's social network.

More recently, Dale has produced a thorough exposition which will be of value to all professionals. It is called the 'negotiating model', because it focuses on negotiation as a key transaction for partnership work and builds upon the consumer and empowerment models:

> It offers a framework for exploring a partnership practice that can embody or respond to the constraints and reality of actual power relations and positions of the parent and professional within present or future societal contexts. (Dale, 1996, p.14)

The 'negotiating model' endeavours not to discriminate against the parents' rights to be involved and consulted, and to advance, through collaboration and negotiated decision-making with all parents and families, to a point where all are mutually happy with the outcomes. The key features of this particular model are:

- negotiation as a key transaction for partnership
- joint decision-making
- resolution of differences
- shared perspective.

The lessons to be learnt from these various models and the last two decades of endeavour on all parts in parental involvement could be summarized in the following list of recommendations to families, schools and also professionals working with either or both parties:

1. Be honest with each other.
2. Be willing to learn from each other.
3. Treat each other with respect and dignity.
4. Be willing to admit you make mistakes.
5. Work collaboratively and cooperatively.
6. Be yourself.

The context for partnership

If we are to work effectively with families, it is important that they know that we value their context – the home. Parents and professionals grow and change. Families also grow and change. The constitution of a family one year may not be the same the next; an older sibling may have married, gone out to work or away to university. This could have a major impact on a family. The child with learning difficulties may not understand where their much-loved sibling has gone. A key supporter in the family is no longer around to help with baby-sitting. The person who listened to the mother's anxieties is no longer there to 'counsel'. Schools need to be sensitive to this. Listening to and understanding each other's points of view is critical. Schools can do much to strengthen parent–child relationships.

Robert reads in a monotone voice, never allowing his eyes to stray from the book. He is 15 years old and attends a unit for pupils who are considered to be within the autistic continuum, attached to a mainstream secondary school. He joins a Year 10 class for English. They are studying Shakespeare's *Romeo and Juliet*.

Robert's parents are concerned that he is increasingly isolating himself at home. Social interaction is less than ever, and his parents cannot decide how much to attribute to his impairment, and how much to 'normal adolescent behaviour'. Robert is an only child and chooses to spend time alone in his bedroom where he has a television. A touring production of *Romeo and Juliet* has come to Robert's home town. The English teacher organizes a visit and invites families to join the theatre party if they wish. Robert's parents do so.

During the performance, Robert's gaze gradually transfers from his hands to the stage. In a series of fleeting glances, he notices the lights, colours, costumes and actors, and hears the words which he has memorized. He becomes increasingly animated during the performance.

At home the next evening, he recalls the events with his parents. They have a sustained conversation, the first in many months.

Since this theatre event, Robert's parents have taken him to the theatre several times. He is preparing a special project on theatres for his English GCSE. His parents feel that at last they have found something they all three can enjoy and share. In this example, the coincidental initiation of a school has impacted upon the home life of the family and improved the quality of that home life. Teachers need to be aware of the potential influence they can have on a child's home: how they can be a supportive and unifying influence on the home. At the same time too much pressure from the school towards the home can be disruptive and disunite families. The balance is indeed a complex one to achieve.

Ways of working

> No attempts by teachers to communicate with parents about their children are a waste of time. (Parent comment in response to a questionnaire about home–school links, 1992)

There are many practical ways for schools to develop relationships with families and offer them support. Clayson (1996) has offered some imaginative ways of using the telephone for home–school contacts. Many other authors have cited ways in which it is possible to work with parents (Hornby, 1995; Wolfendale, 1989). Ways of supporting families demand a broader consideration of the type of activity that will encompass all family members. The following list offers some practical suggestions, which schools may like to use as starting points for evaluating their current approaches for working with families:

1. Home visits.
2. Shared planning and recording.
3. Circles of celebration (achievement certificates, etc.).
4. Playgroups.
5. Parent support groups.
6. Home–school diaries (handwritten, audio [using an Echo 4] or in symbols).
7. Telephone contact.
8. Child's profile.
9. Parents' library.
10. Shared training.
11. Sensory activities.
12. Events for all the family.

Further discussion of these suggestions can be found in Carpenter and Herbert (1994).

Conclusion

> For us the priorities for the home–school partnership are communication, information and involvement'. (Feedback from a parent support group meeting to discuss and evaluate home–school links)

Dale (1996) talks of a whole family approach – how could we apply this to the shared curriculum links we may embark upon with families, or the dialogue of learning they may establish with us? This may not require significant modification of our usual approach. Rather we will need to reappraise the target audience. (Our traditional focus would have been mother and father – or, in reality, mother.) What is the potential contribution of the significant others? Mittler (1994) points out the increasing role that grandparents are playing in the care of their grandchildren. If they are the receiver of the child when they arrive home, is it they who will read the home diary, discuss the child's day with them, share paintings, books, news?

What of brothers and sisters? Glynne-Rule (1995) discovered in her study that after the parents it was the siblings who provided the most within-family support. In the time they spend with their sibling is there some constructive medium for interaction that can be provided by the school? Or is 'play' (leisure) itself intrinsically valuable, offering opportunities for 'intensive interaction' (Nind and Hewitt,1994)? And if it is, should we not tell the brother or sister concerned, and include their contribution in the overall plan? In this context we can borrow and adapt a concept from the IFSP described above. A more holistic overview would enable us to determine learning partners according to task/experience, to match the most appropriate supporter to the naturalistic context, to bring maximum benefit to the child. Children need families; children need schools. By empowering each other we can empower our children.

> The greatest gift we can give to our children is a caring, supportive family.... Parents are often very unsure of the best ways to help their child, and I believe if they are given flexible, responsive and sensitive support, this will not only strengthen their role in the short term but will also increase their capacity for the future.... It is the parents and families who usually provide the most constant ongoing interest and support in a person's life, so any investment of time and energy, by schools and professionals, I believe is well spent. (A parent)

References

Appleton, P.L. and Minchcom, P.E. (1991) 'Models of parent partnership and child development centres', *Child: Care, Health and Development*, 17, 27–38.

Bailey, D.B., Palsha, S.A. and Huntingdon, G.S. (1990) 'Preservice preparation of special educators to work with infants with handicaps and their families: Current status and training needs', *Journal of Early Intervention*, 14, 1, 43–54.

Ballard, K. (ed.) (1994) *Disability, Family, Whānau and Society*, Palmerston North, NZ: Dunmore Press.

Basil, C. (1994) 'Family involvement in the intervention process', in Brodin, J. and Bjorck-Akesson, E. (eds) *Methodological Issues in Research in Augmentative and Alternative Communication*, Jonkoping: University Press.

Brown, C. (1994) 'Parents and professionals', in Ballard, K. (ed.) *Disability, Family, Whānau and Society*, Palmerston North, NZ: Dunmore Press.

Brown, E. and Carpenter, B. (1995) 'Step by step, hand in hand', *Special Children*, 86, 15–19.

Buckley, S. and Bird, G. (1995) 'Early intervention: how to help your child in the preschool years', *Down's Syndrome Trust Newsletter*, 5 ,1, 1–5.

Campbell, P., Strickland, B. and La Forme, C. (1992) 'Enhancing parent participation in the individual family service plan', *Topics in Early Childhood Special Education*, 11, 4, 112–24.

Carpenter. B. (1995) 'Building an inclusive curriculum', in Ashcroft, K. and Palacio, D. (eds) *The Primary Teacher's Guide to the New National Curriculum*, London: Falmer Press.

Carpenter, B. and Herbert, E. (1994) 'School-based support', in Mittler, P. and Mittler, H. (eds) *Innovations in Family Support for People with Learning Disabilities*, Lancashire: Lisieux Hall.

Carpenter, B. and Herbert, E. (1995) 'Including fathers: parent–professional considerations of the role of fathers in early intervention', *Network*, 4, 4, 4–11.

Clayson, V. (1996) 'An audit of links between a school for pupils with PMLD and their parents', Oxford: assignment submission to the B.Phil.(Ed.) course, Westminster College.

Clench, H. (1994) *Empowering Parents of Children with Special Educational Needs*, East Sussex: Psychological Service.

Cunningham, C. and Davis, H. (1985) *Working with Parents: Frameworks for collaboration*, Buckingham: Open University Press.

Cunningham, C.C. and Sloper, P. (1977) 'Parents of Down's Syndrome babies: their early needs', *Child: Care, Health and Development*, 3, 325–47.

Dale, N. (1996) *Working with Families of Children with Special Needs*, London: Routledge.

Detheridge, M. (1995) *The Writing Set: An overview and rationale*, Leamington Spa: Widgit Software Ltd.

DfE (1994) *Code of Practice on the Identification and Assessment of Special Educational Needs*, London: HMSO.

Ferguson, P.M. and Asch, A. (1989) 'Lessons from life: personal and parental perspectives on school, childhood and disability', in Biklen, D., Ferguson, D. and Ford, A. (eds) *Schooling and Disability*, Chicago: NSSE.

Ferrell, K. (1989) *Reach Out and Teach: Meeting the training needs of parents of visually and multiply handicapped children*, Washington, DC: American Foundation for the Blind.

Fitton, P. (1994) *Listen to Me: Communicating the needs of people with profound intellectual and multiple disabilities*, London: Jessica Kingsley.

Gabba, M. (1994) 'Some things are unacceptable', *Special Children*, February, 19–20.

Gascoigne, E. (1995) *Working with Parents as Partners in SEN*, London: David Fulton.

George, J.D. (1988) 'Therapeutic interaction for grandparents and extended family of children with developmental delays', *Mental Retardation*, 26 6, 369–75.

Glynne-Rule, L. (1995) 'Support for the disabled', *Times Educational Supplement*, April.

Hautamäki, Airi (1995) 'Stress and stressors in mothers of children with Down's Syndrome: a cross-Nordic study', paper presented to the International Special Education Congress, Birmingham, UK.

Hebden, J. (1985) *She'll Never Do Anything, Dear*, London: Souvenir Press.

Herbert, E. and Carpenter, B. (1994) 'Fathers: the secondary partners', in. Carpenter, B. (ed.) *Early Intervention: Where are we now?*, Oxford: Westminster Press.

Hornby, G. (1989) 'Launching parent to parent schemes', *British Journal of Special Education*, 15, 2, 77–8.

Hornby, G. (1995) *Working with Parents of Children with Special Need,*. London: Cassell.

Hornby, G. and Ashworth, T. (1994) 'Grandparent support for families who have children with disabilities: a survey of parents', *Journal of Family Studies*, 3, 403–12.

Johnson, C. and Crowder, J. (1994) *Autism: From tragedy to triumph*, Boston, MA: Branden Publishing.

Kimpton, D. (1990) *A Special Child in the Family*, London: Sheldon Press.

McConkey, R. (1985) *Working with Parents: A practical guide for teachers and therapists*, Beckenham: Croom Helm.

McConkey, R. (1994) 'Early intervention: Planning futures, shaping years', *Mental Handicap Research*, 7, 1, 4–15.

Maki, I. (1994) 'Ecological approach and early intervention', in Leskinen, M. (ed.) *Family in Focus*, Jyväkylä: Jyväkylä University Press.

Mattus, M.R. (1994) 'Interview as invention: strategies to empower families of children with disabilities', in Leskinen, M. (ed.) *Family in Focus*, Jyväkylä: Jyväkylä University Press.

Mirfin-Veitch, B., Bray, A., Watson, M. (1996) '"They really do care": grandparents as informal support for families of children with disabilities', Dunedin, NZ: Donald Beasley Institute.

Mittler, P. (1994) 'Early intervention: the way forward', in Carpenter, B. (ed.) *Early Intervention: Where are we now?*, Oxford: Westminster Press.

Mittler, P. and Mittler, H. (eds) (1994) *Innovations in Family Support for People with Learning Disabilities*, Lancashire: Lisieux Hall.

Newson, E. and Davis, J. (1994) 'Supporting the siblings of children with autism and related developmental disorders', in Mittler, P. and Mittler, H. (eds) *Innovations in Family Support for People with Learning Disabilities*, Lancashire: Lisieux Hall.

Nind, M. and Hewitt, D. (1994) *Access to Communication: Developing the basis of communication with people with severe learning difficulties through intensive interaction,* London: David Fulton.

OFSTED (1995) *A Framework for the Inspection of Schools,* London: HMSO.

Olshansky, S. (1962) 'Chronic sorrow: a response to having a mentally defective child', *Social Casework,* 43, 190–93.

Peterander, F. (1995) *Early Intervention: A report to the Helios II programme,* Munich, Germany: Ludwig–Maximilian University.

Powell, T.H. and Ogle, P.A. (1992) *Brothers and Sisters: A special part of exceptional families* (2nd edn), Baltimore: Paul H. Brookes.

Russell, P. (1983) 'The parents' perspective of family needs and how to meet them', in Mittler, P. and McConachie, H. (eds) *Parents, Professionals and Mentally Handicapped People: Approaches to partnership,* Beckenham: Croom Helm.

Seligman, M. and Darling, R.B. (1989) *Ordinary Families, Special Children: A system approach to childhood disability,* New York: The Guilford Press.

Turnbull, A.P. and Turnbull, H.R. (1986) *Families, Professionals and Exceptionality,* Columbus, OH: Merrill.

Wikler, L. (1984) 'Chronic stresses of families of mentally retarded children', in Henninger, M.L. and Nesselroad, E.M. (eds) *Working with Parents of Handicapped Children,* Lanham, MD: University Press of America.

Wills, R. (1994) 'It is time to stop', in Ballard, K. (ed.) *Disability, Family, Whānau and Society,* Palmerston North, NZ: Dunmore Press.

Wolfendale, S. (ed.) (1989) *Parental Involvement: Developing networks between school, home and community,* London: Cassell.

Chapter 20

Access to the System: The Legislative Interface

Philippa Russell

Introduction

The past decade has seen major developments in terms of policy and practice for families with children with disabilities and special needs. The principles of family-based services and inclusion are widely recognized. But the rhetoric and the reality do not always match. Complex assessment systems and changes in the management of child health, education and social services have improved the actual commissioning of services but – in an increasingly contractual culture – have created major challenges to families in terms of understanding the system.

It is estimated that there are about 360,000 children with disabilities aged 16 and under in the UK (around 3 per cent of the child population) (OPCS, 1989). Of these children, all but 5,500 live at home. It has been estimated that 13.4 per cent of the school population are regarded as having special educational needs (SEN). Just under 11 per cent of all pupils are registered as having SEN but no statements – this figure varying from between around 3 per cent to 25 per cent for different authorities. The proportion of pupils with statements has been rising and now is around 2.7 per cent.

Although accurate figures on mainstream education are difficult to obtain, there is a marked overall trend for pupils with new statements to attend a mainstream school. The number of special schools is falling (primarily through closure of hospital schools) but there is a growing number of children with very complex difficulties and disabilities, largely due to the improving survival rate of very premature or sick infants.

Currently, 16,550 children with SEN are attending residential schools, with the largest number – 8,000 – in schools for children with emotional and behavioural difficulties. Many residential schools are under increasing pressure to provide 52 weeks a year residential care. This trend has to be offset against gradual but encouraging increases in mainstream school placements for all children with disabilities and a recognition that parents are expecting more community-based services which enable them and their children, in the words of the Children Act 1989, to lead lives which are 'as ordinary as possible'.

There has been growing concern about the impact of disadvantage, family problems and health issues on the education of both children with disabilities and/or statements of SEN and on the education and development of children 'in need' under the Children Act 1989. The current acrimonious debate about difficult and disruptive children and the growth of exclusions from the mainstream and special school sectors highlights the need for better understanding between health, education and social services and the need to adopt 'whole child' approaches based on a clear understanding of the legal basis for entitlement to services and the purchasing arrangements within different agencies to meet individual needs.

SEN in context: helping parents to help children

> Partnership with parents – it's a wonderful concept, but the theory is better than the practice. Everyone wants to be your partner, when you have a child with special needs. But by the time I've done the paired reading, I've done the speech therapy and the physio programmes (and oh dear, he *does* hate those callipers!), when I've worked through the developmental play activities there's not time for anything else. But I've got three other children, a mortgage, a cat and an elderly mother – and I think my husband is about to lose his job. I really *would* like to pop up to the school again, just to talk through the IEP. But really, it's me who needs the IEP not Paul. If only the *professionals* would get their jobs (and their Acts) together, life would be much easier. Partnership? Well really, I think I am a nice cheap treatment resource.' (Parent attending parent workshop; Russell and Flynn, 1994)

There has been a growing recognition that the effective education of a child with SEN will not only depend upon the quality of the special educational provision made to address those needs, but upon the interface between education services and the health and social services which may enhance the effectiveness of any educational provision and provide direct support to parents and carers. The pressures placed upon young families by the care needs of their children with disabilities or SEN is well documented. A study by Glendinning (1983) found that out of 361 young children with disabilities, 50.1 per cent could not be left alone for even ten minutes in a day. A later study by Beresford (1995), using Family Fund data on the lives of families with children with a wide range of disabilities, special needs and medical conditions similarly found many families isolated and unaware of practical or financial sources of help and therefore frequently less able to cope. Beresford's study echoed that of Wilkin (1979) on the lives of families with children with severe learning difficulties (SLD), which found that there was little significant help from relatives, friends or neighbours in terms of day-to-day caring. Many parents in consequence felt themselves to be less able to be active partners in their child's education and correspondingly felt less valued as parents and carers and more anxious about their child's future.

Poverty has become an increasingly common agenda item for many families, with the corresponding negative impact of poor housing, the social stigma of unemployment and the greater risk of mental health difficulties and family breakdown. As the OFSTED report, *Access and Achievement in Urban Education* (1994) noted: 'Beyond the school gate are many factors which directly impact upon a child's education, such as poor housing, unemployment and poverty and parental ill health'.

The OFSTED report, like the Audit Commission's report, *Seen but not Heard* (1994) on cooperation between health and social services in provision for children 'in need' (including children with disabilities and special educational needs), concluded that many families were in need precisely because there was poor professional awareness of:

- The opportunities offered by complementary legislation and by the social security system to support vulnerable families;
- The need to acknowledge that positive partnerships with parents (and the optimum development of a child) frequently necessitated the provision of information and advice in order to access services;
- The importance of recognizing the interrelatedness of health, education and social care and the challenges experienced by many families in managing complex and often protracted assessment systems;

The past decade has seen the implementation of a wide range of legislation which directly affects the effective implementation of both the 1993 Education Act and the *Code of Practice on the Identification and Assessment of Special Educational Needs* (DfE, 1994). The Children Act 1989 provides an over-arching legal framework which gives parents (and children) rights and responsibilities in decision-making; refocuses attention away from parents as 'owners' of children to children themselves as autonomous beings; acknowledges children with disabilities within mainstream children's legislation; prioritizes child protection and promotes cooperation between health, education and social services in carrying out their statutory duties. At the same time, the *Code of Practice* acknowledges the interface of arrangements for assessment and review of special educational needs with decision-making and provision emanating from social services and child health services. In practice the rhetoric has been better than the reality but the parallel debates about 'care in the community' and the management of difficult and disruptive pupils within schools have highlighted the impossibility of finding single solutions for 'pupils with problems' and the need to identify and meet the needs of parents and carers in order to support their children.

The Children Act 1989

The Children Act 1989 has been widely welcomed for bringing together most public and private law relating to children and for establishing a new and unified approach to local authority services for children and families in England and Wales. Many of the changes (and challenges) of the Children Act 1989 will be most apparent in services for children with disabilities and their parents. Historically, such services have been provided through health as well as local authorities, with confusing variations in local management and many conspicuous gaps in service. The Act restores the leadership to social services departments and importantly requires that 'every local authority shall have services designed:

  a) to minimise the effect on disabled children within their area of disability, and
  b) to give such children the opportunity to lead lives which are as normal as possible.
  (Schedule 2, para 6)

Many children with disabilities or special needs will require health and social care, both at home and in educational contexts, if they are to achieve their full potential. However, a 'single door' approach to services can only happen if definitions of 'need' and assessment arrangements dovetail, and inter-agency support systems for individuals are complementary, well organized, of good quality and convenient to user families with no waste of resources. There is growing interest in joining purchasing strategies with shared operational and strategic guidelines across the three main statutory agencies. But such an approach requires careful negotiations at local level, to reconcile different priorities and 'cultural differences' between agencies and to create incentives to work together in the future (Audit Commission, 1994; Russell, 1996).

The Children Act 1989 introduces a new concept of children in need. This is defined as meaning that a child will be regarded as being in need if:

    a) he is unlikely to achieve or maintain, or to have the opportunity of achieving or maintaining, a reasonable standard of health or development without the provision for him of services by a local authority under this Part (of the Act);

    b) his health or development is likely to be significantly impaired, or further impaired, without the provision for his services; or

    c) he is disabled.

A key theme in the Children Act 1989 is that of partnership with parents and children, with an emphasis upon basing all decisions not only upon parent participation in decision-making but upon the ascertainable wishes and feelings of children – a challenging concept for children with disabilities or special needs (Russell, 1995).

The Children Act 1989 has been widely welcomed in providing a new legal framework for the inclusion of children with disabilities and SEN within a wider framework of legal powers,

---

The Children Act 1989

For the first time in UK legislation, the Children Act 1989 requires local authorities to provide services for children with disabilities which are designed to minimize the effects of the children's disabilities and to give them the opportunity to lead lives which are as normal as possible.

These requirements are based upon the 'five great principles' which must inform *all* local authority working with children, namely:

- *The welfare of the child.* Local authorities have new duties to safeguard and promote the welfare of children in need, those they are looking after and those who are living away from home.
- *Partnership with parents.* Local authorities should try and support parents without the use of compulsory powers.
- *The importance of families.* Children should be brought up in their own families (immediate or extended) wherever possible
- *The importance of the views of children and parents.* Local authorities have duties to ascertain and take account of their wishes and feelings
- *Corporate responsibility.* The Children Act is addressed to the local authority *as a whole* and not just to social services departments.

Local authorities have new duties to provide a range of services for children 'in need' and their families. These include:

- advice, guidance and counselling
- practical and financial assistance by grant or loan
- occupational, recreational or social activities
- home help (including laundry services)
- help with travel in order to use a service
- day care and supervised activities (including after-school and holiday programmes)
- accommodation (which includes respite care).

The local authority has a duty to prevent neglect and abuse and to avoid court proceedings if possible. The authority has new powers to provide for young people over 18 but under 21, if they have continuing needs.

duties and protection which relate to the welfare of all children and in that context see that all children are literally children first. Section 17(1) of the Act sets out the general duty of every local authority to safeguard and promote the welfare of the children within their area who are in need, but also makes a range of new and specific requirements with reference to children with disabilities. The boxed text summarizes the key message of the Act.

Children' services plans: a collaborative approach to children's services

The Children Act 1989 has a strong inclusive principle. Schedule 2, paragraph 6, does not explain to local authorities how they may provide services for children with disabilities which will minimize the effect of their disabilities upon them, nor does it attempt to describe an 'ordinary life'. But the ordinary life principle runs through all the Act's procedures, including those relating to the courts, where children have new rights to emphasize their own preferences about where they wish to live, who they wish to live with and how their lives should be organized. The Act assumes that local authorities will 'promote access for all children to the same range of services' but Volume 6 of the guidance on the Act (DoH, 1991) notes the importance of avoiding simplistic notions of inclusion and acknowledging that some children *can* use ordinary services, but may need support to do so.

Access to good quality local services for families with children with learning disabilities has always been problematic, not least because children with disabilities and SEN will inevitably constitute a minority within any local authority planning system and because their needs will equally inevitably be met through a multiplicity of different agencies. The Children Act 1989 requires local authority social services, in partnership with the relevant LEA and health services, to create and maintain registers of children with disabilities as the basis for planning coherently for children with disabilities and any associated special educational needs. From 1996 local authorities have a mandatory duty to develop children's services plans, which set out the local authority's planning arrangements for children's services, with annual targets and specified review arrangements. Within these plans, the local authority must include children with disabilities and special needs and must use the register of children with disabilities as the basis for such planning.

Children's services plans must include arrangements for education, health and social services provision within a locality and therefore provide major opportunities for ensuring that there is a planning (and legislative) interface between all providers for children with disabilities or special needs. Their importance is underlined by the radical changes in the organization of children's services within some local authorities following local government reorganization. With some authorities merging education and social services provision for children and young people within unified children's departments, clarity about both the legal interface for the provision of services (particularly for children with low incidence special needs or disabilities) will be critical. Hence the Children's services planning process must be seen by LEAs as well as social services (the lead agency) as a crucial strategic process and one which will have a direct impact upon the operational roles and responsibilities of schools.

Family support

The Children Act 1989 places great emphasis upon supporting children within their natural families wherever possible. Initially, implementation focused in many authorities on the statutory procedures relating to child protection. But Bullock (1996) has highlighted the danger of focusing wholly upon interventionist approaches at the expense of preventive work, earlier intervention and family support. For children with disabilities or special needs, 'family support' may be defined in a variety of ways and may include day or holiday services; respite or short-term care; the provision of special equipment or aids; help in the family home and access to information. As Baldwin and Carlisle (1994) note in a review of the research literature on services for disabled children, any support services provided through the Children Act 1989 must be based on key criteria, namely accurate information, integrated assessment and planning arrangements, and commitment at all levels to listening to parents and children about the services they need.

The Children Act 1989 importantly acknowledges that family support will require an integrated approach towards assessment, specifying that such assessments may be combined with assessment procedures under the Education Act 1993. the Disabled Persons Act 1986. the Chronically Sick and Disabled Persons Act 1970 and the NHS and Community Care Act 1990. Linda's story below reflects the importance of assessing need as broadly as possible and the positive outcomes of schools and LEAs understanding the powers and responsibilities of health and social services in supporting children with special educational needs.

LINDA is 6 years old and has a metabolic storage disease with a poor prognosis. Her condition (and her educational achievements) are both beginning to deteriorate. Her parents, after genetic counselling, have had her brother tested for the same condition. The result is positive. Linda's father has now left home and her mother is clinically depressed. The house is dirty; Linda's own physical care is unsatisfactory and she sometimes appears hungry. She is also frequently late or absent from school. Her social services team with responsibility for services for children with disabilities have ensured that Linda is on the register of children with disabilities. Linda's mother has the right to refuse registration but has agreed and is pleased with the range of information she now gets on local services.

Linda has been introduced to a family link (short-term care) service and spends regular enjoyable weekends with another family with a child of a similar age. Her brother sometimes accompanies her. Her mother says she 'feels better for the break'. The family have been encouraged to join a local parent support group, with a range of weekend activities for parents and children. The group members have helped Linda's mother, and given her advice on benefits and local sources of help. The school in turn has sought advice from social services on supporting a family with two children with potentially terminal conditions and on the kind of practical information on local services they should provide.

The social services department has used its powers under both the Children Act 1989 and the Carers (Recognition and Services) Act 1995 to plan for Linda and her mother's special needs. When and if Linda survives into adolescence, her transition plan will link the family with the Disabled Persons Act 1986 (via the Transition Plan) and with the Chronically Sick and Disabled Persons Act 1970 if the family need special equipment such as a telephone or building adaptations.

Because Linda has ongoing special health care needs, which will increase over the coming years, her annual reviews will contain a regular contribution from her consultant paediatrician, and the school nurse has been alerted to assist with any practical health care needs. The health service support for Linda's special educational needs is arranged through the health authority's designated medical officer.

The role of child health services

The implementation of the NHS and Community Care Act 1990 has led to major changes in the organization of child health services, with a general endorsement of the need for an integrated child health service for all children. The Department of Health (1996a) defines an integrated child health service as:

a) The provision of a full range of health services for children, including primary health care, health promotion and surveillance arrangements; the care of children with special needs and disabilities and the treatment of serious illness.

b) Continuity of care for children and parents, with easy referral between different parts of the system.

c) Constructive working relationships and good communication between different parts of the NHS and in other statutory and voluntary agencies with whom they may need to work.

d) Promotion of parental (and child) involvement in assessment, decision making and care in keeping with the principle of a 'patient led' NHS with education and health services.

e) The provision of medical advice and support to community services (including schools) on the special health care needs of children with complex needs.

f) Clarification of the continuing role of the NHS with regard to respite and longer term health care.

Health and nursing services will be crucial for many children with SEN if they are to participate in ordinary community activities and in particular to attend school. There is evidence that more very severely disabled children are now surviving serious infectious illnesses and living longer with some of the rarer metabolic and genetically determined diseases – but with very significant medical and nursing needs. A number of health authorities are beginning to provide community outreach schemes, but there have been few direct replications of some of the support programmes for 'medically fragile' children which are developing in the USA. The Jackson, Florida, medical care programme provides an individualized nursing care plan as well as a child care plan (Hochstadt and Yost, 1991) for children with profound and multiple learning difficulties who need additional support from the health service. These plans support children in the home and the school community and ensure easy referrals between primary and more specialist services. In the United Kingdom, the NHS and Community Care Act 1990 has separated the purchasing and provision of services, with district health authorities (DHAs) 'purchasing' local services through a range of providers (usually NHS Trusts). More recent changes in the health service are moving towards what is often described as a primary health-led NHS in which GP fund-holders (general medical practitioners with a delegated share of the NHS budget) receive a greater share of delegated budgets in order to directly purchase health services for their patients. The rise of the GP as a 'purchaser' has considerable implications for children with special needs, and education services need to be aware of the changing context of health care and ensure that their designated medical officers (who will liaise between education, the purchasers of health care, i.e. the DHA and the provider services, are fully informed about the level of health care needs for individual children and education services within their locality.

All health authorities make annual statements of their purchasing intentions, which in future may complement the children's services plans for local authority services within their area. Provision within the NHS is generally divided into 'tiers', which consist of:

Tier 1: primary or direct contact services (e.g., the GP, the school nurse).

Tier 2: Interventions by individual professionals in the community (for example a community paediatrician via a child development centre).

Tier 3: interventions by teams of specialist staff helping children with more problems – for example child and adolescent mental health team.

Tier 4: Very specialist interventions and care, for example referral to a hospital working with children with cardiac problems, or neurological difficulties.

Many schools and families are finding themselves confused by the new purchaser/provider arrangements in some health authorities. Divisions of opinion about who pays for nursing care (such as injections or tube feeding) have meant some children being refused respite care in a local authority or voluntary care setting. Ultimately the otherwise welcome shift from a 'medical' to a 'social' model of care poses the important question as to how children with very complex health care needs can best be supported and the extent to which joint commissioning arrangements between local and health authorities can be achieved. However, some health authorities are moving towards the joint commissioning approach for assessment of and provision for SEN and disability, and there is growing awareness that schools and LEAs must ensure that their needs and perceptions of optimum health services in an educational context are shared with their local 'purchasers'. In particular it is worth reflecting that new guidance on community child health services (DoH, 1996a) anticipates greater specificity in defining the health contribution to educational assessment and will require individual contracts for health care of children with special needs in 'out of authority' residential schools. In effect the planning system will become tighter and more specific, but has the capacity for reconciling different legal duties and policy expectations across all three statutory services.

The Carers (Recognition and Services) Act 1995

Both the Children Act 1989 and the NHS and Community Care Act 1990 have highlighted in their implementation the importance of looking after the carers as well as the child or adult with the disability or special needs. Similarly, the introduction of parent partnership schemes through Grants for Education Support and Training (GEST) funding, with the aspiration of achieving both real parent partnership and a positive role for 'named persons' as envisaged by the *Code of Practice*, has demonstrated that partnership is a process and not achievable without a real recognition of the challenges and difficulties encountered by many families in being 'positive parents'.

The Carers (Recognition and Services) Act, implemented in 1996, covers:

- adults (people of 18 and over) who provide or intend to provide 'a substantial amount of care on a regular basis';
- children and young people (under 18) who provide or intend to provide a substantial amount of care on a regular basis; and
- parents who provide or intend to provide a substantial amount of care on a regular basis for disabled children.

Although the term 'disability' is used (as defined in the Children Act 1989 and the preceding Disabled Persons (Representations and Services) Act 1986 and the National Assistance Act 1948), the Act covers 'intensive supervision and emotional support' for adults or children who have serious medical conditions such as HIV or neurological disorders, cancer or mental health problems. It acknowledges that the caring role may vary over time and that parents and carers are not a single homogenous group. Very importantly, the Act acknowledges the impact of support in caring on children and young people in education or training and, for the first time in legislation, the role of the young carers.

Many schools (and indeed LEAs) are well aware of the tensions and conflicts which can arise between the wishes and needs of parents and carers, and the children and young people towards whom an educational assessment is directed. The Practice Guide to the implementation of the Act (DoH, 1996b) notes that:

> Assessment...is a skilful process, the aim of which is to support family and other caring relationships and to assist individuals in finding their own solutions...the care plan should be a result of careful discussion with the user and carer and where differences arise these should be recorded. In certain cases some thought might need to be given as to whether the carer and user should have separate records in view of possible conflicts of interest and confidential information each may give.

Assessments under the Carers (Recognition and Services Act) will be triggered by an assessment under the NHS and Community Care Act 1990 or Children Act 1989 – but the guidance emphasizes the need to give carers and parents the opportunity for private discussions with the local authority about their caring role, separate to discussions with their son, daughter, or other relative. It also notes that educational assessment may be an important opportunity to ensure that families are aware of local support services and that any care needs are dealt with appropriately. The Audit Commission (1994) and others have noted the poor coordination of assessment systems and the feelings of many parents that their own unmet needs were not addressed until a crisis occurred. Ellie's story illustrates the consequences of being an unsupported young carer.

Ellie is 13. She has a hearing impairment, but has done well in a unit within a local comprehensive school. However, her work has recently fallen off; she has periodic absences and her teachers' have noticed her falling asleep in class. Ellie has been a very active member in a local youth group for young people with hearing impairments and has been a regular attender. The youth leader has now contacted the school to ask why she has dropped out and apparently abandoned her Duke of Edinburgh's award. At her annual review (not attended by her mother), Ellie breaks down and cries. Her mother has multiple sclerosis. There are no other relatives. Ellie has become a carer, and is terrified that her mother might be moved to a residential home and she will be sent 'away to school'. Her school is aware of Ellie's right to her own assessment under the Carers' Act and arranges for this to take place. The local authority assesses her mother's needs and, using powers under the Chronically Sick and Disabled Persons Act 1970, provides a range of equipment (in particular bathroom equipment) to lessen the care required. A home help three days a week and a Crossroads Care attendant three evenings a week enable Ellie to go back to her youth club, to do her homework and to understand that no one is suggesting she should leave home. The school, with Ellie's and her mother's permission, contacts the GP to obtain information on multiple sclerosis and Ellie visits the local association. Her annual review notes that she has care responsibilities and that her transition plan should ensure that she is receiving sufficient support to enable her to attend school regularly and do her homework and other activities as she moves towards GCSE and career choices.

From children's services to community care: The Disabled Persons Act 1986

When a young person with a disability reaches the transition period, his or her needs will be assessed and provision made under the Disabled Persons Act 1986, the Chronically Sick and Disabled Persons Act 1987 and the NHS and Community Care Act 1990. The Disabled Persons Act 1986 has important provisions in Sections 5 and 6 which offer opportunities for joint assessment and forward planning, and which parents and teachers should utilize in looking towards the future on school-leaving.

Under Sections 5 and 6 of the Disabled Persons Act 1986, at the first annual review after a child's fourteenth birthday, LEAs must seek information from social services departments as to whether the child with a statement under Part III of the 1993 Education Act is disabled (as defined in the Children Act 1989 and the National Assistance Act 1948) and may require future services from the local authority social services department, on leaving school. The transition plan, replacing the old 13-plus re-assessment, is an important exemplar of the new move towards genuinely inter-agency assessment and planning – but is also illustrative of the problems in reconciling duties under different legislation, which may even define the end of childhood at different chronological points.

The Disability Discrimination Act 1995

The past decade has seen a groundswell of feeling amongst organizations of disabled people on the urgent need for anti-discrimination legislation to ensure that disabled people are not disadvantaged or discriminated against and to give them equal legal rights to those applying on grounds of gender or race. The Disability Discrimination Act 1995, (monitored by an independent National Disability Council) will be implemented in 1996 and will have major implications for health, education and social services as it is implemented incrementally over the next few years.

The government consulted widely on anti-discrimination issues and the Act is designed to ensure that disabled people have equal opportunities in terms of access to employment, buildings and the environment in general, and to services. Although much of the legislation relates primarily to adults, Sections 29 and 30 of the Act refer to education services. Section 29 in particular complements the existing duties of schools with regard to their school SEN policies and will require all schools in the maintained or grant maintained sectors to:

● explain their arrangements for the admission of pupils with disabilities;
● state how they will enable these pupils to gain access to the school (and curriculum);
● state what action they will take to ensure that these students are treated equitably;
● report on these arrangements within the school's annual report.

Section 30 of the Act refers to further and higher education institutions funded by the Further Education and Higher Education Funding Councils. They will also have to publish disability statements which contain information about facilities for disabled people and how they propose to ensure that disabled students gain access to the educational facilities offered by the institution in question.

The Act relates to disability not to SEN, but it defines disability very broadly (including a range of medical and mental health problems), and schools and education services will be directly affected.

The Code of Practice on Access to Services (currently out for consultation) makes it clear that at least in the initial years of implementation, employers and others will have to demonstrate that they acted reasonably if accused of discrimination. For example, it would probably be unreasonable for a school to have no access plan, to be unwilling to make minor adaptations to the physical environment which would make access easier, or to make arbitrary decisions about, for example, refusing a disabled child the opportunity to go on a school visit or to take part in certain activities simply because it would be inconvenient.

In conclusion

The last ten years have seen major developments in creating more family-based services for children with disabilities and special needs. Integration – or inclusion – has become a primary objective, but the ultimate challenge remains the balance between meeting special needs in the most natural environment for child and family.

The DfEE (1996), looking at children's services planning, comments that:

> The [Children's Services Plans Order 1996] requires local authorities to consult with health authorities; NHS Trusts; LEAs; governing bodies of grant maintained schools; voluntary organisations; the police and the probation service. These are the main players...but local authorities may wish to look at children in terms of the 'whole child' and consider other services such as transport, housing, leisure, the environment – all of which impact on their lives and help the child to reach his or her true potential. ...Effective consultation requires a formal framework as well as information contact. Whatever forum is set up between the main agencies, it will be the key to agreeing values and objectives.

The same guidance concludes that:

> Local government reorganisation will create more authorities who will not be self-sufficient in all services. Planning children's services will be crucial and will present opportunities and challenges for innovative inter-agency working and planning. All authorities have equal responsibility for planning and providing children's services.

In effect, 'getting the Acts together' has never been more important – or more challenging in terms of access for all children (and in particular those with disabilities or special educational needs) to optimum opportunities for a full and valued life.

References

Audit Commission (1994) *Seen but not Heard; Coordinating community child health and social services for children in need*, London: HMSO.

Baldwin, S and Carlisle, J (1994) *Social Support for Disabled Children and their Families: A review of the literature*, Edinburgh: Social Work Services Inspectorate, HMSO.

Beresford, B. (1995), *Expert Opinion: Services for severely disabled children*, York: The Family Fund/Joseph Rowntree Trust/Community Care.

Bullock, R. (1996) *Child Protection: Messages from research*, London: HMSO.

DfE (1994) *Code of Practice on the Identification and Assessment of Special Educational Needs*, London: DfE.

DfEE (1996) *Children's Services Planning Guidance, Interagency working with Children in Need*, London: DfEE.

DoH (1991a) *The Children Act 1989: Guidance and regulations, Volume 6, Children with disabilities*, London: HMSO.

DoH (1991b) *Welfare of Children and Young People in Hospital,* London: HMSO.

DoH (1996a) *Community Child Health Services; A practice guide,* London: Department of Health.

DoH (1996b) *The Carers (Recognition and Services) Act 1995; Policy and practice guide,* London: Department of Health.

Glendinning, C. (1983) *Unshared Care: Parents and their disabled children,* London: Routledge and Kegan Paul.

Hochstadt, N. and Yost, D, (1991) *The Medically Complex Child: The transition to home care,* New York : Harwood Academic Publishers.

OPCS (1989), *Office of Population and Census Surveys of Disability in the UK, Report 3: Prevalence of Disability among Children; Report 5: Financial Circumstances of Families; Report 6: Disabled Children: Services, Transport and Education;* London: HMSO.

OFSTED (1994) *Access and Achievement in Urban Education,* London: HMSO.

Russell, P. (1995) *Positive Choices: Developing services for children with disabilities away from home,* London: Council for Disabled Children.

Russell, P. (1996), *The Children Act 1989: Children and young people with learning disabilities: some opportunities and challenges,* Manchester: National Development Team for People with Learning Disabilities.

Russell, P. and Flynn, M. (1994) *Future Services for Families with Children with Learning Disabilities,* Report of Parent Workshop, Manchester: National Development Team for People with Learning Disabilities.

Social Services Inspectorate (1994) *Services to Disabled Children and their Families: Reports of the national inspection to disabled children and their families,* London: HMSO.

Wilkin, D. (1979) *Caring for the Mentally Handicapped Child,* Beckenham: Croom Helm.

Chapter 21

Issues in Teacher Training

Jill Porter

Introduction

The recent presentation of the report of the Special Educational Needs Training
Consortium (SENTC, 1996) to the Secretary of State represents a culmination of some six
years of lobbying by those concerned at the diminution of training opportunities for
teachers of pupils with special educational needs (SEN). The report, funded by the DfEE,
puts forward a number of key recommendations aimed at ensuring a good supply of
appropriately trained teachers, including the establishment of a body to monitor the
supply and quality of training. It remains to be seen however how the Secretary of State
will respond to these recommendations, although as we can see if we trace the steps
leading to this report there has already been official recognition of many of the concerns.

In the last 25 years there has been an important shift in the way in which we view
professional development for teachers.. Historically the emphasis was placed on training,
centrally funded with the needs of an individual given the focus of attention. Almost
invariably the training courses were accredited, leading to a recognized qualification.
Training was instigated by an individual, possibly as part of a longer-term career plan,
and support was sought from the local education authority (LEA). The legitimacy of this
training was clearly stated in the James Report (DES, 1972) which suggested a model of
in-service education and training (INSET) that would 'reflect and enhance the status and
independence of the teaching profession' and set out expectations that teachers would
have regular access to these opportunities. A report from the Advisory Committee on the
Supply and Training of Teachers (ACSTT) entitled *Making Inset Work* (DES, 1978) was
already pointing to a parallel concern to look at the needs of the institution as well as
those of the teacher.

In the 1970s and early 1980s training for the individual teacher might build on
specialist training gained through initial teacher training or provide teachers with an
appropriate training to move for the first time into special education. Even at this time
however, the needs of some groups of teachers were better served than others. For
example, the Advisory Committee on the Supply and Education of Teachers (ACSET)
produced a 1984 report which lists some 15 first degree courses with an option or
substantial element of special needs training, and a further 24 courses leading to a Post-
Graduate Certificate of Education (PGCE). Courses were available for those wishing to

specialize in teaching 'slow learning' or remedial pupils, those with learning difficulties, including severe learning difficulties (SLD) and those pupils with a sensory loss. Of particular relevance to this chapter, there were a further 24 in-service diploma courses for pupils with learning difficulties, including ones for teachers of children with mild, moderate and severe learning difficulties.

Threats to this form of professional development came from a number of directions. Concern had been expressed that teachers did not generalize or maintain the new skills, knowledge and understanding that they had acquired on the course, although these criticisms can be counterbalanced by arguments that LEAs and schools did not always capitalize on returning teachers' new abilities. Consequently, courses often provided teachers with a catalyst to change schools and also LEAs. From an LEA perspective they were funding teachers with little expectation that they would return to utilize their skills to the advantage of their employers. Those teachers who did enthusiastically return to their jobs were often faced with trying to implement change in an unsupportive environment where their colleagues might be suspicious and resentful of the opportunities they experienced for professional development. The cost of this form of training was consequently viewed as high compared to the gains for the school and LEA.

One of the consequences was a review of existing training provision, by ACSET, commissioned by the Secretary of State in 1983. The demand for this arose from a new piece of legislation, the 1981 Education Act; in the case of the SENTC report, the impetus came from the introduction of the *Code of Practice on the Identification and Assessment of Special Educational Needs* (DfE, 1994). The recommendations included the importance of preparing all student teachers to identify SEN, to be able to 'adapt teaching methods and materials', to understand the importance of working with parents and to know about the full range of specialist services. It also brought about the demise of all courses designed to prepare 'students to teach in specific types of special school or in remedial departments'. These 39 courses therefore had one intake after 1984. It also recommended that there should be a rationalization and expansion of in-service courses to provide additional training for those with recognized positions of responsibility. To those working within the field it has always been unclear why the recommendation for an increase in SEN for all teachers was incompatible with the additional specialization of a few teachers. Nor was it clear why teachers who were trained to work in *both* mainstream and specialist settings should have more limited career opportunities than those trained only for mainstream.

The expansion of in-service courses was expected to offset the loss of initial teacher training. In the case of children with SLD, this required some 200 teachers to be trained annually through in-service provision (Mittler, 1993). A number of factors mitigated against the fulfilment of this target, many of which derive from mechanisms of funding. The ACSET recommendation that INSET should be planned and systematically managed was taken up in a series of changes in the way INSET was funded. The Manpower Services Technical and Vocational Education Initiative (TVEI) provided a model in the shape of TRIST (TVEI- related in-service training) for the DES to develop the LEA Training Grant Scheme (LEATGS) (DES, 1986). This scheme was subsequently replaced by GEST (Grants for Education Support and Training) in 1991. INSET was now on course to be based ultimately on national priority areas, centrally funded, and accessed by LEAs through an annual system of bidding. The result of these shifts in the system of funding was to substantially change the nature of in-service provision:

- from personal professional development to meeting the needs of schools/LEAs
- in the negotiators of course content

- in focus from training being course-based in colleges of higher education (HE) to a mixed parentage
- in type and mode of courses.

The changes have been met down the years with the raising of a number of concerns, largely by those who design and deliver training courses. First and foremost was concern at the increase in LEA involvement in decision-making with a move towards short courses targeted specifically at the needs of the LEA/institutions. (e.g., Daniels and Sandow, 1987; Daniels *et al.*, 1988; Mittler, 1986) where issues of price outweighed those of quality. One outcome was a negotiation of content between the consumer and supplier with course providers designing packages of in-service training in collaboration with LEAs (e.g., Daniels *et al.*, 1988; Hornby, 1990; Norwich and Cowan, 1985). The course delivery was likely to be both LEA- and HE-based, with the mode of attendance largely determined by the level of funding. Whereas in the past colleges of HE had largely dominated in designing courses, their areas of expertise were now challenged. Non-award bearing courses were fashionable with both LEAs and the DES but not with teachers who wanted recognition of their commitment (Watson, 1988).

More directly, we can also chart the impact on the training of teachers in specialist areas. One of the significant aspects in the early days of LEATGS was that some courses were singled out for a higher rate of funding, including those courses for teachers of children with SLD. However, other groups, notably those teachers of pupils with moderate learning difficulties (MLD) were funded at a lower rate (Daniels and Sandow, 1987; Daniels *et al.*, 1988). Indeed the review of LEATGS by Glickman and Dale (1990) recognized the shortfall in some areas of training and recommended that the grants be linked to the numbers of teachers *requiring* such training. When GEST was introduced to replace LEATGS, it was accompanied by a DfEE survey of the take-up in training in minority specialist areas (mandatory, areas of sensory loss and SLD). These areas were initially ring-fenced, but this safeguard to training disappeared from GEST funding in 1993 despite considerable concerns that the area required protecting (Miller and Porter, 1994). In recognition of the continued shortfall, the DfE eventually reminded LEAs about the importance of training teachers in these group in an accompanying letter to the GEST allocation. There was continued uncertainty about the criteria used by the DES to award funding (Mittler, 1986) with the result that teachers on courses which were delivered over two years had no certainty of continued funding.

There were also some recognizable gains from the new system. These include:

- the introduction of five non-contact days
- identification by schools in their development plans of staff development needs
- more flexible attitude of both colleges of HE and LEAs to training opportunities
- increased access to training through the development of distance learning courses
- a closer relationship with what is happening in classroom through the types of training opportunities and action research
- widening the range of teachers who are eligible for GEST funding.

Thus we can see that *in general* teachers were likely to be receiving more INSET than they had ever before and that where this was good it was well planned and linked closely to classroom practice (OFSTED, 1993a). If, however, we look at the outcome for particular groups, these gains are offset by other factors.

A review of the current situation with regard to the training of teachers of pupils with learning difficulties reveals overall a shortfall in opportunities for specialist training. First and foremost it is notable that no group has been monitoring the availability of training for teachers of children with MLD. In many ways this group continues to be the Cinderella with funding through GEST accounting for only 3 per cent of the total grants in 1994–5. There is no indication that this figure will increase although only two years figures are available with 1992–3 level indicating that 4 per cent of the grant was spent on MLD training. The level of SLD appears more satisfactory given the lower level of incidence with 10 per cent of the funding being given to training for this group in 1993–4. However, DfEE figures reveal that only half the teachers in SLD schools have had specialist training (DfEE, 1995) and training continues to fall short of the 200 newly trained teachers who entered the SLD field each year until 1988. Figures provided by the Professional Development Network for the academic years 1989–90 through to 1994–5 (see Table 21.1) reveal an ongoing fall in the numbers of teachers undergoing recognized training and a shift from full-time to part-time modes of study.

	1989	1990	1991	1992	1993	1994
Numbers of students– FT	96	82	74	37	7	3
Numbers of students– PT	16	24	30	63	147	117

Table 21.1 Numbers of teachers on one-year equivalent SLD courses. Figures produced by Professional Development Network of SLD Tutors

A shortfall in the supply of trained teachers has a knock-on effect for future opportunities. First, headteachers are unable to find appropriate supply cover and therefore are disinclined to release teachers during the day time. Part-time twilight attendance on courses is probably least attractive to women with family commitments. Second, over time there is a drop in the expectation of training opportunities, and teachers become resigned to this shortfall. With no opportunities there is no attempt to identify need. In short, specialist training becomes a thing of the past.

At this time more than any other it is important to reflect on the values of teacher training and on the strengths and limitations of different forms of delivery. Historical prevalence is an insufficient justification for such forms of training and many of the original concerns of trainers now appear almost naive as they have had to adapt to the current economic and political climate. The remainder of the chapter therefore has selected three important issues to consider in depth. First, we need to consider what factors motivate teachers to seek training and therefore, as a consequence, how we can best ensure that these needs are met. Second, we turn to consider how and where training should take place. Inevitably this leads us to consider who should or could best deliver different aspects of training. Finally, we turn to consider issues of quality control – how we can ensure we meet the diverse range of teacher needs whilst providing appropriately equitable outcomes.

Why train?

Given the overall emphasis of training on the job, through collaboration with qualified teachers and the lack of official recognition that teachers of pupils with learning difficulties require specialist training, we must ask why there is a need for training. Why, for example, is there a mandatory requirement for the teaching of pupils with a sensory impairment but not for those with the most complex needs (often including a sensory loss)? Without recognition that there is a need for training by all parties – funders, providers and consumers – the development of appropriate courses is likely to be severely limited.

First, if we consider the current demands on teachers in special schools, we can see that these are unprecedented. Indeed, it could be argued that training for teachers is as essential now as it was when responsibility for pupils with SLD moved from health to education in 1971. The introduction of the National Curriculum has called for a degree of subject knowledge that exceeds that of primary school teachers. For example, in an SLD class, pupils' ages may cross two or even three Key Stages. A teacher, therefore, not only has to feel confident in ten curriculum areas but conversant with the programmes of study of a broad age range. With a smaller teaching staff, who may well have not been appointed on the basis of their subject knowledge, there may be little available support from colleagues in a number of curriculum areas. This has been pointed out in relation to MLD schools (HMI, 1990). With a fall in the number of teachers within the school who have received specialist training, guidance on the process by which one can meet the needs of a diverse group of pupils within a subject lesson may be severely restricted. Those teachers who *are* able to do this may not feel sufficiently confident to impart these skills and knowledge to others in the school, even if they are in an appropriate position to do so. In addition to this expertise, teachers are also required to meet individual pupil priority needs. It is noteworthy that a recent survey of effective teachers in special schools (OFSTED, 1996) gives priority to the characteristic of 'subject knowledge and expertise'. Those who come into the field from mainstream with this subject expertise may however be poorly placed to adopt a child-centred approach to assessing a pupil's strengths and needs. Thus whilst they may be very knowledgeable with the subject area they may be unable to make the modifications and adaptations which ensure that individual needs are met. As Jordan and Powell (1995) have indicated, this task becomes even more difficult where there is no underpinning understanding of child development in initial teacher training.

At the same time as this, it is important to recognize that the population of pupils in many special schools is changing. HMI (1990) pointed to the fact that special schools were now addressing a more complex range of needs. Surveys carried out by Male (1996a; 1996b) indicate that MLD schools are likely to be required to meet the needs of a diverse population, ranging from those who, in the head teacher's opinion, would be well placed in mainstream to those with physical difficulties, sensory loss, language and communication difficulties, emotional and behavioural difficulties and SLD. Significantly, 92 per cent of the schools surveyed felt that there had been a change in the range and type of special educational needs of pupils they catered for. Unsurprisingly, if MLD schools are found to provide for some pupils with SLD, then the population of pupils in SLD schools was also found to have changed. A greater proportion of the school was seen by head teachers to have profound and multiple learning difficulties, severe challenging behaviour, 'degenerative and life threatening conditions and complex medical conditions' (Male, 1996b).

Teachers are therefore facing unprecedented challenges, both in relation to the curriculum and to meeting pupil needs. It is clear that even those teachers who received initial teacher training are facing new demands. Consequently, there is clearly a need both for initial teacher training where teachers have no specialist training, and also, for those who trained a decade or more ago, a need to update their expertise. It is perhaps indicative that a recent survey of stress in teachers showed that those working in SLD schools experience the greatest level (Male and May, 1996).

One of the challenges of the current system is to meet the differing needs of these two groups of teachers. Whilst teacher trainers may find it convenient to think of similarities in their needs, it is unlikely to be entirely shared by the teachers. Those who require an update in their training may be unmotivated either by the type of content they view at one level to be familiar, or equally, by training which is accredited towards a qualification that they already possess. Schools, colleges of HE and other providers, must think carefully about how they meet the needs of these experienced teachers. Recognition and use of the knowledge teachers bring to courses is essential and can be done in a variety of ways, through the methods by which courses are delivered, through the types of learning tasks which are set and through the accreditation of prior learning.

The training of experienced teachers highlights the degree to which courses may be viewed with anxiety. Exposure to new learning is risky, with new expectations and the challenging of old beliefs. The development of more interactive modes of training which are centred around teacher contribution, where there is an expectation that course members make presentations, may fill some teachers with alarm. Above all, there is a risk of failure at worst, or being seen as performing at a 'below average' or poor level.

The advent of inspections by OFSTED has served to identify areas in which schools have the greatest need. One of the overriding requirements is for schools and individual teachers to be able to readily articulate their teaching – to explain why they are utilizing particular approaches, materials, types of classroom organization, etc. and how these relate to the needs of their pupils. For many, these aspects are ingrained in practice and not easily explained without conscious reflection. For some teachers this will be the first occasion on which their practice in a special school has been scrutinized and graded. Clearly, teachers who have received some specialist training will be in a better position to meet these demands. OFSTED will also serve to identify teachers whose teaching is considered to be poor. It is to be hoped that headteachers will be able to pre-empt this process and provide the appropriate mechanisms for support.

It is important that training is used to best advantage, that teachers enter a course with good expectations of what they hope to achieve from it. This suggests that training should link with appraisal to ensure that teachers are clear about their needs and that these complement the needs of the school. These expectations should be discussed with the course providers prior to registration to ensure, first, that these expectations are well matched to the course aims, and second, to locate the opportunities within the course for fulfilling these primary goals. In my experience, training is most effective where it is viewed by the course member as a positive opportunity which opens doors rather than a form of punishment or escape!

Where and how?

As we consider the advantages and limitations of different forms of organization it becomes clear that to gain full advantage from a course it should be provided in different modes. Evaluations carried out by Watson (1988) for example provide us with good insights into the advantages of one-year full-time courses. These include the opportunities to be gained from being part of a group which stimulates thought and reflection and enables the sharing of experiences. There are also clearly more opportunities for reading and reflection (Miller, 1996) and therefore quite possibly a deeper level of thinking which might well lead to greater long-term gains. Such a course can also provide the chance to make visits and see a variety of good practice in operation. This aspect is particularly valued by teachers (Hornby, 1990). It is also likely that full-time courses have been planned as a whole and therefore with greater opportunities for coherence and progression to the teachers' learning. The limitation of such courses lies with the greater difficulty of linking theory to practice. Whilst course designers can be creative in ensuring that courses are assessed through practical work carried out in school, of necessity this is often done as a visitor. If the course member is carrying out work in a new school and broadening their experience, it can be difficult for them to negotiate particular aspects of this practical work. They may also find it difficult to access information where their temporary colleagues have limited time to stop and discuss aspects of practice. Unless areas of choice are planned for, course members can also find themselves uncertain about areas for in-depth study.

Part-time study on the other hand is more likely to guarantee that useful aspects are applied in practice, and the constraints of doing a course and holding down a job can mean that course members become well-focused in their selection of options. Whilst this may feel limiting, it does remove the stresses and delays of decision-making. There are, however, particular difficulties when the part-time study is undertaken in twilight hours following a hard day at work (Hornby, 1990; OFSTED, 1993b). This difficulty may be exacerbated when tutors are also less fresh! The advantages of applied practical work can be counteracted by the lack of opportunities for visits and for in-depth reading and reflection.

A third mode of study is provided through distance learning. The strengths of this have been well discussed by Miller (1994; 1996). Drawing on her own experience of providing a distance course in teaching pupils with language and communication difficulties, she points to the important advantages of being able to work at one's own pace, without the need to travel and at a time of the day/week that is convenient. Whilst course materials can be shared with all the school, course members may feel constrained by the lack of regular access to a library and thereby a variety of materials. This mode may indeed be the only viable option for those with family commitments and/or for those who live in areas not well served by course provision. Like all modes of study, students need good preparation and support to utilize the course to the best advantage.

As we have seen, the most common mode of study now appears to be part-time courses with an increased trend towards twilight teaching. There is, however, recognition that full-time courses have a role to play (HMI, 1990) but it is unlikely at the current time that many colleges will be able to recruit a viable student group to run these as an independent option. More commonly, full-time courses will survive if provision is interwoven with part-time provision and further supported by distance elements. Thus course provision and attendance is often dictated purely by pragmatic elements rather than by matching content to mode. One alternative is to divide course content into elements which are then matched to mode of study. For example, skill-based aspects may best be delivered in part-time mode, while those elements which demand a good underpinning of theory with time for reflection would best be delivered in full-time mode. Finally, those elements in which the course member pursues their own interests in depth may be best addressed through distance provision supported by tutorials. If this model were adopted, teachers would be enabled to experience the best of each aspect of provision. This type of staged approach has been established in the north-east (Hornby, 1990), in this instance coupled with a hierarchy of award. Ideally this form of provision could meet concerns about the development of a reflective practitioner whilst also enabling teachers to gain important practical skills.

One of the recommendations of the SENTC report (1996) is for consortia of schools to put in bids for 100 per cent funding in areas of national shortage, such as training in SLD. These are to be based on a five-year plan, thus offsetting concerns that teachers will not be able to finish their training. This suggestion enables schools to consider individually the needs of teachers and the levels of training required. This is not incompatible with the costing of a mixed mode of attendance depending on the needs of individual teachers and the school.

Quality assurance

Finally we turn to the third issue: ensuring that teachers have access to equal quality of training. Since the recommendations of the DES (1978; 1986) for the evaluation of in-service training, we have seen a greater awareness of the need to monitor the effects of training. This monitoring has tended to rely on the perceptions of course members with questionnaires being the main tool of data collection (Hornby, 1990; Sebba and Robson, 1987; Watson, 1988). Using this method, course providers have been able to establish consumer satisfaction, although this will be affected by the stresses outside the course, etc. (Miller, 1994). Some course providers have extended their evaluation to take pre-course as well as post-course measures. One of the continuing frustrations for course providers is to establish those views which are particular to the current group and those aspects which indicate important developments for future groups.

These measures do not address the important issue of the effectiveness of courses in actually changing teaching practice and, even more importantly, the gains which are brought about to pupil learning as a result of access to specialist trained staff. A recent study by Ware and Porter (1996) of the effectiveness of induction training highlighted the need for such measures to be carefully linked to the course aims and objectives. The importance of taking baseline measures of pre- and post-course practice was also established. The move towards establishing training competences may serve to support such evaluation measures.

We can see that when we look at how competences are often established, there are important areas of contention. In this country the establishment of competences is relatively new in education. The reform of initial teacher training (DfE, 1992; 1993) called for 'defined levels of professional competence' which were sufficiently precise that they lent themselves to assessment. The establishment of competences for special education is characteristic of a number of other countries, including Canada, Australia, New Zealand and the United States (Advisory Council for Special Educational Needs, 1990; Ramsey and Algozzine, 1991; Servis and Swan, 1992; Westwood and Palmer, 1993). Characteristically these have been established through either looking at the agreed content of training courses or at establishing the views of educators, rather than looking at what strategies, skills and understanding teachers require to maximize learning opportunities.

There is also considerable debate about the ways in which competences are expressed (Jordan and Powell, 1995). For example, the notion of prescriptive behavioural competences suggests that teachers' roles can be broken-down and defined in terms of standard behaviours arranged in a checklist. A slightly less prescriptive approach can be seen when the approach is based upon a functional analysis of the skills required by a teacher. These are less tightly tied to specific situations. A third alternative is to include recognition of the knowledge, understanding, and experience as well as ability to perform. It reveals the processes by which teachers make decisions about appropriate responses in a given situation and is likely to be underpinned by a particular set of values. The interested reader is directed to Reynolds and Salters (1995) for further discussion.

It is informative to compare the models adopted by other countries. For example, Ramsey and Algozzine (1991) provide a survey of teacher competence tests in the United States of America. If we look at which aspects had 100 per cent agreement across the 46 states, we find included: historical developments, main principles and regulations of Public Law 94–142, identification and characteristics of six groups of pupils (learning disabled, mentally retarded, emotionally disturbed, speech handicapped, hearing handicapped and visually handicapped), the process and procedures of assessment, the development of responsible behaviour, types of special class placement, vocational training and finally, community-based facilities. Whilst there was not complete agreement, the inclusion of behavioural learning techniques formed a significant part of the content of competences for many states. The emphasis is on specialist methodologies and diagnosis. Learning theories are dominated by behavioural and information-processing approaches, i.e. individualistic and largely mechanistic approaches to learning. Sceptics will not be reassured either by the precise level of detail put forward by Servis and Swan (1992), with a mere 107 competences put forward as 'essential for all beginning special education teachers'.

It is important to remind ourselves about the rationale for competences in this context, namely that consumers (including funders) can select a course which matches their needs and that they can be assured that the course will fulfil those needs. The development of finely graded competences which include specification of the means by which these competences will be achieved will lead to an agreed syllabus with little to choose between courses. Choice can only occur where there is variety between offerings. For the consumer to be provided with quality *and* some elements of choice requires the statement of general competences which include aspects of skill, understanding, knowledge and attitudes rather than those which are very detailed and highly prescriptive. If we look at the recommendations put forward by SENTC (1996), we can see that the competences fall largely within this category:

> Teachers should demonstrate knowledge and understanding concerning… the nature and effect of a special educational need on a pupil's development and on the learning process. (SENTC, 1996, p.33)
> Teachers should demonstrate knowledge skills and understanding to enable them to…apply the successive cycles of teaching and evaluation proposed in the Code of Practice in order to meet individual needs and in the formulation of Individual Educational Plans. (SENTC, 1996, p.34)
> Teachers should demonstrate knowledge skills and understanding to enable them to… implement and evaluate whole school approaches through staff development activities….(SENTC, 1996, p.35)

One of the additional aspects of setting competences is that not only does it serve to meet quality assurance concerns but it also draws attention to the fact that assessment is likely to take a number of different forms. For example, assessment based purely on a sample of observed practice can only provide indirect evidence of understanding. It needs to be supported by evidence of the teacher's ability to reflect and convey his or her decision-making in a given situation. Teachers need to be able to articulate their practices and to share their rationale with others. Teachers capable of sustaining high levels of reflection are likely to continue to learn and develop as result of their experiences.

Conclusion

The changes in the way teachers are funded on courses have had a number of ramifications and have led both directly and indirectly to a current shortfall in the supply of teachers with additional training in either moderate or severe learning difficulties. This has been monitored closely in the latter field; we can only speculate on the outcome in the former. We do know, however, that there are unprecedented demands on teachers working with both groups of pupils. It is therefore more important than ever that teachers are given access to quality training. The shift in form and type of training means that for the majority of teachers this is unlikely to be provided in full-time courses. In this chapter we have pointed to a very real need to provide a system by which the diverse range of teacher needs can be met, and that this is done through mixing the modes of study according to the type of training outcomes. One way of helping consumers identify courses which match their needs is through the use of training competences. It is suggested that these should be stated in terms which recognize the need for the development of skills, knowledge understanding and positive attitudes, and result in a reflective practitioner able to utilize these abilities in a broad range of contexts.

References

ACSET (Advisory Committee on the Supply and Education of Teachers) (1984) *Teacher Training and Special Educational Needs*, London: HMSO.

Advisory Council for Special Educational Needs (1990) *The Way Ahead: Meeting a wider range of educational needs in regular schools. Implications for preservice teacher education*, Spring Hill: Guidance and Counselling Services.

Daniels, H., and Sandow S.(1987) 'Will Circular 6/86 frustrate the 1981 Act?', *British Journal of Special Education*, 14, 1, 10.

Daniels H., Porter J. and Sandow S. (1988) 'New issues in in-service education', *British Journal of Special Education*, 15, 3, 127–9.

DfE (1992) *Initial Teacher Training (Secondary Phase)*, Circular 9/92, London DfE.

DfE (1993) *The Government's Proposals for the Reform of Initial Teacher Training*, Circular 14/93, London: Department for Education.

DfE (1994) *Code of Practice on the Identification and Assessment of Special Educational Needs*, London: DfE.

DfEE (1995) 'Survey of LEAs' use of GEST Grant 12 (Training for Special Educational Needs) in 1994–5', unpublished.

DES (1972) *Teacher Education and Training* (The Report of the James Committee), London: HMSO.

DES (1978) *Making Inset Work: In-service education and training for teachers: a basis for discussion*, London: HMSO.

DES (1986) *Local Authority Training Grants Scheme: Financial Year 1987–88*, Circular 6/86, London: HMSO.

Glickman, B.D. and Dale, H.C. (1990) *A Scrutiny of Education Support Grants and the Local Education Authority Training Grants Scheme*, London: DES.

HMI (1990) *Education Observed: Special needs issues*, London: HMSO.

Hornby, G. (1990) 'A modular approach to training'. *British Journal of Special Education*, 17, 4, 156–60.

Jordan, R. and Powell, S. (1995) 'Skills without understanding: a critique of a competency-based model of teacher education in relation to special needs', *British Journal of Special Education*, 22, 3, 120–24.

Male, D. (1996a) 'Who goes to MLD schools?', *British Journal of Special Education*, 23, 1, 35–41.

Male, D. (1996b) 'Who goes to SLD Schools?', *Mental Handicap Research* (submitted for publication).

Male, D. and May, D. (1996) 'Burnout and workload for teachers of children with severe learning difficulties', *Mental Handicap Research* (submitted for publication).

Miller, C. (1994) 'Professional development and distance education', paper presented to the SENTC Working Group, 21 April.

Miller, C. (1996) 'Relationships between teachers and speech and language therapists: influencing practice by distance education', *Child Language Teaching and Therapy 12*, 1, 29–38.

Miller, O. and Porter, J. (1994) 'Teacher training: settling the bill', *British Journal of Special Education*, 21, 1, 7–8.

Mittler, P. (1986) 'The new look in in-service training', *British Journal of Special Education*, 13, 2, 50–51.

Mittler P. (1993) *Teacher Education for Special Educational Needs. Policy Options for Special Educational Needs in the 1990s*, Seminar Paper 3, Stafford: NASEN.

Norwich, B. and Cowan, E. (1985) 'Training with a school focus', *British Journal of Special Education 12*, 4, 167–9.

OFSTED (1993a) *The New Teacher in School: A Survey by Her Majesty's Inspectors in England and Wales 1992*, London: HMSO.

OFSTED (1993b) *The Management and Provision of Inservice Training Funded by the Grant for Education Support and Training (GEST)*, London: HMSO.

OFSTED (1996) 'Effective teaching in special schools', presented at HMI Invitation Conference, Peterborough, 11 March.

Ramsey, R.S. and Algozzine, B. (1991) 'Teacher competency testing: what are special education teachers expected to know?', *Exceptional Children*, 57, 4, 339–50.

Reynolds, M. and Salters, M. (1995) 'Models of competence and teacher training', *Cambridge Journal of Education*, 25, 3, 345–59.

Sebba, J. and Robson, C. (1987) The development of short, school focussed INSET courses in special educational needs', *Research Papers in Education 2*, 1, 3–30.

Servis, B. and Swan, W.W. (1992) 'The CEC common core of knowledge and skills essential for all beginning special education teachers', *Teaching Exceptional Children*, 25, 1, 16–20.

SENTC (1996) *Professional Development to Meet Special Educational Needs: Report to the DfEE*, Staffordshire County Council.

Ware, J. and Porter, J. (1996) 'Evaluating teacher training', paper presented at the IASSID Conference, Helsinki, July.

Watson, J. (1988) 'One-year courses: the teachers' views', *British Journal of Special Education*, 15, 2, 79–82.

Westwood, P. and Palmer, C. (1993) 'Knowledge and skills for special educators in the 1990s: perceptions from the field', *Australian Journal of Special Education*, 17, 1, 31–41.

Chapter 22

Changing Public Attitudes

Christina Tilstone

In December 1995, Bengt Lindqvist, the UN Special Rapporteur of the Commission for Social Development on Disability, wrote:

> In all societies of the world there are still obstacles preventing persons with disabilities from exercising their rights and freedoms and making it difficult for them to participate fully in the activities of their societies. (Lindqvist, 1995, p.2)

Such obstacles will naturally vary in accordance with the religious, cultural and political influences in society. Many are due to the ways in which the physical world is organized, and as our physical environment has been developed and we have become more sophisticated, the steps, stairs, and narrow doorways which we use to extend our living space or to gain access to other levels have created a handicapping environment for many people. A child with a mobility problem in an African village, where houses are single storey and on a level with outside walkways, will not be as handicapped as a child with a similar disability in a developed country who may have to negotiate not only steps from the house to the footpath, but also stairs to the upper storeys.

Modern technology has, however, enabled the development and provision of aids and appliances which help a disabled person to live more efficiently and happily in the community, but the consequent disability industry highlights the limitations of individuals. In education, the 'special needs industry' is seen by many (Barton, 1988; Norwich, 1990; Tomlinson, 1982) as providing opportunities for professionals to perpetuate their own vested interests, with their numbers growing in order to highlight and deal with the limitations of individuals. Oliver (1996) argues that the problems are not created by the limitations of individuals; rather they are due primarily to society's failure to take account of the needs of the disabled in its social organization. An obstacle to socialization is the structure of the physical, as it can either limit or extend opportunities, but a much more serious one, which keeps persons with disabilities apart in society, is the attitude of members of the general public towards them

Unfortunately, historical events have not helped the so-called able bodied to recognize the common humanity which they share with the disabled. The assumption that the handicapped are social rejects and should be cared for in asylums and institutions which, on the one hand provide protection but on the other, permanent segregation, has left its mark (Cole, 1989; Pritchard, 1963; Tilstone, 1991). In the UK alone, despite government policy to close long-stay hospitals, more than 15,000 people with learning difficulties still live in institutions (Ward, 1995). Media coverage of the conditions and practices in some long-stay institutions has led to the general view that hospitalization represents a degrading and inhumane treatment of the majority of those with learning difficulties. But there is still a belief that there is a need to provide a way of life separate from the rest of society for those with profound and multiple disabilities or with complex and severe challenging behaviours (Collins, 1995).

Even people with less severe disabilities are not tolerated in some everyday situations and are therefore segregated in many aspects of their daily living. One airline, for example, still keeps all disabled passengers in a separate lounge!

Research undertaken in the 1950s confirmed that some disabilities are easier for society to accept than others and that it is possible to construct a hierarchy of disability (Kvaraceus, 1956). In the main, UK society finds those with hidden impairments least unacceptable, then the visually impaired or the blind, and next the physically disabled, as long as they are not facially disfigured. Although as a society we are conditioned to the Hollywood model of beauty (slim and perfectly formed), it is often facial appearance which determines our responses. Unusual facial features due to genetic abnormalities or neurological damage can result in negative attitudes, and the aetiology, not the essential humanness, becomes the focus. We also tend to draw inferences about a person based on a single prominent characteristic, which Wright (1974) termed the 'spread phenomenon'. The BBC's programme 'Does he take sugar?' and SCOPE's advertising slogan: 'One in nine of us have a disability. Too many of us see it as no ability' (*The Observer*, May 1995) have helped to highlight the dangers of the spread phenomena but there is no room for complacency. People who are perceived as 'slow' or who behave 'inappropriately' are the last in the acceptance list, and are often labelled.

Many of us can remember the effects of being called 'thick', 'stupid', 'an idiot' or 'hopeless' at some point in our lives, but to be perpetually referred to in this way is a constant reminder of personal inadequacy, which reinforces feelings of failure and rejection in the adult or child, and may result in stereotyping (Tilstone and Visser, 1996).

Why change attitudes?

The stereotypical images and labels which are a form of public degradation are hard to eradicate, but the title of this book, *Enabling Access: Effective teaching and learning for pupils with learning difficulties*, assumes more than merely access to a common curriculum and the legal right to quality education. It presupposes that the staff of schools, and the pupils within them, have an obligation to press for access to society in order that all people with disabilities, including those with learning difficulties, can be included. The statement from the Salamanca World Conference on Special Needs Education in 1994 stressed:

> A change in social perspective is imperative. For far too long, the problems of people with disabilities have been compounded by a disabling society that has focused upon their impairments rather than their potential.(UNESCO, 1994, p.7)

The statement goes on to emphasize that quality special needs education must start from the assumption that human differences are normal and that schools are the training ground for a 'people-oriented society that respects both differences and the dignity of all human beings'. Schools must, therefore, challenge negative attitudes, and changing attitudes must become a structured part of their curricula.

Where do we start?

In order to effect change it is important to understand *what* we are changing. What *is* an attitude? The following definitions suggest that it consists of cognitive, affective and behavioural components which interact with each other:

- a mental view or disposition, especially as it indicates opinion or allegiance (*Collins*);
- settled behaviour or manner of acting as representative of feeling or opinion (*Shorter Oxford*);
- a habitual mode of thought or feeling (*Chambers*).

Put simply, our feelings in the presence of someone with an obvious impairment, or who may not be acting in a conventional or acceptable way, may be irrational, and often fearful; our response: withdrawal. McConkey (1991) reminds us that such reactions are rarely based on first-hand experience, and that around three-quarters of the population have never met a person with severe learning difficulties (SLD). Numbers are low: '1 in 250 people are markedly affected...' (McConkey, 1991) and it was only recently that people with severe learning difficulties began to live in the community. In addition, the historical label of 'mental handicap' is still used to describe people with severe learning disabilities and is often confused with mental illness. Images of locked rooms, doctors, psychiatrists, and violent behaviour are all too quickly conjured up. Of crucial importance, however, is the fact that attitudes are not only acquired in the present, but are strongly influenced by the feelings, reactions and beliefs of the past and, unless challenged, are handed down from generation to generation.

What research tells us so far

In order to change perceptions and views, it is vitally important to learn from research. The pioneer in the area is McConkey, who has rigorously and systematically explored ways in which the public can be better informed and involved in the inclusion of people with learning difficulties into their communities (McConkey, 1987; 1991; 1994; 1996; McConkey and McCormack, 1983; McConkey *et al.*, 1993). McConkey's work indicates that any attempt to prepare communities or groups to accept others whom they perceive as different, will have positive effects, and that positive experiences shape positive attitudes. He also stresses that there are certain key elements in bringing about attitude change: planned personal contact; interesting and relevant information; and multi-media presentations.

McConkey's work has encouraged people with learning disabilities to give their views on *who* needs educating about disability and *how*. The importance of listening to children with special educational needs has been highlighted by the passing of the Children Act (1989) and the Code of Practice (DfE,1994), both of which require us to take account of pupils' views on their education. As a result, books and articles are appearing which document the rich data received, and emphasize the value of using them to shape all aspects of education, from curriculum development and delivery, to educational organization (Davie and Galloway 1995; Lewis, 1995; Roffey *et al.*, 1994; Wade and Moore 1992; 1994). Although the importance of listening to adults with disabilities is also being stressed, it is salutary that no disabled person was invited to speak at the major national consultation conference on the draft Code of Practice (Corbett, 1996) and that people with learning disabilities are rarely consultants to the charities which purport to support them. McConkey's workshops and other initiatives are vitally important if we are serious about ensuring that people with learning difficulties are to become valued members of society.

Not surprisingly the workshop participants stressed that anyone who has not been involved with a person with a disability needs to be educated, and gave the following a special mention:

- Influential people: MPs and councillors;
- School kids, Pre-schoolers, Students, Teachers;
- DSS people;
- Police;
- Social workers, Community workers;
- Doctors, nurses, medical people, medical profession;
- Bus companies;
- Licensed victuallers association;
- Shop owners (access problems);
- Local residents and communities;
- Planners and architects;
- Potential employers;
- People in media, newspapers, children's TV presenters;
- staff in services 'who don't listen to you'.

(McConkey, 1994)

So where do we start? Certainly not by trying to change everything immediately, but by adopting policies and practices which are possible and practicable. I would suggest that we need to:

1. acknowledge that attitude change is vital if people with learning difficulties are to become part of the social organization of society,
2. recognize that schools have an obligation to work on changing attitudes;
3. ensure that such work needs to be undertaken in a structured and systematic way and therefore must become a major part of the policy, administration and curriculum of the school;
4. work from the evidence already available from research;
5. ensure that pupils with learning difficulties are a valued part of the of the organization of the school, are listened to and consulted, and are able to influence decisions about the school's management and organization;
6. work on aspects which are feasible, and are already part of the working practices of the school;
7. monitor and evaluate the work.

Although these seven needs are considered in this chapter, it is important to pay particular attention to the third, and to reverse the usual order of starting with 'policy development' and moving to 'practice', by focusing on the curriculum itself.

Structured attitude change: the curriculum

Two aspects of the curriculum, already in place, are crucial to attitude change, but are often undervalued. The first is the teaching of self-advocacy to pupils with learning difficulties; the second, more carefully planned and structured links between mainstream and special schools.

Self-advocacy

People with learning difficulties are their own best advocates and, as it is essential for them to have a say in educating communities, they need to acquire the skills and confidence to enable them speak for themselves. The acquisition of these skills is inevitably a lengthy process and must be at the heart of the curriculum of any school. The components of self-advocacy include: choosing; decision-making; problem-solving; interacting and communicating with others; listening; being assertive without aggression; and taking responsibilities. Self-advocacy may appear as a subject within the Personal and Social Education (PSE) curriculum for older children, but the basic skills are embedded in all aspects of the curriculum from the beginning of the child's school life.

The ethos and attitude of the school must reflect the fundamental principles of empowerment for all children. Embedded in the notion of empowerment is the way in which the school promotes the feelings of self-worth in all its pupils and the ways in which the staff show respect for each child on a day-to-day basis. Showing respect involves listening to the language that we use to describe and talk to our pupils. Language is power and is often used both consciously and unwittingly to suppress and devalue children (Corbett, 1996). The vocabulary of special needs not only draws heavily on medicine (e.g., epileptic), and psychology (e.g., cognitive impairment), but on the negative labels of history (e.g., mentally handicapped). Although it is unlikely that the latter label will be used in schools, labels *are* used, albeit unintentionally, in classrooms and staffrooms as a shorthand to point out children's shortcomings. A recent example was the teacher in a special school who described some of the children in his class as 'four Down's, one spastic and a hyperactive-autistic'. Hardly the vocabulary which values and empowers!

The methods used to teach the curriculum are important, and often unconsidered, factors in empowering pupils and encouraging self-advocacy. Fortunately, school staff have progressed from the days when instruction was the prescribed method of teaching. The prescriptive and constraining approach to teaching rooted in behavioural theory has been replaced by practices which encourage pupil participation at every level. One of the major advantages of the National Curriculum is that it is has forced us to consider the most effective teaching approaches for all aspects of the whole curriculum (Rose *et al.*, 1994; Sebba et al., 1993), and the complexity of the new and evolving curriculum inevitably requires a variety of approaches and methods. Different groupings for learning and class management are needed to teach the subjects of the curriculum, and the aspects of the whole curriculum, which ensure the total maturity of the child.

The benefits of early intervention approaches, such as High Scope, where the child has the opportunity to exert control over both the learning situation and the teacher (Weikart, 1989), are being recognized in mainstream and special schools (see Mitchell [1994] for an account of the work with children with SLD). Nind and Hewett's (1994) unorthodox approach with children who are either at an early stage of development, or whose behaviour challenges the school system, is an imaginative attempt to encourage children to become their own advocates in the learning process.

Although Hinchcliffe (1994) emphasizes that no reference to self-advocacy can be found in the National Curriculum programmes of study (PoS), Byers (1994), reminds us that the PoS for many of the orders contain the words 'explore', 'investigate', 'find out about', which: 'suggest that pupils should be active in the learning process, engaging their curiosity and creativity, as well as being taught new skills and knowledge' (p.86) and, if properly planned, should provide a sound basis for pupils to become self-advocates.

The curriculum and approaches to teaching are two of the aspects of school life which will encourage people with learning difficulties to become self-advocates. Others foster the notion of the truly inclusive school by encouraging children with learning difficulties to make a contribution to every aspect of its running: from formulating school rules to developing all major policies, including equal opportunities.

Given the tools to speak for themselves, as McConkey's research shows, they have much to tell us which should be used both at the micro level of changing local attitudes and at the macro level of influencing governments. In 1992, for example, Barb Goode, a Canadian, became the first person with learning difficulties to address the General Assembly of the United Nations. Her speech centred on the importance of pushing forward the rights of those with learning difficulties in order that they could take their place as equal citizens, living and working in their own communities (Ward, 1995).

Planned personal contact

In theory there is now a greater commitment to the inclusion of children with the full range of disabilities in mainstream education, and Mittler (1995), writing from an international perspective, reminds us that Rule 6 of the 22 rules on the Equalization of Opportunities for Disabled Persons put forward by the United Nations in 1993, emphasizes that:

> States should recognise the principle of equal primary, secondary and tertiary educational opportunities for children, youth and adults with disabilities. They should ensure that the education of persons with disabilities is an integral part of the education system. (p.106)

The special schooling which children with learning difficulties receive in Britain is certainly part of the education system, and in most cases is of the highest quality, but for many it is still exclusion from mainstream.

The idea that children, whatever their needs, should be educated together and share resources, continues to be attractive, but in practice a shared campus or building does not necessarily lead to full and meaningful participation in the life of the school (Carpenter et al., 1991). There may be sound academic reasons for educational segregation at the present time, and certainly one would not want to emulate the chaos in Italy where special schools closed almost overnight. Although I firmly believe that many children educated in special schools will do equally well, socially and academically, in mainstream schools, I do not agree that special schools are 'coming to the end of their shelf-life'. In a society committed to 'education for all', there will always be a small proportion of children who will need the protection of a sheltered environment, but many children at present are excluded from mainstream due to fear and prejudice. If we are serious about people with learning difficulties becoming a truly valued part of the social organization of society, special schools and mainstream school must join together to make greater attempts to break down the barriers to interaction and acceptance

McConkey's research shows that *any* attempt to prepare communities or groups to accept others whom they perceive as different will have a positive effect (McConkey, 1996). Preparation is likely to be most effective if ordinary children are introduced to those with learning difficulties at an early age. They are the ones whose attitudes in the long term will be instrumental in creating the future for people with learning difficulties. It is worth challenging perceptions, however, at any age, and link schemes between mainstream and special schools involving pupils of all ages have proved a powerful and efficient way of developing positive attitudes.

Their programmes have been developed over many years (Jowett *et al.*, 1988) and, despite fears that the new legislation and financial cuts would obliterate such schemes, of 898 special schools taking part in a recent survey, 83 per cent were involved in collaborative arrangements with ordinary schools (Fletcher-Cambell, 1994). Such figures, however, give no indication of the quality of the involvement. Some teachers are reporting that a shortage of time and other pressures have forced them to cut back on the careful preparation and planning of these programmes

Link schemes vary from one-way visits (either to the special or mainstream school); reciprocal; regular but infrequent; to weekly or daily. Although contact in an integrated setting can bring about improved attitudes Lindoe (in Carpenter *et al.*, 1991), Lewis (1995), Shelvin (1992), Shelvin and Walsh (1994) and Walsh and Shelvin (1991) show that attitude change can be accelerated by encouraging shared activity based on common interests. In Lindoe's studies, for example, a mainstream pupil and a pupil with SLD from a special school were encouraged to work together if they had a shared enthusiasm for football and, as part of a planned integration programme, they were allowed, either formally or informally, to develop this interest together.

Simply sharing an interest may, however, result in the domination of the activity by the mainstream pupils, and 'learned helplessness' by the pupil with learning difficulties (Lewis, 1995). Using the interest as the basis for initial contact, it is important to ensure that the power base is more evenly weighted, and that the pupil with learning difficulties, either alone or with his or her classmates, is given every opportunity to take the lead in activities. Lewis suggests that teaching Makaton signing or the use of specially designed computer aids and programs are ways in which pupils with learning difficulties could shine. She also emphasizes that linking children more closely by developmental, rather than chronological age, is a proven method of redressing the power balance.

One of the important elements in attitude change, which McConkey (1994) identifies, is that of giving information. Lindoe's work (reported in Carpenter *et al.*,1991) has alerted us to the importance of not only giving mainstream children basic information on disability as part of the preparation for link schemes, but allowing them to take part in 'sanctioned staring'. By showing video films of children who are physically different, or whose behaviour indicates slowness, she encouraged the mainstream children to ask questions and to articulate the negative feelings which surround physical and facial 'difference'.

Lastly, and most importantly, she monitored and evaluated the attitude shift. Using a simple questionnaire at the beginning and at various stages throughout the project she was able to record the positive changes which occurred. Gash and Coffey (1995), in a comparative study involving mainstream pupils and pupils with moderate learning difficulties (MLD), also found that the mainstream pupils (in this case girls) who experienced structured meetings through integration, were more pro-social, more mature in their outlook, and more positive in the way they talked about the children with MLD, than the control group.

Structured attitude change: administration

It is not possible to explore every aspect of attitude change in one chapter and therefore I have chosen to interpret administration as a process which directs the affairs of the school and to concentrate on a small, but crucial, component which is vital to altering opinions.

Working with the media

As stereotype and prejudice are socially learned, the media have an important influence on attitudes to people with learning disabilities (Philpot, 1995). There has been a shift in the way in which films and TV portray people with difficulties in learning, and some TV programmes are employing people with learning difficulties as actors and presenters in their own right. Educational programmes are being sensitively constructed as teaching aids for those who find learning difficult. Interestingly, it is in the 'moral dilemma' programmes where the most bigotry and prejudice can be found. A recent BBC programme on abortion focused almost exclusively on the prevention of Down's Syndrome. One wonders what those with the extra chromosome felt! I do not wish to labour the point, but I would like to see the following quotation from Williams (1995) above every doctor's desk:

> To treat Down's Syndrome as a disease to be 'prevented' entails taking action to remove *a type of person* from society by preventing their birth. (p.48)

Writing to producers of such programmes pointing out negative impressions should have an impact, but it is likely the staff of schools will have more control over what is presented in their local newspapers. Schools often contact the papers to publicize fund-raising activities, celebrate successes or emphasize special events. The words and pictures used to make a 'good story' can give the 'wrong messages'. Journalist are unlikely to be any better informed than the general public, and sensation sells papers. We know, however, that the media influences thinking, and therefore as part of policy on changing attitudes, schools have a responsibility to help the media to present children with learning difficulties in the most positive way.

As a former journalist interested in this area, Shearer (1996) emphasizes the importance of showing children with learning difficulties in normal environments (not just in specialized environments such as multisensory rooms); interacting with other children (without and with learning difficulties); and engaged in activities (rather than lying doing nothing or smiling at the camera) and speaking for themselves. Shearer stresses that school staff and pupils are in the best position to work with journalists to change attitudes and offers the following important messages:

- get to know the key person who will be responsible for the stories you offer or generate;
- when you have a story, think ahead about its presentation;
- will publicity which is intended to shock end up reinforcing negative images?
- feedback is important, an appreciative letter when a story turns out well helps a positive climate;
- the United Nations document, *Improving Communications about People with Disabilities,* is designed specifically to encourage positive presentations in the media and is useful for all schools;
- keep on trying even when the going seems difficult. The influence of the media is too important to ignore.

(Adapted from Shearer, 1996, pp.217-8)

It is not only images in newspapers that are important but the messages sent out directly by the school. Newsletters, home/school diaries, the school's prospectus, are all designed to inform parents and the general public. Are we sure that the messages they convey are concerned with dignity and respect?

Structured attitude change: policy

I have purposely left comments on policy until the end, as people tend to remember the last thing they read, and as the practices in schools must be driven by policies which outline the philosophy and intentions of each school, a policy on changing public attitudes is vital.

In the present climate of change (including the introduction of a new National Curriculum, the *Code of Practice*, OFSTED inspections, and other external pressures) morale in schools is low. As Byers and Rose (1996) point out, there may be a tendency for schools to concentrate in the first instance on developing policies which they feel will satisfy outside agencies, and they urge schools to 'defend their autonomy and their right to develop a philosophy which is unique to themselves' and consequently:

> Policies should further be regarded as a means of communicating the purpose of the school to those who have a vested interest: pupils, teachers, parents and the local community. (p.16)

If the purpose of any school is, as the Education Reform Act (1988) states, to 'prepare pupils for the opportunities, responsibilities and experiences of adult life' (p.1), the policies which enable pupils with learning difficulties to benefit must be in place, the most important of which will remove existing barriers and allow all pupils to be valued and respected members of society. Thus, to return to Bengt Lindqvist (1995), they must be enabled 'to participate fully in the activities of their societies'.

References

Barton, L. (1988) (ed.) *The Politics of Special Educational Needs,* London: Falmer Press.

Byers, R. (1994) 'Teaching as a dialogue: teaching approaches and learning styles in schools for pupils with learning difficulties', in J. Coupe O'Kane and B. Smith (eds) *Taking Control; Enabling People with Learning Difficulties,* London: David Fulton.

Byers, R. and Rose, R. (1996) *Planning the Curriculum for Pupils with Special Educational Needs,* London: David Fulton.

Carpenter, B., Moore, S. and Lindoe, S. (1991) 'Changing attitudes', in Tilstone, C. (ed.) *Teaching Pupils with Severe Learning Difficulties,* London: David Fulton.

Cole, T. (1989) *Apart or A Part? Integration and the growth of British special education,* Buckingham: Open University Press.

Collins, J. (1995) 'Moving forward or moving back? institutional trends in services for people with learning difficulties', in Philpot, T. and Ward, L. (eds) *Values and Visions: Changing ideas in services for people with learning difficulties,* Oxford: Butterworth Heinemann.

Corbett, J. (1996) *Bad-Mouthing: The language of special needs,* London: Falmer Press.

Davie, R. and Galloway, D. (eds.) (1995) *Listening to Children in Education,* London: David Fulton.

DfE (1994) *The Code of Practice for the Identification and Assessment of Special Educational Needs,* London: HMSO.

Fletcher-Campbell, F. (1994) 'Special links? Partners in provision? Collaboration between ordinary and special schools', *British Journal of Special Education,* 21, 3, 118–20.

Gash, H. and Coffey, D. (1995) 'Influences on attitudes towards children with mental handicap', *European Journal of Special Needs Education,* 10, 1, 1–16.

Hinchcliffe, V. (1994) 'A special special needs! Self advocacy, curriculum and the needs of children with severe learning difficulties' in Sandow, S. (ed.) *Whose Special Need?,* London: Paul Chapman.

Jowett, S., Hegarty S. and Moses, D. (1988) *Joining Forces: A study of links between special and ordinary schools,* Windsor: NFER/Nelson.

Kvaraceus, W.C. (1956) 'Acceptance: rejection and exceptionally', *Exceptional Children*, 328–33.

Lewis, A. (1995) *Children's Understanding of Disability*, London: Routledge.

Lindqvist, B. (1995) 'Europe should take the lead', *Helioscope*, Winter, 6, 2.

McConkey R. (1987) *Who Cares? Community involvement and handicapped people*, London: Souvenir Press.

McConkey, R. (1991) 'Changing the public's perception of mental handicap', in Segal, S. and Varma, V. (eds.) *Prospects for People with Learning Difficulties*, London: David Fulton.

McConkey, R. (1994) *Innovations in Educating Communities about Disabilities*, Chorley: Lisieux Hall Publications.

McConkey, R. (1996) 'Seen through a glass darkly: modifying public attitudes', in Mittler, P. and Sinason, V. (eds) *Changing Policy and Practice for People with Learning Disabilities*, London: Cassell.

McConkey, R. and McCormack, B. (1983) *Breaking Barriers: Educating people about disability*, London: Souvenir Press.

McConkey, R, Walsh, P.N. and Connelly, S. (1993) 'Neighbours' reaction to community services: contrasts before and after services open in their locality', *Mental Handicap Research*, 2, 131–141.

Mitchell, S. (1994) 'Some implications of the High/Scope Curriculum and the education of children with severe learning difficulties', in Coupe O'Kane, J. and Smith, B. (eds) *Taking Control: Enabling People with Learning Difficulties*, London: David Fulton.

Mittler, P. (1995) 'Special needs education: an international perspective', *British Journal of Special Education*, 22, 3, 105–8.

Nind, M. and Hewett, D. (1994) *Access to Communication*, London: David Fulton.

Norwich, B. (1990) *Reappraising Special Needs Education*, London: Cassells.

The Observer (1995) *Supplement* (in Association with SCOPE), 7 May.

Oliver, M. (1996) *Understanding Disability from Theory to Practice*, Basingstoke: Macmillan.

Philpot, T. (ed) (1995) 'What the papers say: media images of people with learning difficulties', in Philpot, T. and Ward, L. (eds) *Values and Visions: Changing ideas in services for people with learning difficulties*, Oxford: Butterworth Heinemann.

Philpot, T. and Ward, L. (eds) (1995) *Values and Visions: Changing ideas in services for people with learning difficulties*, Oxford: Butterworth Heinemann.

Pritchard, D. (1963) *Education and the Handicapped 1760–1960*, London: Routledge and Kegan Paul.

Roffey, S., Tarrant, T. and Majors, K (1994) *Young Friends: Schools and friendship*, London: Cassell.

Rose, R., Fergusson, A., Coles, C., Byers, R. and Banes D. (eds) (1994) *Implementing the Whole Curriculum for Pupils with Learning Difficulties*, London: David Fulton.

Sebba, J., Byers, R. and Rose, R. (1995) *Redesigning the Whole Curriculum* (2nd edn), London: David Fulton.

Shearer, A. (1996) 'Think positive! advice on presenting people with mental handicap', in Mittler, P. and Sinason, V. (eds) *Changing Policy and Practice for People with Learning Disabilities*, London: Cassell.

Shelvin, M. (1992) 'Fast friends: shared classroom activities for students with and without learning disabilities', *Frontine Magazine*, Summer, 10–11.

Shelvin, M. and Walsh, P.N. (1994) *On Equal Terms*, Dublin: St Michael's House Research.

Tilstone, C. (ed.) (1991) *Teaching Pupils with Severe Learning Difficulties*, London: David Fulton.

Tilstone, C. and Visser, J. (1996) 'Learning difficulties' in Varma, V. (ed.) *Coping with Children in Stress*, Aldershot: Ashgate Publishing.

Tomlinson, S. (1982) *A Sociology of Special Education*, London: Routledge and Kegan Paul.

UNESCO (1994) *The Salamanca Statement and Framework for Action on Special Needs Education*, Paris: UNESCO.

Wade, B. and Moore, M. (1994) 'Feeling different: viewpoint of students with special educational needs', *British Journal of Special Education*, 21, 4, 161–5.

Wade, B. and Moore, M. (1992) *Experiencing Special Education*, Buckingham: Open University Press.

Walsh, P.N. and Shelvin, M. (1991) *Fast Friends: A users' guide,* Dublin: St. Michael's House Research.

Ward, L. (1995) 'Equal citizens: current issues for people with learning difficulties and their allies', in Philpot, T. and Ward, L. (eds) *Values and Visions: Changing ideas in services for people with learning difficulties,* Oxford: Butterworth Heinemann.

Weikart, D.P. (1989) 'The High/Scope curriculum in practice', *The High/Scope Project : Perspectives 40,* Exeter: The University of Exeter, School of Education.

Williams, P. (1995) 'Should we prevent Down's Syndrome?', *British Journal of Learning Difficulties,* 23, 46–50.

Wright, B. A. (1974) 'An analysis of attitude, dynamics and effects', *The New Outlook for the Blind,* 68, 108–18.

Part IV:
Conclusion

Chapter 23

Preparing for Self-advocacy

Peter Mittler

> We hold that education has certain long term goals... they are first, to enlarge the child's knowledge, experience and imaginative understanding, and thus his awareness of moral values and capacity for enjoyment; and secondly, to enable him to enter the world after formal education is over as an active participant in society and a responsible contributor to it, capable of achieving as much independence as possible. (DES, 1978, para 1.4)

The challenge of self-advocacy

This chapter aims to stimulate discussion on ways in which the foundations for self-advocacy can be laid by schools. How can schools prepare young people for adult life by helping them to develop the skills and confidence to speak for themselves, to be self-assertive, even militant when this is necessary? How can this be incorporated into the activities of the school and into the day-to-day interactions which take place in the classroom and the playground? How early should this process begin?

In considering ways in which they can prepare their students for self-advocacy, teachers need to appreciate what it means to live as a young adult 'in the community', the demands, expectations and stresses which society places on all young people who may be disadvantaged in any way.

Discrimination and oppression take many forms. Disabled young people have much in common with other oppressed minorities, such as those disadvantaged by poverty, chronic ill health, membership of an ethnic minority group or culture, or by the interaction of any or all of these with the additional discrimination that arises from gender.

Nearly all adults with learning disabilities will be living in poverty. Such income as they may receive from welfare benefits will be deducted to contribute directly or indirectly to living or service costs, leaving them with little or no money of their own. If they are attending day services, they are likely to receive between £2 and £4 a week – rates which have hardly changed for 20 years – though some will receive even less or be charged for the service.

In order to set the role of schools in context, we begin by summarizing the origins of the self-advocacy movement, the goals which self-advocates are struggling to achieve, and the obstacles which they encounter.

Origins of self-advocacy

The core components of self-advocacy have been summarized as follows (Further Education Unit, 1990)

- being able to express thoughts and feelings with assertiveness, if necessary
- being able to make choices and decisions
- having clear knowledge and information about rights
- being able to make changes.

The self-advocacy movement affirms the right of disabled persons to enjoy the same basic human rights as their fellow citizens. It has developed in reaction to the obstacles placed in the way of disabled people in expressing choice and self-determination.

The movement can be seen as part of a struggle to redress the gross power imbalance between professionals and service users which, almost by definition, is potentially greater and more damaging in the field of learning disabilities than in most others. It is this power imbalance which renders them particularly vulnerable to well-meaning and experienced professionals who claim to speak on their behalf and understand their needs and who act in the light of this knowledge in planning service provision or in regulating their day-to-day lives. It is this powerlessness which also makes them particularly vulnerable to oppressive and abusive practices, including repeated sexual abuse and the emotional abuse that springs from neglecting ordinary human needs for personal relationships and for the expression of feelings.

Griffiths (1994) lists the essential elements of successful self-advocacy practice. These include:

- an understanding of choice
- a feeling of being regarded
- a better understanding of the world, its possibilities and difficulties
- a feeling of self-worth
- the development of skills and competences
- competence in risk-taking
- a feeling of safety which makes risk-taking possible
- a feeling of confidence
- a feeling of being encouraged and supported as they develop towards autonomy.

Obstacles and frustrations

It is a salutary experience for teachers to make contact with former students, to try to experience something of the quality of their day-to-day lives as they move around the community and to talk with members of their household or family about their situation.

They may be surprised at how well many of them have developed since leaving school. A few will be living in ordinary houses with support tailored to their individual needs, perhaps in full-time supported or sheltered employment; others will be attending FE colleges. Many who had not acquired literacy skills before leaving school will have learned to read competently. A few will have formed stable long-term relationships and some will have married or become parents.

But they will also be depressed by the paucity of service provision for most school leavers. Many will still be attending day centres with poor staffing ratios and little or no possibility of continuing with the learning programmes initiated at school. Some will be living with their parents, who are becoming increasingly frail and anxious about the future. Some of the residents of group homes or sheltered housing schemes are leading lonely and isolated lives, sometimes victimized, exploited and abused by their neighbours (Flynn, 1988).

Pervasive underestimation

Young people leaving school are likely to encounter major obstacles to their participation in society over and above any difficulties arising directly from their disability. Perhaps the biggest obstacle is the continuous pervasive underestimation of their abilities by society and its representatives and by the public at large. Even parents and professionals with many years of experience are in danger of such underestimation, believing it to be in the best interests of the young person to be 'realistic' and 'not expect too much'. Such sentiments, however well-meaning, need to be challenged, as they can create additional barriers for young people moving into adulthood. They also act as a self-fulfilling prophecy by fuelling further underestimation.

One way to combat underestimation on the part of the general public as well as professionals and parents is to publicize examples of outstanding achievement and excellence of any kind. Who would have predicted 30 years ago that the time would come when individuals with Down's Syndrome or labelled as experiencing severe learning difficulties would go through five years of secondary education in the ordinary class of a comprehensive school, achieve several GCSE passes, hold down a full-time job, live independently, get married, and address the United Nations General Assembly?

These and others successes may, at least for the present, be exceptional but they are real, not token achievements. They raise questions about how many more individuals are capable of beating prediction. By the same token, such achievements should lead schools to ask themselves whether there are students in their charge now whose abilities may be being underestimated.

Tracey Samutt is a 16-year-old actress with Down's Syndrome who is known all over Australia for her starring role in a soap opera. This is what she told an audience of special educators in Darwin last year:

> People should set higher goals and maybe they would be surprised by what we can do.
> I think I could do better if I was pushed a bit more but the teachers are afraid I might fail.
> If I did something wrong, it was not because I made a mistake but because I had Down's Syndrome.
> I can get there. I might need more time; I might need repetition. But once I've got it, I've got it for life.

Traditionally, much emphasis has been given by schools to equipping young people with the skills which they will need to live and work in the community, e.g., understanding and using money, shopping, budgeting, using public transport. More emphasis has recently been given to personal and social education and to issues concerned with sexuality and sexual relationships. These are all essentials which need to be nurtured in partnership between teachers and parents and with young people themselves. But this is not enough. In particular, we need to take account of the initiatives which young people themselves have taken to shape their own future, what they have said about their schooling and their own rights and aspirations to achieve independence and autonomy. The self-advocacy movement reflects their determination and their ability to find a voice.

The frustrations and aspirations experienced by young people found expression in the growth of organizations of people with learning disabilities. Williams and Shoultz (1982, 1991) have traced the origins of these organizations in Sweden, Australia, the USA and the UK; more recent accounts of developments in the UK are available in Flynn and Ward (1991) and Whittaker (1996). In the USA, strong People First organizations have been set up in most of the states but there is also a national organization which has run international conferences of self-advocates.

As early as 1982, 'student committees' were established in more than a quarter of all adult training centres in the UK. By 1988 the proportion was higher than a half (Crawley, 1988). Some of these committees persuaded social services managers to change the name of the centre from 'Adult Training Centre' to 'Social Education Centre' and to refer to them as 'students' or 'service users' rather than 'trainees'. Others came into conflict with their managers, for example in applying (successfully) to join the National Union of Students.

Self-advocates, working as individuals, in small groups and at national and international levels, have fought and are still fighting to achieve a number of goals. These include the right to be consulted on decisions affecting their own lives and that of others by means of service users' groups who are consulted on major as well as minor issues. They are increasingly involved in the selection of staff, in the evaluation of services and in quality assurance procedures. They have acted as expert witnesses in law courts, giving evidence on compulsory sterilization of women with learning difficulties. Several have produced training materials to help other self-advocacy groups and have acted as consultants and trainers.

Self-advocates have also been a powerful voice on issues of labelling and terminology. In Canada, they were the moving force that led to the change of name from 'Canadian Association for Mental Retardation' to 'Canadian Association for Community Living'. In the UK, they campaigned successfully against the MENCAP 'little Stephen' logo and against negative fund-raising images, and added their voices to the campaign to remove labels from buses.

A recent issue of *Mental Retardation* includes articles by three self-advocates which reflect the need to be heard and valued and the right to be consulted on all decisions which affect their lives (Monroe, 1996; Pacht, 1996; Ward, 1996). Dybwad and Hersani (1996) have now brought together a comprehensive world-wide account of the progress of the self-advocacy movement, using the voices of people with learning disabilities themselves and drawing examples from different countries and settings. Dybwad ends his overview of these developments by writing:

> Thus, people with intellectual impairments have, in my lifetime, gone from 'feeble-minded patients' to empowered agents of social change. They work to make the world better place not just for themselves but for the rest of us as well. (Dybwad, 1996, p.16)

Implications for schools

How, then, can schools prepare their students to become 'empowered agents of social change'?

The present time is an opportune moment to reconceptualize curriculum priorities and to ask questions concerning the extent to which existing practice needs to be modified to support students to acquire and use the knowledge, skills, attitudes and understanding which they will need as self-advocates in the community. The Dearing review of the National Curriculum (SCAA, 1994) has prompted a reconsideration of priorities and, in theory at least, released the equivalent of a day a week for other activities. Moreover, students over 16 are not obliged to follow the National Curriculum.

The Dearing review was broadly in line with what teachers had been pleading for ever since the introduction of the National Curriculum, namely more flexibility to relate the programmes of study and the assessment arrangements to the needs of individual pupils, and more time and freedom to design school experiences accordingly. A mass of evidence is now available in this and other publications which reflects the attempts of teachers to develop a 'broad and balanced curriculum which meets the individual needs of pupils' and to which they are entitled by law. The results of this work are summarized in the present volume and its predecessor (Ashdown *et al.*, 1991) and elsewhere (NCC, 1992; Rose *et al.*, 1996; Sebba *et al.*, 1995; Tilstone, 1991).

The work reported in these books was carried out at a time of crisis for education and for special needs education in particular. Although most schools tried to strike a sensible balance between preserving 'the best of the old' and introducing the 'best of the new', the effort and energy required to keep pace with constantly changing innovation have left many schools exhausted and eager for a period of stability. A recent study of curriculum development in 12 special schools concludes:

> In various ways, the National Curriculum is interpreted as either irrelevant to the special school context or is accepted at the level of rhetoric while making minimal impact on practice (as in the minimal use made of cross-curricular strategies by some schools). (Halpin and Lewis, 1996)

The case for more attention to preparation for self-advocacy is not merely a plea for more time on the timetable. Self-advocacy is not 'just another subject' (Tyne 1996). Aims concerned with opportunities for choice, decision-making and empowerment should be woven into the life of the school and all its activities. Even so, some activities lend themselves particularly well to this aim.

Fortunately, developments in professional practice over the past decade or so, both in mainstream as well as in special schools, are at least in part consistent with preparation for self-advocacy. In general terms, the thrust of developments in the past decade has been towards more holistic pupil-centred approaches, with more emphasis on process rather than product. Although the National Curriculum, with its emphasis on subjects, attainment targets and national assessment was at first seen as a retrograde step, teachers have successfully developed innovative methods of teaching which combine the best elements of an objectives-based approach with a regime which tries to develop relevant individualized plans.

The more positive national trends include the changes brought about in the mid-1980s by the Technical and Vocational Education initiatives (TVEI), particularly the development of pupil-led Records of Achievement (Parker, 1994); the belated and partial return to teacher assessment and to criterion-referenced assessments, recommended by the Task Group on Assessment (DES/WO, 1988), as well as the work done by teacher working parties across the country to provide examples of curriculum access for pupils with severe learning difficulties.

The remainder of this chapter summarizes some of the strategies and opportunities for incorporating curricular aims and activities which, to a greater or lesser degree, are designed to foster skills and experience of self-advocacy both now and in the future. Many of these, as well as others not mentioned, are already elements of good practice. Volumes edited by Coupe O'Kane and Smith (1994) and Garner and Sandow (1995) provide both a radical rationale for self-advocacy in schools, as well as examples of good practice.

Intensive interaction

'Intensive interaction' is the generic name given to a style of teaching which emphasizes the centrality of the pupil-teacher relationship. The main proponents of this approach are Nind and Hewett (e.g., 1994). In contrast with behavioural strategies in which the teacher is held to be firmly in control of what is to be taught, defines the steps to acquisition and the reward system to be used, intensive interaction can follow leads provided by the child. Put simply, the emphasis is on process as much as product.

> Much consideration is given to the learning environment and to the stimulation which is offered but what happens will depend very much on the student, following his/her interests and lead. In this way, the teaching is seen less as technology and more as art. The emphasis is on the exploring, the doing, the discovery. It is the understandings that come as part of this active process that the teacher aims to promote.
>
> Intensive Interaction is concerned with negotiation and participation, as opposed to dominance and compliance. Part of valuing the learner on an equal basis is not imposing on him/her our agenda for action, our style and pace of working and our needs. (Nind and Hewett, 1994, pp.14, 16)

In a recent review of the involvement of pupils with severe learning difficulties in their own learning, Lawson (1996) makes a clear link between interactive teaching, preparation for self-advocacy and the enhancement of self-esteem, respect for people underlying all three. She quotes the FEU (1990) report on self-advocacy as follows:

> self-advocacy can be seen as a relationship in which it is the professional's responsibility to:
>
> - invite and value the learner's self-expression;
> - offer choices and develop decision-making skills;
> - act as an information resource about rights and opportunities;
> - give support as the learners make changes, accepting mistakes and inappropriate behaviour as part of the learning process.

Turn-taking

A number of researchers studying the interaction of mothers and newborn or very young babies have detected patterns of timing and synchronization, in which mother and baby appear to wait for pauses before taking their turn in the interaction. Studies along these lines have been carried out with infants with Down's Syndrome and with young children with profound and multiple impairments.

Goldbart (1988) and Harris and Wimpory (1992) provide useful discussions of the implications of this and related research for classroom practice. Here again, the focus is on the style and nature of adult-child interaction and the opportunities it provides for facilitating successful communication (see also Harris, 1994, for a fuller elaboration of these ideas).

Children controlling their environment

In working with pupils with profound and multiple impairments, it is important to provide them with opportunities to control features of their environment. By this means they learn that certain actions on their part invariably trigger a particular response – an early example of empowerment!

With or without the use of information technology and microelectronics, it is possible to design environments which will be responsive to sounds or movements made by the child, which will in turn trigger a specific response. This has implications for the design of multi-sensory environments (e.g. Snoezelen rooms); instead of or in addition to providing sensory stimulation, opportunities should be available for children to control aspects of their environment through their own actions. Barber (1994), Ware (1995) and Wilkinson (1994) provide detailed accounts of how this can be done.

Opportunities for choice and decision-making

Most schools now try to ensure that opportunities for exercising choice are an integral part of the everyday experience of all pupils, including those with profound and multiple impairments. Numerous opportunities occur in the course of ordinary routines to present pupils with simple choices – tea or coffee, toy bus or toy train, blue or red sweater, story now or later – gradually extending to more complex choices between activities, games, companions, teachers. A videotape of even half an hour's ordinary classroom activities makes it possible to assess how many opportunities for choice were naturally available or were presented by adults or other children; how many pupils were and were not offered such opportunities and how adults and other pupils reacted to such choices as were made.

In the context of a manual on training for self-advocacy, Cooper and Hersov (1986) elaborate on a range of graded choice opportunities which can be provided:

- simple yes/no (conveyed in any medium – speech, sign, non-verbal indication
- choice of two seen alternatives (tea or coffee)
- choice of more than two alternatives
- larger number of alternatives (what would you like to drink?)
- open choice (where shall we go for our outing?; what do you do next?)

Inevitably, providing opportunities for choice and decision-making for school-age pupils reduces the 'authority' and control of the teacher and brings the risk of resentment or conflict. In particular, tensions may arise when teachers (or parents) and the pupil have different priorities about what should be taught. This may include readiness to go out alone, embark on a sexual relationship, live independently, get a job.

One example of such tensions is provided by Griffiths (1994) as part of his proposals for a staff audit of provision. His questions to staff:

> Are you skipping adolescence?
> Are you expecting young people with severe learning difficulties to move straight from childhood to sensible middle age?

are prompted by the following observations, all too familiar to those who have ever shared a home with one or more teenagers:

> Most adolescents do not:
> Dust
> Make sponge cakes or apple pie
> Wear 'sensible clothes'
> Go to bed early (or get up at a 'normal time')
> Behave well towards adults
> Do what they are told without arguing
> Eat sensibly
> Plan carefully

Keep their cupboards, drawers and rooms tidy
Behave in an exemplary way towards the other sex.

A glance at some current 'social education' or 'social skills' programmes would no doubt add to the list.

Personal and social development

In *Redefining the Whole Curriculum for Pupils with Learning Difficulties*, Sebba *et al.* (1995) made a strong case for personal and social development (PSD) permeating all aspects of the work of schools, including pupil-teacher relationships. They are careful to distinguish this from personal and social education (PSE) as traditionally conceived in terms of work on self-help skills, alcohol, sex and drugs.

They see PSD as being concerned with the development of personal autonomy and self-determination, rather than with the acquisition of skills *per se*. Planning a PSD curriculum involves a reconsideration of the nature of the power relationship between teacher and pupil, and the extent to which the aims of schooling should be concerned with 'empowerment and liberation rather than remediation and normalization'. It aims to foster environments which reduce dependency and practices which disempower pupils.

Their arguments represent a radical departure from current special needs theory and practice. But seen from the perspective of the community of adult disabled people, the arguments have a familiar ring because they are couched in the language of disability rights. This is the language that young people are hearing, learning and using. It seems appropriate that teachers should support them in doing so.

Consulting the pupil

Both the 1989 Children Act and the *Code of Practice on the Identification and Assessment of Special Educational Needs* (DfE, 1994) emphasize the importance of listening to the views of children and young people and giving them the fullest possible opportunity to take part in discussions and decision-making concerning their education and key issues in their life. In fact, encouragement to do this was already explicitly provided in DES Circular 1/83 concerned with the implementation of the 1981 Education Act, which stated that the principle of partnership with pupils was as important as that of partnership with parents. Nevertheless, research on the implementation of the 1981 Act indicated that this was extremely rare (Goacher *et al.*, 1988).

Records of Achievement

Records of Achievement record and celebrate all aspects of achievement and are much more than a summative record of educational attainments. They provide a rich source of evidence about a pupil's interests and hobbies, both inside and outside school. Above all, pupil involvement in developing Records of Achievement lies at the heart of the whole process.

Despite lukewarm support from the government, Records of Achievement were developed in secondary and special schools and are now widely used in primary schools as well. Lawson (1996) provides a useful summary of their origins and development and demonstrates how they reflect a more holistic approach to formative assessment than those required by the Education Reform Act or by the Dearing modifications. Parker (1994) describes in some detail the development of TVEI and Records of Achievement initiatives in the West Midlands in general and in one special school in particular.

Key features of the Record of Achievement are summarized by Lawson (1996) as follows:

- assessment is an ongoing process;
- only success is recognized;
- all experiences are important;
- it is participative;
- it enhances learning;
- it provides evidence rather than judgement;
- ownership lies with the pupil.

Code of Practice

Because developments since the early 1980s, particularly Records of Achievement, have created a more favourable climate for the involvement of pupils in their own learning, it is possible that research on the *Code of Practice* will provide evidence that pupils with learning difficulties are being consulted at all five stages of the Code. 'The effectiveness of any assessment and intervention will be influenced by the involvement and interest of the young person concerned' (DfE, 1994). The benefits are

- *practice:* children have important and relevant information. Their support is crucial to the effective implementation of any individual educational programme
- *principle:* children have a right to be heard. They should be encouraged to participate in decision-making about provision to meet their special educational needs.

Schools should consider how they

- involve pupils in decision making processes
- determine the pupil's level of participation, taking into account approaches to assessment and intervention which are suitable for his or her age, ability and past experiences
- record pupils' views in identifying their difficulties, setting goals, agreeing a development strategy, monitoring and reviewing progress
- involve pupils in determining individual educational plans. (DfE, 1994, paras 2.34–2.37)

Individual Educational Plans, annual reviews and transition planning

The involvement of pupils in the process of planning for the future as part of the process of IEP development, for the annual review and most importantly as part of the transition process, is particularly vital.

If such involvement is to be genuine and not tokenistic, a long period of preparation and successful participation in discussion and decision-making is essential. Everything depends, therefore, on the pupil participation policy of the school as a whole and on the nature and quality of the opportunities that have been available to students over a period of years.

Here again, the *Code of Practice* is quite explicit:

Effective arrangements for transition will involve young people themselves addressing issues of:

- personal development
- self-advocacy
- the development of a positive self-image
- the growth of personal autonomy and the acquisition of independent living skills.

Wherever possible, pupils should be actively involved in the review process, including all or part of the review meeting and should be encouraged to give their views of their progress during the previous year; discuss any difficulties encountered; and share their hopes and aspirations for the future. (DfE, 1994, 6.15)

Griffiths (1994) provides a detailed checklist adapted from the Further Education Unit document, *Developing Self-advocacy Skills for People with Disabilities and Learning Difficulties* (FEU, 1990). The checklist is too long to reproduce in full but one section headed 'Negotiation and Choice' is particularly relevant in this context.

1. Are young people always consulted about such basic matters as being touched, lifted or being taken somewhere else if they are in a wheelchair?
2. At the start of a session, do staff seek to gain the young peoples' consent to the content and method of teaching?
3. Is it genuinely acceptable for young people to say 'no'?
4. Is it accepted that young people may have legitimate criticism of a member of staff?
5. Can programmes be changed at a young person's request?
6. Is there always a choice of activities within sessions?
7. Is there alternative provision for young people who want to opt out of a session?
8. Is one-to-one guidance and counselling available?
9. Are there staff guidelines about when to insist that a young person abides by a contract that he or she has made?
10. Is there a policy of gaining young peoples' consent to behaviour modification programmes if that is at all possible?

Student committees

Many schools have established a student committee (e.g., Winup 1994). The nature and quality of teacher support and teacher 'presence' varies considerably from school to school and over time. Some concern themselves with relatively minor issues, others have a considerable impact on the life of the school – e.g., policy on visitors entering the classroom; talking about pupils in their presence; access to records. Whatever is discussed, it is important that students should feel that these meetings are not just a 'talking shop' and that action is taken where it is agreed to be necessary and follow-up action can be taken.

Students learn valuable committee and negotiating skills from membership of committees, for example setting and keeping to an agenda, taking turns, waiting for others to have their say, not interrupting, speaking through the chair, accepting majority decisions, not 'hogging the floor', as well as techniques of persuasion and argument.

Working with families

A parallel paper (Mittler, 1996) explores ways in which families can help to prepare their sons or daughters for self-advocacy.

Because families have their own agendas and concerns, no school-based programme of preparation for advocacy, however well planned and delivered, can hope to succeed without the collaboration and participation of the family. Helping young people to become autonomous adults, to express their opinions and where necessary to insist on them to the point of refusal or militancy, makes it necessary for the family to be involved in the initial planning so that teachers and family members can anticipate difficulties and work together from the outset. This is perhaps the most sensitive area for discussion between parents and teachers (see Chapter 19 in this volume).

Conclusions

Young people with learning disabilities are part of a world-wide movement of self-advocacy, emancipation and 'liberation', initiated by disabled people themselves. They are not content any longer to have others speak on their behalf – whether they be parents, professionals, politicians or leaders of voluntary organizations established to defend and extend their interests, however experienced or well-meaning they may be. They are highly critical of society's low expectations of their capacity to learn and to contribute. They insist on their right to be treated as fellow citizens, with the same rights to have their needs met as any one else.

It is precisely because young people with learning disabilities are now living in less segregated environments that they will have daily experience of discrimination and various forms of abuse and exploitation. They are also likely to lead lives characterized by loneliness and poverty and to lack the means to have access to community leisure and recreational facilities. They may be denied access to certain places of entertainment because of their disability and are at risk of being accused and found guilty of offences they have not committed. In general, their quality of life is likely to be poor.

It follows that young people need to be helped to fend for themselves in environments which may be lonely or hostile. In this context, self-advocacy provides not only a foundation for assertiveness but a means of support and empowerment from others in a similar situation. This process needs to begin in school, if not before. It must also take place in the closest possible relationship with parents and with the young people themselves.

References

Ashdown, R., Carpenter, B. and Bovair, K. (eds) (1991) *The Curriculum Challenge: Access to the National Curriculum for pupils with learning difficulties,* London: Falmer Press.

Barber, M. (1994) 'Contingency awareness: Putting research into the classroom', in Coupe O'Kane, J. and Smith, B. (eds) (1994) *Taking Control: Enabling people with learning difficulties,* London: David Fulton.

Cooper, D. and Hersov, J. (1986) *We Can Change the Future: A staff training resource on self advocacy for people with learning difficulties,* London: SKILL (National Bureau for Students with Disabilities).

Coupe O'Kane, J. and Smith, B. (eds) (1994) *Taking Control: Enabling people with learning difficulties,* London: David Fulton.

Crawley, B. (1988) *The Growing Voice: A survey of self advocacy groups in adult training centres and hospitals in Great Britain,* London: Campaign for People with Mental Handicap.

DES (1978) *Special Educational Needs: Report of the Committee of Inquiry into the education of handicapped children and young people* (The Warnock Report), London: HMSO.

DES/WO (1988) *National Curriculum: Task Group on Assessment and Testing,* London: HMSO.

DfE (1994) *Code of Practice on the Identification and Assessment of Special Educational Needs,* London: HMSO.

Dybwad, G. and Hersani, H. (eds) (1996) *New Voices: Self advocacy by people with disabilities,* Baltimore, Md.: Brookline Press.

Further Education Unit (1990) *Developing Self Advocacy Skills with People with Disabilities,* London: Further Education Unit.

Flynn, M. (1988) *Independent Living for Adults with Mental Handicap,* London: Cassell.

Flynn, M. and Ward, L. (1991) 'We can change the future: self and
citizen advocacy', in Segal, S. and Varma, V. (eds) *Prospects for People with Learning Difficulties,* London: David Fulton.

Garner, P. and Sandow, S. (eds) (1995) *Advocacy, Self Advocacy and Special Needs,* London: David Fulton.

Goacher, B, Evans, J., Welton, J. and Wedell, K. (1988) *Policy and Provision for Special Educational Needs,* London: Cassell.

Goldbart, J. (1988) 'Re-examining the development of early communication', in Coupe, J. and Goldbart, J. (eds) *Communication Before Speech,* Beckenham: Croom Helm.

Griffiths, M. (1994) *Transition to Adulthood: The role of education for young people with severe learning difficulties,* London: David Fulton.

Halpin, D. and Lewis, A. (1996) 'The impact of the National Curriculum on twelve special schools', *European Journal of Special Needs Education,* 11, 95–105.

Harris, J. (1994) 'Language, communication and personal power: a developmental perspective', in Coupe O'Kane, J. and Smith, B. (eds) *Taking Control: Enabling people with learning difficulties,* London: David Fulton.

Harris, J. and Wimpory, D. (1992) *Get Kids Talking,* Kidderminster: British Institute for Learning Disabilities.

Lawson, H. (1996) 'Exploring the relationship between teaching, assessment and research methodology: An inquiry into pupil involvement with pupils who experience severe learning difficulties', unpublished Ph.D thesis, University of East Anglia.

Mittler, P. (1996) 'Laying the foundations for self advocacy', in Coupe O'Kane, J. and Goldbart, J. (eds) *Whose Choice? Contentious issues in the lives of people with learning disabilities,* London: David Fulton.

Mittler, P. and Sinason, V. (eds) (1996) *Changing Policy and Practice for People with Learning Difficulties,* London: Cassell.

Monroe, T.J. (1996) 'We need to educate the professionals', *Mental Retardation,* 34, 122–3.

National Curriculum Council (1992) *Curriculum Guidance 9: The National Curriculum and pupils with severe learning difficulties,* London: School Curriculum and Assessment Authority.

Nind, M. and Hewett, D. (1994) *Access to Communication: Developing the basics of communication with people with severe learning difficulties through intensive interaction,* London: David Fulton.

Pacht, H. (1996) 'My thoughts: self-advocacy, professional organisations and the public', *Mental Retardation,* 34, 123–4.

Parker, S. (1994) 'Taking control with the help of the Technical and Vocational Education Initiative and Records of Achievement', in Coupe O'Kane and Smith, *op. cit.*

Rose, R., Fergusson, A. Coles, Byers, R. and Banes, R. (1996) *Implementing the Whole Curriculum for People with Learning Difficulties,* London: David Fulton.

School Curriculum and Assessment Authority (1994) *The National Curriculum and its Assessment,* Final Report, London: SCAA.

Sebba, J., Byers, R. and Rose, R. (1995) *Redefining the Whole Curriculum for Pupils with Learning Difficulties* (2nd edn), London: David Fulton.

Tilstone, C. (1991) *Teaching Pupils with Severe Learning Difficulties: Practical approaches,* London: David Fulton.

Tyne, J. (1996) 'Advocacy: not just another subject', in Rose, R., Fergusson, A. Coles, Byers, R. and

Banes, R. (eds) *Implementing the Whole Curriculum for People with Learning Difficulties,* London: David Fulton.

Ward, N. (1996) 'Supporting self-advocacy in national organisations: our role and yours', *Mental Retardation,* 34, 121–2.

Ware, J. (1995) (ed.) *Educating Children with Profound and Multiple Learning Difficulties,* London: David Fulton.

Whittaker, A. (1996) 'The fight for self-advocacy', in Mittler, P. and Sinason, V. *op. cit.*

Wilkinson, C. (1994) 'Teaching pupils with profound and multiple learning difficulties.',. in Coupe O'Kane, J. and Smith, B. (eds) *Taking Control: Enabling people with learning difficulties.,.* London: David Fulton.

Williams, P. and Shoultz, B. (1982, 1991) *We Can Change the Future,* London: Souvenir Press.

Winup, K. (1994) 'The role of a student committee in promotion of independence among school leavers.', in Coupe O'Kane, J. and Smith, B. *op. cit.*

Glossary

Attainment targets (AT) Objectives for each core and foundation subject of the National Curriculum. Attainment targets define the expected standards of pupil performance in terms of level descriptions or end of Key Stage descriptions.

Basic curriculum Religious education plus the core and foundation subjects of the National Curriculum.

Code of Practice (on the identification and assessment of special educational needs) This code gives practical guidance to LEAs and the governing bodies of schools on the discharge of their functions in relation to statemented and non-statemented pupils with special educational needs.

Core subjects English, mathematics and science within the National Curriculum.

Cross-curricular elements These run across the whole National Curriculum and are not confined to one subject. They cover dimensions (e.g., equal opportunities), themes (e.g., health education) and relevant skills (e.g., communication).

Department for Education and Employment (DfEE) Central government department with duties and responsibilities relating to the provision of education in schools in England. Formerly known as **Department for Education (DfE)**, and as **Department of Education and Science (DES)** prior to that.

Differentiation The matching of work to the differing capabilities of individuals or groups of pupils in order to extend their learning.

End of Key Stage descriptions These apply to art, music and physical education in the National Curriculum. They set out the standard of performance expected of most pupils at the end of each Key Stage. They are similar in style to level descriptions.

Foundation subjects Usually taken to refer to design and technology, information technology, geography, history, physical education, modern foreign languages, music and art. Strictly speaking English, mathematics and science are both core and foundation subjects.

Individual Education Plan (IEP) Pupils with special educational needs, at whatever stage in the process of assessment recommended by the Code of Practice, should have an IEP which identifies the nature of the child's learning difficulties, action to be taken, staff involved, specific programmes and resources, targets to be achieved within a given timescale, monitoring, assessment and review arrangements and other information.

Inset In-service education and training.

Key Stages (KS) The periods in each pupil's education to which the elements of the National Curriculum apply. They are: KS1 beginning of compulsory education to age 7 years; KS2, 7–11 years; KS3, 11– 4 years; KS4, 14 years until the end of compulsory education. The equivalent year groups are Years R (reception), 1 and 2; Years 3–6; Years 7–9; Years 10 and 11.

Learning difficulties This book deals mainly with pupils with **profound, severe** or **moderate learning difficulties**. Their learning difficulties result from a degree of intellectual impairment, often of organic origin, but compounded by social and environmental factors. These pupils are a minority of the pupil population, perhaps about 2 per cent. Many other children experience less severe learning difficulties.

Local Education Authority (LEA) Parliament has given a number of duties relating to the provision of schools and an appropriate education for all children to these local elected bodies and a range of powers to enable them to carry out these duties. Some of these powers and duties are delegated to the governing bodies of schools which are made up of LEA-appointed people, elected representatives of staff and parents, and local community representatives.

Level descriptions In each National Curriculum subject there are eight level descriptions per attainment target (with the exception of art, music and physical education). Level descriptions indicate the types and range of performance which a pupil is expected to demonstrate for each level. They are used to make summative judgements about a child's performance at the end of a Key Stage. The scale does not apply to Key Stage 4.

Local Management of Schools (LMS), Local Management of Special Schools (LMSS) The arrangements by which LEAs delegate to the governing bodies of individual schools responsibility for the management of their budget share and other aspects of school management.

National Curriculum The core and foundation subjects and their associated attainment targets and programmes of study.

National Curriculum Council (NCC) Former advisory body on aspects of the curriculum in schools. Its functions were taken over by SCAA in October 1993.

Office for Standards in Education (OFSTED) Non-ministerial government department which has responsibility for the inspection of all schools in England. Their professional arm is formed by **Her Majesty's Inspectors (HMI)**.

Programmes of Study (PoS) The Programmes of Study set out the minimum statutory entitlement to the knowledge, understanding and skills for each National Curriculum subject and at each Key Stage.

School Examination and Assessment Council (SEAC) Former advisory body on all aspects of examinations and assessment in schools. Its functions were taken over by SCAA in October 1993.

School Curriculum and Assessment Authority (SCAA) Current advisory body on all aspects of the curriculum and its assessment in schools, as well as examinations.

Special Educational Needs (SEN) Referring to pupils who, for a variety of intellectual, physical, social, sensory, psychological or emotional reasons, experience learning difficulties which are significantly greater than those experienced by the majority of pupils of the same age.

Special support assistants Non-teaching staff who assist teachers, usually within the classroom.

Standard Assessment Tasks (SATs) These may also be called **Standard National Tests**. They are externally-prescribed National Curriculum assessments administered to pupils in the final year of a Key Stage. The methods of assessment vary depending on the subject and Key Stage.

Statements (of Special Educational Needs) Statements of special educational needs are provided under the terms of the 1993 Education Act to ensure appropriate provision for pupils formally assessed as having special educational needs.

Statutory order or Order A statutory instrument which enables the provisions of an Act of Parliament to be augmented or updated. Each National Curriculum subject has its related statutory order.

Whole curriculum The curriculum of a school incorporating the basic curriculum and all other curricular provision deemed appropriate by the school.

Author Index

Subject Index